The Screen Education Reader

The Screen Education Reader

Cinema, Television, Culture

Edited by
MANUEL ALVARADO
EDWARD BUSCOMBE
and
RICHARD COLLINS

Columbia University Press
New York

#26263775

Columbia University Press
New York

Selection, editorial matter and Introduction copyright © Manuel Alvarado,
Edward Buscombe and Richard Collins 1993

Individual chapters (in order) copyright © John Caughie, Steve Neale, Elizabeth
Cowie, Pam Cook, John Ellis, Umberto Eco, John Tulloch, Graham Murdock,
Richard Paterson, Edward Buscombe, James Donald, Manuel Alvarado, Valerie
Walkerdine, Diane Adlam and Angie Salfield, Richard Johnson, Hazel Carby,
Richard Collins, John O. Thompson, Stuart Hall 1993

The essays from *Screen Education* appear with the agreement of the
John Logie Baird Centre, University of Strathclyde, Glasgow.

Library of Congress Cataloging-in-Publication Data
The screen education reader: cinema, television, culture / edited by
Manuel Alvarado, Edward Buscombe, and Richard Collins.
p. cm.
Includes bibliographical references and index.
ISBN 0–231–08110–3 —ISBN 0–231–08111–1 (pbk.)
1. Mass media. 2. Mass media in education. 3. Popular culture.
I. Alvarado, Manuel. II. Buscombe, Edward. III. Collins,
Richard. IV. Screen education (1974) V. Series.
P91.S37 1993
791.45—dc20 92–25729
CIP

Casebound editions of Columbia University Press books are
Smyth-sewn and printed on permanent and durable acid-free
paper.

∞

Printed in Hong Kong
c 10 9 8 7 6 5 4 3 2 1

Contents

Part III   Education

Part IV   Cultural Studies

Introduction

Manuel Alvarado, Edward Buscombe and Richard Collins

It's ten years now since *Screen Education* ceased publication and was absorbed back into its parent journal *Screen*. It had been born ten years before that, in the winter of 1971. It ran for 41 issues, four times a year, until closed down in the spring of 1982.[1] The body which published both journals, the Society for Education in Film and Television (SEFT) had been founded (as the Society of Film Teachers) in 1950 as a grant-in-aid body of the British Film Institute (BFI). Working closely with the BFI's Education Department, SEFT was an organisation representing film teachers at all levels of the education system in the UK. Its first publication was *The Bulletin*, which was expanded later into a 16-page duplicated sheet called *The Film Teacher*. In 1959 this was further transformed into a printed journal, *Screen Education (SE)*, which combined accounts of film teaching with articles about the film industry and about film theory. Issue no 46, September/October 1968, contained a report on a festival of films for children, an article about making films with children, and, a premonition of things to come, an essay by Philip Crick asking 'Is Cinema A Language?' and one by Michael Budd entitled 'Eisenstein's *The Film Sense*: its Relevance Today'.

This issue was in fact the last under that title for some time. The history of SEFT seems to fall neatly into ten-year periods, so at the beginning of 1969 SEFT duly relaunched its journal, this time under the title *Screen*. It announced that 'controversial areas relevant to the study of film and television' would be examined.

1

This proved an accurate prophecy. After some internal convulsions, a distant echo of the seismic shocks that had been reverberating round the intellectual world since 1968, what may be regarded as the first issue of the modern era of *Screen* appeared under the editorship of Sam Rohdie in Spring 1971. Discounting any previous efforts by SEFT to theorise education and film together, its editorial statement pronounced that

> Education and critical practice has for too long remained unconscious and unaware of itself. The development and criticism of theoretical ideas is required to make meaningful, to provide a context for, what has in the past remained at the level of anecdotal accounts of teaching experience.

The editorial board promised, as well as theoretical analyses, 'direct practical information on film extracts, duplicated materials, film conferences, meetings, seminars, books, study units . . .'.

But the commitment *Screen* had made towards the production of a new theoretical discourse about cinema proved a larger and more consuming task than even its ambitious editorial board had anticipated. The first few issues of the new *Screen* found strictly educational questions pushed to the margins. A separate section entitled 'Educational Notes' survived for only three issues. True, the issue of Autumn 1971 included a great deal about education, in response to the crisis which had developed within the BFI Education Department and which had led to the resignation of six of its leading members. But the two following issues, devoted to Soviet cinema of the 1920s and to the question of realism in the cinema, virtually excluded education altogether. It was at this point that *Screen Education Notes* (*SEN*) was born.

The decision to float off education into a separate publication has been represented as a trick whereby the elitist intellectuals of *Screen* managed to slough off their responsibilities to the education constituency, thus allowing them to get on with the more congenial job of remaking film theory:

> Academics were seen to produce knowledge; it was the teachers' job to make it accessible, and to deposit it in students' heads.[2]

Certainly the title *Screen Education Notes* indicates a subaltern status, as does the announced intention in the opening editorial that the purpose is 'to supplement and complement the work of *Screen*'. From the start resources for the newer journal were limited. It took *Screen Education Notes* all of three years to grow up into *Screen Education* (with the double issue nos 10/11, Spring/ Summer 1974) and longer than that to reach the same size as its parent. The early cover design, a reflection of the distinctive fractured lettering designed for *Screen* by Gerry Cinamon, was a further sign of its dependency; only with issue no. 27 did *Screen Education* commission a separate design of its own. And not till the end of the 1970s were the two journals running the same number of pages.

The balance of power between those committed to transforming education and those who thought revolutionising film theory the more pressing task was, surprisingly for a body drawing funds directly from the BFI Education Department, always in favour of the latter. The lion's share of SEFT's resources was secured for the work of *Screen*. Yet despite this unequal provision, there was a practical logic in the decision to separate out education. Since SEFT took seriously the programme of transforming *both* educational *and* critical practice, the best way to ensure that each was given proper weight was surely to have two journals. To see the decision to transfer education into a separate journal as evidence of an intent to remove it from the centre of things is not only something of an insult to the intellects who chose to put their efforts into the new journal rather than the older one. It is fundamentally to misunderstand what the entire project of SEFT in the 1970s was about.

The intention was to investigate the discourse of both writing about the cinema and teaching about it, to uncover the relationships within each between theory and practice, and to relate this to the wider concerns of a progressive or radical politics. Writing about the cinema and teaching about it ought to be thought through together. Teachers needed to be clear what it was they were teaching and why. Theorists in turn (who, it should be remembered, often *were* teachers) needed a meaningful social context for the knowledge they produced. For SEFT film theory could not exist in a vacuum. It was always embedded in cultural politics, and education was one of the most important terrains on which that politics was played out. If any one thing was characteristic of *Screen Education* it is that theory was never justified for its own sake. It was not, in the derogatory sense, academic. Theory was needed – not just any theory, but a critical and rigorous theory – because the prevailing educational discourses about film at the time largely ignored or even opposed theory. Instead they resorted to notions such as talent or taste – categories which were of dubious value in the teaching process. What the new theory looked for was knowledge, since knowledge, unlike taste, was verifiable and transferable.

In the name of a vague and bloodless liberalism, this commitment to theory has recently been caricatured as a hermetic and terroristic theoreticism:

> in the 1970s, SEFT's policing of the 'correct' theoretical line was marked by a degree of arrogance worthy of the sectarian Left at its most doctrinaire.[3]

Doubtless *Screen* occasionally overbalanced into arrogance, though scarcely any of its theoretical positions would have been hailed by the doctrinaire Left of the time, which viewed it with impeccably proletarian suspicion. But it is not a charge that can be seriously sustained against *Screen Education*. There was no attempt to impose a single 'line'. On the contrary, it thrived on debate, as demonstrated by the exchange between Alvarado and Williamson over the merits of so-called child-centred education.

Screen Education now looks like one of the most sustained attempts yet made in Britain to explore the radical implications of teaching about film and television by working simultaneously both on the conceptualisation of a previously unformed or ill-formed subject and on the actual practice of teaching. As its work progressed it frequently found itself caught up in debates which derived, at least in part, from its own success. On the one hand the increasingly institutionalised nature of media studies brought undeniable advantages. There was more material support, and the subject became more securely inscribed into examination syllabuses. Its foothold within the educational system was ever more assured. On the other hand there was the danger that such developments might blunt the intellectual cutting edge which, as a new and iconoclastic field of inquiry, film and media studies had enjoyed. One of the major achievements of *Screen Education* was that the real dangers and strengths inherent in each of these tendencies were recognised and the tension between them explored in such a productive way.

The decision by SEFT in 1982 that it could no longer support two journals was probably unavoidable, forced as it was by a financial crisis. Since *Screen* had the largest circulation (largely as a result of its American sales) there was a certain economic logic in the decision that *Screen Education* should be the one to close. But there were many at the time who thought that *Screen Education* had become the more lively journal, with a more vital and relevant agenda. Since then, much of the theoretical work on film which *Screen* pioneered has been taken up elsewhere, so that *Screen* has become, partly as a result of its own success, just another journal of film theory. It is not so easy to see who or what has replaced *Screen Education*. Hence in our view the relevance of the present anthology.

The principles on which the selection has been made are not based simply on choosing the best writing. On that basis two or three separate selections of equal length and equal quality could easily have been made, each with its fair share of famous names. (*Screen Education* was from the start dedicated to the encouragement of new and untried writers, but it managed to appeal to a good many authors who were already key figures in the field.) Rather, we have sought to represent four main strands of the work of the journal. These are the continuing attempt to rethink our understanding both of film, and of television; the investigation of educational theory and practice – and theory in practice; and lastly what, from the present vantage point, can be seen as a far-sighted move into cultural studies. *Screen Education*'s contribution in each of these fields is considered in more detail below.

Of necessity we have omitted much. In general we have tried to avoid those contributions which have appeared elsewhere (such as the notable analysis by Fredric Jameson in issue no. 30 of *Dog Day Afternoon*). Also, because *Screen Education* was always intensely interested in the here-and-now, many of its articles were occasional, concerned with such matters as new examination proposals or syllabuses, localised policy developments within education, and activities such as conferences and exhibitions. These we have not included. Besides its path-breaking studies of popular television, of the media industries and of institutional structures, *Screen Education* also pioneered work on representation (for example Jean-Pierre Golay's and Jo Spence's work on image analysis, Jim Pines's on racial images) and feminist analyses of films and images (instanced in the work of Christine Gledhill and Griselda Pollock). *Screen Education* sought out examples of media work from other countries, especially in Europe, and also ventured beyond the boundaries of screen studies into other cultural forms. It ran articles on popular fiction by Tony Bennett, on popular music by Simon Frith, Angela McRobbie and Dave Laing, and on photography by Victor Burgin, John Tagg, John Berger and Manuel Alvarado. All this work repays re-reading, but to have included it here would have expanded the present volume to unmanageable lengths. We can only hope that this sampler sends readers back to the complete set of bound copies.

Film Studies

John Caughie's 'Teaching Through Authorship' was published in
Screen Education, no. 17, a special issue on John Ford's film *The
Searchers*. Caughie's article aimed to dethrone auteurism from its
position of theoretical primacy and to identify it as but one among
a number of different approaches to identifying the plurality of
codes which make cinematic meaning. It echoes many of the
motifs of film theory and criticism of the 1970s, notably an aspir-
ation to 'science' (a borrowing from Althusser's reformulation of
Marx,[4] and a consequential identification of theory which stressed
human agency as unprogressive and mystifying. However,
Caughie turns the antimony at the centre of auteurism (between
'structural' auteurism concerned to identify common motifs in
films, and humanistic and evaluative auteurism, which attributed
commonalities to a warm authorial body) into a promising pedagogical strategy well fitted to exploring the 'confrontation of authorial freedom with genre determinism'; that is, to exploring the
role of human agency (personified by the director) in relation to
less individualised forces of meaning-making. Like all the essays
reprinted here, 'Teaching Through Authorship' has both a period
quality (unmasking the 'trick' of the dominant ideology has a very
1970s ring) and enduring claims on the attention of contemporary
readers. It is a fertile provocation to thinking about cinema and
suggests useful strategies for classroom work on *The Searchers*
and other films. Most of all, its unpretentious lucidity makes easy
the reader's access to its arguments and aids the comprehension
of the still pertinent issues discussed by Caughie, notably the
contradiction, well focused in auteur theory, between structural
analysis and evaluative criticism.

Steve Neale's point of departure in his article 'The Same Old
Story: Stereotypes and Difference' is the conventional use of
'stereotype' as a 'boo' word. Such usage, he argues, aids understanding but little. His definition of stereotyping as a process of
formal repetition which reduces a complex heterogeneity to a
single function suggests that stereotyping may be productive as
well as reductive. Moreover, as Neale deftly shows, to identify
the presence of stereotypes in Griffith's *The Birth of a Nation* is
a one-finger exercise, and a demand for 'positive images' is no
more productive of understanding than is an offensive negative
stereotype itself. Though the value polarity of an image may
have been changed, the new, positive, images produce no more
understanding of the processes of representation than did the old,
negative, image. They may empower but they do not emancipate.
Neale's succinct argument illustrates both *Screen Education*'s

accommodation of different lengths and forms of writing and a thoughtful and subversive engagement with conventional wisdom characteristic of the journal. Neale's demonstration of the poverty of the notion 'stereotype' embodies and exemplifies *Screen Education*'s assumption that the politics of education inhere primarily in fostering understanding by clarifying arguments and issues, rather than in the mobilisation of support for a 'correct' programme or slogan.

Similar aspirations are displayed in Elizabeth Cowie's article 'Women, Representation and the Image'. Cowie argues the need to develop more rigorous tools for the analysis of the image, and she provides a valuable exposition of how three key theorists in this field – Roland Barthes, Christian Metz and Guy Gauthier – attempted to negotiate the relationship between connotation and denotation in the image. She goes on to show how feminism has helped to reveal the inadequacy of both formalistic and 'ideological' analyses. Image analysis, she urges, must move beyond looking at the image itself and engage with wider, institutional discourses, such as those of the legal, education and health care systems.

Cowie argues against the 'essentialism' of much work on images, the assumption that the meaning of any image is fixed and given. Instead, she emphasises the importance of active, contextual reading, alert to how specific groups, such as women, generate different meanings as a result of inhabiting their own specific cultural space.

What is also important here is her recognition that it is more productive to trace meanings between and across images than to try to fix direct relations between images and the real world. Returning us to the theme of Steve Neale's article, she writes: 'The problem of stereotyping is not that it is true or false, distorting or manipulated, but that it closes off certain productions of meaning in the image'.

The beginning of Pam Cook's article 'Teaching Avant-Garde Film: Notes Towards Practice' makes explicit the roots of her work and of much of the writing published in *Screen Education* – years of experience of teaching a subject. Through that experience a consequential familiarity with the materials took place which enabled authors (whose knowledge of issues and quality of argument had been refined in the two-way flow of ideas through dialogue and debate with students) to clearly identify the issues central to the matter in question. Cook's article is a fine example of the productive influence of an educational milieu on the contents of *Screen Education*. She raises to an unusual degree of explicitness the importance of a personal experience in the development of an intellectual point of view. She is more forthcoming about the 'determinations' of her analysis and viewpoint than were other writers, but her history has a representative quality. However, her incisive discussion of Michael Snow's *Wavelength* and the persuasive programme she develops for teaching avant-garde cinema are very much her own. It is a programme which testifies to the productivity of influences (notably Peter Wollen's 'Two Avant-Gardes' article),[5] but which is neither bound by them into discipleship, not insistent on demonstrating how much further the writer has advanced from the work of her or his mentor. An exemplary blending of social context, educational discourse, film theory and film practice, the article offers a series of stimuli to further reflection and some eminently useful directions for teaching and learning practice, none of which gloss over the troubled student response which often attends the screening and study of avant-garde cinema.

John Ellis's 'Film in Higher Education' is a crisp and clear-eyed polemic for film education. Ellis argues that film studies may, should, serve as a seed-bed from which a new critical intelligentsia will spring. Ellis vigorously lists the characteristics of film study which will promote the intellectual emancipation of students and the beneficial consequences that may flow. His *terminus ad quem* for film education, providing students with 'intellectual equipment and the means of thinking through problems that they will inevitably encounter after the end of their formal education', fore-shadows the concern in educational policy and theory during the 1990s for the cultivation of 'transferable skills' in higher education students. It is representative of a concern, shared by many contributors to *Screen Education*, that film, television and media studies be ultimately directed more towards a general educational and social goal than to the establishment of film and media studies as an academic subject in and for itself. Ellis defines explicitly what was customarily implicit in other contributions: the educational aim of producing a 'critical intellectual of a practical kind'.

Television Studies

In 'Can Television Teach?' Umberto Eco resumes, neatly and intelligibly, the formulations about the mediated nature of communication, the uncertainty of media effects, the conventionality and cultural specificity of codes, which have been the core of film and television studies. His exposition is clear and elegant, a notable excursion by *Screen Education* into a field, television

studies, which it did much to develop. Eco refers to Thames
Television's *Viewpoint* programme, one of British television's
excursions – not so common in those days – into self-examination
and a programme which was analysed in *Screen Education*, no.
19 (and doubtless influenced by it, for Douglas Lowndes, the
'author' of *Viewpoint*, had been Head of Education at the British
Film Institute). The programme also occasioned *Screen Education*'s most explicit political intervention: the publication of a
leaked Independent Broadcasting Authority (IBA) memorandum
on the curtailment of the *Viewpoint* series at issue. The editorial
decision to publish was a difficult and perhaps irresponsible one.
Though none of the fearsome consequences foreseen in the long
editorial discussions about whether or not to publish, and consequently risk court actions for breach of confidence or copyright,
ever materialised, even a threat of legal action might have had
terminal consequences for the journal.

John Tulloch's 'Gradgrind's Heirs – the Quiz and the Presentation of "Knowledge" by British Television' prefigures several
themes developed in later issues. Tulloch cites Pierre Bourdieu –
Screen Education, no. 28, in 1978 was one of the earliest sustained
presentations of Bourdieu's work in British journals – and draws
together arguments consistently made elsewhere in *Screen Education*; notably, that both television and education present a view
of the world and not the world itself. Tulloch neatly argues that
television's quiz shows express society's educational values: stressing facts not analysis, reification not relationships, and rapid recall
rather than considered judgement. Tulloch's commentary on the
social profile of quiz contestants and the rhetorical forms of knowledge which pertain to the class-stratified television quizzers of
Mastermind and *Sale of the Century* is rich in insights. Moreover,
his distinction between the programmes on grounds of their social
class composition is eloquent of an equivalent dualism in the
formal education system. Tulloch has written an illuminating essay
which judiciously highlights the salient characteristics of two television programmes and generates successive clarifications of the
ideological operation of both the education system and television.
Appropriately, the theme of Tulloch's essay is 'Screen Education'
and, like the journal from which the essay is selected, it both
illuminates the structural characteristics of the systems which are
its subject and indicates directions for change and reconstruction.

Graham Murdock's 'Authorship and Organisation' is a key article. Murdock's elucidation of the ideological and structural framework within which television drama in Britain is produced (and
of the role of drama within the political economy of television)
draws on the two main currents within British media studies:

literary critical interest in textual production, and social scientific concern with the social shaping of textual production and the role of texts in shaping consciousness and society. Murdock was not an author principally associated with *Screen Education*, but his 'Authorship and Organisation' would have graced the pages of any communication or cultural studies journal. It exemplifies not only *Screen Education*'s commitment to publishing lucid writing, but also its continuing concern with exploring the relationship between cultural production in general (and film and television in particular) and social structure and reproduction. Ten years on, Murdock's article remains the best orientation to drama's role in British television and to the shifting field of forces which shape the relationship between television drama and the institutions in which it is located.

Richard Paterson's 'Planning the Family: The Art of the Television Schedule' shared the pages of *Screen Education*, no. 35, with Murdock's article and half a dozen other pieces on television drama. It introduces issues concerning the reception and consumption of television, themes of unchallenged importance but ones which entered the pages of *Screen Education* too seldom. The work of Dorothy Hobson, Charlotte Brunsdon and David Morley, published in the early 1980s, triggered the wider interest in reception which now forms one of the central foci of media and cultural studies in the UK. It also led to the welcome development of a dialogue between professional audience researchers (notably in the research departments of the BBC and the then IBA) and the academic community. Paterson's article foreshadowed these developments but his emphasis is somewhat different. He is primarily concerned, not with what audiences do with television, but rather with how conceptions of the audience shape the practice of programme schedulers, whose work then constructs a particular television audience profile and pattern of consumption. As Paterson states, this relationship 'between programme format and audience is not a simple one' and is moreover in constant flux. Paterson's article documents and makes intelligible the arcane practices of broadcasters in the late 1970s and also gives us a general understanding of the practice and importance of such relationships.

Edward Buscombe's essay 'Broadcasting from Above' is representative of what became a characteristic feature of *Screen Education*: the review essay. Reading *Screen Education*'s reviews is one of the best ways to track the journal's responses to new intellectual initiatives and to contemporary issues such as broadcasting policy, which received a good deal of attention in the review pages. *Screen Education*, no. 37, which published Buscombe's meditation on British broadcasting, its relation to the state and on history and historiography (taking Asa Briggs's fourth volume of *The History of Broadcasting in the United Kingdom* as a starting point) also featured illuminating review essays by Stuart Hood and Ian Connell. Buscombe's commentary focuses on two issues, each of which were continuing concerns. First, the relationship between broadcasting and the state, and second, the necessity for the study of programming to go hand in hand with the study of institutions. Without both emphases we understand too little of television. And, as Buscombe rightly pointed out, the history of programming still remains to be written.

Education

Screen Education was, as its title suggests, a journal centred on image-making and on education: broad fields, though the journal limited them by principally focusing on large-scale systems of image and educational reproduction, that is, on the mass media and the formal education system, and by examining the ideas and assumptions which informed and underpinned them. Within a framework which recognised the productiveness of Marxist ideas while not necessarily being bound by them, the journal investigated the interaction of images and institutions. One distinctive feature of *Screen Education* was its absence of a hard editorial line, which enabled editors and editorial board to remain open to new ideas and initiatives and to accept and encourage work from a range of contributors across a developing community of media teachers and scholars. *Screen Education* excluded contributions only on criteria of quality of argument and writing, not on whether articles adhered to what counted as a 'correct' viewpoint. There was also a consistent endeavour to expand the circle of contributors to the journal. As part of the wider process of media education in which *Screen Education* participated, the Board attempted to publish at least two new writers in every issue; as a result many subsequently productive scholars learnt their writing and explored new ideas through their contributions to *Screen Education*.

It also meant that *Screen Education* was neither intellectually debilitated by adherence to hard-edged interior orthodoxies nor riven by factionalism. Rather than emphasising, or insisting on, the priority of material determination, or the autonomy of discourse, or a particular normative conception of the relationships between state, capital and ideology, *Screen Education* explored the relationship between these forces.

James Donald's article 'Green Paper: Noise of Crisis', a critique and 'reading' of the Department of Education and Science's (DES's) 1977 Green Paper *Education in Schools*, was certainly the longest single article published by *Screen Education* and is published here in an abbreviated version. Donald shows how difficult are concepts like 'state' and 'policy', and how important are the meanings – the systems of ideas – which are implicit in these taken-for-granted terms. Donald begins by reviewing the forces marshalled by each side in the 'battle of ideas' represented by Prime Minister James Callaghan's Great Debate about education, and by examining the nature of the linkage each side poses between industry and education. Donald appropriates Barthes's model of textual analysis in *S/Z* to deconstruct the DES Green Paper. His remorseless demonstration of the woolliness of the Green Paper's argument provides him with a secure position to assault the programmes of 'piecemeal social engineering' which, he argues, have animated Labour educational policy, and to attack the vacuous cultivation of a Pollyanna-like 'creativity' distinguished by its anti-intellectualism and emphasis on manual skills.

What next? Donald's answer is more and better theory; specifically 'a theory of ideological struggle' and the translation of such a theory into collective consciousness and action through agencies such as SEFT. Donald's argument, reduced to its most basic propositions, is that intellectuals should stick to their knitting, for no one else can knit for them or for the rest of the community. Quite simply, Donald argues, ideas are too important not to be fought over.

Much of the contemporary liveliness and continuing usefulness of *Screen Education* stemmed from its participation in the wider struggles in the UK about political culture. Of course battle was often joined between comrades in arms who disagreed on tactics or strategy or sometimes even on the purpose and rules of war. Such a, more-or-less comradely, disagreement unfolded between Manuel Alvarado and Judith Williamson. Alvarado advanced his position, from the perspective of secondary education, in two articles, in *Screen Education*, no. 22, and in a review essay in *Screen Education*, no. 38, occasioned by Len Masterman's *Teaching about Television*. Judith Williamson (and Len Masterman) responded, from a further or higher education perspective, in *Screen Education*, no. 40. The terms of the exchange echo those used by Donald in his 'Noise of Crisis' article. Alvarado, in both his articles, argues that child-centred education (though this is not a term he uses) is misconceived, for children's frame of reference comes not from an anterior and immanent pure consciousness, but from the dominant culture which surrounds them. The role of education is therefore not to confirm but to challenge this frame of reference and to cultivate students' ability to reason critically. By introducing students to systems of ideas and enabling them to make ideas their own, students will be, Alvarado argues, intellectually emancipated.

He develops this argument in his review of Masterman's book *Teaching about Television*. The core of Alvarado's position is that a central task for education is the development of students' intellectual skills. Child-centred education cannot do this for two reasons: first, the acquisition of cognitive skills is hard work, and students who learn in a child-centred classroom that work is pleasant and easy are unlikely to acquire these techniques of emancipation. Second, the endowment of knowledge which students bring to a classroom is likely to be insufficient, false and flawed. Student acquisition of a more powerful, empowering, heuristic toolkit is more likely, Alvarado considers, if teachers recognise that their professional responsibility is, in part at least, to provide the conceptual and theoretical parameters which will enable students to make uncontextualised knowledge their own. Clearly Alvarado's conception of good pedagogy – cultivating students' independent habits of mind, their ability to reason independently and critically and to selectively acquire knowledge when not all knowledge has equal status – is hard to realise. But, as he says, people's interests are seldom best served by defining only easy tasks for them.

Judith Williamson did not wish her response to be republished here. This is unfortunate because she slides her knife through several chinks in Alvarado's armour. She argues for a pedagogy that takes students' ideas and experiences as its starting point – surely unexceptionable. Williamson's common sense leads her to concur with Alvarado that ideas foreign to students' experience and the active intervention of a well-informed and confident teacher are indeed necessary elements in a classroom experience. Out of this exchange a series of unexceptionable conclusions can be derived, for both parties clearly have at least some of the truth on their side. But Alvarado's position is, for better or worse, the more characteristic of *Screen Education*'s overall position on pedagogical questions. He and Donald are united in their advocacy of the role of ideas, the importance of disciplined study and their view that the central emancipatory project of education is the development of students' ability to reason independently. *Screen Education* thus neither espoused a utilitarian pedagogy nor saw social engineering as a sufficient purpose for education.

Valerie Walkerdine's article 'Sex, Power and Pedagogy' echoes two themes present in other articles collected here: Alvarado's (and Donald's) rejection of child-centred or 'progressive' education, and Donald's conception of social relationships and identities as a shifting plurality of discourses and ideologies. Walkerdine introduces powerful new arguments in her discussion of sex, power and pedagogy. Taking one instance of classroom relationships, Walkerdine demonstrates the power of children's ability to resist and refuse the teacher's authority and shows that this infantile power may well have intolerable consequences. For children's power is unequally distributed between boys and girls, and boys' power (coupled with the teacher's conception of herself as a child-centred educator) is, at least in the incident discussed by Walkerdine, sufficient to challenge and insult the teacher as a legitimate authority and as a woman. This encounter demonstrates for Walkerdine the fallacious nature of progressive education, which reproduces unequal and intolerable patriarchal relationships. Although Walkerdine's evidence is vulnerable to the criticisms of other British studies of language use in the classroom made by Adlam and Salfield (see below), it is, surely, sufficient to demonstrate that gender is a decisive factor and that men and women do indeed have distinct loci of power which children appropriate and struggle over in play.

Put thus, Walkerdine's article sounds like a documentation of the obvious. But, the obvious is often invisible to those who view it, as we all do at times, through the optic of a well-established ideology (in this instance progressive education). Walkerdine demonstrates that patriarchal ideology disadvantages women even in classroom relationships between 'innocent' male pre-school children and an experienced woman teacher. She also (in a fascinating aside) uses her understanding of patriarchal relationships within the classroom to speculate on the reasons for the gendered nature of children's achievement in primary schools and to propose self-critically that her notion of the way ideology and power are related may be flawed. As she states, 'certain problems of determination do not seem to be totally resolved by this analysis'. Walkerdine points both to the pressure of a hierarchy of importance, of power, among ideologies, and to the complex connections between that hierarchy and the material world.

Diane Adlam and Angie Salfield, writing in *Screen Education* no. 34, review the main currents in socio-linguistics, a subject which has contributed to educational theory and to classroom practice in a variety of ways, notably by establishing linguistic difference as an explanation of the mutual incomprehension and hostility between teachers and learners and of the different levels of educational achievement displayed by different individuals and distinct social groups. Adlam and Salfield take Harold Rosen as one of their starting points. Rosen's work is notable for its pragmatic, political and progressive impact. His advocacy of an educational practice based on evaluating the different linguistic performance (and cultural, educational and pragmatic performance) displayed by different linguistic and cultural communities as 'separate but equal' has been extremely influential but is, the authors argue, mistaken. Adlam and Salfield's argument against a conception of pupils as innocent centres of value and competence and against the experiential, child-centred and progressive educational strategies rooted in such conceptions is consistent with other contributions to *Screen Education*. Here is the distinctive unifying feature of *Screen Education*'s explorations of educational theory and policy.

Adlam and Salfield argue that the theoretical basis of work such as Rosen's is weak; they comment acidly on his refusal to reflect on his conceptual assumptions and the discrepancy between his 'flamboyant moralising' and the findings of his researchers. Studies in this tradition are, they believe, prone to 'become merely studies in impression formation'. None the less, the work of Rosen and those like him has become established as a powerful legitimising ideology for pervasive contemporary educational policy and classroom practice, in spite of its reliance on 'bits of spoken language from supposedly random individuals'. There is, in British educational policy and practice, a pervasive notion of the 'equal validity of all experiences and cultures'. This leaves quite unanswered the question of why and how one particular linguistic/cultural nexus (post-Renaissance European rationalism) has achieved its unparalleled social dominance and its demonstrable power as a heuristic tool and instrument of human control of nature. Adlam and Salfield's challenge to the idea that distinct linguistic (and cultural) practices are equal and equivalent is salutary and persuasive. They argue, as do other *Screen Education* contributors whose work is reprinted here, for the vital importance of 'teaching children something which directly conflicts with their cultural identity and experience' and against the sentimental sanctification of the assumptions and ideolects of subordinate groups. Adlam and Salfield offer a well-grounded and clearly argued critique of a dominant educational ideology. The policy implications of their argument are as clear as its intellectual cogency. Both are representative of the overall project of *Screen Education* and are paralleled and substantiated by the work of other contributors to the journal.

Cultural Studies

The editorial to *Screen Education*, no. 34, 'Cultural Perspectives' (from which most of the articles about cultural studies reprinted here come), tells us that the category 'culture' has at least 164 meanings. No matter the number, it's clear that culture is both a much-used notion and a remarkably slippery one. Richard Johnson agrees, and sensibly recognises both the need for a pragmatic tolerance of conceptual imprecision and the usefulness of whatever advances in precision are able to be achieved. What he terms 'theoretical absolutism' may be as disabling as really sloppy thinking. But however promising 'culture' is as a site for investigation (and Johnson reminds us that, because it suffuses experience, it is therefore to hand for study in every classroom), it has customarily been approached from an overly specific position. 'The first problem', he states, 'is the tendency to approach culture within the narrowly disciplinary or theoretical frame'. The two principal frames of reference used in British cultural studies are the 'old New Left' (Richard Hoggart, Raymond Williams, E. P. Thompson) and the 'moment of theory' (Louis Althusser, Michel Foucault, formalism). Other important currents could be instanced, such as those drawing on Gramsci's work (see, for example, Geoffrey Nowell-Smith's article in *Screen Education*, no. 22, and Philip Simpson's in no. 28) and feminism (see numerous articles in *Screen Education*, including Angela McRobbie's, outlined below, which we are unable to republish for contractual reasons).

Johnson offers an analytical commentary on these diverse, sometimes congruent, sometimes conflicting, currents in British thinking about culture. From this incisive ordering of the field he draws useful conclusions, conclusions which constitute a rationale for cultural studies itself. Notably, that understanding how beliefs become principles of action in modern societies demands that we 'attend both to public representations and lived cultures' and also to the structural and historical processes which have made and remade beliefs and cultures. The materials through which these questions can be addressed are everywhere to hand. In the classroom the mass media are pervasive, but so too is the equally pertinent resource of students' own experience. The diversity of these experiences (the different impact of sexism on boys and girls, of racism on blacks and whites) needs to be recognised and understood if education is to take place. Here is the role of cultural studies in informing general education practice, and these experiences offer, Johnson reminds us, a unique resource for the educational practice of cultural studies itself.

Multi-culturalism is the official social doctrine of several nation states – Australia and Canada among them – formulated in response to their polyglot and heterogeneous social and cultural composition. Although not elevated in the UK to such a commanding position in public policy, the notion of multi-culturalism has, none the less, underpinned such political strategies as the Greater London Council's creation of a 'Rainbow Coalition' and the classroom practice of many schools. However, Hazel Carby argues that both the concept and the practice of multi-culturalism mystifies the real social relations of domination and racism which suffuse schools and society in Britain. She equates 'multi-culturalism' with 'national interest', seeing both as false, ideological notions affirming a spurious communitarianism and equality in order better to maintain real structures of oppression and exploitation. For her the liberal tolerance which informs multi-culturalism is a system of comforting self-deception, enabling members of dominant groups (or 'cultures') – that is, whites – to feel good about their progressive attitudes. The maintenance of multi-culturalism as a semi-official ideology is possible only in so far as the burning uppermost experience of humiliation and oppression suffered by subordinate groups – notably blacks and, most of all, black women – remains unrecognised and unacknowledged.

Carby herself makes connections with articles by Richard Johnson and James Donald reprinted in this volume. One could also make a link to Angela McRobbie's 'Settling Accounts With Subcultures: A Feminist Critique', in the same issue, *Screen Education*, no. 34. (Like McRobbie and Johnson, Carby was a member of the Centre for Contemporary Cultural Studies at Birmingham University.) McRobbie argues that the emphasis in cultural studies on the male experience has magically made the experience of women and girls invisible. Carby and McRobbie share a perspective which affirms that subordinate groups are able to subvert and re-appropriate the motifs and relationships generated by dominant groups. For Carby and McRobbie the experience of blacks and women is different from male groups; customarily they lack the power to re-make culture on terms of their own choosing. Carby's proposition that the doctrine of multiculturalism simply repositions subordinated blacks within white society is representative of a general historical shift in the conceptual paradigms of cultural studies, and in the practices, both in and out of the classroom, which follow from them.

In *Screen Education*, no. 31, entitled 'Interventions', the editorial considers the nature of the cultural interventions which are to 'bring about changes in practices and so in the disposition of social forces'. Much of *Screen Education*'s publishing was so directed. However, its 'interventions' generally had a specific character, for they were informed by direct experience of education practice. The distinct 'social shaping' of the core contributors to *Screen Education* by their work as teachers meant that the journal's intellectual 'interventions' were mercifully seldom marked by the donning of political certitudes like the team colours before a football match. Rather they were 'developed and reworked in the actual process of engagement'. The 'Interventions' editorial justly observed that *Screen Education* was neither programmatic nor 'a prioristic', and refers to an antecedent 'intervention', that of *Scrutiny*, the British journal of cultural critique and literary theory indelibly associated with F. R. Leavis and which was published from 1936 to 1952.

'Interventions' was not the only echo of *Scrutiny* in *Screen Education*. John Ellis's essay on film studies (reprinted in this volume) argues that film studies possesses an educational potentiality and vocation not far removed from that which *Scrutiny* claimed for the study of literature. And Richard Collins's article in *Screen Education*, no. 22, 'Revaluations', not only explicitly echoes the title of F. R. Leavis's book on English poetry but focuses on Leavis's (and *Scrutiny*'s) influence on media and cultural studies. *Screen Education*, no. 22, like *Screen Education*, no. 34 (from which the articles by Hall, Johnson and Carby came), also published several articles on the study of culture. As Collins observes, the orthodoxy in screen studies was (and is still) hostile to Leavis, whose influence was (and is) seen as closing off the mass media and popular culture from serious scholarly attention. Collins argues rather that Leavis (and many of the 'school' who clustered around the journal *Scrutiny*) opened up useful approaches to the media and popular culture. For Leavis and *Scrutiny*, unlike the mainstream of the British tradition of cultural theory, argued that cultural production and cultural consciousness were finally shaped or 'determined' (though that is not a word *Scrutiny* used) by economic and productive relationships. Whilst therefore sharing ground with Marxist analyses of culture, *Scrutiny* and Leavis insisted on more autonomy for the cultural realm than contemporary Stalinist Marxism was prepared to concede it. Such a position, Collins argues, offered a useful conceptual platform for culture and media studies, although he concedes that most film and media scholars working within a Leavisite paradigm (notably Robin Wood) grounded their work, not in this early moment of *Scrutiny* and Leavisite theory (which essayed a thoroughgoing survey of the mass media and other agencies of ideological reproduction), but in Leavis's later fetishisation of an autonomous realm of culture – a fetishisation, Collins argues, that advocates of the mass media, as a genuinely popular culture, reflect in an inverted form. Neither the fetishisation of high culture by Leavis's epigones, nor of mass culture by post-*auteur* theory film critics, constitute a useful model for the study of the mass media (including film) and their social impact. Collins argues rather for a totalising model of media and cultural studies which recognises the institutional and political-economic shaping of meaning as well as the distinctive, relatively autonomous, nature of the production and consumption of culture.

Collins's emphasis was shared by other commentators in *Screen Education*. Nicholas Garnham, for example, in his review essay in *Screen Education*, no. 22, comments on the similarities between *Scrutiny* and the structuralist Marxist position. And in issue no. 34, Stuart Hall (whose essay is reprinted here) referred approvingly to Raymond Williams's testimony to Leavis's 'cultural radicalism'. The editorial of *Screen Education*, no. 31, compared their journal's project to *Scrutiny* as being both different and the same. Collins's early essay testifies to *Screen Education*'s commitment to the investigation of numerous conceptual currents and to the assessment of a variety of intellectual paradigms. *Screen Education*'s contributors essayed – with some success as the selection of articles reprinted here demonstrates – the construction of new paradigms which were applied to emergent subject areas. The moment of *Screen Education*, though prematurely terminated, was one of a great deal of intellectual development, of exploration of new territory in film, media and educational studies, and of the growth of new scholarly talent.

One of the overarching influences on film and media studies in the 1970s was a quest for theory: for domestic precedents which could legitimise and direct these new subjects (hence the importance of Williams's recovery of a British tradition), and for foreign theory which addressed the central vexed question of the relationship between symbolisation and reality. The influence of Althusser (and Jacques Lacan) on contributors to *Screen* is perhaps the most obvious but far from the only example. John O. Thompson's essay 'Up Aporia Creek' reviews the contribution twentieth-century German Marxists offered to British media and cultural studies. Its object and tone exemplify a representative shift away from the Althusserian/Lacanian paradigm. Thompson reviews *Aesthetics and Politics*, New Left Books' collection of translated essays and commentaries by German Marxist aestheticians of the inter-war years (Ernst Bloch, Georg Lukács, Bertolt Brecht, Walter Benjamin, Theodor Adorno). He administers summary judgement on two recurrent characteristics of Marxist writing on politics and culture. He justly pillories its obscurity of language and consequential imprecision (or absence) of thought. And he trenchantly anathematises its relentless quest for a normative model, an authoritative text which would 'be not only equal to the world but equal to changing it'. Anyone who has the most cursory familiarity with film and cultural analysis of the period will know how much this will-o'-the-wisp haunted the pages of film and literary journals. Thompson's delightful image of 'a large Marxist machine called an Effectometer' eloquently punctures the pretensions of those who saw, as many did, comprehensive social change following struggle on the 'cultural front', and a reader or viewer experiencing a Damascene change in their world vision following upon their exposure to some sanctified 'Perfectly Progressive Text'. Thompson's article, replete with good sense, command of the literature, penetrating analysis and acerbic humour, had too little influence at the time of its first publication. Its message remains relevant and its wit retains its barbs. With luck the influence it may achieve in the 1990s through reprinting here will surpass that which it achieved in the 1980s in consequence of its first publication in *Screen Education*, no. 31.

Stuart Hall's essay on the interviews with Raymond Williams conducted by *New Left Review* is perhaps the best example of how productive was *Screen Education*'s distinctive review essay format. Hall's publications and his institution-building work in the 1970s and early 1980s took the Centre for Contemporary Cultural Studies (established at the University of Birmingham by Richard Hoggart and handed on to Richard Johnson by Hall) to an unchallenged eminence. This makes his commentary particularly interesting, since his subject, Raymond Williams, was no less important. As Hall acknowledges, his own work, and thus the course of British cultural studies in general, was orientated by Williams's pioneer explorations. Particularly interesting is the autobiographical element in Hall's review – provoked of course by the same characteristic in Williams's work – an element which is customarily absent in men's writing. But the kernel of Hall's commentary is his discussion of Williams's engagement with the vexed question of culture's relation to politics. The title of the Williams interviews, *Politics and Letters*, signals this theme, which was both the major theme of Marxist cultural theory and overwhelmingly the central issue addressed in British cultural and communication theory and in film and media studies of the 1970s and early 1980s. For 15 years the point of intersection between humanities and social sciences in British academic life was dominated by this question. It was posed particularly acutely in the emergent fields of cultural and communication studies and nowhere more so than in film and television studies – the main focus of *Screen Education*'s attention. Exploration of the relationships between representation and politics centred on the direction and extent of the determination of one by the other (or to make the point in a less Marxist way, on the nature – if any – of the causal connections between politics and culture). It involved a comprehensive archaeology, sifting the bones of German, Russian and Italian theory, and (where the bones retained some meat) translation.

But archaeology was neither confined to exotic sites nor the whole game. Some interesting and lively British skeletons were disinterred and much new theorising produced. Williams's work in *Culture and Society* and *The Long Revolution* – with all the idiosyncratic emphases noted by Hall – dug the ditches and laid the foundations for an understanding of the British tradition. Williams's quirks still influence the architecture of later constructions but it is in large part due to Williams that there is any contemporary construction at all. For without him (and the notable skeleton of Leavis which Hall's review rattles) the fields of cultural studies, of culture and society would long have remained fallow. Moreover, as Hall acerbicly remarks, Williams offers many salutary rebuttals of the prolific contemporary canards which dogmatically fetishised modernism and read off political effect from formal structure. Hall testifies to the most important and enduring lesson to be learnt from Williams – the necessity to think, to revise, rework and reject unsatisfactory models: especially when they are one's own.

Viewed through this optic, *Screen Education*'s absence of a 'line', of a hard-edged easily-summarised theoretical position, becomes one of the journal's distinguishing features. Because of its permeability to ideas and writers 'from below' (though as essays by Hall, Murdock, Eco and others demonstrate, *Screen Education* also attracted excellent contributions 'from above'), from contributors who for the most part were classroom teachers in schools and in higher and further education, *Screen Education* tended not to regard positions as closed. Its pages offered a continuing engagement with issues of cultural and educational theory, policy and practice, and the journal played a major part in opening up new areas such as television studies, feminist cultural and media analysis, and issues around representation. The questions which *Screen Education* addressed have not ceased to be relevant, nor have the fundamental theoretical problems been authoritatively resolved.

Notes

1. Reflecting, perhaps, the tentative nature of its beginnings, the first few issues are confusingly numbered. In the unlikely event that there are covetous bibliophiles whose search for a complete run is frustrated by apparent discrepancies, let us clear up any confusion surrounding the initial sequence. The first issue (of what was then called *Screen Education Notes*) appeared with no numbering. The second issue appeared in Spring 1972 as no. 1. The third issue appeared in the Summer of 1972 as no. 3. After this the journal was numbered sequentially.

2. David Buckingham, 'Lessons From SEFT', *Initiatives*, no. 11, 1989.

3. Ibid.

4. See, for example, Louis Althusser, *Lenin and Philosophy and Other Essays* (trans. Ben Brewster) London: New Left Books, 1971.

5. 'The Two Avant-Gardes', reprinted in Peter Wollen (ed.) *Readings and Writings: Semiotic Counter-Strategies*, London: Verso, 1982.

Part I
Film Studies

Chapter 1

Teaching Through Authorship*

John Caughie

The 'auteur theory' is still with us; still being kicked around, and still refusing to go away. What this article proposes is neither yet another attempt to make it go away, nor another attempt to resurrect or reconstruct it as a theory. Rather the article seeks to clarify the confused development of an approach which has posed as a theory while refusing coherent theoretical definition; and, centrally, it seeks to locate the uses and limitations which this approach may have in a specific teaching practice devoted to *The Searchers*.

Three points are worth making here. The first is a terminological clarification between 'auteur theory' and *auteurism* on the one hand, and 'authorship' on the other. Where the terms of 'auteurism' are used the reference will be specifically to those critical practices which have gone under the banner of either 'la politique des auteurs' or the 'auteur theory', and when reference is to 'authorship' the term is used in as neutral a sense as possible, without involving it in the critical practices of *auteurism*. I make this point since it seems to me that much of the confusion of *auteurism* derives from critics who have made fundamental adjustments to the approach, without allowing these adjustments to appear in the terminology. The result may be a misleading impression of consistency.

The second point is that the article proceeds from a position

* *Screen Education*, no. 17, Winter 1975/76.

unsympathetic to the centrality which *auteur* criticism gives to the director as creative source of the film. At the same time, it seems to me overreactive to dismiss the director as *one* of the points at which meaning enters the film, and, therefore, as one of the *potential* producers of meaning within the film. But while some understanding of how notions of authorship affect our reading of the film seems essential, equally essential is the realisation that authorship does not possess the final key – it does not provide the definitive reading. So what uses this article may propose for an authorship approach are to be considered as partial, requiring the verification and attestation of other approaches set out in this issue – genre, industry, image analysis, and so on.

The third point to make is that what is being suggested is a teaching strategy, rather than a theory of film, and the uses of authorship which are offered are to be situated within a strategy of teaching *The Searchers*. This point, however, has to be made with some hesitation. Much of the longevity of the '*auteur* theory' may be attributable to a number of critics (Bazin, Sarris, Wollen)[1] who have been willing to justify the 'theory' on its positive, empirical results, without insisting on a theoretical validation. Such an approach tends to ignore, or at least devalue, the negative 'blockages' which *auteurism* has erected within film criticism. As in criticism, so also in educational practice, and while authorship is offered as a strategy, the theoretical implications of the strategy need to be revealed, and it is for this reason that the following brief consideration of the development of the '*auteur* theory' is offered.

Development

The task of commenting on the development of *auteurism* has been made considerably easier by Edward Buscombe's article, 'Ideas of Authorship'.[2] Since an extended critique of *auteurism* is outwith the intentions of the present article, and since such an extension would largely involve a restatement of points already clearly articulated by Edward Buscombe, the following discussion contents itself with providing a context for authorship – isolating the dangers, and locating channels of usefulness – while encouraging the reader to turn to 'Ideas of Authorship' for amplification of the essential points.

Auteurism is rooted in the practice of the critics of *Cahiers du cinéma* – Truffaut, Rohmer, Godard, Bazin *et al.* – in the 1950s. The '*politique des auteurs*' was what its title proclaims it to be – a policy – initiated by *Cahiers* with the specific polemical intent of placing consideration of film on the same level as consideration of 'high' art, and giving film the artistic status of any cultural product stemming from a single, identifiable creative source – the *'auteur'*. The choice of an apparently literary term did not imply literary values within film, but rather indicates an attempt to place film, by analogy, within art. The term *'auteur'* was taken to imply an artist who was individually responsible for his creation and who created out of his own personality. *Cahiers*, in the 1950s, was enthusiastic rather than radical, and its aesthetic credo accepted, more or less without question, the elevation and celebration of the values of personal expressiveness and individual creativity. The 'policy' of *Cahiers* involved the separation of directors into *'auteurs'* and *'metteurs-en-scène'*, the latter being those directors who, more or less skilfully, translated given material onto the screen, while the former were those who were able to inject into the material an expression of their own creative personality and their own 'world view'. The distinction was evaluative, rather than descriptive. Having established a policy on an attitude towards individual expressiveness, the more enthusiastic of the critics then attempted to project it into theory, at least in so far as they refused, it seems, empirical evidence. The theoretical projection resulted in such claims as, (a) that, since it involved a personality, the worst film of an *auteur* must, necessarily, be of greater value than the best film of a *metteur-en-scène*, and (b) that, since artists matured, and since film directors were artists, the later films of a director were necessarily of greater value than the earlier. Though theories admit exceptions, the weight of empirical evidence against these claims demonstrates the difficulty which comes from giving an evaluative attitude the force of a theory.

A statement of André Bazin, in his critique of the excesses of his colleagues, directs attention to the strengths and the weaknesses of the *Cahiers* position. He refers to his unease at 'the naiveté of the assumption whereby . . . the intentions and the coherence of a deliberate and well thought out film are read into some little "B" feature'.[3] It was precisely the 'naiveté' of the *Cahiers*' search for *auteur* even among the despised depths of the 'little "B" feature' that produced the highly positive effect of bringing the 'B' feature to critical attention. The limitation of the search was that they rejected the films which did not reveal the intentionality and consistently expressed personality of an *auteur*. The danger of the literary analogy implicit in the terminology of *auteurism* has always been that it places consideration of film outside consideration of its conditions of production, treating the intentionality and individuality of literary production, and the industrial and popular basis of film production as if they were the same thing.

As a policy, locating *Cahiers* as a film magazine operating in a specific cultural context and wishing to transform that context, *'la politique des auteurs'* can retrospectively be viewed with some sympathy, and as a polemic it can be seen to have borne fruit in the attention it gave to unrecognised work, particularly the work of Hollywood directors. What is now most suspect is the 'theory' which has been fabricated out of the *Cahiers* reviewing practice. This *'auteur theory'* is the responsibility of Andrew Sarris, who with considerable licence, and parenthetically, translated the French *'politique'* into the American 'theory' ('Henceforth, I will abbreviate *la politique des auteurs* as the *auteur* theory to avoid confusion'.[4]) The weakness of Sarris's reformulation of *auteurism*, and it seems so fundamental that it is difficult to see why he should have been given such prominence in subsequent critical writing, lies, first, in his mystical refusal to 'fix' film (a film's 'tone cannot be fixed by anybody' and 'why all the fuss about talking and writing seriously about something one loves',[5] and second, more crucially, in his insistence on 'criteria of value', an insistence which he might himself admit indicates his interest as being the distribution of directors along a hierarchical scale of value, rather than the more theoretically-based investigation of how precisely the director produces meaning within the film. 'Ultimately, the auteur theory is not so much a theory as an attitude. . . .'[6] The one hint which might be drawn out of Sarris's 'attitude' and placed in an eventual theory might be contained in his notion of 'interior meaning' which he defines as the meaning 'extrapolated from the tension between a director's personality and his material'.[7]

The most useful attempt to develop *auteurism* as a means of understanding film (as opposed to classifying or evaluating film) has been made by Peter Wollen in both the 1969 edition of *Signs and Meaning in the Cinema*, and in its 1972 revision. Wollen's approach – *'auteur*-structuralism' – depends on revealing, within the work of a single director, a structure of meanings and relationships which run as a cohering thread throughout the work. Once this thread, this 'core of meanings', has been revealed in the work of a director, it can be activated as an interpretative agent in approaching a single film by that director, possibly uncovering a level of significance which would not have become apparent if the film had been treated as a discrete, autonomous unit. 'By a process of comparison with other films, it is possible to decipher, not a coherent message or world-view, but a structure which underlines the film and shapes it.'[8] As an interpretative tool, this approach has obvious value – value which is indicated, but not exhausted, by Wollen's own account of Ford and Hawks. His position occasionally drops into strange evaluative traps: to characterise Ford's work as 'richer' than that of Hawks because of the shifting relations between antinomies seems possible, even if unnecessary; but to go on to say that these shifting relations make Ford a 'great artist', beyond being simply an undoubted *auteur*' reintroduces a hierarchy of values which is out of place in structural analysis. But these evaluative 'slips' are uncharacteristic, and do not form the focus of the later work.

More limiting, if not crippling, to Wollen's *auteurism* is his tendency to see this structural core as constituting 'the film'; the business of *auteur*-structuralist analysis being to 'decipher' or 'decrypt' 'the film', discerning it from those elements which are not 'the film'. 'A great many features of films analysed have to be dismissed as indecipherable because of "noise" from the producer, the cameraman or even the actors'.[9] Such a view, ignoring such producers and qualifiers of meaning as genre conventions and iconography, studio practice, camera and acting, and thrusting towards the 'core of meanings' presumed (though not proven) to be produced by the director, offers monumental blind spots. Fortunately, they are blind spots which Wollen sees (if not 'sees through'). The *auteur* theory, he says in his 1972 conclusion,

> cannot be applied indiscriminately. Nor does an *'auteur'* analysis exhaust what can be said about any single film. It does no more than provide one way of decoding a film, by specifying what its mechanics are at one level.[10]

Later Wollen adds: 'I do not believe that the development of *auteur* analyses of Hollywood films is any longer a first priority'.[11] Perhaps the most positive development which Wollen's version of the *auteur* theory offers is the notion that the structure which is revealed in the film(s) through analysis is not necessarily the intentional product of a conscious director, but may equally enter the film as an unconscious meaning, unintended by the director. The implication of this is a reversal of the view of the director struggling to impose his personality on material, and leads to a view of the director, 'John Ford', as an identification of a particular structure, an identification made after, and on the basis of, a viewing of the films, rather than John Ford, a personalised identity who exists in the real world prior to, and independently of, the films. Thus the director is seen not as creative source, imposing on the film, from outside, a personality or a vision, but as a 'sub-code' within the film, a sub-code constructed out of experience of other films by the same director. The activity of the critical spectator is then directed, not towards discerning the thread of personality in the work of a director, or placing him on an evaluative scale, but rather towards investigating the way in which the directorial sub-code operates within the film, how it interacts with, modifies, and is modified by the other codes and sub-codes which also operate.

To summarise this necessarily simplified account of *auteurism*, the main thrust of the critique would be against placing the director outside cinema, separate from the film – as creator, free from the determinisms of the medium and its means of production, determined only by the need and the responsibility to express his personality; against the assumption of a 'knowable' personality, and its elevation into a criterion of value; against the assumption that this personality finds its way into the film in an unproblematic way; and against the view that the essential focus of critical activity is toward evaluation and/or interpretation, without accounting for the ways in which meanings and readings are produced.

Ford, accepted for the last 20 years as an 'undoubted *auteur*', and identified always as a strong personality ('Pappy'), has been particularly available to *auteurism*, an availability from which his work has probably suffered more than it has benefited. The work has gained from the emergence of a clear pattern, but the *auteurist* tendency to identify this pattern with a strong personality (supported by anecdotes and interviews) making statements 'freely' about the world, has thrown the focus of the attention on to the personality, obscuring the position of the director within the relations and conditions of production, and within ideology. For a clear view of Ford, and, more importantly, of film, it seems essential to drop the assumptions of centrality inherent in *auteurism*, and consider instead, investigatively, the operations of authorship within the film, as a sub-code, situating these operations, ultimately or immediately, in the context of the operations of the other determinants of the film's meaning.

Authorship and Teaching

The concern of the remainder of this article will be with the implications of the critical activity associated with authorship for teaching practice: specifically for a teaching of *The Searchers*. The theoretical injunctions are there, however, to qualify and define the practice. What I have tried to argue above is that the operation of the director within the film is not unproblematic, and statements about the director's role have to be qualified by some knowledge of the operation of the industry, of the medium, of genre, and of ideology. An authorship study, in other words, has to be situated within a comprehensive study of film, has to be qualified by the other components of a film course, and has to be clearly presented as being partial.

Given this understanding, the point of an authorship study is to discover how knowledge of the authorial sub-code affects the reading of a film. It offers an approach to the understanding of a film through reference to the director's established concerns and techniques. My own view, based on the belief that the object of a course is not to 'learn about the director' but to 'learn about the film' (or better still 'about film'), is that while the 'style' of the director and its effect on reading may be usefully approached in the classroom by process of discovery, the actual structure of concerns of the director might be indicated as a given – a point of departure for the course rather than the object of search. The 'given' structure can be presented in its simplest, basic form – with Ford, the antinomy of Desert and Garden; with Hawks, loyalty and the male group – allowing for verification and elaboration through exposure to the films; but its presentation at the outset allows the study to concentrate, not on the search for a pattern ('*auteurism*'), but for the way in which the pattern operates in the film ('authorship'). (On a purely practical level, the search for patterns in a presumably limited number of films seems, in any case, like a fairly artificial exercise, requiring strong, if concealed, direction from the teacher.) For this reason, strategically, the director selected for authorship study should be one whose authorial presence within the film is, as far as possible, uncontroversial – Ford and Hawks rather than Ray. Once more, the point is not to establish *auteur*, but to study operations of patterns.

Ford and Hawks recommend themselves, again, as directors working within genre. The confrontation of author and genre seems like an essential strategy, since it offers a means of examining the status of the director as producer of significance when the material which he is using already has its own associative significance. The director inflects conventions, but the existence of conventions usefully questions the limits of the director's 'free' expression. Classroom discussion can be directed, towards questioning which sub-code – generic or authorial – is enabling a reading to be made. The point is not abstruse or overly sophisticated, but it is crucial. Films operate within conventions; effectiveness of expression is determined by competence and expectation. The confrontation of authorial 'freedom' with genre determinism ('the tension between an author's personality and his material'?) offers an explicit and accessible way of approaching this potentially difficult area. Thus, again strategically, Ford, operating within explicit genre conventions, rather that Hitchcock, whose determinisms are more concealed.

Authorship and *The Searchers*

The ideal context for the specific study of authorship in *The Searchers* is taken to be a course which includes at least two other Ford films. Though a course consisting only of *The Searchers*, supported perhaps by slides and extracts, seems perfectly feasible, in an authorship course the presence of secondary feature films provides, at least, the opportunity for verification. Since the object is to look at the operation of authorship, rather than to discover the complexity of the director's thematic concerns, the 'supporting features' might best be Westerns, allowing an elaboration of the confrontation of Ford and genre. My own choice would be for either *Stagecoach* or *My Darling Clementine* (*Stagecoach* for its 'classicism', and because there is a valuable and adequate extract from *Clementine*) and *The Man Who Shot Liberty Valance*. The course would be supplemented by slides and extracts, not all from Ford films. Again ideally, the authorship study would presume a prior study of genre and of industry. If these had not been covered as separate studies they would have to be built centrally into the course, over and above their position there as qualifiers.

The following treatment attempts to narrow the focus to *The Searchers*, avoiding the assumption of 'supporting features', but assuming the availability of slides and the *Clementine* extract. It offers three areas for consideration: style, and thematic concerns – which, more or less, conform to the levels of form and content – and ideology. While the three are placed under headings for ease of presentation, it is obvious that there is no autonomy among them, and in teaching practice it should be neither desirable nor necessary to preserve the illusion of autonomy. Rather, it is important to reveal the operation of each on the others, and the position of the director within them all, neither creating, not ultimately controlling, but inflecting, at least potentially.

Style

There is a temptation implicit in the centrality which *auteurism* gives to the 'core of meanings' to privilege content (the 'indicator' of an *auteur*) over form (the 'indicator' of a *metteur-en-scène*); to treat style as transparent, 'through which' meaning is seen, but not itself producing meaning. Not only has this to be avoided, but it seems that style might usefully be placed at the beginning, as a way into the film, and as an opportunity for the close analysis which might provide the basis for the study of authorship at other levels. The point of this stylistic analysis should not simply be to illustrate some of the formal visual and narrative characteristics of Ford's films, though it has to be established that there are 'typical' characteristics in his work; not should it be to validate, simply, Ford's credentials as a creative artist. Much more it should be directed towards investigating the ways in which Ford ('Ford') uses existing visual and narrative conventions, articulating the spectator's previous experience of film language to produce meaning.

The first 'act' of the film, up to the funeral sequence, offers a great deal of varied, but accessible, and important material for analysis. Within this long section, having discussed its general significance in establishing the foundations of the narrative, and such particular significances as Ethan's rejection of kinship with Martin, and the verbal suppression of the relationship between Ethan and Martha, certain sequences can be isolated for closer study:

1. *The arrival/return of Ethan* – The extreme formality of the opening shots has to be discussed – not merely noted, but examined for its effect on our subsequent reading of the film. (A 'commutation' – what else would have changed if this opening had been presented differently?) The *Clementine* extract of the church social might be introduced as another instance where Ford uses a highly-stylised, almost ceremonial, presentation. Both sequences show people coming from the desert to the community, both show a family community. How does the style place the community within our reading of Ford's film(s)?

Slides from the beginning and end of the film would isolate not only the formal composition of the images, but would also show the cyclical structure of the film. Formal composition is matched by formal narrative structure. Why is formality important?

The more confined, less-obtrusively stylised presentation of the family within the homestead, engaging in the rituals of the meal and the sharing of gifts (and payment of debts), could be treated, in contrast, as an example of 'invisible' style. The contrast itself could be talked about. The impression is not of a carefully constructed scene, but close examination will reveal the function of camera placement, character groupings and unobtrusive editing in the presentation of relationships. The moment of Ethan's raising of Debbie might be pin-pointed, and compared with the later occasion when the gesture is exactly replayed.

2. *The massacre sequence* – The starting point might be the camera movement in on Ethan's shadowed face, looking out over his horse's back, almost, it seems, 'at' the massacre. The point is an elusive one, perhaps, but examination of the precise effect of this one camera movement might lead to useful discussion and insight. It can be established that camera movements in Ford films are, typically, infrequent and concealed. It might also be drawn out from discussion that this particular camera movement into close-up is usually associated with flashback, or some other form of interiorisation. Discussion can then go on to the precise meaning which might be produced by this relatively obtrusive use of a convention which has an associative significance. Does the association carry over to give Ethan's look the force of an interiorisation of the massacre? The point would seem to be born out by the 'unreal' lighting of the massacre sequence itself.

The stylisation of the massacre sequence is a fairly obvious point, but it might be directed towards discussion of verbal suppression – the fact that everything is taking place below the verbal level. This seems to be a feature of the film, and the opening shots could be used here as another example. More crucial, but more difficult to introduce at this point, is the verbal suppression of rape and sexual relations between whites and Indians which are talked around rather than about, in sentences which trail off or are cut off.

Also the effect of the very stylised appearance of Scar should be discussed.

3. *The graveside sequence* – This would best be approached through slides of other Fordian gravesides – *Grapes of Wrath, Young Mr Lincoln, Liberty Valance* – to establish its typicality within Ford, and of gravesides in other Westerns – they are part of the iconography, with slides available from *Shane* and the Italian Westerns – to establish its typicality within the genre. The comparison with other Ford movies can point to the specific inflections in this film, and the comparison with other Westerns points to the general Fordian inflection.

Under style, Ford's narrative strategy might also be considered – particularly in *The Searchers*, his use of an epic, highly formal structure. While many Westerns are referred to as epic, the reference is usually to scale, but in *The Searchers* the structure itself seems to be specifically epic, the features being the totally non-naturalistic compression of time and place, and the circuitous

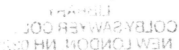

intertwining of the fates of the protagonist and the antagonist (the sense that their paths have crossed before), both of which features are definitive in classical epic. Again, how does the refusal of narrative naturalism affect our reading, and, crucially, what are its limits? At what point, and with what ideological results, is naturalism reintroduced?

Finally, Ford's treatment of landscape has always been seen as a central element of his style, and in *The Searchers* attention has to be drawn to the function of the landscape, and to the way in which figures are presented within it. The sense of a community is strong, but it is represented visually by two homesteads isolated in the desert. Comparison might again be directed toward the *Clementine* extract, where there is the same sense of a community sprouting in the desert, and contrast could be made with *Liberty Valance* where this is a central thematic concern, but the movie itself is predominantly made on studio sets.

Also, in considering landscape, the question might be raised of the motivation for, and the effect of, departing from natural locations, in the approach through the pond to the Indian camp, and in the shoot-out with Futterman. Discussion of this apparently simple point could be directed towards discussion of the way in which the industry works, and even of the way in which realism works.

Thematic concerns

Since the opposition of the Desert and the Garden seems to me, following Peter Wollen and others, central to Ford's films (though not, of course, unique to Ford), consideration of the formal presentation of the landscape provides a useful bridge into the thematic concerns, particularly useful since it contains the demonstration that thematic concerns are not something separate, but are already present in style and formal arrangement.

It is one of the propositions of this article that the antinomy of the Desert and the Garden be presented by the teacher (following, ideally, some discovery of its presence at the formal level) as an element of Western mythology, and the introduction of the relevant issues in Henry Nash Smith's *The Virgin Land*[12] provides a way into this mythology.[13] The recognition of a mythology points to an awareness of Ford working within a structure of meanings, rather than Ford as creative source of all the meanings.

The apparent simplicity of this structural principle, the antinomy of the Desert and the Garden, conceals a considerable degree of interpretative and analytical potency. In the first place, it extends itself into important ramifications – related antinomies which, as is indicated by Jim Kitses,[14] are definitive characteristics of the Western genre. Central to *The Searchers* are the clearly related antinomies, Savagery/Civilisation and Nomad/Community, specific inflections within this film of Desert/Garden. (One of the 'uses' of *Liberty Valance* within the course is that it refers specifically, and explicity, to the Desert becoming the Garden.)

In the second place, the antinomy and its inflections do not exist simply at the level of overall content (they are not, simply, what the film is about), but are distributed through a film at a number of levels, making them available to analysis as much as to interpretation.

We have already seen how the central antinomy is present in the visual presentation of homestead and desert landscape. Developing out of this, inflections can be seen to be present at the level of the structural (as opposed to the psychological) formation of the characters – not only between the characters, but also within the character. Thus, if the polarities of the antinomy are seen as being Family Community and Scar ('scar', precisely, on the community and within the characters), the characters caught between the polarities are seen to be suspended in tension between the two, possessing elements and functions of each: Ethan, protecting the community but not belonging to it, a white man who scalps Indians; Martin Pawley, belonging apparently to the white community but eighth part Cherokee, first seen in moccasins, riding bareback; Debbie, first seen, dressed in blue-check calico (almost a cliché of the West), within the family, next seen in Scar's tent dressed in skins and holding the pole of scalps; Captain Reverend Clayton, a soldier-priest; and Mose Harper, racially ambiguous, half crazy, wandering with the Indians (protected by his craziness) but longing for a rocking chair. The action of the film leads to the resolution and non-resolution of these tensions; Debbie, Martin and Mose, recuperated into the community, and Ethan (the most 'scarred') returning to 'wander between the winds'. The scope of the film is that it locates the antinomy as a tension within character as well as a social tension, and it compares usefully again with *Liberty Valance* where the concern is more socio-political. As a teaching strategy, the structural consideration of how each character fits a pattern, offers a way out of the psychological consideration of character 'as if' they lived in the real world.

Yet again, the concern is not with Ford creating meaning out of the air, but of the specific articulations which Ford makes of a structure which is recurrent in his own work, but which is also present in genre. An interesting point can, in fact, be made here which illustrates a crucial distinction between this approach to authorship and the more traditional *auteurism*. In the book *John Ford* by Michael Wilmington and Joseph McBride,[15] a book which follows exactly an *auteurist* principle of tracing values to Ford's personality and background, the interpretation centres on the notion of miscegenation. The section on *The Searchers* is one of the best things in the book, and the interpretation is persuasive; at one level, miscegenation is what the film is about. Where it seems to me to limit itself, however, is that it stops short at the meaning which it is presumed Ford intended (the way in which his personality and values expressed themselves in this film) without going on to relate this to the structural antinomy which pervades Ford's work, and which is a feature of the Western. Such an extension of the *auteurist* interpretation into the structural analysis of authorship would reveal the theme of miscegenation to be yet another inflection (an 'objective correlative'), specific to this film, of the antinomy of Savagery and Civilisation, which is itself an inflection of the antinomy, general to Ford and to Westerns, of Desert and Garden. It is this extension of the reading process which an authorship study should aim at, and, in the classroom, discussion has to be directed beyond a simple interpretation of what this single film is about, towards Ford's status within the structure of meanings which exists already within genre and mythology.

Ideology

The examination of the operations of ideology is both an essential task in film teaching, and a difficult one: essential, since film is one of the, as yet, relatively unaccommodated areas in which ideology can be tackled; and difficult, since, though the educational system works to make students aware of form and content, it does not work to make them aware of ideology, and the film teacher may find himself taking on a larger task than merely teaching film. (Analyses of this are offered by Nell Keddie and Jim Grealy in *Screen Education*, no. 15, Summer 1975.[16]) Initially, at least, and particularly in an authorship study, it may be necessary to approach ideology obliquely; and the danger of this (in an authorship study) is that it is liable to come out looking like personal values. The task, then, is to 'situate Ford in ideology', to see the way in which the 'Fordian world-view' is not simply a system of personal moral and social values, but is a mediation of the dominant ideology; and, crucially, to see the ways in which the spectator is 'tricked' into seeing the presentation of the world as being natural, and therefore unassailable: tricked, not by Ford, who may himself be the 'victim' of determinants, but by form, and the satisfaction of the spectator's own formal expectations.

The ideological analysis of *The Searchers* seems to me to be complex, not least because of the already mentioned characteristic of verbal suppression, which places meaning below the explicit level of what is said, but there are areas which can usefully be discussed in a teaching project.

The nature of the community, the status of the family, and the status of women within the family are important areas, and discussion can focus on the way in which the family community is defined by the mother (Martha – mother, and, implicitly, lover; and Mrs Jorgensen – mother, and explicitly, teacher), but the Desert is defined by men, the active participants in struggle. The nature of the reverence for the mother, typical, again, of Ford and genre, the nature of its limitations, and the extent to which both are statements of a general perspective, are vital parts of the discussion of ideology in the film.

In relation to Ford's cavalry films and to the traditional notion of the US cavalry, the position of the army in this film is interesting. As an institution, the army is criticised for its brutality, and satirised for its rigidity, the comparison being weighted in favour of the roughness and readiness of Clayton's Rangers, a preference which is more populist (Goldwater) than anti-militarist. The point has to be drawn out that, whereas, in the sequence of the discovery of Look's body, we see the consequences of the cavalry attack, but not the attack itself, in the sequence of the Ranger's attack on Scar's camp, we are excited by the attack, but 'protected' from its consequences.

Central to discussion of the film in ideology is the position on race and the relationship between races. It has frequently been urged that the film is, to some degree at least, sympathetic to Scar, and it is illuminating to discuss how this impression is gained. The point is that Scar is a highly stylised figure, 'dignified' but uncomplicated, who derives his sympathy not from what he does, which is brutal, but from what has been done to him. If Scar is sympathetic, it is because Ethan, his antagonist, shares his brutality. It seems indicative of our expectations of the presentation of Indians in Westerns that this stylised (in real terms, caricaturised) presentation of the 'noble savage' is enough to produce the impression of sympathy. This seems to be an accessible point at which students could be made aware of the way in which their own acceptance of film convention qualifies their ideological reading of the film, and, potentially, of the world.

Equally, discussion of the recuperation of Debbie back into the family community offers a possible point at which the formal determination of ideology can be approached. The explicit 'message' of the film seems to be that Debbie was content in Scar's household ('unscarred'?), and that Ethan was wrong in his expectation of her brutalisation by the experience. But the resolution of the film is the recuperation of Debbie into the white community – whites remain white, and Indians remain Indian. In a sense, this recuperation, put forward, and generally accepted, uncritically, as natural, seems to redirect the moral thrust which the film might have followed. Thus, even if the 'intended meaning' of John Ford was a critique of the racism latent in white society, the need for a narrative resolution, a tidy and happy ending, forces the resolution of the 'confusion' of racial mixture, removing the sting from the critique by asserting what is dominantly assumed to be the natural order. The demands of narrative, compliance to which is itself ideologically determined, in turn determine ideology, and John Ford can be seen as the victim of form, rather than its creator.

The point of the ideological component of an authorship study is, yet again, to indicate crucial limitations on the author's capacity freely to express his individual personality, and to place both the author and his audience in society.

Conclusion

The authorship study of *The Searchers*, then, is directed not only to revealing the ways in which the structures associated with John Ford produce meaning within the film, but also towards discovering the limits on Ford's (and hence, any author's) free individual expressiveness. If the second part of this project seems negative, my own feeling would be that, in a system of cultural education which has always placed its stress on the individually responsible and free creator, to show an alternative would be a positive proposition.

The limitations of authorship study itself have been stated throughout – supplementation and qualification from consideration of genre, industry, star system, acting, technology, and so on, have to be made – but, at the same time, there seems no reason why consideration of authorship should not be given at least equal status with each of these individual items in the progression towards a total study of film, and the investigation of the effect of the author on the reading of a film forms a strategically-useful and educationally-necessary part of film study.

Notes

1. André Bazin, 'La politique des auteurs' in Peter Graham (ed.) *The New Wave*, London: Secker & Warburg, 1968. Andrew Sarris, 'Notes on the Auteur Theory in 1962', *Film Culture*, no. 27, 1962–3, also reprinted in *Film Theory*, Mast & Cohen, OUP, 1974. *The American Cinema*, E.P. Dutton, 1968. Peter Wollen, *Signs and Meaning in the Cinema*, London: Secker & Warburg, 1969, 1972.

2. Edward Buscombe, 'Ideas of Authorship', *Screen* vol. 14, n. 3, Autumn 1973.

3. Ibid, p. 139.

4. Ibid.

5. Andrew Sarris, 'Where I Stand on the New Film-Crit', *Village Voice*, 11 August 1975.

6. *The American Cinema*, p. 30.

7. Ibid.

8. Peter Wollen, *Signs and Meaning*, 1972, p. 167.

9. Ibid, p. 104.

10. Ibid, p. 168.

11. Ibid, p. 173.

12. Henry Nash Smith, *The Virgin Land: The American West as Myth and Symbol*. Cambridge, Mass.: Harvard University Press, 1950.

13. Also useful in this area are: Jenni Calder, *There Must be a Lone Ranger*, London: Hamish Hamilton, 1974; Frederick Jackson Turner, *The Significance of the Frontier in American Life*, first published 1893, reprinted by Prentice-Hall in *Frontier and Section*, a selection of Turner's essays.

14. Jim Kitses, *Horizons West*, London: Secker & Warburg, 1969 (note particularly p. 11).

15. Michael Wilmington and Joseph McBride, *John Ford*, London: Secker & Warburg, 1974.

16. Nell Keddie, 'What are the criteria for relevance?' and Jim Grealy, 'Film Teaching and the Ideology of the Educational System', *Screen Education*, no. 15, Summer 1975.

Chapter 2

The Same Old Story: Stereotypes and Difference*

Steve Neale

The term 'stereotype' has been widely used in attempts to understand racism and sexism in films and in other artistic texts. In this
article, I want to draw out and challenge some of the implications
of this approach by examining the limitations of the problematic
within which it is inscribed. In particular, my concern is that
certain uses of the concept (above all the tendency to think of
'stereotypes' as empirical entities) can actually block the productive analysis of the bodily differences central to categories of
race and gender.

As a critical concept, stereotyping is applicable almost solely to
the analysis of character and characterisation; to that extent it is
concerned with only one set of elements within the structure and
functioning of a text. In addition, the characters and characterisation within any one text are treated as exemplary of a process
of *repetition* which links the specific text (and the characterisation
within it) to other texts and other discursive forms. According to
this problematic, a stereotype is a stable and repetitive structure
of character traits. The verification of its existence is therefore
dependent, first, upon the analysis of a range of texts; second,
upon a reduction of the scope of the analysis to those elements
within the texts which concern the construction of character; and

Screen Education, nos 32/33, Autumn/Winter 1979/80.

third, upon a further restriction to those characters and modes of characterisation (and to those aspects of character and characterisation) that appear to be relatively constant from one text to another. At each stage, the specificity of the texts being analysed will be lost or ignored, just as the multiplicity of their systems and operations will be drastically underestimated. In other words, such analyses will tend to do precisely what stereotypes themselves are supposed to do – they reduce the complexity and heterogeneity inherent in a process and its relations to a single, homogeneous (and repetitive) function.

When the concept of the stereotype and the methodology it implies are used for purposes of ideological analysis, their reductiveness can easily obscure or even erase altogether those features of a text and its systems which are not only equally pertinent to the analysis but could also open up further areas of enquiry. To take just one example[1] *The Birth of a Nation* has, quite rightly, been characterised as a racist film. But there are a number of ways of discussing its racism. One would be to catalogue the ways in which the black characters within it are restricted to a narrow range of demeaning stereotypical roles; those, for instance, of the dangerous savage, the faithful servant and the plantation comic. This will confirm, from the perspective adopted, that *The Birth of a Nation* is racist. But it will tell you very little about *The Birth of a Nation* itself, since these stereotypes can easily and readily be found in other contemporary films and in vaudeville acts, plays and novels. And it will tell you very little about racism itself, other than the fact that it involves stereotypes. Since sexism, for example, also involves stereotypes, and since, moreover, it could be said that the white characters in *The Birth of a Nation* are just as stereotyped as the black ones, and since it could equally be said that this is a feature not only of the 'Southern plantation myth', upon which the film draws, but also of the melodramatic form which it deploys, then you are still left with a number of important and complex issues either unresolved or not addressed at all.

Another way of discussing *Birth of a Nation* in terms of its racism would be to examine its overall structure and, in particular, the 'neuralgic' points within it. The emphasis here would be less on character than on *narrative* and *fantasy*. If one were to do this, account would have to be taken above all of the role and significance of the family within the film, of the fact, in particular, that all the 'troubles', conflicts and divisions that produce its drama are specified in family terms – even (especially) the Civil War. The source of the film's racism would emerge as acute anxiety in the face of the possibility of miscegenation, since miscegenation is characterised simultaneously as a threat to the integrity of the family and as a threat to the sign of its purity – its white, virginal daughter. I certainly wouldn't want to claim that this exhausts the possibilities of a reading of the significance of the stress on racial difference in the film. Even within the kind of approach suggested, there would have to be detailed analysis of the precise links made between the family, between the national division represented by the two sides in the Civil War, between the racial division that the war exacerbates and between the family romance that it elaborates and the fetishisation of virginal purity that it produces. But at least this approach does address the specificities of the film and would lead, in my view, to engagement with some of the wider issues raised by racism, particularly in so far as it involves the significance of anxieties that centre on bodily difference and, hence, castration and fetishism – something, I suspect, which is of particular importance in racist fantasy and ideology.

Stereotyping

I want now to look at some of the problems involved in the ways in which the notion of stereotyping is embedded in ideological analysis and argument, and at what happens once a stereotype has been identified and discussion moves from the level of description to the level of aesthetic and ideological evaluation. Two basic positions can be identified here.

The first involves measuring the stereotype against what is conceived of as 'the real'. Stereotypical characters are evaluated negatively to the extent that they are not like 'real people', to the extent that the characters do not appear as complex individuals living complex lives in a complex society. A variant on this position is able to take social groups and categories like blacks, gays and women into account. Here the stereotype is measured against the reality that the category itself is held to reflect. It is found wanting in so far as it is not fully adequate to the heterogeneity and complexity of the reality to which the category refers – a reality which consists, like the category, of real, concrete individuals with all their different personalities, attitudes and experiences. The problem with this position is its inherent empiricism. Although it claims that the stereotypes it identifies (which are, incidentally, not simply there in the texts examined but are constructed and classified in analysis) are measured against 'the real', the actual object of comparison is other discourses *about* the real. Castigations of stereotypical characterisations on the grounds that they do not approximate to the complexities of real, concrete individuals are in fact covert demands for one particular form of analysis rather than another – a popular generic narrative, for example, might be evaluated according to the canons of the bourgeois novel. Thus attacks on stereotypes of blacks or gays or women because they do not correspond to the variety of personality, attitude and experience that those categories include often indicate an implicit appeal for realist characterisation: the categories themselves are treated as reflections of a pre-given reality instead of as categories constructed and defined within specific modes of discourse. As a result the distinctions marked by the categories are treated as non-pertinent. What ultimately matter, from this point of view, are not the groups *as groups* but only the individuals within them.

The second position differs in that it measures the stereotype, not against 'the real', but against an 'ideal' – against a characterisation which would act as a 'positive' rather than a 'negative' image for, say, blacks, gays or women. This position therefore recognises the positive effectivity of images, discourses and texts, that they are interventions rather than reflections. In this, it is dependent upon a negative evaluation of stereotypes, upon the fact that the term stereotype itself has negative connotations. However, if those connotations are removed, what in fact is being demanded is the replacement of one set of stereotypes by another. Thus the problem here is that of the concept of the stereotype in general – the failure to recognise both the limits of a stress on character and the limits of those conceptions of character upon which it draws. Basically, the argument is that identification is, or can be, ideologically and politically progressive, since it seeks to replace one form of identification (with the stereotypical image) and another (with the 'positive' or 'ideal' image). My own view is that identification as the goal of an artistic practice can never be progressive since it fails to produce knowledge or to allow for the inscription of the potentiality of transformation, both of which are dependent upon the inscription of difference and of distance. Moreover, what is rarely considered is the textual mode within which either 'positive' or 'negative' characterisations are, have been or can be produced. Here the limiting effects of a concentration on character and characterisation at the expense of attention to textual systems and modes of address become particularly apparent. Secondary forms of identification (such as identification with a character) achieve their effect and their meaning through their inscription within textual systems and strategies: in most forms of cinema, these depend in turn upon an identification with the text itself. It is this primary identification that provides the basis of the spectator's relationship to the text and its characters and so requires initial attention and analysis.

Difference

This returns us to the problem with which we began, that of focusing upon character at the expense of the text as a whole and of the global systems that traverse and articulate it. My argument is that one way out of this impasse may be to recast analysis of racism and sexism that is currently limited by the 'stereotype' problematic by shifting attention from *repetition* to *difference*.

The notion of the stereotype acknowledges repetition, but it tends either to ignore difference altogether or to reduce its role simply to the provision of variation, without thinking through what the status of variation might be. Quite clearly, there is a sense in which there is an important recognition here of the discursive economy of, say, popular mainstream cinema. But the crucial and central significance of difference with that economy tends to be missed. Difference and variation are not optional extras, they are not there to make repetition less evident, to conceal it behind a palatable surface. Nor are they added on to repetition. Rather, they are part and parcel of its fabric. They are necessities, absolutely basic to the production and provision both of meaning and of pleasure. Although in one sense each instance of the appearance of, say, the 'dumb blonde' character is a repetition of the same, there is also a sense in which each instance is always new, always different. It is not only that the narrative within which the character is constructed will be different each time or that the text within which the character is constructed will be different each time: in a more general and fundamental theoretical sense, pure repetition, either within or across different instances of signification, is impossible. However simple the point, it is also worth noting here that, within any one text or within any one corpus of texts, a character or character type always assumes its identity and its meaning in so far as it is distinguishable from other characters and character types. It assumes its identity and meaning in so far as it is different, and in so far as the differences are marked – textually – as pertinent ones. It is at this point, I think, that the use of the stereotypical problematic in analyses of racism and sexism tends to break down and makes it more difficult to think through the issues that it wishes to address.

As Elizabeth Cowie has pointed out, the designation of a text as sexist depends not upon a recognition of elements always already present in the text, but upon a reading of those elements through the concepts and meanings located in other discourses. The concept 'sexism' is not located in the text that is analysed but in the discourse used to analyse it. It is hence in the interaction between this latter discourse, the text itself and the other discourses in relation to which a text inevitably locates itself that meanings will be produced which may or may not be labelled sexist.

Sexism in an image cannot be designated materially as a content in the way that denotative elements such as colours or objects in the image can be pointed to. Rather it is in the development of new or different definitions and understandings of what men and women are and their roles in society which produce readings of images as sexist; the political perspective of feminism produces a further level of connotative reading. Sexism is not always already there in the image but is produced through the process of signification in the coming into play of a number of connotative levels.[2]

The same applies to racism. A text can only be read as racist if the discourse through which it is read contains that term and, hence, an explicit or implicit definition of it.

Both sexism and racism are dependent upon the existence of bodily differences. They both function by marking certain specific differences as significant and by inscribing those marks and their significances into ideological and political discourses and relations such that they become the basis for systematic discrimination across a variety of social institutions and practices:

The problem of sexism is not that men and women are different but that that difference is inscribed politically and ideologically, and feminism as a political movement opposes that inscription within our society as presently constituted.[3]

Returning now to the analysis of specific texts – and remaining at the level of character and characterisation to which the problematic of stereotyping addresses itself – it is possible to propose a different approach in which the functioning of repetitive characterisations of blacks, gays and women can be understood. Here one would look, first, for the extent to which the sexual or racial traits of the characters are textually marked and, second, for the significance that the text attributes to them: in other words, for the extent to which and the way in which a text *constructs* sexual and racial differences with respect to its characters and for the extent to which and the ways in which it *produces meanings* around them. From here it would be possible to examine a range of texts and to note the links between them. The significance of restricted and repetitive modes of character and characterisation in terms of race and sexuality is likely then to be that such modes are not there, so to speak, in and for themselves, but rather as a means by which specific forms of difference can be marked and re-marked in accordance with the racial and sexual distinctions and discriminations constructed by the discourses that traverse and articulate the texts being analysed. Stereotyping (if the term is to be retained) will emerge not, or not simply, as a function of repetition, but rather as a crucial part of a process of differentiation. It is to that process that attention needs to be drawn.

Notes

1. For another, see Rosalind Delmar's remarks on *The Maltese Falcon* in 'Gays and Film: Le Gai Se Voir', *Screen Education*, no. 26, Spring 1978.
2. Elizabeth Cowie, 'Women, Representation and the Image', *Screen Education*, no. 23, Summer 1977, p. 19.
3. Ibid.

Chapter 3

Women, Representation and the Image*

Elizabeth Cowie

The study of images in schools and colleges has been widely promoted over the last few years. Developing in conjunction with the growth of film studies in the past ten years, the concern with images and how they produce meaning draws on similar concerns of those of film education: how images are constructed, how they are read and produce readings, the implications of the various determinants of construction, the development of 'visual literacy' in students. Image-work, too, seemed to show a way of presenting the discoveries of semiotics through the use of its concepts and tools in the analysis of images in schools. Already established as an area of work by J. P. Golay (though he himself was not a semiotician), it was developed in particular through the work of Roland Barthes, Stuart Hall and Guy Gauthier.[1] Work on images in this way has not only enabled many of the concerns of the film teacher to be introduced in courses without the expense and timetabling of a proper film course, but has also opened up areas of work on the still photograph, which itself has been incorporated into work on film – through the kinds of teaching materials such as *Teachers' Protest*[2] introducing notions of editing, framing, and narrative construction through the combination and ordering of still images. The developing interest in, and work on, image analysis by photographers can be seen in a variety of specialised courses, and also in schools where photography as an examined

Screen Education, no. 23, Summer 1977.

subject is increasingly taught, as well as in magazines like *Camerawork*,[3] and articles such as the one by professional photographers Terry Dennett and Jo Spence in *Screen Education*, no. 21, Winter 1976/77.

However, the work has produced a number of problems:

1. The tendency (a hopeless cause) for work on images at the denotative level to develop into a search for a 'language' of images.
2. The problem that, having established with students operations of the image at the denotative level – the constraints of production and reproduction of the image and implications of its context of viewing – in fact little more has been achieved than produce a 'developed sensitivity' in students to images – to see more in them.

(This is a potential danger in the kind of work outlined by Richard Eke in *Screen Education*, no. 21, Winter, 1976/77.) Further, when connotative readings and analyses are then engaged in, other problems arise: Andrew Bethell wrote in *Screen Education*, no. 13, Winter 1974/75:

we need to develop an entirely different form of analysis, one which allows us to come to terms with the formal qualities of the medium, ie how it works to get its message across, while at the same time making us aware of its ideological qualities, ie what does the message really mean in terms of where it has come from and where it is being received?

Here a separation is being made between how a message-image signifies – conveys its message – and what the message means. However, such a separation cannot be made except theoretically; where Roland Barthes writes in 'Rhetoric of the Image' of the 'literal image', identifying this as he does with the 'denotative message', he qualifies the argument by noting that 'the viewer of the picture receives the "perspective" message and the cultural message *simultaneously*', and indicates that the distinction 'has however an operative validity, similar to that which allows us to distinguish, in the linguistic sign, between a signifier and a signified'.

Barthes's interest in a 'literal' image is linked to his argument of 'a message without a code' which he attributes to the literal image (this is the third in his schema of messages within the image: the linguistic message; the coded iconic message – cultural or symbolic; the uncoded iconic message – literal or denoted):

the signifieds of this third message are formed by the actual objects of the scene, the signifiers by these same objects photographed, for it is clear that in analogue representation the connection between the signified thing and the signifying image is no longer arbitrary (as it is in language).

Hence, Barthes says:

> This peculiarity is found again at the level of the knowledge invested in the reading of the message: for 'to read' this last (or first level) of the picture we only need the knowledge attached to our perception . . . This message corresponds in a way to 'the letter' of the picture and we will agree to call it the literal message, as opposed to the preceding message, which is a 'symbolic' message.

However, the operative validity Barthes argues for does not seem entirely proven, especially in the light of subsequent work. It remains arguable how far perceptual knowledge is uncoded or 'anthropological' and in any case this has the effect of making the denotative level of the image mechanical and quickly irrelevant to further analysis. This places on to connotative analysis much greater weight without producing conceptual tools for proceeding – for instance we are, I think, little nearer the 'massive inventory of systems of connotation' Barthes calls for elsewhere in that article. In any case, while it remains important to specify particular systems of connotation, an inventory as such assumes the possibility of some fixity (at least, in so far as it is available as an item within an inventory) in relation to connotation whereas it now seems necessary to reformulate the problem of connotative meaning itself. Moreover Barthes's distinction, excluding from the denotative, as it does, the codes of production – framing, lighting, and so on – of photography, becomes a formalist attempt to 'match' the mode of the analysis of the image to that of the linguistic sign. The problem hinges on the nature of the analogical properties of the photographic image which Christian Metz has posed as follows:

> There is good reason [with regard to the *impression of reality*] to recall the partial similarities between filmic perception and everyday perception (sometimes called 'real perception'), similarities that certain authors (including the present author) have sometimes misinterpreted. They are not due to the fact that the first is natural, but to the fact that the second is not; the first is codified, but its codes are in part the same as those of the

second. The *analogy*, as Umberto Eco has clearly shown [*A Theory of Semiotics*[4]] is not between the effigy and its model, but exists – while remaining partial – between the two perceptual situations, between the modes of decipherment which lead to the recognition of the object in the real situation and those which lead to its recognition in an iconic situation, in a highly figurative image such as that of film.[5]

There is no pure moment of perception, in fact, since the 'modes of decipherment' are themselves already part of culture; Gauthier argues against the notion of 'a message without a code' in 'Initiation to the Semiology of the Image': 'The over-hasty conclusion is that the photograph is an analogical message which functions through a reference to the real and that it is therefore a universal language'. Gauthier says that while this might appear to be the case in terms of the photograph operating as a universal language between the French and Germans (who are, of course, located within the same Western European capitalist structure), this is not true for (his example) Australian Aborigines. Even if it refers to elements of the real, the organisation of these within the image may not correspond to the way in which 'real objects' (those elements) are recognised in that culture: 'Working with photography is, whether one likes it or not, the manipulation of symbols.'

Barthes's distinctions are then reformulated by Gauthier as between *description* – level of denotation, and *interpretation* – level of connotation. Gauthier then argues that the units of signification in the visual message constituted by a single photograph can be isolated but that these units have no existence outside the message in question: 'Any analysis can only be *descriptive*'. While the designation of these two levels has been important in opening up the image to analysis beyond that of simply its contents, it can lead to a different problem once questions concerning the ideological are raised. Andrew Bethell was precisely concerned with this in the passage already quoted – the images' 'ideological qualities' – and this is especially crucial as soon as work is proposed on 'Images of Women' or 'Images of Blacks'. What is at issue here is the point (and mode) of intervention of the ideological in the image. However, the separation out of the ideological as a 'level' in the image enables one to continue with a notion of a 'pure' image prior to, or coexisting with, the corrupted 'ideological' image; this has all the problems of Barthes's 'message without a code' and obscures the importance of image analysis as a question of *reading* rather than of producing 'essences' of the image (of an ontology of the image rather as Bazin sought). Further,

the positing of an ideological 'level' in the image suggests that
one can analytically disengage the ideological from something
non-ideological and that, having located the ideological, one can
establish what the image 'really means'. However, 'meaning' in
the image is notoriously unstable and highly dependent on *interpretation*, that is, what the reader brings to the image rather than
what the image constructs for the reader. There are particular
difficulties in this area which have been shown by Gauthier: 'the
interpretation of the image depends on the experience of the
receiver; its meaning is diffuse and rarely arguable'. Nevertheless,
Gauthier argues for the possibility of image analysis because
'photographic technique has opened the way for a rhetoric which
directs interpretation: in some cases the photographic message
seems capable of being analysed into signifying units which cannot
exist independently of the context'. Yet the danger is then of a
concentration of image analysis on formal qualities on to which
'ideological' qualities are grafted. The point of production of the
ideological qualities cannot be grasped, existing either within the
individual – the experience of the receiver, or as manipulation by
those controlling the images – 'where the image comes from'.
Hence in this schema all one can do is establish the markings of
ideology on the form of the image – its symptoms – the levels of
coding are then readable only through social knowledge. The
modes by which interpretation is made can be exposed but not
analysed – this is the substance of the later projects in Gauthier's
text.

Two implications of this are particularly important. First, in
relation to the educational use and value of work on image analysis, Andrew Bethell writes:

> if children can be encouraged to realise that the image has many
> meanings and that often these meanings are not immediately
> obvious, they will better be able to analyse and understand the
> thousands of images which they encounter every day.

The importance of this statement however, is not just that students
appreciate and better locate the multiplicity of meanings in images
through image-analysis, but that such work exposes some of the
parameters of the production of those meanings, within the image
itself and within other signifying systems. Less a question of
'inoculation' than of learning that images have no 'necessary'
meanings except as produced in the process of viewing (reading)
and that this production always exists both within the image and

between the image and larger signifying systems, for instance, the advert within advertising, the news photograph within journalism.

A second implication arises when one starts to look at images in terms of a connotative level whose 'interpretation' is systematically organised according to specific notions which can be seen represented elsewhere in the society, that is, for example, in terms of sexism or racism. It is then not only a question of the multiplicity of meanings – polysemy – of the image but their organisation through the intervention of codes extrinsic to the image and located in the society producing the image. The polysemy of the image which Barthes posited in 'Rhetoric of the Image' was never a plurality of endless or arbitrary meanings produced in the image. Rather, the endless potential signification of the image is always, and only, a *theoretical possibility*. In practice the image is always held, contained in its production of meaning or else becomes meaningless, unreadable. At this point the concept of 'anchorage' is important: 'there are developed in every society diverse techniques intended to *fix* the floating chain of signifieds so as to contend with the terror of uncertain signs: the linguistic message is one of these techniques'. The image is in fact rarely seen without some linguistic text, supporting or contextualising the image; even the painting or expressive photograph has a title, or introduction explaining its moment of production. The other techniques, Barthes suggests, have hardly been explored at all, for example, the repetition or re-marking of connotative levels in the image. It is such operations within the image itself which are important for arguments which designate the image sexist or racist. Following Jim Pines's argument,[6] that 'The concept-image "black" is heavily value-loaded' and his discussion of the difficulties arising 'out of the problematic of the racial image itself, i.e. its highly emotive content and context', it is possible to argue that the forms of 'anchorage' of meaning in the image may also be constituted through certain connotative levels being located in other social practices, to the extent that they become extremely 'stable'. In the instance of women, the point of 'origin' of the codes organising the image, and the kinds of connotative levels produced – that is, patriarchy – may still not be fully understood but their effects can be clearly pointed to.

The study of images of women arises out of a position that women in our society constitute a specific category characterised by the particular legal, administrative, educational and economic definitions accorded women and which constitute discrimination as against the definitions accorded men. Work on images from the position of feminist politics has been variously called 'Images of Women' or 'Women and Images', and the argument has been concerned with the 'sexist' nature of the images, or their potential or actual non-sexism. These two headings, however, mark two quite different strategies, on the one hand relating to a content, women as represented, whether in the visual image or ideational image of literature, and so on; on the other hand, to form, the images as specific photo-cinematic form to which in talking of 'Women and Images' one is posing a specificity not only to 'image' but also to 'woman'. Here indicating both a content – objectively, images of women – and as well, suggesting that the form of representation of women has implications for that representation in a way that is not simply reducible to an ideological reading/ critique, that is, sexism.

The concern of this strategy is to designate and oppose the production of images which are found to be sexist. This is dependent on (a) the image having a homogeneous content or meaning which can be evaluated; and (b) definitions of sexism – sexist images and so on – by which the meaning or content can be evaluated. I have separated the two problems because the first is part of the problem of how an image as such is theorised, that is the relation of content/meaning to its form and the problem of 'interpretation' suggested already in the discussion above of Gauthier. The second problem relates to the questions being explored by feminists of how sexual difference is constructed in our society and the way it is institutionalised, ideologically and materially, to produce women in a subordinate relationship and with inferior access to social, political and economic structures.

In the *Non-Sexist Code of Practice for Book Publishing* (produced by the Women in Publishing Industry Group and approved by the NUJ Book Branch and ASTMS Publishing Branch) it states that 'Sexism refers to discrimination based on gender', and similarly Terry Dennett and Jo Spence in *Screen Education*, no. 21,[7] say it is 'systematic discrimination on the grounds of sex'. What becomes critical, then, is the notion of 'discrimination'; this is, of course, meant in the pejorative sense of 'discriminatory practices' rather than as distinguishing difference as such (the dictionary's definition). The problem of sexism is not that men and women are different but that that difference is inscribed politically and ideologically, and feminism as a political movement opposes that inscription within our society as presently constituted – thus the *Non-Sexist Code* also used the notion of '*oppressive stereotyping* of men and women' (my emphasis).

Sexism in an image cannot be designated materially as a content in the way that denotative elements such as colours or objects in the image can be pointed to. Rather it is in the development of new or different definitions and understandings of what men and women are and their roles in society which produces readings of images as sexist; the political perspective of feminism produces a further level of connotative reading. Sexism is not always already there in the image but is produced through the process of signification in the coming into play of a number of connotative levels. For instance, an image itself might be 'innocuous' but its point and mode of presentation produces its reading as sexist – the linguistic anchorage in particular can provide this function, but also the 'techniques', for example, framing, lighting and especially choice of lens and aperture in, for example, the use of soft focus.

Returning to the problems of the relation of content/meaning to its form, and of interpretation, it must be argued that images cannot, in fact, be treated as having a homogeneous content or meaning which can be taken as a given. This quickly becomes apparent when feminist analysis of images is undertaken: for instance, an image of a woman and child can be attacked for reproducing notions of femininity wholly defined by motherhood (the relationship of a woman to a child is readily assumed to be that of mother), of representing women only in this role, drawing on a wealth of connotative systems, from the archetype of the Madonna and Child, to concepts of the 'earth mother' in touch with her body and hence in harmony with nature, the 'natural' carer of children. On the other hand it can be argued that the same image instead presents a positive image of women – affirming their roles as mothers in society which treats as second citizens those who are involved in the care of children.

The 'meaning' of the image always exists both as a production within the image and beyond the image, in the intertextual space of all the other images of mothers and children. The image 'means' not only in and for itself but also connotes its place in other discourses. It is in this sense that other, positive, images of women can be thought; not as different or alternative in themselves but through their changed insertion in that intertextual space. This seems to me to be part of the project of the film *Riddles of the Sphinx*[8] whose narrative deals with motherhood as a problem, both cultural and practical. Thus, while the image does not enclose a homogeneous meaning, neither is it permanently open; readings remain the production of the intertextuality, as well as intra-textuality, of the image. 'Alternative' readings are then not just a question of a new content, or a changed 'consciousness' but a result of a different strategy of production of the image in relation to its intertextual space.

If there is then a problem of the relationship of the form of images which can be designated, to the meaning of images which are interpreted, where should questions arising from notions of sexism be addressed? It is here that the questions of the second strategy suggested earlier are placed. At stake are the forms of representation; the meaning of the image lies not in its 'objective content' the objects and so on, depicted (a content which, I have argued, can only be posited theoretically), but in the articulation of those 'objects' as image, including any accompanying linguistic message, and the context or placing of the image (in a magazine or journal, its relationship to accompanying images and text or articles). That is, the meaning cannot be fixed in relation to referents within the image but is produced through their relationships not only as referents within this image, but also in all other images. The depiction of a table in an image signifies not just this table but also all the kinds of tables it might be but is not, and all the uses tables represent. The image of the table is then not only the signified 'table' but is also part of a chain of signification in which the signified becomes the signifier of 'eating' or 'writing' or 'kitchen' or 'dining-room' which in turn involve further levels of signification.

Sexism cannot, therefore, be 'read off' images – there is neither a given unity of meaning to enable this, nor a simple evaluative system for defining sexism. Because of this the study of images of women (images and women) can never be in isolation from work on signification in images generally, and indeed raises questions as to whether only images of women are sexist, or whether images of men or even of objects can also be understood as drawing upon connotative levels which bring into play notions of roles and relationships oppressive to women (and men).

Work on signification (in structural linguistics, in the work of Lacan in relation to psychoanalysis and in the work of *Screen*) has shown that the signified does not exist except as a function of a particular signifying system. Meanings do not pre-exist their organisation within a chain of utterance, and equally, signifieds become signifiers for further chains of signification. Questions remain, however, concerning the form of relation between the means of representation – signification – and the determinants of the practices entailed in the action of the means of representation. To designate those determinants 'ideological', and then also to place the means of representation – signification – as ideological, produces a teleology dependent on definitions of ideology – whether as 'false', 'imaginary' or just pernicious. Ideology becomes a monolith covering all sins and virtues, and more importantly it places the production of meaning as an effect (reflection, reproduction, conveyor belt) of a pre-existent meaning. Rather, signifying practices, such as the image, are the moment of production of ideology; ideology is not simply pre-existent, detach-

able through analysis to leave the image pure. Sexism (as ideology) is produced, not just reproduced or represented, in the
process of signification. Nevertheless, the determinants of that
production – the practices entailed in the action of the means of
representation – have still to be understood.

Also raised here are questions about the status of the image
in relation to 'reality' which is particularly important given the
appearance of resemblance to reality – capturing the concrete
world which has been the object of the gaze of the camera – its
verisimilitude, which the photograph produces. However, it has
been argued earlier that the meaning of the image is not constructed on the basis of its reference to 'real objects' but on the
organisation of objects within the image in relation to other chains
of signification – rather than other real objects. The introduction
of the *Non-Sexist Code of Practice for Book Publishing* poses
some of the problems of the status of 'reality' for the image
or representation when it talks on the one hand of 'oppressive
stereotyping of men and women', which refers specifically to one
of the means of representation, and on the other hand of 'the
dishonest way in which women and men, girls and boys are frequently presented', which contains the notion that the image lies
when it could have told the truth.

Unfortunately, the conventional representations of women –
stereotyping – are 'real', in the sense that most people agree with
such representations, and in that it has a relation of verisimilitude
to the 'real world'. For example, the *Non-Sexist Code of Practice
for Book Publishing* argues against vocational stereotyping:
'women should not only be shown as home-maker or secretary,
indeed fifty-four per cent of women work; forty-two per cent of
mothers with children under five go out to work'.

However, the example chosen of vocational stereotyping, 'the
housewife is protesting at higher food prices', *is* more realistic, in
the sense used within the Code, since women, whether they work
or not, continue predominantly to carry responsibility for shopping, meals, housework, and so on. While here seen as sexist, the
discrimination between 'housewives' and the alternative suggested
in the code of 'shoppers' in fact reveals what is much more sexist
– the sexual division of labour within the home.

The problems of representing sexual (and racial) difference in
language are rather different from those of the image. For instance
The Times recently reported that eight British people had been
arrested in Holland in connection with kidnapping charges; the
eight included 'two women and a Jamaican' (is the nationality of
the women and the Jamaican different from the other five
people?). The *Evening Standard*, on the other hand, reporting on

the arrest of 21 young people in Deptford and Lewisham on 30 May on 'conspiracy to rob' charges carefully chose *not* to mention that all but one was black – in this case the racist implications of the event (unwarranted police brutality, nature of charges) are denied, while in the first case, *The Times* produces a racist (and sexist) implication where there presumably had been none. (Interestingly, *Time Out*'s more progressive reporting on the police action fell into a different trap; they reported 'The arrests of twenty black youths and one white woman . . .' The sex of the black persons is designated presumably by 'youth' which also denotes their age – that is, young; the woman is left ageless.)

The 'reality' behind the news stories reported by *The Times*, *The Evening Standard* and *Time Out* respectively is coded by the language system itself (apart from the 'interpretations' of the reporters). Equally in the visual message, reality is coded. While the age, sex or colour of the persons shown may be represented as such – denoted (though age in particular is notoriously difficult, for instance a recent colour supplement feature on 'Jane Fonda at Forty' signified no specific age, let alone that of 'middle age') – since the message of the image is rarely just the signified age, sex, colour, the denotative elements are always organised connotatively: 'Black is beautiful' or 'Young black muggers' or 'female and *feminine*', 'Young and Forty'. The denotative is always a coded representation, not only through the techniques of photography, lighting, framing, and so on, but also through the relationships produced between the denoted, the objects included, the actions shown, the clothing worn. Stereotyping then becomes a function of the systematic coding of the image. 'Housewife' is pre-eminently a stereotype; no woman is actually (legally) married to a house, rather the term is constituted on notions of the role and duties of the 'wife' which are defined around the maintenance of a home and its services. The problem of stereotyping is not that it is true or false, distorting or manipulated, but that it closes off certain productions of meaning in the image.

The image is a point of production not as origin but in the setting into play of all other images and other significations from which it is distinguished as alike or not alike. The image will draw upon elements from other images, and will use notions, concepts, myths, and so on, already available in the culture. The image will not just 'reflect' these, however, but in re-producing them will re-form them, producing new meanings as it sets in play its connotative system – its 'rhetoric'.

What remains problematic is not simply the relationship such 'notions' and 'myths' have to the image, but the ways in which these function and are produced in a society. Again, in relation to women, this is the question of patriarchy posed earlier; it is also the problem of the 'determinants of the practices entailed in the action of the means of representation' similarly raised earlier. It is a point at which the ideological – signification or the means of representation – engages with the political and economic. For instance, the law distinguishes between the earnings of a husband and those of his wife for tax purposes; a man can claim tax allowances for his wife but a woman cannot reciprocally, or instead, claim for her husband. Equally it can be seen that the status and meaning of a man's (husband's) wage in our society is more important than his wife's (a woman's). He is seen by the law, and the culture, as the 'breadwinner'.

Work by feminists and on the Left has to investigate the way in which such notions can be produced as legal constructions and cultural myths, and also to engage politically with both the institutions of law and those of signifying systems – the media – in raising questions about the basis of these notions. To approach image analysis in relation to the questions raised by feminism must always take one beyond, however, the single image, or even institutions of images – advertising, news, fiction, comic-strip, and so on, into the analysis of other structures and their discourses. The law and education are obvious examples, but important as well is the health service. For instance, in the Dennett and Spence article referred to earlier, is included a drug-manufacturer's advertisement which places workers, medically – as 'depressives' requiring the wondercure of 'Vivalan'. A videotape made by Glasgow Women's Group uses a similar drug-manufacturer's advert to show that while here at last is an image presenting women 'realistically' loaded down with shopping, children in tow, tired and hassled, the advertiser's message is that with their drug these women will once again be the ideal mothers and housewives the image shows them failing to be.

Within image-systems it is nevertheless important to distinguish the specificity of the image being addressed. The kind of organisation of meaning presented in the advertising image, in terms of who it has been produced by (not a specific individual but as the collection of forces involved: the advertising firm, the manufacturer, its sales department or company board) and who it is produced for, with what purpose (the drug adverts were directed entirely at the medical profession), is quite different from that involved in a news photograph or government information poster. The 'genre' of the image will affect the way the reader understands and treats information-persuasion offered by the image (and text). The 'verisimilitude' of the photograph is, presumably, understood differently in relation to the news photograph of, for example,

Northern Ireland bombing compared with a fashion photograph or the kind of photographic image currently used in Benson and Hedges 'Silk Cut' cigarette advertisements.

In analysing images this is important not only in terms of the veracity the image and its text is credited with ('Things happen after a Badedas bath' compared with 'Smoking Kills'), it is also important for the kinds of presentations the image offers. For instance, in understanding the variety of images *of women*, the kinds of images presented in magazines like *Jackie* or *Nineteen*, the photos of nude and semi-nude women in newspapers like *The Sun* or *The Daily Mirror*, the representation of women in the TV programme *Within These Walls* are obviously not equivalents. Moreover they exist together with the images (positive or negative) women already have of themselves, their mothers, and women generally. In marking the *differences* between the images offered in all these ways is not to pose one as a truth against the other but to present a range of determinants of 'reality' in relation to 'images of women' available to us.

Notes

1. Jean-Pierre Golay, 'Introduction to the Language of Image and Sound', *Screen Education Notes*, no. 1, Winter 1971, now available as an advisory document from the Education Department of the British Film Institute; Roland Barthes, 'The Rhetoric of the Image', *Working Papers in Cultural Studies*, no. 1, Spring 1971; Stuart Hall, 'The Determinations of News Photographs', *Working Papers in Cultural Studies*, no. 3, Autumn 1972; Guy Gauthier, 'Initiation to the Semiology of the Image', available as an advisory document from the Educational Advisory Service of the British Film Institute (BFI).

2. *Teachers' Protest – an experiment in editing*, devised by Andrew Bethell and Mike Simons and available from the Society for Education in Film and Television (SEFT).

3. *Camerawork* is a photography magazine published by the Half Moon Photography Workshop.

4. Umberto Eco, *A Theory of Semiotics*, Indiana University Press, 1976.

5. Christian Metz, *Language and Cinema*, The Hague: Mouton, 1974, p. 275.

6. Jim Pines, 'The Study of Racial Images: A Structural Approach', *Screen Education* no. 23, Summer 1977.

7. Terry Dennett and Jo Spence, 'Photography, Ideology and Education', *Screen Education*, no. 21, Winter, 1976/77.

8. Laura Mulvey and Peter Wollen. Distributed by The Other Cinema. The script of the film is published in *Screen*, vol. 18, no. 2, Summer 1977.

Chapter 4

Teaching Avant-Garde Film: Notes Towards Practice*

Pam Cook

It may be helpful to begin with a definition of a central term and an explanation of the structure of this article. I use 'avant-garde' to refer to that body of work which engages with questions of film language and the relationship of film-maker and spectator to film, but which is also produced in opposition to the dominant system of production, distribution and exhibition and is therefore part of independent cinema. This is a limited and debateable usage, but my argument here is that the changes in conditions of production implied by the practice of independent cinema are important to the activity of thinking through the social practice of the avant-garde. These notes are part of a process of reflection upon three years' experience of teaching avant-garde and independent cinema to mixed groups of adults on the British Film Institute (BFI) University of London Extra-Mural course in Film Studies from 1976 to 1979. In one sense they are 'thoughts after the event', the rationalisation of a process of testing and transforming positions on 'the avant-garde' and 'teaching' which were not clearly formulated in the first place. This is an opportunity to hesitate, to reassess that work and its underlying assumptions in the light of certain historical changes over the past five years or so which make reassessment important. Inevitably the notes are the result

* *Screen Education*, no. 32/33, Autumn/Winter 1979/80.

of more than just the work of teaching, which has been extremely limited in my case. They emerge from my involvement in many other areas of practice and from the process of history itself – hence the combination of theoretical reflection and personal digression. Such hesitations are an important part of any materialist cultural struggle which challenges existing social relations of dominance and subordination by refusing to take for granted the divisions on which they are based.

The BFI Extra-Mural course is a specific instance of film study within the formal education system. In the past three years it has been in a state of transition because of organisational restructuring. As an apprentice teacher I was placed within these institutional determinations as well as within the wider determinations of historical shifts in film culture in general. These two sets of determinations were not compatible, and I want to trace some of the gaps and contradictions produced by the attempt to bring them together, rather than provide guidelines for the future.

* * *

In 1975 Peter Wollen's article 'The Two Avant-Gardes' appeared in a special issue of *Studio International* on avant-garde film;[1] it argued polemically for the timely convergence of radical formalist aesthetics with radical political concerns. Since then various historical shifts have taken place. It is now possible to look at the polemic in the context of an emerging body of work by filmmakers which engages with that polemic, and of a critical discourse which begins to recognise the importance of such a filmmaking practice for materialist cultural struggle.

The process of bringing together politics and the avant-garde is slow and difficult, symptomatic perhaps of a society which has a great deal invested in keeping one in a subordinate relationship to the other. Formalism and politics don't mix: this resistance runs through British film culture from Grierson's insistence that a cinema of experiment and individual artistic concerns should be channelled into a propaganda cinema at the service of a benevolent democratic state,[2] to the commitments to a necessary relationship between art and society in Free Cinema, and surely the thread of social realism running through British commercial cinema, extended now into television, manifests the same puritanism, the same view of 'politics' as a higher state.[3] In this context marginal figures like Len Lye, Humphrey Jennings and Michael Powell stand out in isolation, symptoms of what has been suppressed. Although it is outside the scope of this article, the extreme marginalisation of avant-garde cinema in Britain needs to be understood in the light of the relationship of artistic production to the state in British culture. This is also the historical context for understanding the implications of Peter Wollen's polemic for the importance of a radical formalism to a materialist counter-cinema. Some puritanism remains in this argument, in its condemnation of the so-called 'self-referential' avant-garde to the endless tautology of an 'ultra-left Utopianism', thus denying the process of uneven development in history.

In retrospect, the 'Two Avant-Gardes' article seems to mark a moment at which a growing number of activities in London and the provinces in the late 1960s and early 1970s came together and took off.[4] In 1975 the London Film-Makers' Co-op received its first substantial grant from the British Film Institute, enabling it to rationalise its previously precarious organisational structure; the 'First Festival of Independent British Cinema' held in Bristol showed the extent to which avant-garde film-makers had invaded the art schools as students and teachers, and their films were increasingly funded by Arts Council and BFI Production Board grants. 1975 heralded the beginnings of an activity around independent cinema, its production, distribution and exhibition. Partly through the Independent Film-makers' Association (IFA) founded in 1974, film-makers, writers, teachers and others involved in cultural struggle were mobilised to organise from a marginal and impoverished place for a radical oppositional intervention in British film culture. This eruption of political activity makes demands on institutions at many levels – on the government (the IFA's proposals for the British Film Authority), for instance, or on central cultural institutions like the BFI – with inevitable repercussions. This burgeoning activity raises important questions about the status of any history of the cinema which excludes an account of independent and avant-garde film, relegating it to a marginal place outside historical process. Rewriting the history of cinema is of primary importance in generating a discourse of independent film which will help bring it into productive contact with film culture in general, out from the so-called 'safe place'.

* * *

My own encounter with avant-garde film took place against a background of historical and theoretical shifts; to trace my own history, therefore, might indicate what some of those changes were. In 1972 the revised edition of *Signs and Meaning in the Cinema*[5] introduced the idea of the historical importance of modernism in the building of an oppositional cinema: the '*coupure*' which shifted the polemic towards that of language itself. The influence of French avant-garde theory, structuralism, semiology and psychoanalysis had had a profound effect on British film theory, particularly after the publication of the analysis by *Cahiers du cinéma* of *Young Mr Lincoln* in 1972,[6] which posited the film text as the site of contradiction of a multiplicity of different elements. In 1973 Nöel Burch's book *Theory of Film Practice*[7] appeared in Britain, and Nöel Burch himself was teaching film history at the Royal College of Art and the Film Unit of the Slade School of Fine Art. I came to the Slade Film Unit in 1973 committed to the primary importance of theoretical work on Hollywood cinema as the dominant popular cinema, and with a distrust of avant-garde film based on notions about its 'formalism', 'elitism', 'inaccessibility', 'individualism' and 'defensive marginality'. I thought that popular commercial cinema offered within itself, within its contradictions, the possibility of social criticism and formal self-reflexiveness without abandoning the all-important element of pleasure. I was interested in those directors who consciously or unconsciously presented a critique of bourgeois American society by manipulating the language of dominant cinema.[8] In the institutional context of a School of Fine Art this seemed at the time like a positive intervention on behalf of Popular Culture. It was important to assert the validity of a theoretical practice which took account of the dominant system of representation without rejecting it on puritanical grounds, and so conceptualise a new oppositional cinema based on confrontation rather then disavowal. In other students and teachers I met different positions, coming out of deep and long-term commitments to the struggle for alternative film-making practices, both avant-garde and political, a commitment which in turn led to a distrust of the dominant system. It seemed that our differences were based on a straight opposition between the argument for a cinema of confrontation and an alternative 'marginal' cinema.

Although it did offer an important challenge to the idealist notions of ideology as monolithic and non-contradictory on which many alternative film-makers and critics based their analysis of the dominant system, the polemic rested on a positivist view of history. This led to a particular kind of prescriptive theory which is not very productive because it polarises issues in order to privilege one set of political priorities at the expense of others. Prescriptive theory may seem to avoid the pitfalls of liberalism, but it also avoids the process of learning, investigation and transformation of ideas so important to a materialist view of history.

The two years between 1973 and 1975 at the Slade Film Unit were formative in many ways. Because of the Unit's historical place within the School of Fine Art we were taught, among other things, to look at the history of cinema from the perspective of modernist art movements like German Expressionism, from the perspective of technological development, and from the perspective of 'primitive' cinema. It was not only the body of 'knowledge' gained that was important, but precisely this change of perspective, a shift in point of view which made it possible to understand the position of those involved in a practice of film-making marginal to the dominant system. A series of theoretical seminars on semiology and psychoanalysis, which were more directly related to my own project on women and representation, produced ideas on subjectivity and language which seemed to connect with this marginal film-making practice in ways I didn't clearly understand. Strangely enough in an Art College, avant-garde film was placed as an option for fine art students on Friday afternoons, when only the devoted could attend. Under pressure from the film students screenings and discussions of modernist film practice were included in the main curriculum of the post-graduate diploma course in film studies in 1974, and continued until the diploma course closed down completely in 1978 as a result of the cuts in expenditure on education.

The selection of films in the modernist programme ranged from the French and German avant-gardes of the 1920s to the post-war New American Cinema and the contemporary British avant-garde. It became clear to me that a large area of film history remained submerged, a film-making practice which defined itself explicitly in opposition, not only to the forms of dominant narrative cinema, but also to its system of production, distribution and exhibition. The sheer extent of the work and multiplicity of projects made this absence hard to believe.

* * *

One of the first films shown in this programme was *Wavelength* by Michael Snow (1966–7). It was an appropriate introduction to the project of a structural/minimalist cinema.

> Michael Snow utilises the tension of the fixed frame and some of the flexibility of the fixed tripod in *Wavelength*. Actually, it is a forward zoom for forty-five minutes, halting occasionally, and fixed during several different times so that day changes to night within the motion . . . The room, during the day, at night, on different film stock for colour tone with filters and even occasionally in negative is gradually closing up its space as the zoom nears the back wall and the final image of a photograph upon it – a photograph of waves. This is the story of the diminishing area of pure potentiality. The insight of space, and, implicitly, cinema as potential, is an axiom of the structural film.[9]

A different argument would be that *Wavelength* does more than explore the limits of cinematic potential. There is another story

in the film, the remnants of a thriller, a drama over a death and
the discovery of a body. This is narrative reduced to a set of
arbitrary coded events, displaced and replaced by a complex
drama of filmic process. What 'takes place' in *Wavelength*, then,
is a pleasure in the process of displacement of dominant forms, a
breaking up of homogeneity in favour of a different type of discourse, one which challenges the place of the spectator as privileged participant, invisible guest, and demands an activity of
reading. This process of displacement marks the shift from history
to discourse which characterises the avant-garde text.

> Discourse and history are both forms of enunciation, the differ-
> ence between them lying in the fact that in the discursive form
> the source of the enunciation is present, whereas in the histori-
> cal it is suppressed. History is always 'there' and 'then', and its
> protagonists are 'he', 'she' and 'it'. Discourse however, always
> also contains, as its point of reference, a 'here' and a 'now' and
> an 'I' and a 'you'. Benveniste cites as examples of the historical
> form in language on the one hand the statements of historians
> proper, and on the other hand passages from novels represent-
> ing events . . . Discourse, by contrast, is always marked by the
> presence of a subject of the enunciation – whether this be the
> author/speaker as person or not.[10]

The shift in emphasis in *Wavelength* is not from narrative as
history to the simple presence of Michael Snow as the subject of
the enunciation, since, precisely, the 'author' of the film is also
displaced, subject-ed to the structural rigour of the zoom and the
drama of filmic processes. It is through the spectacular display of
process that the discursive comes about: the film exhibits itself as
process and transformation, refusing the masquerade of history.
It constructs the spectator as the one who is looking at the film,
as the 'you' addressed specifically and immediately, in a shifting
relationship with the 'he', 'she', 'it', 'there', and 'then', which are
still there held at a distance in a process of negation.

> The film, therefore, can hold a discourse towards the spectator
> as that which exhibits itself to be seen, or for that matter, as
> that which enables the spectator to see (identification with the
> camera as voyeur) or as an alternation of the two. Not only is
> exhibitionism, as Metz notes, 'of the order of discourse, not
> history' (which incidentally means that *what* is exhibited is to
> some extent irrelevant). It is also discursive articulation. History
> becomes discourse in so far as the exhibitionist/voyeurist

relation (or, more simply, the relations of seeing and showing) presides over the construction of the film.[11]

There is a movement in *Wavelength* away from the body *in* the film towards the body *of* the film and the question of the spectator's relationship to that material body. Its importance resides partly in the extent to which it provides a metaphor for the modernist *'coupure'* itself: the break with the dominance of history in nineteenth-century representation and the foregrounding of the problem of the relationship of the subject of language. The subject in *Wavelength* is decentred, dispersed, calling to mind the subject of Marxist theory decentred from the stage of history and the subject of Freudian psychoanalysis dispersed across language in the intersubjective relations of meaning construction.

* * *

I have traced a particular conjunction of my encounter with avant-garde film and more general historical shifts within independent cinema in order to suggest the contradictory social conditions in which my own critical practices changed. At the same time, this conjunction marks a transitional moment at which there began to emerge an independent film-making practice in which avant-garde work on form has played a major part, and a critical discourse around the questions raised by this independent cinema which has attempted to support and assess its political potential. What, though, are the implications of this new film-making practice for social practice in general?

The enormous diversity of projects covered by the term 'independent cinema' makes it difficult to be prescriptive about what kind of work *should* go ahead. It seems to me more productive to be aware of differences, to proceed on the basis of difference. Different projects require different audiences; the very diversity of aims is a potential challenge to a commercial cinema geared to profit and therefore to repetition of the same rather than recognition of difference. The projects of independent cinema are produced in many different situations,[12] and this also presents a potential challenge to a system based on hierarchical division of labour which has excluded women in particular from the industry. The radical heterogeneity which characterises independent cinema makes it possible to conceive of an activity of opposition and confrontation from multiple points of view, to activate a discursive productive questioning as part of a process of political transformation. The emphasis on productive confrontation is precisely what marks off this conception from the liberal attitude of tolerance, which in effect avoids confrontation in favour of pluralism.

Work on discursive articulation in cinema opens up the question of sexual difference. 'In a world ordered by sexual imbalance', Laura Mulvey points out, 'pleasure in looking has been split between active/male and passive/female'.[13] There are some crucial questions for feminists here. Should we proceed by reversing this relationship, by positing a 'women's language' as a discrete area which mirrors the sexual divisions of 'patriarchal' society, or should we exploit the contradictions at work in discursive articulation to question those divisions? How do we disturb the system in which the active/passive heterosexual division of labour controls narrative in favour of the male as active 'bearer of the look' and the female as 'object of the look', closing down on the heterogeneity of the drives? How does the decentered subject of discursive articulation relate to the personal politics of the women's movement? There are no immediate answers to these questions, but already some films emerging from independent cinema are beginning to work on these areas; many of them are made by women, for whom the independent sector offers the possibility of access to the process of production denied by the industry. Discursive articulation, by foregrounding the material existence of the recording process and the critical reading of the spectator, by foregrounding shifts in point of view, can break down the illusion of objectivity and truth (history) in dominant language, posing itself in opposition to sexual division in favour of the problematic of sexual difference, and against its collapse into sexual division in narrative cinema.

The challenge here is based on confrontation which involves working on the forms of dominant language to transform them: a counter-cinema. Other areas of work within the avant-garde are more concerned with the material of film and the process of signification itself. This work, defining itself as alternative rather than oppositional, may not seem to represent a direct challenge to the dominant system. Nevertheless, the idea of an alternative practice has been historically important in opening up space in which independent facilities for film production, distribution and exhibition have been established (through co-operative workshops, for instance). We need to recognise the historical value of all these different practices so that we are not reduced to a utilitarian view of cultural struggle in which a view of what might be possible is subordinated to the 'reality' of a hierarchy of political priorities which constantly defers long-term considerations. What is 'alternative' and what is 'oppositional' in effect cannot be determined *a priori:* these areas of challenge offered by independent cinema are therefore *potential.* It would be idealist to argue for this cinema without understanding the material conditions in which it must work and political analysis of the institutional framework is a vital part of the work of independent film-makers and others working in cultural production.[14] An equally important area of work is at the point of consumption: the task of building audiences for independent cinema is a difficult struggle which already has a history within avant-garde and political film-making. Independent facilities for distribution and exhibition need to be supported by a critical discourse around independent cinema which brings into play its radical heterogeneity, rather than simply reproducing it as an object for consumption. This implies, I think, a reconsideration of the social and political function of teachers and writers.

I would identify three main models of teaching practice which seem to be in fairly general use:

1. *Re-presentation*, in which the teacher gathers a coherent, pre-existing body of factual information and presents it to the students for them to consume and to be reproduced in some form.

2. *Mediation*, in which the teacher re-works information for easier assimilation by the students, and for them to reproduce.

3. *Provocation*, in which the teacher re-works information so that the students can be provoked to think, ask questions, analyse and produce coherent arguments.

These models do not take account of different institutional contexts. Classroom teaching in schools, seminars in Higher Education, Extra-Mural classes and Workers' Educational Association courses all require different methods, but it's probably true to say that most teaching involves one or more of these approaches in varying combinations. They all assume the need to master and reproduce a body of knowledge. Similarly, they tend to ignore the actual context of teaching, a nexus of contradictory relationships between students and teachers in which these abstract models are continually shifted and undermined.[15] A fourth model might be proposed: the *argumentative* or *discursive*, in which the notion of an autonomous, coherent area of work (which depends upon a division between subject/consumer and object of study/consumption) is broken down to allow for productive conflict between different areas of work. This would also involve a different relationship between teacher and student in which the positions of each would be identified and open to criticism, and the breaking down of discrete subject categories to include interdisciplinary work. In my extensive experience as a student, and limited experience as a teacher, the discursive approach is extremely rare. Discourse is always present in teaching, of course, but subject to the contract by which scientific knowledge and method, on which qualifications are based, are passed on from teacher to student. There is a concrete, immediate 'end in view' which imposes an economy on the proceedings. Even if that end in view is 'politics', for instance, teachers and students are still caught in the same system of exchange and reproduction for use. There is a closing down of space for work on the language and subject positions at play in the formal teaching situation itself: there are only 'good' and 'bad' teachers, 'good' and 'bad' students, those who master (more or less) and those who do not. Yet film is a multiple system: as well as the specifically cinematic codes film contains ideas and influences from a variety of other arts. The process of assemblage which produces a film clearly lends itself to the discursive mode, since it suggests that the combination of elements is never finally fixed. Avant-garde work brings into play the shifting relationship between elements, the complexity of the process of combination, and the relationship of intertextuality between film and the other arts.[16]

* * *

Looking back to 1976 when I began teaching on the BFI Extra-Mural course with Ian Christie and Simon Field (both experienced campaigners for the avant-garde), the profound effect of the 'Two Avant-Gardes' article becomes apparent. Like all good polemics it brought together apparently incompatible categories in a way that made it possible to re-think both terms of the opposition and their relationship. By locating avant-garde film within the general context of modernism, it revealed a body of work, and a history of that work, which had never been written into film history. Finally, it inserted avant-garde film-making practice into film theory in Britain, which up to that point had implied that practice in its theoretical work, but had not actually come to terms with it. Although that polemic had far wider repercussions, I will limit myself to its implications for our teaching on the third year of the Extra-Mural course.

At that time the Extra-Mural Course consisted of three years' study (two-hourly sessions one evening a week for 24 weeks) leading to a Certificate. Students could then go on to complete a fourth year of study in a specialist area to gain a diploma. There were no rigorous selection procedures, but students were expected to produce certain amounts of written work to a required standard, and to take an exam. There was a choice in the first two years of the Certificate course between alternatives within general headings such as *Realism and Anti-Realism, Authorship and Genre;* in the third year students concentrated on a particular area of study in depth. I think I am right in saying that the emphasis was on mainstream cinema, although some attention had been paid to Russian cinema, to Surrealism, Neo-Realism and Godard, and there had been a pioneer course on Women and Cinema. The flexibility of this third year enabled us to construct a course more or less as we wanted. Our primary concern at that point was to redress the balance of film history to take account of modernism, and then to engage critically with some of the formal issues raised by the avant-garde in relation to dominant cinema. The course was called simply *Avant-Garde Film*, reflecting the emphasis on formal concerns, and was explicitly informed by the 'Two Avant-Gardes' argument. The first term's films from the French and Russian avant-gardes of the 1920s were intended to link up with the students' work in the first two years, placing it in the different historical context of modernism in the arts. In the second term we introduced difficult and unfamiliar structural/minimalist work from the post-war New American Cinema, set against films by Godard and Straub-Huillet. In retrospect, we undoubtedly applied the argument too literally. In the absence of any general discourse about the avant-garde in film studies which might have placed it historically, students understandably polarised themselves against the radical formalism of the New American Cinema in favour of the political avant-garde, exemplified by Russian cinema, and the work of Godard, and encouraged by our chronological approach, regarded these two historical moments as 'golden ages' for the political avant-garde. Also we failed to take adequate account of the students' unfamiliarity with the work and the concepts. They were in no way prepared for what they saw in the second term. Our own commitment to the avant-garde and our specialised knowledge of its history and theory made it difficult to deal with the resistances of the students, particularly in the context of a two-hourly session one evening a week.

In the light of this experience we reformulated the course in 1977 as *Avant-Garde and Independent Cinema*. We abandoned chronology in favour of juxtaposing avant-garde work from different periods and contexts in each session, bringing forward specific issues such as formal subversion, formal innovation, the activity of reading and 'self-referential' film, so that the films acted as examples of the issues. Some avant-garde film, because of the variations in screening time, is particularly suitable for this kind of juxtaposition, and we were able to avoid the trap of creating a 'golden age' which students could identify as representative of an ideal practice. By placing the films in their specific historical situations, we built up a context for avant-garde film both as an area of work with its own history, and as an area of work defining itself in opposition to the forms of dominant cinema. In the second term we included work from the contemporary British avant-garde, with sessions on the history of British independent film-making. We raised explicitly the question of alternative conditions of production, distribution and exhibition in order to give the work on formal issues seen in the previous term a specific political relevance. We were trying to relate our teaching practice quite directly to what was emerging in British independent film culture at that time through the IFA, and to the then developing interest of cultural institutions like the BFI and SEFT and the Edinburgh Film Festival in the work of the avant-garde. On the whole I think this course was well conceived, but it failed to deal with a different problem for that year's students, who found the emphasis on avant-garde film acceptable because they saw the films primarily as 'art'. They were familiar with a history of art into which the first term's films fitted quite well, and they were able to engage with the formal issues in a sophisticated manner. They saw the politics of independence as a separate area, and since they were not involved in the emerging debates within contemporary British film culture, those issues meant little to them. Again we were faced with the problem of the lack of a general discourse about avant-garde film.

In these first two years we were confronting two basic problems: that of *context*, and that of *constituency* or *audience*. There is very little formal educational context for avant-garde and independent film (except perhaps among film-makers). The teacher is therefore committed to presenting a body of work with which the students will be unfamiliar; this inevitably limits the level of engagement with polemics. The constituency of Extra-Mural evening classes is generally drawn from groups of people who have never encountered avant-garde work before, because it is not widely distributed. On the third year course students are concerned to pass the exam and gain the Certificate: they are therefore under pressure to produced fixed amounts of written work under difficult circumstances, after work and in their spare time. Breaking through the syndrome of consumption and reproduction in this context is not only difficult: it is probably unfair to the students and self-defeating for teachers. It is important, therefore, to be much less Utopian than we were, and to see the task of building an educational discourse around independent cinema as long-term and dependent upon many different historical factors. It is obviously easier to raise polemical issues outside the formal educational system, but it is extremely important to begin to work within that system as well. This means facing the relations of production of knowledge for consumption on which that system rests, and of course it is perfectly possible to teach avant-garde film in this way: as 'history of art' presents its object 'art', for instance. It is not an *essential* feature of avant-garde work to resist this relationship, although it is tempting to believe that its 'difficulty' and historical marginalisation make it so. Its potential for resistance depends on a discourse which produces that resistance, and the institutional context within which its is placed. As long as it refuses to remain silently marginal, but argues vociferously from the margins, avant-garde work can push against the boundaries set for it. But the limitations imposed on that potential by working within formal educational structures must be understood. Because this is a long-term project, it cannot have immediate results in terms of producing new knowledge about the politics of independent cinema which would hold it up as an imaginary goal: rather it depends on a constant process of assimilation and displacement of knowledge, in which all the practices of the cinematic institution are brought together in productive confrontation.

In 1978 we attempted to deal with the problem of audience: this coincided with changes in audience within the Extra-Mural course itself. During the two years that we had been teaching avant-garde film the changes in the first two years of the course meant that they now included examples of avant-garde work. Students reached the third year with some knowledge of the area and, combined with a wider constituency (we now had several film-makers in the class as well as teachers, students and BFI staff) and a growing familiarity with theoretical writings on the avant-garde, this meant that a more lively and direct critical work on the issues was possible. One of the most difficult of these was the problem of pleasure, which had previously been dealt with only implicitly. Students often complained of boredom when faced with 'difficult' films, pronouncing them humourless and didactic. It was clear that they felt that they had lost, or were being denied, something. It is difficult to justify this loss of pleasure in terms of 'the work of the text' or in terms of the subjectivity of pleasure: students still feel deprived. Something radical is happening when this symptom occurs.

'A text of *jouissance* imposes a state of loss. It is a text that discomforts, unsettles the reader's historical, cultural, psychological assumptions, the consistency of his tastes, values, memories, brings to a crisis his relation with language' . . . In the avant-garde text the semiotic produces the dissolution of fixed, uniform subjectivity. Characteristic are those twentieth century texts which minutely examine their own matter: language, systems of signification, and the subject implicated in that signification.[17]

We wanted to confront this process of the unsettling of the unity of the subject by looking first at how the narrative construction of the 'classic realist text' holds the subject in place.

The whole process is directed towards the place of a reader: in order that it should be intelligible, the reader has to adopt a certain position with regard to the text. This position is that of homogeneity, of truth. The narration calls upon the subject to regard the process of the narrative as a provisional openness, dependent upon the closure which the subject expects as the very precondition of its pleasure.[18]

An introduction to the history of the construction of the narrative codes in American cinema from Griffith to the 1940s, with an emphasis on the account given by Nöel Burch[19] of editing codes based on match-cutting, shot:reverse-shot and eyeline match established the basis of the system. We supported this with Laura Mulvey's article 'Visual Pleasure and Narrative Cinema' as an introduction to the Freudian psychoanalytical concept of scopophilia, and its manipulation by narrative cinema in the service of the spectator's position of dominance and transcendence *vis-à-vis* the film. As a 'limit-text' here we used Ophuls's film *The Reckless Moment*, in which the obsessional moving camera dominates the movement of the protagonists in such a way that the 'secrecy' of the process of domination through looking, we argued, is threatened by the overt marking of the camera as representative of the scopic drive itself.[20]

In the previous years of the course we had introduced psychoanalytical theory only tentatively, in relation to the Surrealists, and then in the context of the eruption of the unconscious into language represented by some avant-garde texts. Now it became a central part of our approach to the question of the position of the subject in language.

A genuinely materialist understanding of language and ideology needs an analysis of the process by which fixed relations of predication are produced for/in the subject. It is this necessity which can be met only by psychoanalysis, since positions/identifications are produced in the socio-familial construction of the subject.[21]

We examined the use of moving camera to construct a place for

the spectator in *ciné-verité (The Chair)*, which led to the discovery
of its affinity with the subject construction in the realist narrative,
and compared it with the use of interrupted vision and sound in
The Nightcleaners, Part I to problematise the subject position of
transcendence in conventional documentary film. In one of the
most difficult and interesting sessions a screening and presentation
of *Vampyr* in terms of its unreadability,[22] its system of hesitations,
produced a vociferous demand from most students in the class
that the film should be rendered coherent, its gaps and inconsist-
encies filled by rational explanation. *Vampyr* is an exemplary text
for overturning the relationship of mastery of spectator to film,
radically disturbing the practice of reading as consumption. The
realist text activates the discursive and the play of subject relations
within the limits of narrative and the organisation of discourses
into a hierarchy: a metadiscourse frames and contains the narrative. The avant-garde text, by contrast, activates the discursive at
the expense of narrative, overturning hierarchy, refusing containment, asserting heterogeneity and excess.

> Texts which do not depend on placing the subject in this kind
> of position [of observation, understanding, synthesising] are as
> rare in the cinema as in literature itself. For reasons of con-
> venience, we shall confine our account to literature, where a
> text like Joyce's *Ulysses* appears at certain points to be creating
> 'that breach of the "I" [exhibited in] the explosion of modern
> literature: a plurality of languages, a confrontation of types of
> discourse and ideologies, with no conclusions and no synthesis
> – without "monological" or axial points' (Kristeva).[23]

In the second term we looked at the different forms of discursive
activity exemplified by the post-war American avant-garde, placing the films in terms of the problematic positions constructed for
the spectator, the extent and effect of the disjuncture between
signifier and signified in each, and the different levels of engagement with narrative in *Anticipation of the Night* (Brakhage),
Wavelength (Snow), *T.O.U.C.H.I.N.G.* (Sharits) and *Nostalgia*
(Frampton). We concluded by looking at *Riddles of the Sphinx*
(Mulvey/Wollen) and *Mirror Phase* (Klein) in terms of the possibilities for a political feminist cinema, and a women's cinema,
opened up by avant-garde film practice:[24] its concern with a
critique of the relationship between signifier and signified, with
the splitting of the coherence of the subject, and with the problem
of sexual difference (as outlined above), and, particularly, its
small-scale artisanal mode of production.

This course therefore took two directions. In the first, more formal one, we traced the history of narrative cinema through the building of a set of codes which inscribed a particular place for the spectator, a process of placing which the realist narrative disguises, presenting itself as history. We moved towards a critique of this placing and process of disguise by showing films which appeared to act in opposition to it, but could be seen to support it, and then by showing 'limit-texts', narrative films which pushed at the limits of those codes in such a way that the place of the spectator was disturbed. Finally we looked at avant-garde texts which radically disturbed the dominant codes and the inscribed place of the spectator, displaying themselves as textual process. We then questioned the political potential of this radical formalism from the perspective of more recent films which attempt to combine the project of overturning the dominant codes with a political project, transforming but not receiving narrative. Clearly, at this point, we were still tending to move towards the avant-garde as a kind of ideal practice. This is a contradiction inherent in attempting to introduce 'independent cinema' as an unknown and undervalued area without diminishing its potential implications for existing practices in film criticism and film production. If students were more aware of the history of avant-garde/independent cinema and had seen more of the films, they would be involved in, and aware of, different modes of production, distribution and exhibition. This would allow for a range of diverse practices within the cinematic institution to be brought together in the formal study of film. Within such a structure teachers could obviously argue for their own preferences, which would be open to criticism from students who could insert themselves from their own positions, which would also be open to question.

The other, less clearly 'taught' direction of the course led towards questions of changing conditions of production. We intended to suggest the limitations imposed on meaning-production by producing films within the dominant system, and that this supported an aesthetic of production for consumption. We wanted to show that the development of a 16mm technology made possible an independent system of production, distribution and exhibition, which had important consequences for the transformation of the relationship of spectator to film based on consumption to a relationship of active reading. The argument was complicated by the presence of films made on 16mm which clearly did not contribute to this active critical process (like *The Chair*), and by the presence of narrative films made within the industry which seemed to contribute to it, albeit only in a formal sense. It was difficult to involve students in argument about changing conditions of production even when we included a session where the film-maker was present at a screening and discussion of her film. They were much more prepared to argue about the formal issues. Yet clearly, if we are to think about avant-garde film as social practice, it is important to link the question of work on meaning-construction and the activity of critical reading with questions of the transformation of the institutional framework of production, distribution and exhibition. The displacement of subject positions does not only consist in the rupture of identity between signifier and signified, but in changing social conditions. Although this argument now seems axiomatic to me, it is not self-evident; nor does its exposition guarantee engagement with its terms. None the less, it needs to be built into any educational discourse around avant-garde cinema if teachers are to find ways of reconstituting that cinema other than as an object for consumption.

* * *

It seems opportune, after four or five years which have seen the organised growth of independent film-making in Britain, to look again at the 'Two Avant-Gardes' polemic. Those years have seen the opening up (and in some cases the closing down) of new institutional spaces for the production and consumption of independent films, in the form of independent workshops, cinemas, work in educational institutions, the BFI Production Board and Regional Film Theatres, and the Edinburgh Film Festival, the growth of political groups and magazines and publications devoted to independent film.

The opposition between formalism and politics now seems too simple, especially in the context of an emerging body of work which questions such a division, a significant part of it produced by women.[25] There is a danger in an argument which produces both terms of an opposition as discrete categories, as though 'politics' were an already given area, and as though 'formalism' automatically excluded that area. The problem can now be thought about in a different way. No politics can be taken for granted as self-evident: it has to be constructed, and various kinds of work on form, language and systems of representation are important for that process of construction. The work of the avant-garde is relevant here, but the 'avant-garde' is not a homogeneous area, and understanding of its history in terms of its diverse practices has to some extent been limited by the two 'avant-gardes' division. That wider history needs to be brought forward in order to make the argument about the relationship between form and politics meaningful. We have to start thinking in terms of a materialist politics which understands the historical process of transformation, refusing the temptations of a prescriptive theory which would mirror bourgeois divisions and hierarchies.

This means that the idea of oppositional practice also has to be thought through. The term 'independent cinema', or for that matter 'avant-garde cinema', covers a diverse range of contradictory practices, some of which are not immediately identifiable as 'oppositional'; viewing contexts and audiences are equally diverse and contradictory. Some avant-garde experimental work would obviously fall into the category of long-term projects rather than 'counter-cinema'. On one level we need to argue for the importance of experimental work as part of the longer-term struggle; on another level we need to bring some of the 'purist' or 'essentialist' aspects of this experimental work into productive critical contact with more immediately 'political' work so that we can confront both practices, rather than suppressing one in favour of the other. This is particularly important for feminists, since besides the immediate political struggle against social oppression there are long-term questions of how to understand and oppose the dominant language of 'patriarchal' society and our place within it. In accepting the value of experiment we accept the idea that constructing a feminist politics is a process of struggle which takes nothing for granted: in effect this means confronting and opposing any form of argument which presents itself as self-evident truth, outside criticism. To prescribe one kind of practice rather than others can obviously have an important polemical function at certain historical conjunctures, but this can often obscure the wider social struggle, and it seems to me more productive to bring together contradictory and incompatible practices in a discourse of argument and struggle.

The intervention of avant-garde and independent film-making into the formal educational system not only begins the work of bringing forward that practice into history, with all the difficulties that entails given its unwieldy diversity, it also provides the opportunity to rethink the practice of cultural struggle in terms of a social practice of transformation of the relations of production and reproduction for consumption within institutions, providing that social practice is based on political and historical analysis of the cinematic institution as a whole. Any social practice which imagines itself above transformation by history runs the risk of either sterile isolation or exhaustion and despair. It is in the dialectic between heterogeneity and constraint, between fragmentation and coherence, that displacements occur which open up the space for new knowledge.

Notes

1. Peter Wollen, 'The Two Avant-Gardes', in *Avant Garde Film in England and Europe, Studio International*, November-December 1975.
2. See Alan Lovell and Jim Hillier, *Studies in Documentary*, London: BFI/Secker & Warburg, 1972, pp. 21–2 and 29–30.
3. On 'art' in the service of 'national culture', see John Ellis, 'Art, Culture and Quality: Terms for a Cinema in the Forties and Seventies' *Screen*, vol. 19, no. 3, Autumn 1978; also Steve Neale, 'Propaganda', *Screen*, vol. 18, no. 3, Autumn 1977.
4. See David Curtis, 'English Avant-Garde Film: An Early Chronology', *Studio International*, op. cit.
5. Peter Wollen, *Signs and Meanings in the Cinema*, (rev. edn), London: BFI/Secker & Warburg, 1972.
6. The Editors of *Cahiers du cinéma*, 'John Ford's *Young Mr. Lincoln*', *Screen*, vol. 13, no. 3, Autumn 1972, reprinted in J. Ellis (ed.) *Screen Reader*, vol. 1, London: Society for Edcuation in Film and Television, 1977.
7. Nöel Burch, *Theory of Film Practice*, London: Secker & Warburg, 1973.
8. See, for example, the Edinburgh Film Festival publications on *Douglas Sirk* (Laura Mulvey and John Halliday, eds, 1972); *Frank Tashlin* (Claire Johnston and Paul Willemen, eds, 1973); *Raoul Walsh* (Phil Hardy, ed. 1974); *Jacques Tourneur* (Johnston and Willemen, eds, 1975). Also J. Halliday (ed.) *Sirk on Sirk*, London: BFI/Secker & Warburg, 1971.
9. P. Adams Sitney, 'The Films of Michael Snow', in Annette Michelson (ed.) *New Forms in Film* Montreux: Lausanne Museum of Art, 1974.
10. Geoffrey Nowell-Smith, 'A Note on History/Discourse', *Edinburgh '76 Magazine*, Edinburgh Film Festival, 1976, p. 27.
11. Ibid.
12. See Rod Stoneman (ed.) *Independent Film Workshops in Britain*, Torquay, Devon; Grael Communications, 1979.
13. Laura Mulvey, 'Visual Pleasure and Narrative Cinema', *Screen*, vol. 16, no. 3, Autumn 1975.
14. This point is clearly recognised in Part 2 of Stoneman, op. cit.
15. Roland Barthes draws out some of the complexities of teaching in 'Writers, Intellectuals, Teachers', in Stephen Heath (ed.) *Image-Music-Text*, London: Fontana, 1977.
16. See Wollen, 'The Two Avant-Gardes'. op. cit.
17. Rosalind Coward and John Ellis, *Language and Materialism*, London: RKP, 1977, p. 149.
18. Ibid.
19. Burch, op. cit.
20. See Paul Willemen (ed.) *Ophuls*, London: BFI, 1978.
21. Coward and Ellis, op. cit., p. 7.
22. See Mark Nash, '*Vampyr* and the Fantastic', *Screen*, vol. 17, no. 3, Autumn 1976.
23. Coward and Ellis, op. cit., p. 50.

24. For an elaboration of these questions see Simon Field, *Stan Brakhage: An American Independent Film-Maker*, London: Arts Council of Great Britain, 1979; Laura Mulvey, 'Feminism, Film and the Avant-Garde Film' *Framework*, no. 10, Spring 1979; Pam Cook, 'The Point of Expression in Avant-Garde Film', in E. Cowie (ed.) *British Film Institute Production Board Catalogue, 1977–78*, London: BFI 1978.

25. The opportunity to see some of this work, in all its diversity, was presented at the *Feminism and Cinema* event at the 1979 Edinburgh Film Festival.

Chapter 5

Film in Higher Education*

John Ellis

The key difference between British and US university arts faculties is that student essays have to be typed in America, whereas a typed essay from a British student is received with general wonderment. This demonstrates two features about British universities. First, they (erroneously) assume their students to be living on a hand-to-mouth basis, with no money for obtaining typewriters, individually or collectively. Second, they have no conception of their activity as one of training intellectuals for modern society. Their product is the 'British literary intellectual', a species of little use other than colour supplement journalism, whose stock in trade is the ability to produce an urbane quotation from the classics to fit any occasion whatsoever. Most arts graduates find careers in areas for which their training in this *salon mode* is singularly inappropriate: news journalism, civil service administration, social work, various kinds of management. Typing is an essential skill for most of these careers, as is the ability to understand complex technological processes (or at least their potential); the intricacies of particular sectors of the economy; the role of the state; the organisation of tasks into a systematic articulation of functions; the actual experience of working within such processes; the organisation of unions and shop-floor solidarity and so on. Instead, the arts undergraduate is offered the model of the lonely scholar ferreting out facts from a mass of evidence, and that of the author

---

* *Screen Education*, no. 38, Spring 1981.

starving in a garret until he (sometimes she) emerges into the world of the select coteries of his or her time, and the pantheon of the greats after death. The notion of the individual working alone is posed as the privileged route to Truth. Any technical or social intervention in this process is held to distort it. Typing places a machine between the self-expressive personality and the expressed truth itself; handwriting is held to embody the direct expression of the mind. Hence teachers' wasted hours of trying to decipher handwritten essays.

Film studies erupts into the middle of this ideological complex. Its object is an industrial art form, the product of a technology, a division of labour, particular forms of institutional organisation. English literature teaching is able (massively) to forget the institution of publishing; film studies has to have some explanation of how and where films come from and go to, even if this remains (as often) in the form of a myth like 'Hollywood = constraints': 'Europe = individual creative freedom'. Film studies throws into relief many of the repressed questions which relate directly to the intellectual formation that higher education gives its students. Film studies is incapable of breeding the 'British literary intellectual'. At least it is capable of questioning such an attitude; in favourable circumstances it could be capable of producing a rather different form of intellectual, provided with skills that could produce progressive changes beyond education.

Film studies gains its potential from both its object of study and the necessary ways of approaching that object. The object throws into relief questions of production, of collective labour (film producers and film audiences), of the nature of 'art' and so on. The approach to the object 'film' inevitably involves an examination of different disciplines and a close attention to the reliability of texts and 'facts'. The range of attentions potentially demanded from a student are therefore wide: they involve an awareness of technology as well as of aesthetics; an awareness of the partiality of approaches and the tendency of historians to make and perpetuate mistakes. Film studies therefore can challenge the 'natural attitude' of the British intellectual in its (usually dismal) moment of formation. The challenge takes place in a number of ways: by bringing together separate disciplines; by producing disruptions within disciplines by this encounter; by questioning the creation of knowledge and the attitude that it involves; by challenging various specific ideologies within the field of aesthetics; and by raising more general ideological problems across this whole process.

Bringing Together Disciplines

Inherent in an understanding of the filmic medium is some simple science: a certain amount of optics, a knowledge of the way photographic emulsions work, an understanding of the methods of sound reproduction. The importance of such a background knowledge can be demonstrated to students when they encounter the history of the introduction of sound technology, the question of why cinema appeared when it did, or the various and demonstrably different modes of colour photography. The technological basis of cinema relies upon certain ideas from the area of science that many students will have abandoned as 'incomprehensible'. The economic exploitation of this technical knowledge shows how pure science becomes specific technology. Here again a series of knowledges which do not normally enter into many humanities subjects have to be taught. The history of Hollywood is the history of the move from small-scale speculation for immediate gain towards full integration with American financial capital. At each point the form of organisation of the production process is a major factor in determining the kinds of choices made: choices at the level of specific sorts of films (length, marketability, level of investment, and so on), and at the level of possible future developments (for example Hollywood's rush to buy an appreciable part of its retail outlets: theatres). Yet this economic construction on the basis of certain scientific knowledges does not explain the cinema. The particular kind of product has to be explained if the particular economic forms adopted to regularise its production (stars, genres) are to be understood. Hence aesthetics enters: the area of particular theories of the artistic process (creation, catharsis), of the nature of the aesthetic object (realism, semiotics), of the role of entertainment and art. Included in this notion of 'aesthetics' (itself not 'a' discipline) is therefore a certain amount of sociological speculation, as well as some intellectual currents that are scarcely welcome even now in more conventional arts subjects: principal amongst these being semiotics.

Thus film brings together major concerns from a series of disciplines which usually maintain themselves largely as separate. Yet this cannot be a happy encounter: each theory or approach having its own little patch to cultivate, with film studies a benevolent landowner. Problems are created for each discipline by this encounter, and these problems can easily enrich or enliven the approach that students can then bring to other subjects that they may be studying. These problems are of two kinds: those where different kinds of accounts contradict each other, and those where the inadequacies of existing disciplines are revealed.

Disruption of Disciplines

A sociological account of the reactions of an audience, their expectations and their view of the role of cinema has little in common with a particular account of a film generated by close textual analysis. Yet both can be seen by students as valid methods of approach, and to some extent they can coexist. But when they are put side by side in detail, this coexistence begins to break down. Textual analysis always avoids the quantifiable and the concretely measurable in favour of the ineffable and the potential of the text. Descriptive sociology tends to miss the process of viewing with its complex displacements of attitudes in favour of the convenient memory-image that members of the audience retain from that experience. The two approaches construct different questions and criteria for answering those questions. They coexist simply because the questions and answers are radically different. Comparison between them, using the student's own relatively untheorised sense of cinema, can reveal from where such accounts come and why they are different. This reveals that the coexistence between them is a matter of their respective blindness rather than that they are simply 'worlds apart'. This is a relatively sophisticated procedure that relies on the forced marriage in film studies of different regional methodologies to give students an explicit awareness of the ways that different disciplines construct their own problematics.

A more simple, and more devastating, procedure also tends to take place in some areas of film studies teaching. Film studies in practice tends to reveal the blindness and lacks of different disciplines by the very questions it has to ask. For English Literature teaching, certain concepts, like that of the individual creative genius, rest unquestioned; and other considerations, like that of the nature and effects of the institution of book publishing, remain unexplored. Rare are the courses which tackle these problems, and fortunate the students who attend them. Film is forced to study the industry that produces it as it has had demonstrable effects at every level. The availability of feature film finance has not been the same in every country at every time; film genres have a determining effect upon the possibilities for narrative filmmaking: state intervention has had the effect (USSR, Weimar Germany) of producing a particular conception of 'art cinema'. Examining these questions is commonplace for film studies; for literature the examination of the financial structure of the nineteenth-century novel publishing industry is something that is generally considered an irrelevancy to students. Again, authorship is a simple category for literature: one person sits, quill in hand,

and writes, and there you have the author. For film, a series of arguments about the process of production, responsibility for work, creative contributions, and so on, have to be deployed before even this position can be reached. It is further challenged by the arguments put forward by Peter Wollen in *Signs and Meaning in the Cinema* and various writers in *Screen*,[1] so that it ceases to be tenable for many students as anything other than a particular method of organising and reading texts constructed against the grain of the industry producing those texts. Hence students who combine literature with film can return to literature with unquestioned literary attitudes productively questioned in their work on cinema.

For students combining orthodox historical studies with film, the nature of 'evidence' can be called into question. Film history is a mess and is likely to remain so as the tasks of clearing a way through the accumulated myths is a complicated and sometimes delicate one. Nevertheless, for all the historiographic disasters to which the area is prone, film history still has to be taught. Students have to distrust printed sources (for example, the innumerable retailings of the myth of the introduction of sound by a 'bankrupt' Warner Bros. so effectively dispelled by Doug Gomery).[2] They have demonstrated to them the inadequacy of primary sources in some areas, as with the haphazard preservation of films and the consequent neglect of Vitagraph as an innovative company. They see constantly before them film historians who cannot remember films accurately, and can then measure these memory lapses against their own and those of their teachers. They find different accounts of the prehistory of film, the early history of the cinema, of the whole process of innovation and change. They have to face these differences because of the very lack of writing in many areas, which means that no overall account with any theoretical homogeneity has yet been constructed, even on a reading list. The production of film history can then be shown to be the result of a complex of determinations. This includes the aesthetic principles of archiving policies (for example, Iris Barry's Griffith-obsessed policies at the New York Museum of Modern Art); the promotional role of the film critics; the industry's own conceptions of artistic merit and the use-value of films; the fetishism inherent in the activities of certain film historians[3] as well as more general ideologies of history. The very inadequacy of film studies in the realm of serious and detailed historiography can be turned to advantage: film studies can pose to history the question of history's own methods and presuppositions.

These two brief examples demonstrate differing ways in which film studies can pose awkward questions for other disciplines,

disciplines which are prone to being combined with film studies in various academic institutions. For English Literature, it poses the questions that conventional literary studies repress; for history, the lacks in film history can be turned into a demand addressed to history for a sense of direction and purpose. Further, these examples begin to reveal another role for film studies: that of questioning 'knowledge' and the attitudes it involves.

Knowledge

Our culture presents knowledge as an empirical procedure: one of constructing in thought a model that coincides exactly with the real that exists beyond thought. This is a process that is usually considered to fall short of its aims, but nevertheless the aim remains and is held to be achieved rarely. Yet what I have said up to this point demonstrates that film studies can conform with such a model only with considerable difficulty. Film studies is not so much a discipline in the process of self-creation (generation of specific problematics and procedures) as sociology or anthropology were in the second half of the nineteenth century: it is more the convergence of a series of disparate problematics and procedures upon a particularly recalcitrant object. This situation sets up a series of problems within its area that radically question the dominant notion of knowledge. First, we have the deficiencies of many approaches: some texts are 'wrong . . . but for a reason', others are 'unreliable, but better than nothing'. This sense of treating texts with caution⁴ assessing their status as writing can be extended by providing back-up material in the form of press books, reviews, and so on, harvested from the British Film Institute (BFI) Library. Then there is the way that disparate problematics cannot 'see' each other's objects: the model of textual functioning generated in semiotics (narrative movement through disruption and heterogeneity towards a final reintegration of significations) conflicts with the notions of a static and exhaustible content that are implicit in most audience surveys. Knowledge can be seen as a function of the questions that are asked and the way material gathered from asking those questions is integrated into a particular system of understanding. Knowledge is then a function of problematics rather than of the clear vision of the (voyeuristic) analyst(s) towards the world. The empiricist position is therefore revealed as a repression of these questions in favour of placing the analyst in such a voyeuristic position. As a result connections can be made with the critique of the ideology of the visible and of vision upon which much cinema trades.

Film studies, then, are very explicit about theory. Even the most conventional of film history courses has at some time to encounter the construction of films explicitly from a theoretical basis. Such is the impact of Russian montage theories, where theoretical writing has to be mobilised in the very least to 'explain what they were trying to do'. Similarly modernist theories have to be deployed to understand what we glibly call 'the avant-garde'. A course can hardly avoid the realist theories of a Bazin, the formalist notions of Reisz or Burch. It is difficult to avoid the conclusion that certain films can be read from within more than one theoretical construction, with different perceptions of its textual functioning as a result.[5] This is the only possible conclusion that students can be guided towards which does not provide a hopeless eclecticism (that is, each to their own theory) on the one hand, or a notion of the historical and social specificity of each theory that denies their currency and possibilities in the present (for example, 'Montage was OK for the Russians, but it's an out-of-date irrelevancy now'). It has moved very far from simple notions of the relationship of knowledge to its ostensible objects, providing a series of doubts about the position of empirical 'fact-finding' without totally destroying the possibility of analysis. Knowledge is shown to be knowledge from a position: the position that claims an objective truth for its knowledge is an impossibility.

The final problem for an empiricist conception of knowledge is the nature of film itself. The movement and productivity of any single film always escapes the possibility of exhaustive analysis. The constant movement and mutation of any film makes each text an 'unattainable text' in Raymond Bellour's phrase.[6] Quotation in analysis is impossible when the analysis is written. Long seminar hours can be devoted to analysing the components of particular scenes, and then the whole activity shown to be a process of naming from which the contingent nature of the significations has escaped. Over all of this hovers the question of memory, the radical impossibility of a recall of a film, especially one constructed along the most conventional lines: Hollywood classic editing. Any detailed analysis or reviewing of a sequence is enough to demonstrate the fallibility of memory.

Film studies has the potential to demonstrate that knowledge is not absolute or empiricist: that it is constructed from within particular positions and can never aspire to being final or exhaustive. Knowledge is put in its place as necessary but not absolute, decisive but never final.

Specific Ideologies

So far, I have dealt only with the way in which film as a particular subject area operates as a re-articulation and therefore questioning of approaches from established disciplines. At its furthest point, this can take the form of deconstructing the specific ideology of intellectuals: the primacy and power of knowledge. In such a way, film studies can contribute to the formation of a critical intelligensia that could be capable of producing an analysis of its own social position and role. Film studies also deals with a particular area of intellective activity: the area of audio-visual significations and the forms that they have taken and could take. In this area certain very specific ideologies operate, constructing notions of truth based in the mimetic function of the image, and notions of the form of current society in which 'entertainment' exists as a separate and licensed playground. These are the major ideologies of film in which film studies is caught: one specific to the photographic media, the other to the whole realm of the production of fictions.

Realism is one variant of a supple form which forges a connection between the realm of vision and the ideal of truth. The whole physical arrangement of cinemas in the West is based upon the separation/implication of the spectator in the spectacle. What is seen is separate, whole and complete; the seer is able to view everything that is needed in order to decipher the truth of what is shown. This voyeuristic position for the viewer in relation to the photographic image lies behind the conception that the photographic image has some privileged relation to the truth of the real. The link is particularly strong when applied to documentary filming, television news or newspaper photos. It exists for most students as a kind of 'practical Bazinianism' in relation to fiction and narrative. For teaching, a number of criticisms of this attitude can be launched, beginning with the common-sense approach which demonstrates the amount of fictional editing involved in TV news interviews of the simplest kind (the filming of cut-aways as cover after the end of the interview, often extended to the re-filming of the journalist's questions); to the complex forms of staging and pre-dissection of action that many documentary and all fiction modes necessarily involve. Another approach demonstrates that the photograph is a signifying practice itself. This can begin from a demonstration of advertising (obvious in its use of significations) using a text like Judith Williamson's *Decoding Advertisements*,[7] and then moving to more complicated examples of specific filmic significations. A third approach involves the use of films which confront the textual construction of reality: particularly revealing of aspects of sound mixing (the silent aid to creating a seamless fiction of reality) are the films of Straub/Huillet, refusing to grade sounds across a cut, and usually insisting on the use of the appropriate sound take with each shot used. The particular variants of the ideology of the visual and the audible can thus be revealed as variants of an overall ideological approach. This approach accords to the photograph the status of truth so long as the photographic procedures place the spectator in a position of voyeurist contemplation.

Another major ideology in which cinema is particularly caught is that of 'entertainment'. This term can be opposed to 'work' or to 'art', with very different results. Work is necessary, serious and unpleasurable; entertainment is unnecessary, frivolous and pleasurable. Thus runs one ideological tendency. Art is serious, uplifting and humanising; entertainment is lightweight, ennervating and ultimately condescending to its audience. Thus runs another tendency. In each of these characterisations, most of cinema, certainly most American cinema, is 'entertainment'. Students will partake of these tendencies spontaneously, without understanding their implications for the course of study they are taking, let alone the kind of society they inhabit. On the one hand, the ideology of art can be shown to have produced forms of cinema whose aesthetic presuppositions now seem obvious if not facile (for example, many American attempts at 'the art of the film'); it can also be shown to link to a whole complex of ideas about the role of art in society that are becoming increasingly untenable. The division between entertainment and work similarly reveals the operation of a puritan ethic of work that rules out any examination of the social construction of the individual. It also tends to conceal the work and economic organisation involved in production of entertainment. Study of film tends to turn the category of 'entertainment' inside out, asking questions of its place and social role as well as of its potential.

General Ideological Problems

Any course can raise problems in the general ideological arena if it feels like it: the problem is one of providing the basis which makes such questioning profitable. A facile anti-capitalism is a stock-in-trade of most arts undergraduates, who are quite willing to be cynical about 'the men with the money'. Indeed, this is precisely the basis of the division between the film producer (always hated) and the artist-director (always loved). Equally, it is fairly easy to get students to designate certain films as sexist or racist. But to persuade students into such activities of moral labelling is nothing more than the creation of a temporary sense of togetherness for a seminar group. It is more difficult to produce a genuinely political mode of thinking amongst students.

The discussion of films inevitably raises major ideological questions. Examination of the film industry and its forms can be used to demonstrate different forms of capitalist enterprise, different forms of and rationales for state intervention. A comparison of the Hays Office and methods of censorship in the USSR reveals remarkably few fundamental differences between them (something students are for some reason unwilling to accept). The question of the wide dissemination of American films, their sheer numerical weight in the world market, raises the question of 'hegemony' and imperialism. Similarly, questions of sexism (and indeed what sexism does and can mean) are easily raised in relation to most narrative films. Yet what eventually defines the form that such discussions take is the attitude that the students have to bring to bear upon them. Across each discussion of (for instance) whether a particular film can be said to be sexist or not is the elaboration of categories of thought, criteria of comparison and evaluation. It is this procedure, undertaken across the reception of 'facts' and 'knowledge', that will eventually produce facts and knowledge.

I have deliberately limited this short exposition of the possibilities of film studies in higher education to the question of intellectual attitude. It may seem to many to be theoreticist rather than political. The kind of teaching that I am describing aims to provide students with intellectual equipment and the means of thinking through problems that they will inevitably encounter after the end of their formal education. It conceives of higher education as producing intellectuals in the Gramscian sense: individuals whose primary social role is one of organisation, coordination of activities, the production of representations and patterns of actions in and for others. Teaching in higher education can take a number of attitudes to the training of intellectuals. It can adopt a Leavisite approach and inculcate values which it hopes will undermine the effectivity of such intellectuals in the rough world of modern commerce. It can choose to ignore this function entirely and produce individuals with a range of particular knowledges in a particular self-defining subject area. Or it can, as I am suggesting, move from the basis of providing knowledge about a specific area (in this case film studies) towards providing an assessment of the production of knowledge and the realm of thought itself. This involves realising the specificity of thought as a process: its limitations as well as its potentials, the blindnesses of certain approaches and the reasons why such blindnesses occur. Such an approach will produce critical intellectuals of a practical kind. They will be suspicious of romantic approaches which value thought and 'Culture' above work and industry. Yet they may also be open to socialist currents, to the development of new forms of organisation of work and personal life. Their intellectual training will have produced this openness; it cannot guarantee the production of young left-wingers. That conception of education is a fantasy of the power of the intellect that has to be criticised.

It has to be acknowledged that this kind of intellectual training is very different from that which produces the traditional British literary intellectual. The literary intellectual is constituted as a figure who can comment, who knows, who sees the truth, but is incapable of action from that position. The training given to many students to produce such an intellectual attitude typically has to be supplemented by further training such as journalism courses, management training schemes, or even the 'year or two messing around before settling into a job' that many university arts graduates undertake. Arts degrees have given such students a large degree of knowledge on many topics, but have failed to give them an attitude to knowledge that would enable them to move into different areas. Higher education acts as a finishing school or as a licensed playground where sensibilities can be sharpened, and personal attitudes explored. Film studies has been constituted against many of the tendencies inherent in such an education: against literary tendencies that see film as a 'bastard art form'; against historians who point to its lack of critical or historiographic reading matter; against plain academic conservatism and disdain for anything connected with popular taste. It is inevitable that the subject area, painfully constituting itself in such an environment, should take one of two options. Either it aggressively identifies itself with those tendencies which seek to destroy it ('Film is an art form embodying fundamental values just like yours'), or it tries to undermine the intellectual basis of the attacks made upon it. Film studies, then, can be at present a place from which the formation of the traditional literary intellectual can be challenged. The force of such a challenge is that it upsets assumptions about the relation between knowledge and its objects, producing a questioning of the adequacy of current modes of thought.

Notes

1. Edward Buscombe, 'Ideas of Authorship' *Screen*, vol. 14, no. 3, Autumn 1973; Stephen Heath, 'Comment on "Ideas of Authorship" ',

Screen, vol. 14, no. 3 Autumn 1973; Michel Foucault, 'What is an Author?' *Screen*, vol. 20, no. 1, Spring 1979.

2. J. Douglas Gomery, 'Writing the History of the American Film Industry: Warner Bros. and Sound,' *Screen*, vol. 17, no. 1, Spring 1976'; J. Douglas Gomery, 'Failure and Success: Vocafilm and RCA Photophone Lunorate Sound', *Film Reader*, vol. 2, January 1977.

3. For example, seeing the writing of history as the prolongation of promotion of the pleasure derived from watching (a) film, demonstrated clearly in the case of Kevin Brownlow.

4. This is particularly true of the disparate pieces included in Tino Balio's collection *The American Film Industry* (University of Wisconsin Press, 1977), which was acutely reviewed by Vincent Porter in *Screen Education*, no. 24, Autumn 1977.

5. Welles's *Touch of Evil* provides one such example: an *auteurist* construction, a generic (*film noir*) interpretation and a semiotic reading looking at the textual production of meaning, can all be produced.

6. Raymond Bellour, 'The Unattainable Text', *Screen* vol. 16, no. 3, Autumn 1975, pp. 19–27.

7. Judith Williamson, *Decoding Advertisements*, London: Marion Boyars, 1978.

Part II

Television and Media Studies

Chapter 6

Can Television Teach?*

Umberto Eco

Eight or nine years ago, when my daughter was beginning to watch the world through the window of a television screen (this screen has been called in Italy 'an open window on a closed world'), I once saw her religiously following a commercial, which, as far as I remember, was assuming that a certain product was the best in the world, and was able to satisfy all your needs. Educationally alerted, I tried to teach her that this was not true and, to make my argument simple, I informed her that television commercials usually lie. She understood that she shouldn't trust television (since for oedipal reasons she was yearning to trust me). Two days later she was watching television news, informing her that it would be imprudent to travel on the northern highways because it was snowing (information that met my profound wishes, since I was desperately trying to stay home that weekend). She glared suspiciously at me, asking why I was trusting television as I had suggested, two days before, that television does not tell the truth. I was obliged to begin a very complicated dissertation in extensional logic, pragmatics of natural languages and genre theory in order to convince her that *sometimes* television lies and

*   This article is based on a talk delivered to the conference sponsored by Thames Television (in association with the Independent Broadcasting Authority and the London University Institute of Education) on *Schools Television*, held in London on 1 and 2 June 1978. We are grateful to the sponsors for permission to reprint the text.
Screen Education, no. 31, Summer 1979.

sometimes it tells the truth. For example a book begins 'Once upon a time there was a little girl called Little Red Riding Hood and so on . . .' doesn't tell the truth when on its first page it attributes the story of that girl to a gentleman called Perrault. Only the psychiatrist that my daughter will probably summon on arriving at the age of wisdom will, I suppose, be able to say to what extent my pedagogical intervention has damaged significantly her mind or her Id. But this is another story.

The fact is, and I definitely discovered it on just that occasion – if you want to use television for teaching somebody something, you have first to teach somebody how to use television. In this sense, television is not so different from a book. You can use books to teach, but first you must teach people about books, at least about alphabet and words, and then about levels of credibility, suspension of disbelief, the difference between a novel and a book on history and so on and so forth. In reality, I wonder whether there is a real difference between teaching people to read books and using books to teach people. Apparently in schools we distinguish primers, spelling books and grammars (which teach how to read other books) from, for example, a handbook on chemistry or Roman history. We think that the first kind of book speaks about other books, while the second speaks about the world. I am not sure that things are just like that.

A handbook of chemistry mainly speaks about the language of chemistry and a book on Roman history, especially when it is written for children, has to be approached with great circumspection. It tells the truth when it says that Rome was founded in 735 BC, but it has to be made very clear that, for Julius Caesar, this piece of information was devoid of any sense because of a different way of recognising the flow of time, while for Theodor Mommsen, it was endowed with sense but merely fanciful. If this book assumes that Rome was founded by Romulus and Remus, the book has lied. Nevertheless, many children's books do that and when they say that Caesar was actually murdered on the Ides of March, the first thing I would like a schoolboy to realise is that this fact is historically true only according to a series of intepretative decisions concerning the reliability of certain literary sources. It happens thus that history books also speak about other books. I am not trying to advocate an education based on sceptical assumptions, but I think that the first duty of a teacher is, if not to say, 'Don't trust me', at least to say, 'Only trust me within reason'. I think in fact that this attitude is one that every reasonable person takes when watching television.

If television news says that an event, X, happened in Lebanon, my first reaction is that it *probably* happened and it *may* be that it happened the way the screen is showing, but I would prefer to check it from other sources. When instead of a piece of straight information, however, television communicates an opinion or a more complicated definition of interrelation among events, then our reaction frequently is rather 'dull': 'What does it mean?' or 'Do I understand exactly what they want me to understand?' There are, finally, felicitous cases in which we realise that the secret thought of the sender is, 'I know you believe you understand what you think I said, but I am not sure you realise that what you heard is not what I meant'. If such is the situation which defines a mature reaction on the part of the adult viewer, why then should we hope (or act in order to make possible) that for children, television messages are univocal and plainly readable? And when we have something important to say to them that we can communicate through television, why should we assume that they understand it in the same way we conceived it?

I think that the problems concerning the educational use of television are the same as those concerning its supposed perverse effects. It may be possible that television, as well as other media, corrupts the innocent, but undoubtedly it achieves this in a way which was not the one foreseen by many educators (or by many corrupters). Let's suppose that a Martian tries to extrapolate the impact of television on the first generation to grow up under its influence – people who began watching television at the age of say 3 in the early 1950s – our Martian could begin with a content analysis of television programmes of the 1950s. Fed with programmes such as *$64,000 Question*, soap operas, Mary-Alcott-like serials, Coca-Cola ads and John Wayne movies about the Second World War, that generation should, by 1968, have acquired a dignified position in a savings bank, a crew cut and a white collar. They would have believed in law and order and be looking for an honest marriage with the girl/boy next door. On the contrary, if I rightly remember such a prehistorical event, it happened that in 1968 this 'television generation' tried to kill not the Japanese but university professors, and smoked grass instead of Marlboro, practised yoga, transcendental meditation, macrobiotics and so forth. Let me add when television proposed long-haired people smoking marijuana and putting flowers into guns, as the new model of a 'young' lifestyle, this next generation cut their hair, began to fire guns and prepare bombs. This suggests that youngsters read television differently from those who make it. I don't believe that this happens at random, I believe there are rules governing the gap between the emission and the reception of a television programmes. One must know these rules and one must, above all, attempt to teach people, and mainly young people, about these rules.

Let me try to outline a sort of elementary grammar of communication since, from the most ancient times, to teach first meant to transmit the fundamental elements of a grammar. The most optimistic view of mass media suffers because of an over-simplified diagram, according to which to communicate is to make a *message*, emitted by a *sender* through a *channel* so that it arrives at an *addressee* (supposedly able to understand the message according to the same system of interpretative rules – or codes – as the one shared by the sender). The first diagram is very simple and optimistic and false. In reality, and according to major researchers in theory and mass media, the diagram should be written as in the second diagram.

SENDER	MESSAGE (CHANNEL) MESSAGE CODE		ADDRESSEE

Diagram 1

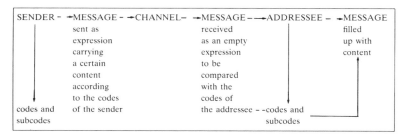

Diagram 2

We have the sender 'S', who has his own set of codes and subcodes, with an entire universe of competence. He or she produces a message 'M', which is a physical expression endowed with meaning according to the system of codes and subcodes that he or she, the sender, recognises. The message travels through the channel and arrives at the output ready to be absorbed by the addressee, as 'ME', that is message as expression. At this point 'ME' can be perceived as an empty physical expression, to be compared with the codes and subcodes (and entire competence) of the addressee. Subsequently the addressee produces the actualised message as content, filling it up with the meanings provided by his or her own system of competence.

In order to make clear the umbrella term of code and sub-code, let me say, for instance, that the linguistic code can be reduced to take the formation provided by a dictionary, but it is complicated by a set of subcodes to be analysed in format of an encyclopaedia. Suppose I am communicating with the members of a culture which has subdivided animals and vegetables in the same way as a standard European culture does, distinguishing chickens from cats and frogs from dogs, Indian corn from buckwheat and so on. Both cultures, however, at the higher level of meaning, may reorganise these cultural units, distinguishing what is edible from what is non-edible in two different ways. For certain Asiatic people, dogs are edible. For others, arguably less savage, the French and Italian custom of eating frogs is looked upon with horror. Thus alternative cultures, even when sharing a certain basic code, establish different sub-codes. A frog is categorised within the same zoological unit for the Englishman as for the Frenchman, but to the first it means non-edible, whilst to the second it means a dainty morsel.

Let's imagine an Oxford Professor speaking with an immigrant taxi driver in Piccadilly Circus and using a sophisticated lexical competence, elaborated understatements, Wildian ironies, maybe whimsical oxymorons, along with subtle allusions to Chaucerian characters. Well, we have a reasonable picture of a communicational interaction in which, even though the two are speaking the same English language, a network of mutually impenetrable sub-codes are conflicting with each other. Consider that I have spoken so far of linguistic, verbal devices. It is enough to add to our picture other semiotic phenomena, such as gesture or facial mimicry, and Piccadilly Circus has become the Tower of Babel. Do not forget that Ludwig Wittgenstein gave up with the principles of his *Tractatus* when the Italian economist, Piero Sraffa, during a conversation in a train from London to Cambridge, innocently asked him, 'What is the meaning of this gesture?' – simultaneously producing one of Neopolitan tradition, with a number of meanings. Wittgenstein thus began to think out his *Philosophical Investigations*, in which communication is viewed as a hard and problematical game.

Sociologists who studied mass media in the 1940s and 1950s already knew very well such phenomena as the *boomerang effect*, the influence of *opinion leaders*, the necessity of reinforcing message by a *door-to-door control*. They knew that between the sending and the receiving point there are many filters sensitised by psychological and social or cultural screens. The first tests after the arrival of television in suburban and depressed areas in Italy demonstrated that a lot of people watched all the evening programmes as a continuum, without any discrimination between shows, television news or drama. Everything was taken at the same level of credibility in a total mish-mash of genre competence. For years and years television corporations have relied on various kinds of ratings, have been content to know how many people like a given programme (certainly an important piece of information from a commercial point of view), while basically ignoring what the audience readily *understood* about a given programme. Nevertheless, the communicational gap I have outlined above is more complex than that.

We ought to consider not only the differences in codes between sender and addressee, but also the variety of codes distinguishing certain groups of addressees from other groups of addressees, according to their social status and their ideological attitudes. And we should consider, even from this more flexible point of view, that the picture is still incomplete since we should also take into account the fact that a given subject belongs to different groups according to the programme and to the hour of the day. I mean that the given person X can rank as a politically sensitive worker (therefore, endowed with economic and political competence) when watching the news. However, the same person, X, can assume the competence of a middle-class philistine when watching a serial, keeping frozen his own sensitivity about sexual roles, women's liberation or class struggle, though he was able to awaken this sensitivity when his television set was speaking about wages, strikes or human rights. We should be aware that the same phenomenon happens with children. Children can be extremely sensitive to ecological values when television arouses their underlying and already acquired competence about respect for animals, in a broadcast about wild life. But the same child, when watching a Western movie, will participate in the excitement of the cowboy riding at full gallop to pursue the outlaws, without suffering for the *tour de force* of the horse, so mercilessly exploited. Can we say that even in this case we are witnessing a difference in codes? Can we say that according to the situation and to an aroused competence about genre, the same person responds according to different cultural codes? It depends on our agreement apropos the notion of cultural code. Suppose that during a broadcast someone pronounced the word 'metempsychosis'. One can guess that a given per cent of the audience doesn't share a correct competence about this piece of lexical information. There is undoubtedly a code gap, but the gap can be filled by further education. Let's suppose that our broadcaster is so smart as to be able to insert in the course of the programme the explanation of that critical word. No problem, in this sense television can be used educationally.

But what happens in the case of the boy who watches a Western movie and, once accepted, its genre rules fail to activate his competence about animal abuse? I cannot imagine the movie stopping while a speaker appears and says, 'Pay attention to the unethical behaviour of the hero'. I mean, I can imagine a situation like that but not as a grammatical intervention, as in the case of 'metempsychosis'. Rather, it would be a procedure of decontextualisation or deconstruction.

We can imagine such an operation in two ways:

1. A movie which is a false Western and which has been narratively conceived as an education story about horses. In this case the boy is no longer watching a Western movie.
2. A special broadcast in which a normal Western movie is submitted to ideological analysis.

In both cases we have implicitly recognised that in order to make our boy switch from one type of ideological competence to another type, we have been obliged to switch from one genre to another. In other words, we have been obliged to switch from one type of text to another in order to arouse a different kind of textual competence. One is thus led to assume that under the umbrella term of codes and sub-codes, one is not only gathering something similar to verbal, lexical or grammatical competence, but also something more akin to rhetorical competence. At the same time, one realises that the potential of such competence cannot be made explicit in the format of a set of grammatical rules but resides rather in the format of a storage of previous texts. An inter-textual competence plays a great role in our way of using mass media. We understand the verbal languages, road signs, communications by flags in the Navy and other semiotic systems, by way of so-called grammatical competence. It seems we possess a set of combinational rules, to be applied to a set of clearly distinguishable, expressive units, in order to produce a series of recognisable content units, such as orders, names of things, precise warnings and so on. But in many other cases we do not perform a grammatical competence but rather a textual competence.

Take the Bible. Sometimes it says, 'Do that or that, don't eat pork, don't kill your brother', and so on, by providing precise rules. But at other times – as a matter of fact in the majority of cases – the Bible offers to us examples of possible behaviour, tales or life models. It doesn't communicate through general grammatical rules, to be applied in many different cases, but through model texts. If you like, this is the difference between so-called Roman law and Anglo-Saxon common law. The former provides precise rules for precise cases, duly registered and coded. The latter provides a series of cases along with their solutions, to be compared to new cases in order to extrapolate the similar solutions. Roman law has a grammatical structure, common law a textual structure. Our competence in decoding mass media bears more relationship to common law than to Roman law. Perhaps it is not by chance that television started in Anglo-Saxon countries.

Orson Welles's radio production of *The War of the Worlds* was explicitly presented as make-believe, with many explicit warnings on the part of the speaker. It was received by many, as you know, as live news. The framework of the evoked textual model (*news*) was so strong as to overwhelm every blatant warning on the part of the broadcasters. Our culture makes precise distinctions between tragedy, comedy and drama. One cannot conceive of a story which begins with the classical language and typical situation of a tragedy and then ends with the protagonists triumphing over their enemies and living happily ever after. If one had to produce such a provocative broadcast or play, one would have to over-emphasise the tragic language in order to prepare the audience for the paradoxical denouement. But even irony, parody and paradox require an audience able to detect certain rhetorical signals (the ancient rhetoricians spoke of pronunciates, a sort of inflection of the voice) otherwise those figures of speech are taken literally. Children watching television can easily mistake comedy for tragedy, and vice versa, when the genre signals are ambiguous or when their competence is not trained enough. But even in the adult world, the different behaviour of Don Quixote and Sancho Panza, *vis-à-vis* certain events, is a beautiful example of a gap between two different genre competences. A society dominated by mass media is the playground of such misunderstandings. Sometimes the situation is purposefully used by the sender to induce, through the manipulation of textual rules, ideological consensus. Given the usual structure of the happy ending comedy, much disturbing information can be given according to this textual scheme.

Two years ago, research by Italian scholars on the general structure of television news in different countries from Japan to Sweden, Italy and the USA and so on, proved that they follow the classical scheme of Russian Fairy Tales, analysed decades ago by Vladimir J. Propp. Thames Television has produced a programme, *Viewpoint*, no. 5, just to explain this kind of phenomenon. While the grammatical competence can be taught in the form of a handbook, and grammatical ambiguities are easily understood and disambiguated when one knows the basic

elements of a code, textual ambiguities remain frequently unde-
tectable. Maybe, just because of their evidence, Molière's Mon-
sieur Jourdain spent his life speaking in prose without realising
it. To make him conscious of his competence, Molière was obliged
to make him compare his everyday prose with poetry. I mean that
our underlying textual competence can be made conscious only
by violently contrasting different texts and/or different interpretations of the same text. I have seen one of the *Viewpoint* programmes and I have read the description of the others. I think
that these programmes represent very clever examples of how
to use television in order to teach about television. They are
'deconstructive' in the good sense of the word. They show the
internal devices of that clockwork orange that young viewers
usually consume without worrying about its chemical composition.
I mean that if I had to make a programme about television
manipulatory techniques, and as a matter of fact, I have prepared
a programme like that in Italy, I would follow the same pattern.
But, at this point, we have a problem to face. Let me call 'normal'
programmes, as usually broadcast by television, *gross programmes*
or *gross messages*. And let me call a *net programme* or a *net
message* a programme about television, a metalinguistic or meta-
televisional programme – like *Viewpoint*. A television programme
speaking about television programmes is still a television programme. As such, even a *net* programme falls under all the structures I have listed above, apropos the impossibility of a univocal
reception and the variety of competences which make a given
broadcast like more broadcasts, according to the social, cultural
and even psychological situation of the viewer. Programmes like
Viewpoint provide teachers with a bibliography and other orientat-
ing material for use as opinion leaders. But, even in this case, one
cannot avoid the typical situation of every mass communication
process. The message is emitted by a sender, more or less belonging to the dominating cultural milieu, who foresees the possible
competence of his or her addressee, but since the message travels
through a highly sophisticated technological channel, and is supposed to reach an undifferentiated audience, there is never a face-
to-face control, there is no feedback. That's very well known.
And, even the most critically orientated educational television
cannot escape from this mass mediological cul-de-sac. Now, notice
that the core of the problem resides in who takes the initiative of
deconstruction of the message and of controlling the variability
of competences. This agent must have both metalinguistic capability, the capability of emitting *net* messages about *gross* messages, and feedback control. This agent cannot be the author of
the *net* programme but is rather the teacher, physically present in

the classroom. The teacher should be the real sender of the critical *net* message. Once this is realised, it is no longer necessary that the television message be a critical one. It can belong to the normal production. It becomes the object of the process of deconstruction.

I have fixed on this point for a precise theoretical reason. A *net* television message can focus the way in which *gross* messages produce meaning, opinions, ideologies, world views – but only if we assume the meaning is definitely contained within the message. This is the limit of traditional content analysis and of many analyses of values, ideologies and so on. In the diagram I have proposed, the meaning (the final meaning, the message as content, filled up with the content) doesn't only depend on the syntactic structure of the message and on its semantic value such as it has been conceived by the Sender. The meaning is a *social* product which is produced in the framework of the entire pragmatic process. This process concerns the emission of the original message. Its reception is a still empty form; its comparison rests with the addressee's competence and its definitive actualisation as content. The *production of meaning* takes place all along this whole process. Now, even a *net* message can be emitted only as the starting point of such an interpretative chain. One can expect that it will be understood in a unique way. Therefore even a critical programme such as *Viewpoint* should elicit a series of active critical operations on the part of its young addressees. Once seen as the *net* message analysing *gross* messages, children should acquire a moviola (a good editing table) and could continue to manipulate the film in order to produce directly, by themselves, different treatments of a piece of news, for example. (Along with the film, a sort of kit could be given to encourage them in continuing to produce.) They could have a soap opera, or a situation comedy, and try to rewrite the original treatment in order to produce a different pedagogical message. They could compare television material with other media, from comic strip to publicity. They could make explicit a lot of their underlying textual competence.

But I fear that an educational *net* message still comes from nowhere and is still confused with that constant halo of paternal authority which accompanies every *gross* television message. It is exactly this sort of magic which needs to be broken by an educational enterprise, since a *net* programme runs the risk of appearing as magic, as already endowed with truth as any other *gross* programme. The next educational step ought to consist of transforming children from passive spectators of an educational programme into active protagonists of a critical endeavour. To do that, *net* programmes would not be, in principle, so indispensible.

It would suffice a trained teacher able to use directly *gross* programmes as 'negative' school books.

Television is the school book of modern adults, as much as it is the only authoritative school book for our children. Education, real education doesn't mean teaching young people to trust school. On the contrary, it consists of training young people to criticise school books and write *their own school books*. It was like that at the time of Socrates, and I don't see any reason for giving up this attitude. Therefore, teachers should have the courage to take *gross* television as the basis of their teaching. To use *gross* television means to teach about the entire pragmatic process of communication and not only about the emitted messages. In this way, to teach about television not only means to teach about the starting message, but about the concrete situation of its interpreters, about their competence and about the socially-rooted differences among competences. In analysing *gross* programmes, children become aware both of the way messages are manipulating them and of the way they are necessarily manipulating messages. Now the problem is, are the teachers prepared to do that? I don't think so, at least in general. It is at *this* point I see the real function of educational *net* messages. They should be projected primarily for teachers. Teachers constitute a most homogeneous body of viewers and their different competences can easily be foreseen by the authors of *net* messages. Teachers can recognise the metalinguistical proposal of the *net* message and avoid a charismatic effect. Their participation in the critical project can be reinforced by various sorts of reading material. To produce *net* messages for teachers is the sort of job capable of taking years and years of activity for any educationally orientated television corporation.

I am not saying that such programmes as *Viewpoint* should not be watched by students, on the contrary, the students can observe through them, the way their teachers are invited to deal with *gross* messages. This sort of participation can increase their active attitude. But the real educational operation begins later, when children are actively involved in their own task of analysing *gross* programmes. Only at this point can they become aware of the object of their analysis, not only of the *gross* message in itself, but also of their way to react to it. This kind of teaching could be particularly useful for classes where there are children of different social or ethnic origin.

Educational television has had many merits. A programme like *Sesame Street* has taught millions of young Americans that black English is a dignified language which can express joy, wit, compassion, concepts. But I would like to see a programme teaching the teacher how *to use*, for instance *The Johnny Carson Show*, in order to predict what it says to a young Puerto Rican, to a young black, to a young white Anglo-Saxon Protestant. Probably each of them sees something different in that programme. None of these interpretations is in itself a case of 'aberration'. The real aberration is that all these children do not realise that the programme is the same, but the interpretations are different. Every interpretation reflects a different cultural world with different codes. These codes, even if contrasting with each other, can be mutually compared, translated one into the other when possible, or recognised as incommensurable when they are so, and, when it is educationally necessary, that even their mutual incommensurability becomes a matter of critical discussion. To compare codes with each other doesn't only mean to deal with lexical competence, verbal fluency, knowledge of syntactical or rhetorical rules. It doesn't only mean, as I have previously insisted upon, to deal with narrative and genre rules. It also means to make clear various levels of visual competence. Take, for example, iconographical sub-codes: different styles of clothing mean different historical periods, different cultures, different social classes. To what extent does previous education in visual arts allow one better to detect visual references which (in their turn) are indispensable in order to understand given narrative situations? Take aesthetic sub-codes; there are different models of beauty, in the human body as well as in furniture, cars and houses, depending on national tradition, class association, extra-television exposure to other models and so on. It is important to show that a given programme makes use of stereotypes, but it is also important to see whether these stereotypes have the same effect for every child in the class.

Take erotic sub-codes (don't worry, I'm not advocating striptease in schools): even children recognise a beautiful girl or a beautiful boy when a situation comedy introduces her or him as an appealing character. Models of sex appeal are culturally rooted and I think it can be very educational both for boys and girls to recognise to what an extent our way of detecting beauty, and especially feminine beauty, is due to previous models imposed by mass media and based on the commercial notion of women as an erotic object. Children belonging to a racial minority frequently suffer because of the gap between their original aesthetic models (shared by their parents and coming from their cultural, ethnic tradition) and the models imposed on them by the mass media. One of the duties of an educational enterprise is also to demonstrate that there is no straight opposition between beautiful and ugly but that there are different criteria of beauty; that, if the models of their racial groups are different from those proposed by the mass media, they are 'alternative' rather than 'negative'. To show a variety of cultural codes also means to rediscover 'suffocated' values. I've been speaking so far of iconographic and erotic codes but there are many other systems of unconscious conventions. There are rules for manipulating sounds. Music is used in television to arouse fear or excitement, hope, sadness or emotion. It does so in accordance with cultural models which must be recognised as such. A child must become able to recognise when an image elicits his fear, not because it is dreadful in itself, but because it is accompanied by 'dreadful' or *dread-inducing* music. Moreover, it can happen that mass media are proposing as dread-inducing certain musical modes which, in another culture, convey feelings of joy, vitality and happiness. I can obviously continue to list other levels of cultural conventions that can be analysed by using *gross* television as a school-book (even though a negative one). But it is not so important to make this list complete. What is important is to understand that only in a particular classroom where the teacher knows the social origin and the cultural level of his students, can this comparative job be performed.

A critically-oriented education has to recognise the fact that television exists and is the principal source of education for adults and young people. But a critically-oriented education has to make teachers use *gross* television as a piece of the world in the same way as they use weather, seasons, flowers, landscape to speak about natural phenomena. At this point my proposal for an educational television concerns, I suspect, not only children but also a permanent adult education. Just two days ago, the German Prime Minister Schmidt wrote a long article in *Die Zeit* to show his preoccupations about television, which absorbs most of the free time of his countrymen, stopping every possibility of face-to-face interaction, especially in families. Mr Schmidt therefore proposed that every family decide to devote one day a week to the rite of keeping the television turned off. A day a week *without* television. Probably Germans will be so obedient as to accept this proposal. I only hope they don't switch off their television sets just at the moment their government is promulgating a new law! However, were I in Mr Schmidt's shoes, my proposal would be different. Friends, Germans, Countrymen, I would say (but the proposal is also valid for Englishmen), one day a week, let us meet with others and watch television critically together, confronting our reactions and speaking face to face about what television has taught us or has pretended to teach us. Don't switch off television, switch on your critical freedom.

Chapter 7

Gradgrind's Heirs – the Quiz and the Presentation of 'Knowledge' by British Television*

John Tulloch

British television presents, with few exceptions,[1] a view of knowledge that can be termed 'objectivistic', 'which disguises as given a world which has to be continuously interpreted'. It is a presentation which characteristically pretends *not* to be a presentation, not (say) a *version* of events but those events themselves. It is a notion of 'knowledge' that seems to me part of an ideology which is common to both our educational system and the media.

The genres of news and documentary production are those in which this view of knowledge is most clear cut, though embedded and asking to be 'taken for granted'. And in these forms it has been subjected to considerable recent analysis. But the same notion of what knowledge constitutes seems to me to be a feature of different television genres as well – genres which are frequently regarded as trivial.

One programming form that *explicitly* concerns itself with 'knowledge' whilst claiming at the same time the status of 'enter-

* This is a shortened version of a paper published in *Explorations in the Politics of School Knowledge*, edited by Geoff Whitty and Michael F. D. Young, Driffield: Nafferton, 1976.
Screen Education, no. 19, Summer 1976.

tainment' is the television quiz. Bearing in mind Murdock and Golding's dictum that 'It is not sufficient simply to assert that the mass media are part of the ideological apparatus of the state, it is also necessary to demonstrate how ideology is produced in concrete practice.[2] I will attempt to indicate how that ideology is reproduced in two current quiz programmes. My principal assumption is that even seemingly trivial broadcast forms – forms that invite and depend on us taking them for granted – play an important part in structuring consciousness and thereby ensuring the continued reproduction of social contradiction. My argument also depends on an assertion of the representative character of the programmes I have chosen and a very reduced account of the historical development of the genre – for reasons of space the assertion must stay at the level of an assertion. I pursue the history elsewhere.

The current television quizzes – such as *University Challenge, Top of the Form, Ask the Family, Sale of the Century* and *Mastermind* – command vast audiences. The genre provides some of the most durable television programmes and – apart from occasional allegations of rigging – among the least problematic for the broadcasting agencies.

There are two strands to be discerned in the genre – what I shall call the *intellectual* and the *populist* forms of the quiz.[3] They appear to offer radically different forms of entertainment. But, whilst their respective styles and the values they affirm seem to be contradictory, I shall argue that they function in such a way as to complement each other. The analysis which follows is an attempt to articulate this argument in a concrete way by examining a representative show from each strand of the genre.

The Two Strands Compared – *Mastermind* vs *Sale of the Century*

> dominant in the culture . . . is the demand to be able to think and act quickly, a demand most clearly revealed (and success rewarded) in the exam system.[4]

'How did it all begin?' asks the executive producer of *Mastermind* in a recently published collection of questions from the show.

> It began in the quiz-unit offices of the Entertainment Department of Outside Broadcasts – a unit that has been responsible for *Television Top of the Form, Quiz Ball* and *Transworld Top Team.* We produced a television version of the *Brain of Britain* some years ago, but I had always thought that television ought

to be able to produce an intellectual quiz that was entirely original.[5]

It may be unfair to ascribe too much weight to Mr Wright's use of the term 'intellectual' in a passage from what clearly sets out to be a light-hearted introduction. But the usage is significant. The dominant sense is that given in the Oxford English Dictionary (OED) of 'appealing to or engaging the intellect'. But it has other resonances in British culture. The chief of them is concerned with the holders of intellectual powers – what the OED drily defines as 'an intellectual being; a person possessing or supposed to possess superior powers of intellect'. The carefully expressed ambiguity of 'possessing or supposed to possess' points to what Raymond Williams has recently described as a 'social tension around the word'.

> ranging from an old kind of opposition to a group of people who use theory or even organised knowledge to make judgements on general matters, to a different but sometimes related opposition to elites who claim not only specialised but directing kinds of knowledge.[6]

Mr Wright's statement is a claim for cultural legitimacy for a form relatively low in status. In a sense it is a gesture at what are felt to be 'serious', 'legitimate' intellectual fields. Pierre Bourdieu suggests that this concern is a characteristic of Western culture.

> in a given society at a given moment in time not all cultural signs – theatrical performances, sporting spectacles, recitals of songs, poetry or chamber music, operettas or operas are equal in dignity and value, nor do they call forth the same approach with the same degree of insistence . . . the various systems of expression from the theatre to television are objectively organised *according to a hierarchy independent of individual opinions that defines cultural legitimacy* and its degrees.[7] (My italics)

Mr Wright's statement is also useful in revealing something of the pressures on producers to create an 'original' form of the same formula. This form, he says 'gradually took shape from the basic concept of a single contestant with an interrogator firing questions'. Entertainment and education uneasily nudge elbows here. The basic concept is a dramatic one – the formula, for instance, of innumerable war films, courtroom dramas, and so on. Clearly the formula has obvious advantages for television – supplying that element of visual drama presumably lacking in quiz shows directly translated to television from radio.

But the concept also carries resonances of a particular type of educational relationship – one not apparent to Mr Wright but undeniably there. A good embodiment of this relationship is located in the novel to which my title refers. 'Girl number twenty . . . Give me your definition of a horse . . .'. In M'Choak-umchild's classroom there is only one 'right' answer to that question:

> Quadruped. Graminivorous. Forty teeth, namely twenty-four grinders, four eye-teeth, and twelve incisive. Sheds coat in the spring; in marshy countries sheds hoofs too.

What are the implications of this kind of educational relationship? John Holt illuminates the link between 'right answers' and the formation of attitudes.

> Practically everything we do in school tends to make children answer-centred. In the first place, right answers pay off. Schools are a kind of temple of worship for 'right answers' and *the only way to get ahead is to lay plenty of them on the altar.* The chances are good that teachers themselves are answer-centred . . . One ironic consequence is that children are too busy to think.[8]

Later in his introduction, Mr Wright defines the necessary qualifications for a contestant on *Mastermind*.

> To qualify as *material* for *Mastermind* you have to know your chosen subject thoroughly to stand any chance at all. Couple the degree of excellence in a given subject with a *sharp, decisive and concise mind* and you have the qualifications required to enter for the title 'Mastermind of the United Kingdom'.

The reification of the participant – 'Mastermind material' – goes hand in hand with the reification of knowledge in this statement. Common-sense notions of what constitutes intellectual ability – 'sharp, decisive and concise mind' – are linked to the notion of a delimited 'given subject' in which 'excellence' can be displayed.

The gesture at 'intellectual' status is a characteristic of *Mastermind*. It is always pre-recorded at a university – a location emphasised in pre-programme trailers and during the show itself. The programme adheres to a rigid ritual. Left of frame on the establishing longshot sits chairman Magnus Magnusson, at a desk facing an empty chair right of frame. The four contenders – Mr Magnusson so describes them – sit together in the front row of the audience.

Contenders are called individually to the chair facing Magnusson. The same introduction is made for each contender each week in the form of an interrogation – 'Your name?, Your occupation?' On the night I took detailed notes the contenders described themselves as: a systems analyst; a law student; a chartered surveyor and a coal-miner. Such a range of contestants is untypical for the programme on at least two counts. The great majority of programmes include contenders from the educational professions – university or college lecturers and teachers. And contenders from working-class occupations are in a tiny minority – indeed the programme that night rather stressed its coal-miner in the way the Open University in the past has stressed the 'steelmaker from Scunthorpe' among its students.

Contenders must first answer questions on a 'special subject' of their own choice. In the second part of the show they answer 'general knowledge' questions. The systems analyst opts for 'The Life and Works of Isambard Kingdom Brunel'. Questions range from 'Why was he turned upside down?' to 'At what age did he master Euclid?' and 'How many cigars did his cigar box hold?' Having opted for 'The City of Rome' the law student is asked a series of 'historical' and 'topographical' questions such as 'What happened to the bronze panels in the Pantheon?'

During the interrogation the auditorium lights are dimmed whilst a spotlight illuminates the contender. The principal shot during question and answer sessions is a medium closeup of the contender, with the score superimposed left of frame. The dominant imagery therefore is that of an isolated individual under pressure, performing 'well' or 'badly' according to the rules of the game, competing with others in the same situation.

One intriguing aspect of the show's design is the way that it directly penalises thinking – in the sense of hesitation or pauses for thought, consideration of possible alternatives, and so on. The main pressure contenders face is time – those who pause to think lose time and points. As a winning tactic it is better to 'pass' than risk a 'wrong' answer and a time-consuming correction from Mr Magnusson. To paraphrase John Holt, one ironic consequence is that contenders appear to be too busy to think. As Trevor Pateman observes: 'To speak without thinking implies unselfconsciousness of what one is saying, its status and even the very fact of speaking'.[9] In the same way the quiz also penalises long descriptions, in line with Mr Wright's prescription for ideal Mastermind material – 'sharp, decisive and concise'.

Both producer and programme make certain implicit claims

about the nature of knowledge. In *Mastermind*'s terms, knowledge is a *thing* which can be *possessed*. Possession is demonstrated by skill and agility in the use of 'facts'. The overview of knowledge implied is that of a constellation of rigidly defined 'subjects' with a content of 'facts'. With few exceptions, the bulk of these facts fit easily into a traditional, received, liberal definition of the 'Humanities' – principally History and Literature.[10] (Subjects in a recent collection of *Mastermind* questions range from French Literature to Scandinavian Mythology, Tudor History to Assassination and Murders, the Sea and Ships and the History of Aeronautics.) The components, in fact, are those of a 'middlebrow' culture, with the popular forms of the biography, the novel and the colour supplement article. Science is present in Chemistry, Mammals and Astronomy but is much less frequent as a category – I suspect that this is a result of pre-programme planning on the programme-maker's assumption that only a relatively small proportion of the audience will have much acquaintance with science at all.

Within the restrictions of the programme's format it is difficult to see how questions could be cast in anything but a fixed 'How? When? and Where?' format of 'convergent' questions. Expecting 'Why?' questions is like demanding conversational answers to a crossword puzzle. It is true that 'Why?' questions do appear, but in a particular, restricted form – that is, 'Why? (for what one reason did)', and so on. Thus 'Why was he (Brunel) turned upside down?'

Such a view of 'knowledge' abolishes explanation. Inside such a definition of intellectual competence there *can* be no explanation, rather as though the historical continuum was defined as the Chronicle of Events in *Pears Cyclopedia*. The type of verbal exchanges that go on in *Mastermind* are akin to what Postman and Weingartner call 'Guess what I'm thinking questions'. In the teaching situation they outline: ' . . . what students mostly do . . . is guess what the teacher wants them to say. Constantly, they must supply the Right Answer'.[11] They attempt to define certain 'messages' that come out of such situations:

Recall is the highest form of intellectual achievement, and the collection of unrelated 'facts' is the goal of education.
The voice of authority is to be trusted and valued more than independent judgement.
There is always a single, unambiguous Right Answer to a question.
English is not history and history is not science and science is not art and art is not music. (My italics)

Within the format of *Mastermind* both questions and answers are curiously devoid of meaning in themselves. What is the meaning of the 'fact' that Isambard Kingdom Brunel's cigar case held a certain number of cigars? The answer can only be that its meaning resides in its context – that is, it is the answer to a crossword puzzle, the occasion for a certain kind of performance that stands for the notion of knowledge and what it is to be knowledgeable which the programme presents.

This view of knowledge presents itself in an institutional context. It derives its legitimacy from an educational system that broadly promulgates the same view of knowledge. If this is not the case, how else can the fact be explained that *Television Top of the Form* employs real schools – with presumably enthusiastic support from the relevant authorities – or that *University Challenge* pits real universities against each other?

In the same way *Mastermind* roots itself on actual university campuses (including the Open University!) and in 'subjects' with questions supplied by 'authorities'. (For example, questions for the subject 'British Politics since 1900' were set by Dr David Butler).[12] The view of intellectual competence that the programme presents grows from, and is buttressed by, a dominant social notion of what constitutes the 'intellectual'.

Sale of the Century represents the second, populist strand in the genre. Occupying a time slot early on Independent Television's Saturday evening (*Mastermind* is broadcast on BBC2 on a weekday evening) its audience is roughly three times that for *Mastermind*.

There appear to be few similarities in format between the two programmes. In *Sale of the Century* the three contestants sit in a row behind desks adorned with score panels facing the questionmaster. But the 'score' is numbered in pounds rather than points. Contestants compete in answering questions posed by the quizmaster, Nicholas Parsons. The first contestant to press their buzzer in response to each question gets the chance to answer.

Questions are linked to sums of money and are arranged in the widely used 'starter' and 'bonus' system. At certain points during the show the flow of questions ceases and a curtain goes up to reveal a particular prize item 'on offer' at a 'price' that is a fraction of its market value – a feature emphasised in the description given of each item. Contestants use their buzzers to 'buy' the revealed object in competition with each other. Thus they amass cash and consumer goods in exchange for cash. But there are advantages in 'saving' money by not 'buying' goods, for at the end of the show the contestant with the highest cash total 'wins' and is given the chance to buy the star bargain which is worth several hundred pounds. As the title suggests, the claims that the show makes for 'intellectual' status are minimal. Instead of competing for a title such as 'Mastermind of the United Kingdom' – a prize in a sense external to the show – contestants in *Sale of the Century* compete for the visible cash and goods presented forcefully within the show. Any status element involved is implicit in the cash and – more strongly – the consumer goods available, with their associations of an affluent lifestyle. *Sale of the Century* is *about* people winning things, acquiring goods.

If *Mastermind* makes large claims for 'intellectual' status, *Sale of the Century* is concerned to underplay any 'intellectual' pretensions that the quiz might have. Instead it aims to excite what the programme's devisers assume to be two conflicting impulses in their large, predominantly working-class audience – the desire to 'snatch up' an outrageous bargain, and the countervailing impulse to ignore blandishments in the hope of amassing some savings or acquiring an even more substantial bargain.[13] To this end the show presents a fantasy that could be called the apotheosis of 'consumer sovereignty' – the individual spending his cash in a series of seemingly open choices, the Bargain Hunter of commercial mythology writ large.

Nicholas Parsons acts the reverse of an inquisitorial figure, indulging in non-stop patter, contriving to be 'jolly' and implicitly condescending at the same time. His first words are 'Hello and Welcome'.[14] He uses the first names of the contestants. On one night I watched, Eileen was a secretary with a design centre, Frank a clerk with the Customs and Excise. Crudely speaking *Mastermind* and *Sale of the Century* tend to draw their contestants from different social groups. *Mastermind* contenders tend to come from the 'professions' with a very large constituency of teachers and lecturers. *Sale of the Century* contestants are chiefly drawn from the lower middle class.

The form that questions take in *Sale of the Century* is best illustrated by a typical example:

What happened to Rembrandt's painting 'The Night Watch'? – It was slashed. . . .
– Yes and what a sad and tragic event that was. . . .

The viewing audience is constantly apostrophised with statements by the quizmaster such as 'What will they do? Will they take the money or spend it?' Much time is devoted to descriptions of the goods that can be 'bought'. Such decisions also act as occasions for patter. At one juncture Frank opts for the bicycles and Parsons comments: 'You've got two children so the bikes will come in useful'. It is a performance of considerable – if nauseating – skill. At the commercial break there is a surprising lack of hiatus between advertisements and programme. I suspect that this is because both are concerned to sell lifestyles in the shape of consumer artefacts – selling, that is, the prospect of a more comfortable life transformed by the goods and the status that goes with them.

At the end of the show Frank has amassed £127 answering questions such as 'Where is the tomb of Napoleon?' and 'With what do you associate Thomas Sheraton?' Parsons comments that 'It could have been anyone's game'. The show reaches its finale. 'Now Frank take your £127 and spend it with me in the *Sale of the Century*'. Frank faces a royal blue car for £125, a dishwashing machine, a stereo and a full-length palamino mink coat. The items are lovingly described. 'Will you buy a lovely mink coat for your wife, the stereo or the washing machine? Or will you buy the car? Frank, you've got ten seconds to decide.' Frank takes three seconds to opt for the car. Attendant girls put their arms around Frank and lead him to the car. They all get in. Closing shots show smiling Frank in the driver's seat.

Although the questions posed in *Sale of the Century* take a similar form to those in *Mastermind* they serve different purposes and are embedded in a radically different context. The comparative 'easiness' of the questions (to a middle-class viewer with 15 years of state education) can be presumed to be a spur to the identification of the majority of viewers with the contestant. The questions tend to be generally available to a working-class audience in a way that *Mastermind* questions are not. For the programme is not concerned with *displays* of knowledge. This becomes clear in those isolated instances when the implicit rules of the programme are transgressed. One programme provided some particularly clear examples. On that occasion a contestant answered correctly something like 90 per cent of the questions. Both the other contestants achieved very low scores. To make matters worse the dominant contestant bought up every good revealed *before* the curtain was fully raised. It was a very instructive situation. Predictably the quizmaster took to mocking him on the few occasions when he answered wrongly with comments such as 'Ah, you were a bit too fast there'. A feeling of considerable hostility was generated, with the studio audience appearing to support the quizmaster's line.

What the unfortunate (though well-rewarded) contestant was infringing was that sense of solidarity – of no contestant being exceptional or 'too clever' or 'too greedy' – that the populist show has to cultivate if it is to succeed. For if Everyman is too fast in his replies or too clever, he comes perilously close to being *Mastermind* instead. So by mocking the contestant I believe that the quizmaster was trying (perhaps intuitively) to rescue the situation, sponsoring what he may have suspected to be the reaction of the viewers.

What happens in *Sale of the Century* might be described in Marcuse's terms as 'the transplantation of social into individual needs'.[15] When the viewer is asked 'what will they do?' he is not being invited to regard the contestants as 'experts' or 'intellectuals' or even as people with whom to compete. He is not being asked to admire their knowledge. Instead the show makes a simple (but cleverly calculated) appeal to the viewer to identify with the contestant – 'if I was him I'd keep the money' is one way the looked-for response could be described. Placing contestants in a situation where goods that represent hard saving, hire purchase debts or wistful dreams to a large part of the audience are available at 'give-away' prices is a superb stroke of gimmickry. In a sense it is a delivery of the promises that advertisers make.

Marcuse regards this conversion of social into individual needs as one of the principal forms of social control under late capitalism. Describing what he calls the rational character of the system's irrationality he says:

> Its productivity and efficiency, its capacity to increase and spread comforts, to turn waste into need, and destruction into construction, the extent to which this civilisation transforms the object world into an extension of man's mind and body makes the very notion of alienation questionable. The people recognise themselves in their commodities; they find their soul in their automobile, hi-fi set, split-level home, kitchen equipment. *The very mechanism which ties the individual to his society has changed, and social control is anchored in the new needs it has produced.*[16] (My italics)

Some Tentative Conclusions

I find I know more than I thought
I feel I have improved myself
I feel respect for the people on the programme
I think over some of the questions afterwards
Educational.
(Extract from a cluster analysis of statements relating to TV

quiz programmes from McQuail, Blumler and Brown, *The Television Audience, A Revised Perspective.)*

McQuail, Blumler and Brown are concerned in their essay to demolish the 'escapist' theory of television viewing – that is, the tradition of research and writing about television which assumes a fundamental division in broadcast output between 'reality-seeking' genres such as 'news, documentaries, interviews, public affairs programmes and educational television' and genres such as the 'soap opera', the serial and the quiz show that are presented by the tradition as serving an escapist and fantasising function for the audience:

> The effect is to exclude from serious consideration (of television materials in the domain of reality) a wide range of television content which could have an important bearing on the individual's perception and understanding of the real world without appearing in an explicitly cognitive form.[17]

Basing their tests on *University Challenge, TV Brain of Britain* and *Ask the Family* (which they describe as quizzes 'involving genuine tests of knowledge rather than . . . parlour games with big prizes, gimmicks and a prominent element of chance') they analyse what they see as four basic types of gratification afforded by the TV quiz – 'a self-rating appeal' a 'basis for social interaction', an 'excitement' appeal and an 'educational' appeal.

One of their conclusions is that 'working-class fans' are more concerned to 'rate themselves' through quiz programmes than middle-class viewers. Their analysis also rates highly what they term the 'educational appeal' of the quiz programmes which they say is 'strongest for those individuals with the most limited school experience'. They interpret the cluster of statements that I have placed at the head of this section as 'expressive of the function of quiz programmes in projecting and enforcing educational values'.

One of the many valuable aspects of this analysis is the attempt to articulate the 'cognitive' features of the quiz show, which usefully shifts the focus of discussion away from the unhelpful categories of 'information, education and entertainment' – the categories by which the broadcasting agencies tend to describe their output. But this attempt is a *refocusing* rather than a fundamental rethinking of the social categories of description. Marcuse poses the question 'Can one really distinguish between the mass media as instruments of information and entertainment, and as agents of manipulation and indoctrination?'[18] – that is, of social control. McQuail, Blumler and Brown adopt in their analysis, with some misgivings, the dominant notion of 'educational values' which quizzes, as a broadcast form, support and affirm. Consider, for instance, the notion of a 'genuine test of knowledge' and the hierarchical idea of the quiz genre implied in their distinction between 'tests' – what I have termed the 'intellectual', middle-class strand of the genre – and 'parlour games'. (The question of the celebrity 'TV parlour game' is, I think, a separate issue.)

What are these 'educational values'? Questions may serve a different function in the intellectual and populist quiz, but both forms are based on the assumption that 'facts' are in a 'neutral' domain, that they are significant. The intellectual quiz affirms its intellectual status by making these 'facts' stand as the content of a 'subject'. In the quiz facts stand 'in themselves', immutable, unquestionable objects rent from the social and historical process.

A related assumption common to both forms is that all questions have unambiguous 'right' answers. As Postman and Wein-gartner observe, society conditions us to suspect that an instant, fluent response to a question denotes status:

> One does not 'blame' men, especially if they are politicians, for providing instant answers to all questions. The public requires that they do, *since the public has learned that instant answer-giving is the most important sign of an educated man.*[19] (My italics)

Educational values of a particular type are also 'enforced' by the form of relationship between quizmaster and contestant presented by shows in each strand of the genre. These relationships are suggestive of that wider system of communication situations through which knowledge is mediated in British society. The supply of 'right' answers must come from a 'right' – that is, a legitimate – source. The trappings of Academe with which *Master-mind* clothes itself *serve to legitimate the relationship between quiz-master and quizzed*. The quizmaster's immediate position as 'the man with all the answers' in *Mastermind* and the intellectual quiz depends on certain implicit assumptions about *where* the answers are coming from. Answers are supplied in *Mastermind* and the intellectual quiz generally by recognised 'authorities' – the aca-demic, the media exposed 'expert' and (in many cases) the *Ency-clopaedia Britannica*.

The populist quiz tends to adopt different strategies to legitimise its supply of right answers. Here the quizmaster is a different type of 'authority' figure – he is, in fact, invested with the authority of the showman, the performer, the 'professional'. Typically this involves the presentation of a seemingly 'classless' type of deference relationship between the (amateur) contestant and the (professional) quizmaster – the man who is fluent, who has 'all the answers'. Thus the status of a quizmaster like Hughie Green in a populist quiz show has very little to do with corpuses of knowledge and a lot to do with the way in which he 'orchestrates' the situation. This is in strong contrast to the quizmaster in the intellectual quiz, buttressed by 'authorities' and in his way as much an authority figure as the teacher – in common-sense terms the person who 'controls' (rather than 'orchestrates') the situation, who possesses the right answers, who defines the rate at which questions are put, who 'interrogates'.[20]

If the intellectual quiz weds 'knowledge' to the man who controls the situation it also creates the occasion for a performance by contestants of varying degrees of 'skill'. Contestants on *Mastermind* and on intellectual quizzes generally are predominantly middle-class, professional people. Many of them can provide the 'right' answers in an appropriately 'sharp, decisive and concise' way. So the relationship of the working-class viewer to the intellectual quiz may indeed involve the deference expressed in the statement 'I feel respect for the people on the programme', which rephrased might read 'they know more than me'. Indeed, the assumption that 'knowledge' is a possession which confers status (such as the title Mastermind of the United Kingdom) underpins the intellectual quiz. '*Mastermind* . . . is the contestant's chance to pit his knowledge against a leading professional in his particular subject' runs the blurb on the back of the first selection of questions from the show published by the BBC.

Whilst the objective of competing on *Mastermind* is, for the individual contestant, purely status, the objective of competing on a populist show like *Sale of the Century* must be the things that can be won. Thus in the populist show what you know is directly translated into things – and in a sense cash and consumer goods legitimise the operations of the populist quiz in an analogous way to the legitimation of the intellectual quiz by its 'intellectual' pretensions. It could be argued that the populist quiz is an exercise in curriculum relevance, providing tangible benefits and advantages from the use of 'knowledge'. Up to a point this line can be sustained, but it encounters what is, perhaps, the major underlying assumption in the form – this is that 'knowledge' is essentially trivial, not the key feature of the show, not what it is 'about'. To be available to Everyman, the curricula of the populist quiz show must be resolutely non-academic. To appear in the guise of celebrating solidaristic values it must place a low value on competition, whilst having prizes, reassure its contestants with a showman/quizmaster who can control and sustain a seemingly 'classless' type of relationship with each contestant which maintains a due deference on their part to facilitate the smooth running of the programme and 'package' each individual. 'Now Frank take your £127 and spend it with me. . . .'.

Yet the 'knowledge' contained in the intellectual quiz can be regarded as equally 'trivial'. If questions such as 'What happened to Rembrandt's painting "The Night Watch"?' are placed alongside 'How many cigars did Brunel's cigar case hold?' it is clear that the only significant difference lies in the size of audience to which the question can be presumed to be available – popular newspapers have larger readerships than biographies of great Victorian engineers. The difference lies in the context in which the questions are put.

A further feature links both forms of the quiz, associated with the notion that facts stand in themselves as an index of 'knowledge'. For to the extent to which this reflects the dominant ideology of contemporary scholarship and the mass media – the tenacious Namierite position that 'facts speak', the interview that promises the 'real facts' about the subject, the picture that 'says it all' – it can be expected that questions will focus on what this scholarship and media foreground – a view of the social process that concentrates on individuals rather than groups, events rather than processes, leaders rather than classes, professionals, 'experts', politicians, journalists, trade union leaders, and so on, rather than people.

Notes

1. Geoffrey M. Esland, 'Teaching and Learning', in Michael F. D. Young (ed.) *Knowledge and Control*, London: Collier-Macmillan, 1971.

2. Graham Murdock and Peter Golding, 'For a Political Economy of Mass Communication', in Ralph Miliband and John Saville (eds), *The Socialist Register*, London: Merlin Press, 1973.

3. One root of the intellectual quiz is the 'display of knowledge in a casual form' that started with the *Brains Trust*. Another root for the form lies, perhaps, in the long-established parlour games of the middle classes. The *Brains Trust* was, of course, an important source for other programme forms – the chat show, for example, and was translated into television. The origins of the populist quiz can be seen at roughly the same time in the hugely successful '*Have a Go*' programme – which, of course, was a lot of other things as well. Thus by the mid–1940s we find a type of quiz show emerging that is about displays of knowledge and stresses performance and competition against a form that treats its contestants – or rather participants – as Everyman.

4. Trevor Pateman, *Language, Truth and Politics*, Nottingham: Jean Stroud and Trevor Pateman, 1975.

5. BBC, *Mastermind*, London: BBC, 1974.

6. Raymond Williams, *Keywords*, London: Fontana, 1976.

7. Pierre Bourdieu, 'Systems of Education and Systems of Thought', in Michael F. D. Young, op. cit.

8. John Holt, *How Children Fail*, Harmondsworth: Penguin, 1964.

9. Trevor Pateman, op. cit.

10. The 'General Knowledge' category might seem an exception – but the vast majority of questions set fall into these categories. Questions are chiefly to do with (for example) giving the name of a 'famous' artist, 'historical figure', and so on (for example, 'His first play was *The Room* in 1957 and his other works include *The Servant*. What is his name?'), a 'date' a definition or a 'place'.

11. Neil Postman and Charles Weingartner, *Teaching as a Subversive Activity*, Harmondsworth: Penguin, 1971.

12. BBC, *Mastermind*, op. cit.

13. Quizes such as *Sale of the Century* are, from the programme-makers' viewpoint, very cheap shows to mount – unscripted, relatively low on labour and performance costs but very popular – despite the 'no expenses spared' aura of conspicuous consumption that prize-giving involves.

14. Although Parsons has been criticised in the popular press (for example, the *News of the World*) for condescension and patronisation towards contestants.

15. Herbert Marcuse, *One Dimensional Man*, London: Sphere, 1964.

16. Herbert Marcuse, op. cit. Marx's discussion of the nature of a commodity in *Capital* is relevant here. 'A commodity is therefore a mysterious thing, simply because in it the social character of men's labour appears to them as an objective character stamped upon the product of that labour'. In a recent paper Dorothy Smith rewrites Marx's account, substituting 'fact' for 'commodity' and points out that Marx draws a similar analogy with religion later in the same passage. Thus 'a fact . . . is a mysterious thing simply because in it the social character of men's consciousness appears to them as an objective character stamped upon the product of that consciousness'. (From Dorothy E. Smith, 'The Social Construction of Documentary Reality', a paper presented at the meetings of the Canadian Sociological and Anthropological Associations, Queen's University, Kingston, Ontario, May 1973.)

17. Denis McQuail, Jay Blumler and Roger Brown, 'The Television Audience, A Revised Perspective', in Denis McQuail (ed.) *The Sociology of Mass Communication*, Harmondsworth: Penguin, 1972.

18. Herbert Marcuse, op. cit.

19. Neil Postman and Charles Weingartner, op. cit.

20. I am using 'orchestrates' in something of a similar sense to the OED's 'to combine harmoniously, like instruments in an orchestra' to point up this key aspect of the quizmaster's role as a *performer* in the populist quiz.

Chapter 8

Authorship and Organisation*

Graham Murdock

Commentators who have considered the role of the writer in television drama have tended to start either from notions of authorship and creativity, or from the organisation of production. The first approach stresses the writers' relative autonomy and their pre-eminent role in shaping the final text. In this version they are assimilated to the romantic stereotype of the artist 'working alone to carve a personal vision out of the marble of his sensibility'.[1] Organisationally-oriented approaches, on the other hand, present writers as relatively powerless and enmeshed in a web of ideological and economic pressures which curtail their choices and channel their work in certain directions. In these accounts they appear as craftsmen rather than creators, professionals on a par with journalists and copy-writers, working within well-understood constraints to turn saleable ideas into shootable scripts. The text is no longer the unique expression of the author's sensibilities, but a collective product manufactured by an industrial process and subject to the insistent pressures of time, resources and market competition.

This separation of academic approaches tends to follow the general fault line between the literary and sociological currents within media studies. Despite the battering it has recently received, the idea of authorship still finds a secure niche in literary criticism which can be comfortably extended to accommodate the

* *Screen Education*, no. 35, Summer 1980.

analysis of single plays. This has led among other things, to a search for a 'great tradition' of television playwrights to add to the accredited figures of modern theatre. We don't yet have a *Journal of Potter Studies* to put alongside the *Journal of Beckett Studies* on the library shelves, but it may not be long before we do. In contrast to this focus on authors and texts, sociological studies fix on the relations of literary production and the ways they are framed by economic and political pressures from inside and outside the broadcasting organisations. Although most research in this vein has so far concentrated on news and current affairs production, the general approach is being extended to drama, and more particularly to series and serial production where the organisational pressures are at their most pervasive and the elbow room accorded to writers at its most restricted.[2] The problem is that both camps tend to present the particular instances they are interested in as though they were paradigmatic of television drama production as a whole, thereby evading the issue of the relationship *between* authorship and organisation.

These twin emphases are not confined to academic discussions. They also dominate the way that people working in television talk about drama. Here, for example, are extracts from recent articles by two of the BBC's senior drama personnel – Shaun Sutton, Head of Drama Group at BBC Television, and Roderick Graham, who heads the drama wing of BBC Scotland. Whereas Sutton exemplifies the core assumptions of authorship – the idea of innate talent and the endemic divide between creativity and craftsmanship – Graham employs the equally pervasive vocabulary of budgets, markets and industrial management.

> No one can teach a writer to write well . . . These skills are built-in, emotional, intuitive, and if they are not present in the man (or woman) from the start, then no amount of instruction will force them into fruition. What one can do is teach crafts, the alphabet of the art, the nuts and bolts that hold it together . . . One thing is certain: no amount of advice can, or should, mould a writer's style. This must be personal, developed from within . . . writing [series episodes] is a different discipline, calling for high professional competence and ingenuity, rather than genius.[3]

> Television is an industry – whether we like it or not. Many of us don't like it because of the connotations the word 'industry' has, but if you look at the management techniques and marketing methods used, and the amount of budget involved, it must

be regarded in industrial terms. We make programmes and we make these programmes industrially.[4]

As these quotations suggest, notions of authorship and organisation enjoy an uneasy and problematic relationship within broadcasting institutions as well as within academia. In both spheres this tension is most often resolved by stressing one term over the other, so that the issue is posed as one of creativity versus control, individual expressivity versus structural constraint. Although convenient, this kind of polarisation produces an over-simple analysis. It is not a question of liquidating the idea of authorship as Barthes and others have urged. Nor is it a question of reading off the forms and contents of television drama directly from the dynamics of production. Rather it is a matter of exploring the way in which notions of authorship operate as both an ideology and a practice in different types of production and unravelling their reciprocal relationship to organisational forms and to the pressures which shape them.

At one level the idea of authorship clearly functions as a professional ideology in the way that objectivity operates for journalists. It is, in Gaye Tuchman's phrase, a 'strategic ritual',[5] a weapon which writers deploy in their struggle to fend off unwanted interventions from above and retain a degree of control over their work. However, as the quotation from Shaun Sutton suggests, it is also built into the ethos of broadcasting organisations and plays an important part in their strategies of legitimation. The promotion of authorship and creativity lies at the heart of the broadcasters' presentation of themselves as guarantors of cultural diversity and patrons of the contemporary arts, elements which are central to their claims to responsibility and public service. Nor are these notions purely a matter of political rhetoric or window dressing. They are embedded in the concrete practices of drama production. As a result, writers like Trevor Griffiths or Dennis Potter who are designated as 'authors' are given a good deal of freedom to determine the subjects they will work on and the forms in which they will be presented. This does not mean that the finished programmes are a pure expression of their experiences and commitments. They are still enveloped within wider ideologies and they remain indelibly marked by organisational pressures which range from limitations on location filming to demands for cuts and revisions. At the same time, the existence of this licensed 'authorial' space, means that the writer's biography cannot be entirely discounted in the search for a full explanation of why particular productions turn out as they do. The problem, then, is not whether to jettison the idea of authorship altogether, but how to explain its specific location, role and limits in the current situation. As a beginning, however, we need to look a little more carefully at its rise as a professional ideology and at the ways it has become institutionalised within television drama production.

Inventing Authorship

Our modern notions of authorship and creativity were part of the Humanistic world view which accompanied the rise of modern capitalism in the second half of the sixteenth century. Up until then the idea of creation had been reserved exclusively for God's original act of making the world. Cultural production was seen as a process of making or fabricating, and artists thought of themselves as skilled craftsmen fashioning a range of useful objects. As well as painting the pictures we now associate with him, for example, Botticelli was quite happy to turn his hand to decorating banners and wedding chests.[6] After 1550, however, commentators began to stretch the original meaning of creativity to cover the activities of painters and poets. Creativity was seen as next to Godliness in several senses. First, it was attributed to divine gifts and inspiration or, in the later secular version, innate talent and genius. And second, artists were seen as reproducing the essential act of Creation by inventing completely new worlds by an act of individual imagination and will. This new definition of artistic activity drove a permanent wedge between the notions of creativity and craftsmanship, artistry and artisanship, and since these divisions remain at the heart of conceptions of authorship, we need to unpack them a little before moving on.

Creative activity was seen as the sole prerogative of artists, of whom bona fide authors formed a subgroup. Everyone else involved in cultural production continued to be seen as a craftsman. Craft work is characterised by two essential features. First, it involves a command over technical knowledge and skills which have been acquired through a process of training and apprenticeship. Second, and crucially, these skills are employed to make products demanded by somebody else, either clients and customers or employers.

> The employer understands that the worker possesses special skills and knowledge but regards it as appropriate to have the final say himself as to the suitability of the result . . . Both recognise that the object of the activity is to make something the employer can use for his purposes, whatever they may be.[7]

Creative activity, on the other hand, is defined precisely by its relative freedom from the demands of employers and audiences. 'True' artists are seen as working to realise their personal visions and not to satisfy other people's requirements. They are prompted by their own inner imaginings and convictions rather than external demands for useful and saleable products. While they share the craftsman's skills, their work is seen as transcending technique, or even virtuosity. It is defined by the quality of imagination and vision displayed and the extent to which it bears a distinctive individual stamp. Art, then, is regarded not as an occupation but as a vocation through which people realise themselves and their vision of the world.

These twin themes of creative autonomy and individual express-ivity are central to the Romantic conception which still underpins the ideology of authorship. Over the years it has gathered some unlikely supporters, including Marx. Here he is, for example, contrasting the 'genuine' authorship of Milton with hackwork aimed at a bestseller market.

> Milton produced *Paradise Lost* for the same reason that a silk-worm produces silk. It was an activity of his nature. Later he sold the product for £5. But the literary proletarian of Leipzig, who fabricates books under the direction of his publisher . . . his product is from the outset subsumed under capital, and comes into being only for the purpose of increasing that capital.[8]

As well as exemplifying the now familiar opposition between 'serious' authorship and commercial writing (Tom Stoppard and Solzhenitsyn versus Mills and Boon romances and episodes of *Crossroads*) this passage points to the writer's problematic relation to a literary economy geared to maximising sales in the interests of profitability. As Marx put it elsewhere: 'The writer, of course, must earn in order to be able to live and write, but he must by no means live and write to earn.'[9] But how do writers make a living in a market economy whilst preserving some autonomy and control over their work?

In the case of commercially-oriented production there is no problem since the aim is to give people what they appear to want, as indicated by sales figures and surveys of satisfaction. Success consists of fulfilling the utilitarian goal of the 'greatest happiness of the greatest number', and with modern market research tech-niques it is possible to measure this with some precision. Tele-vision audience research, for example, produces two main types of programme statistics – the total numbers viewing (which pro-vides the basis for the ratings) and an 'appreciation index' showing how much they enjoyed it. In contrast to this consumer orientation, notions of authorship are creator-oriented.[10] Instead of operating with a version of the free market ideology which decrees that consumer demands should determine supply, they work within an ideology of art which argues that creators should be given complete freedom to express themselves through their work. Commercial production aims to turn dominant cultural themes into pleasurable products in the interests of entertainment. Art, on the other hand, aims to challenge dominant assumptions and subvert consumer expectations. It celebrates a conception of authors as an imaginative vanguard, adventurers in the uncharted regions of the imagination, opening them up for subsequent settlement. If audiences gain pleasure and enjoyment from their work, well and good; if they don't, the onus is on them to make the effort. But if authors are mainly interested in giving people what they don't particularly want, how do they obtain support within a market-oriented system? The answer lies in the changing nature of patronage and its complex relationship to the market.

   In the traditional patronage relationship, artists were regarded as servants, skilled labourers whose job was to fulfil the briefs laid down by the patron. The new ideology of creativity shifted the balance of advantage, however, and patrons began to concede control over the productions they subsidised. Increasingly, artists and authors were supported for their talent or promise and left to decide on the subjects and forms of their work for themselves. (Cultural workers who were defined as craftsmen, in contrast, continued to operate in the traditional way, working on projects determined by their employers.) The patron's power was further weakened by the rise of a market economy in cultural goods, although this was a double-edged development as far as writers were concerned. On the one hand, the opportunity to sell one's work to whoever would pay the best price was seen as a release from dependence on a patron, however benign. Indeed, creative *independence* came to be firmly identified with the freedom to work for oneself and to compete in the open market. Publishers therefore displaced patrons at the centre of literary production. They acted as middlemen between writers and the market-place, buying or commissioning works and selling them to the public. 'But theirs was, at best, a kind of antagonistic co-operation' since 'the writer often found that, although he might owe some of his independence to the efforts of his publishers, he was also bound to him by ties nearly as restricting as those of patronage'.[11] Since publishing was a commercial enterprise, publishers not unnaturally wanted to maximise their profits and this led to an unending search for titles which would attract mass sales. But this market logic went directly against the ideology of authorship which decreed that writers should follow their own creative impulses and refuse to become 'literary proleterians' producing whatever would sell. This conflict was resolved by instituting a dual-production system with a 'primary' sector geared to the demands of the mass market, and a 'secondary' sector publishing works with only a minority appeal. These 'secondary' productions were not expected to contribute significantly to sales or profits. Their role was to bolster 'invisible earnings', in the form of the prestige attached to sponsoring works that met with critical acclaim. This in turn helped publishers to retain the loyalty of their established authors and to attract up-and-coming talent. Moreover, since publishing is a form of Russian roulette in which you can never know for sure which chamber contains the sure-fire success, there was always the chance that an unpromising looking title could become an unexpected bestseller. Publishers, then, not only acted as commercial entrepreneurs, they also took over the patron's role of subsidising excellence and promise.

This division between the 'primary' and 'secondary' sectors of production and the consequent tension between entrepreneurship and patronage, is common to all the major branches of the cultural industries, and it provides one of the keys to understanding the way in which authorship has become institutionalised within television drama production.

Institutionalising Authorship

Popular drama, in the form of variety, pantomime and West End theatre, has always belonged firmly in the 'primary' sector of cultural production. It is part of show business and as such it operates with a market ideology which aims for mass appeal. This system revolves around the performers and especially the stars. Their relation to the audience dramatises the relation between demand and supply and every successful performance becomes an affirmation of the fact that the market does indeed give people what they want. Within this system, the writers' main task is to provide materials and settings that will show the performers' talents to advantage. Although this star orientation also operates to some extent in classical and avant-garde theatre (so that we talk of Olivier's *Hamlet*), 'serious' drama is principally located in the 'secondary' sector. Consequently, it operates within the ideology of authorship and tends to find its major audience among the intelligentsia. Just as the stars are the heroes of the market, so authors are the heroes of Art, representing and confirming the expressive individualism which lies at the heart of the intelligent-sia's world view.

Among the major institutions of modern drama, the cinema presents a peculiar case. The fact that it was silent for the first 30 years of its existence led to the elevation of stars and directors and the virtual eclipse of the writer as a significant figure. While the studio publicity machines promoted Charlie Chaplin and Mary Pickford, the intelligentsia celebrated Eisenstein and Pudovkin, and these twin emphases still continue. Despite Richard Corliss's efforts to install screenwriters at the centre of the movie-making process,[12] 'auteur' theory remains securely attached to the direc-tor, while popular commentary continues to revolve around the stars.

By the time that television got under way in the mid–1950s, then, the major ideological and institutional divisions within the cultural industries were already firmly established, and television drama was obliged to accommodate to them. In pursuit of maximum audiences, the popular series and serials took over the performer orientation of Hollywood and the entertainment industry. From the titles onwards (*Dixon, Quatermass, Callan, Lillie*) the whole form of presentation explicitly invited viewers to identify with the central characters and to get involved with their dilemmas week by week. In contrast, single play production derived its ethos primarily from the 'serious' theatre and worked from the beginning within the ideology of authorship. There are several reasons for this. First, it reflects the general emphasis on literary expression in English intellectual culture, together with television drama's early dependence on theatrical material and personnel. And second, it points to the influence of radio drama, which, being a non-visual medium, had already established a model of the writer-as-*auteur* within broadcasting. (The producer-director team of Tony Garnett and Ken Loach does seem to provide a notable exception to the general critical focus on the writer as creator of television drama. But it *is* an exception and can be explained partly by the fact that their most celebrated work is shot mainly or entirely on film and is admired for its 'cinematic' qualities. This makes it relatively easy to accommodate them within conventional '*auteur* theory'.)

In general then, the divisions within television drama pro-duction follow the broad split within the cultural industries as a whole. The 'primary' sector of series and serial production is geared to audience maximisation and confines the writer primarily to the role of craftsman, turning out scripts to other people's specifications; whereas the 'secondary' sector of single play pro-duction operates with an ideology of authorship which nominates writers as the main originators of the text and accords them a good deal of expressive autonomy. As I shall argue, this institutionalisation of authorship has real and important consequences for the range and forms of drama production. At the same time, authorship is also an ideological category and as such it promotes a systematic mis-recognition of the actual process of production. By presenting the writer as the sole or prime creator of the finished text, it bypasses the determining conditions under which production takes place and the pressures that shape it.[13] In examining these conditions commentators have pointed to two main sources of constraint. The first stems from the writer's inevitable envelopment in language and ideology, and the second derives from the economic and political pressures on production.

Paroled from the Prison-house of Language

Whereas the ideology of authorship presents writers as ventriloquists who speak through their works, structuralist criticism, led by Barthes, casts them in the role of dummy, manipulated by the hidden hands of language. 'No longer is the author to be seen as a Subject full of conscious but as yet private meanings who will take advantage of language to make them public'.[14] On the contrary, Barthes argues, 'it is language which speaks, not the author; to write is, through a pre-requisite impersonality . . . to reach that point where only language acts, "performs", and not "me" '.[15] According to this view, writers – along with everyone else – inhabit the prison-house of language and are bound by its immutable rules. It is of course true, as Raymond Williams has recently stressed, that the language writers are born into enters their constitution long before they begin to write and organises their thinking and expression in potent ways.[16] But this argument is too general. It can't explain why specific writers write as they do or why their work differs from that of other writers. It is particularly ironic that Barthes, who insisted so forcefully on the death of the author, should have taken so much care to develop a voice that is instantly recognisable as his. While this is entirely understandable in the context of Parisian intellectual life, where style is a decisive weapon in the struggle for ascendency, it hardly squares with his stress on the relative autonomy of textual codes. If Barthes served a life sentence in the prison-house of language, his works strive remarkably hard to give the impression that he is out on parole. Moreover, this surreptitious individualism leads him to pay almost as little attention to the social and ideological determinants of literary production as the ideology of authorship he seeks to demolish.

These determinants are now being addressed in the developing work on discourse. This is likely to be more productive because it is more specific. In place of Barthes's emphasis on the relative autonomy of signifying practices – 'six textual codes in search of a typewriter'[17] – recent studies have begun to explore the way that television writers work with and within particular historical discourses. Phillip Drummond's analysis of the interplay of discourses about crime, class and sexuality in the Thames Television private eye series *Hazell* provides an example of this developing current.[18] As Ed Buscombe points out elsewhere in this issue, *Hazell* operated with ideological themes that were already familiar to the intended audience – notably the chirpy cockney, the working-class lad on the make, and the 'permissive' society. Similarly, crime and spy series such as *Target, The Professionals* and *The Sandbaggers* can be seen as inhabiting the discourses and ideologies of the law-and-order society and the new Cold War. This orchestration and reworking of common-sense categories is an important ingredient of ratings success. It detonates that shock of recognition that connects the consciousness of the audience with the imaginary world of the text. There is in fact a necessary relation between 'the popularity of a programme and the extent to which it reinforces the ideological position of the majority audience'.[19] That's not to say that popular television is an exhaustive trawl of popular consciousness. It consistently works with the more conservative strands in popular culture which constitute the dominant categories of common sense and plays down or ignores the more radical, combative elements.

Nor does this mean that television writers are simply passive bearers of general ideologies formed elsewhere. As Terry Eagleton has rightly emphasised, the text is always an expression of general ideologies as *actively mediated* through the writer's personal authorial ideology, which is structured in turn by his or her class background, professional career and present situation.[20] Within television, however, this balance between general and authorial ideologies is highly variable and is ultimately decided by the dynamics of production in specific situations. Consequently, while considerations of biography can go some way towards explaining why writers are drawn towards particular themes and why they handle them in particular ways, it cannot account fully for the finished text. To explain this we need to look in detail at the process of programme-making, at the balance of power within production teams and at the complex interplay of political and economic pressures from inside and outside the broadcasting organisations.

The Practice of Authorship

The ascendency of general ideology is at its greatest in serial and series production. Ratings success requires familiar settings, established themes and continuity of characterisation in the central figures. Hence series are habitually 'set against the well-tried backgrounds of crime, hospitals and courtrooms'.

> The attitudes of the leading characters are firmly set, recognisable and familiar, and innovation is suspect. It would disturb the regular viewer if his heroic Chief Inspector of Police suddenly developed dark lustful yearnings for the wives of the criminals he tracks down each week. The long-running series is a secure world, thriving on a comfortable, consistent image.[21]

To achieve this consistency the producer and script editor often furnish prospective writers with detailed specifications of what is required. In the case of *Upstairs, Downstairs*, for example, writers were given the story outline of the episode they were responsible for, told where it would fit in the series and whether it was to be a 'comedy, tragedy or drama', and provided with detailed sketches of the main characters.[22] The emphasis was firmly on craftsmanship rather than authorship, professionalism rather than creativity. As the script editor, Alfred Shaughnessy, later explained:

> Any playwright working on a drama series like this, under such rigid guidelines, with so many things *given*, has to be first and foremost a good dramatic craftsman, able to be given an outline and turn it into a play by sheer technique, with a sense of how long a scene should be, and what you go to next, and so on: the carpentry of making plays.[23]

In this situation there is relatively little scope for authorial mediation on the part of writers, as Fay Weldon discovered when she was commissioned to write the opening episode of the first series. This was a particularly important assignment since the first episode of any new series is instrumental in establishing audience expectations and determining whether or not they will continue watching. Her inclination was to present the view from below stairs and to highlight the latent antagonism between servants and masters. But this was at odds with the conception already decided on. Shaughnessy came from a similar upper-class background to the Bellamy family and his vision of the series drew heavily on his childhood memories of high teas, glittering dinner parties and deferential servants.[24] Moreover, as he later told an interviewer, he had

> very definite views about the theatre and the sort of drama I like – some people think it quite old-fashioned. I believe in what I call the middle-brow, good-quality theatre, the theatre of Priestley, Noel Coward, Rattigan.[25]

Conversely, he felt out of sympathy with what he saw as the agitational approach of much contemporary drama. These social and aesthetic ideologies set the parameters for the series and effectively excluded Fay Weldon's counter-conception. As she has recently explained:

> What I liked, you see, which was what had to go really at the end, was actually the conflict between Upstairs and Downstairs. I mean I really thought they should hate each other, you see. I almost really thought that Downstairs should be putting ground glass in Upstairs' coffee. I was rather pulling in one direction, you see, which wasn't really a totally practicable direction for me to be going if something's turning into, you know, a great commercial success, where other things then have to enter in.[26]

Not surprisingly, she was later dropped from the stable of series regulars in favour of writers who, in Shaughnessy's words, 'absolutely understand the series, and are used to it and are reliable and good craftsmen'.[27] As a result, class antagonism slid quietly out of view and the industrial unrest and Irish 'troubles' which brought England to the brink of insurrection in 1911 were displaced by what the producer John Hawkesworth described as the 'personal and social conflicts of birth control, love (legitimate and otherwise), pederasts, artists, mediums, armament manufacturers, babies (legitimate and otherwise), suicide'.[28] However, these emphases cannot be explained simply in terms of the personal predelictions of the more powerful members of the production team. They must also be seen as logical accommodations to the need for ratings success.

　　As I noted earlier, popular television drama is a branch of show business and as such it works within an ethos of entertainment which promises excitement and emotional engagement rather than intellectual provocation and ideological challenge. Because these values are built into audience expectations, drama which does not fit with the prevailing criteria of entertainment is likely to be defined by most audience members as unexciting and to be avoided. Hence, although *Days of Hope* covered the same period (1916–26) as later series of *Upstairs, Downstairs*, its unremitting focus on class antagonism and political struggles gave it a much lower overall audience and caused a number of those who had begun watching to give up on the grounds that they found it too 'boring' and 'depressing'.[29]

The centrality of market pressures and entertainment values to series production has been further reinforced in the last decade by the growing significance of international sales to the economics of television. In a period of rapidly rising production costs, selling programmes in overseas markets, particularly the massive American market, has become an important way of boosting revenues, and series are among the most popular exports since they are easy for networks to schedule. At the same time, the need to find material that will be intelligible and attractive in a wide range of markets places extra constraints on the popular series' ideological and thematic range. Basically, the international market offers three major options. First, British companies can play the Americans at their own game by turning out action-adventure series with a mid-Atlantic flavour, using international locations and a cosmopolitan cast. Second, they can combine novelty of milieu with familiarity of form by transposing established American genres to British settings. Examples of both types figure prominently in the list of best-selling British programme exports for 1979, with ATV's *Return of the Saint* (type 1) and Thames TV's *Sweeney* (type 2) both selling in over a hundred markets. However, the list also reveals the importance of the third option, which is to give the overseas networks the one fiction commodity they can't get anywhere else – authentically English historical sagas. The breakthrough in this area came with the BBC's adaptation of *The Forsyte Saga* and the series on the lives of Elizabeth I and Henry VIII. But the commercial companies were quick to follow and historical series now make a very substantial contribution to their export effort. The best sellers of 1979, for example, included London Weekend's *Lillie* and *Thomas and Sarah* (a spin-off from *Upstairs, Downstairs); Jennie* and *Edward and Mrs Simpson* from Thames; Granada's adaptation of *Hard Times*, and the Anglia-Trident version of the life of Dickens.[30] As these instances suggest, the drive for overseas sales has certain effects on the range and treatment of historical themes: programmes are obliged to trade off the most pervasive images of historic England and to work within the dominant 'great man' theory of history. This produces, among other things, a concentration on periods that are already internationally familiar from popular fiction and feature films (most recently the reigns of Victoria and Edward), an emphasis on those social groups who are thought of as quintessentially English, the royal family and the aristocracy, and a marked preference for biographical approaches and explanations.

In contrast to series, single plays are not in the front line of the export drive or of the domestic ratings battle. Consequently they are to a large extent exempt from direct market pressures. They are not required to accommodate themselves to dominant currents within popular consciousness or to work within the prevailing ethos of entertainment. On the contrary, they are expected to operate with the ideology of creativity. Hence, where series writers are nudged towards the articulation of general ideologies, playwrights are explicitly encouraged to express their own pre-occupations and commitments. As a result, single plays are one of the few areas within modern television where emergent themes and unorthodox or oppositional views can be presented and worked through. This notion that creativity carries with it a licence to provoke is built into the institutional ideology which broadcasting has taken over from the Art world. According to ATV's Head of Drama, David Reid, the single play 'at best . . . is the individual voice being heard loud and clear which implies that its content and tone cannot be expressed in any series episode'. The Independent Broadcasting Authority (IBA) year-book adds this gloss:

> A play is an opportunity to comment on the society in which we live. It is possible, therefore, that it will deal with subjects that are considered 'difficult' or 'contentious' and it is right that plays should often do so.[31]

These qualities of difficulty and contentiousness mean that single plays generally attract much smaller audiences than series and serials (although they are still massive compared to audiences for the theatre and for many films). But ratings are not the only form of return on investment. There are also what I earlier called 'invisible earnings'. These are of various kinds. By providing writers, directors and producers with a chance to display their talents to prospective employers and backers, single plays perform an important role in an employment market where almost everyone is freelance. Franc Roddam's award-winning ATV drama documentary *Dummy*, for example, was instrumental in launching his career as a feature film director. Critical acclaim and prestige within the profession are also central to the companies' presentation of themselves as supporters of cultural diversity and excellence. This in turn helps to reinforce their claims to a public service role. It also strengthens their hand in the competition for star talent. Moreover, since single plays often deal with emergent strands in social style and consciousness, they provide a kind of early warning system of currents which could be used to refurbish the formulae of popular programming. At the same time, the single play's licence to probe and provoke is by no means infinite. It is limited, first, by what we can call 'the calculus of legitimation' and, second, by the economic logic of cost-benefit analysis.

The Limits of Authorship

Underwriting the ideology of creativity necessarily involves broadcasting organisations in support for work which challenges social and aesthetic orthodoxies. But beyond a certain point, this granting of a licence to provoke conflicts with the search for institutional legitimation, as defenders of the status quo mobilise to question the broadcasters' right to sponsor attacks on established values and institutions. In these situations support for authorial autonomy is always in danger of becoming more trouble than it's worth.

Over the last two decades, single plays have been a major focus for attacks on the legitimacy and responsibility of broadcasters. These have come from various sources. The best known are the various religious and moral pressure groups led by Mary Whitehouse's National Viewers' and Listeners' Association. They claim to represent the silent majority of 'ordinary' viewers and to speak for traditional verities in general and family life in particular. This emphasis on the family neatly capitalises on the fact that, unlike cinema and theatre, television drama reaches people in their own homes and this, as the IBA has recently explained, necessarily imposes certain limits on authorship.

> The problem is that on the one hand there should be freedom of expression for serious writing and on the other hand television is seen by an audience of all sorts and conditions of people in their homes. What might be acceptable in the theatre or the cinema might be less acceptable in the living room.[32]

Apart from making it difficult to address certain themes (such as incest), television's domesticity imposes severe restrictions on the language that writers can use, as Gordon Newman discovered when he was working on *Law and Order*:

These guys punctuate every sentence with 'fuck' and 'cunt' and my scripts were written like that. We had to decide whether to bleep all the words or to cut them out. If we'd have used them, it could have given the BBC a valid excuse to shelve the programmes. I think they suffered as a result.[33]

The case of *Law and Order* also points to a second major source of pressure on single play production – the lobbying of special interest groups who are concerned about the image that television presents of them and their activities. The police, the army and the prison service have been particularly active in this respect over recent years, which is scarcely surprising since during the same period their own legitimacy has come under increasing public scrutiny and attack. Nor are these conflicts played out only in the ideological sphere. They can have important repercussions for future programme-making. Following the original transmission of *Law and Order*, the Prison Officers' Association withdrew their cooperation from BBC film crews. The outcome of these pressures is by no means predictable, however. It depends both on the relative strength and legitimacy of the external lobbies involved and on the balance of power and priorities within broadcasting organisations.

The ideology of creativity can provide a certain insulation for single play production from internal pressures. As Roland Joffe has recently pointed out:

there is an enormous difference between current affairs censorship and play censorship and that's to do with the way our culture has grown. Artists have been allowed a fair amount of freedom . . . the ideas of free speech and art go very importantly hand in hand . . . So a play is a lot more sacrosanct: it's not as safe to interfere with the writer's right, as to say well this journalist did this but we have decided not to put it out.[34]

This ideological insulation is bolstered by the decentralised organisation of play production, particularly within the BBC where producers are given a budget and normally left to commission scripts with minimum interference from above. This is one reason why the axe often falls when productions are either finished or well down the pipe-line. Well-known examples would include Dennis Potter's *Brimstone and Treacle*, Ian McEwan's *Solid Geometry* and Brian Phelan's *Article Five*, which dealt with the use of torture in Northern Ireland. In all three cases the drama department's support for the productions was over-ruled by the senior administration,[35] a factor which points to the potential clash of interests between programme makers and administrators *within* broadcasting organisations.

Where creative personnel celebrate the notions of personal expressivity and authorial autonomy, administrators are more concerned with the 'calculus of legitimacy' – with weighing the possible advantages of transmission in terms of cultural kudos against the disadvantages in terms of a possible political backlash. As W. Stephen Gilbert notes elsewhere in this issue,[36] this difference of perspective comes about in part because most senior television executives are drawn from the worlds of light entertainment, news and current affairs and are consequently not particularly imbued with the ideology of creativity. But it is also rooted in the different structural locations of the two groups. 'Since programme makers in drama are almost all freelance, their major investment in the institution is through the immediate project they are working on'. The writer in particular 'is an outsider, he does not belong, he is a cuckoo, and he is not part of the institution's discipline, not – literally – under control'.[37] Administrative personnel, on the other hand, tend to identify themselves with the institution and are obliged to concern themselves with its long-term survival. In a situation of pressure these differences are likely to come into collision, as writers insist on the integrity of their texts and administrators defend the interests of the institution as they perceive them. As an ex-Head of Plays at the BBC, Christopher Morahan, has noted:

> it seems to me that decisions not to broadcast are usually made for what seem good reasons for professional broadcasters and what seem poor reasons for authors . . . Too often decisions are taken nominally in the best interest of the audience, but in reality in the interests of the broadcasting authority.[38]

However, the balance of these interests in any particular instance also depends on the relative strength and credibility of the external pressure. Here again, *Law and Order* provides an instructive example. Following the controversy which greeted the first showing, the expected repeats were indefinitely postponed and the BBC took the unusual step of declining to sell the series to overseas networks. Recently both decisions have been revised. The series has been repeated and sold abroad. Several reasons can be suggested for these rehearsals. First, there was the adverse publicity surrounding Operation Countryman, the police's own investigation which revealed widespread corruption at all levels of the Metropolitan force. These disclosures severely weakened the original police charge that *Law and Order* gave a highly misleading impression of the extent of corruption. Second, the plays were produced by Tony Garnett, whose production *Spongers* won the best play award at the 1978 Prix Italia for BBC's *Play for Today* – thereby enhancing both his own critical reputation and the Corporation's prestige, particularly abroad.

Such calculations of relative legitimacy are not the only factors in play: there are also insistent pressures of cost-benefit analysis. Although single plays are to some extent removed from the ratings battle, they are not exempt from cost inflation. All drama is expensive to make and single plays are particularly so, since unlike series and serials, sets and costumes cannot be used in the next episode. Once again there comes a point where the benefits in terms of prestige are outweighed by the economic costs. This point was recently reached at London Weekend Television where Jim Allen's two-part film drama *The Commune* was abandoned at an estimated cost of £100,000, despite his own high reputation and the critical standing of the director, Roland Joffe, and the makers, Dennis Potter and Ken Trodd, who had sold the project as part of a nine-play package from their independent production company PFH (Pennies From Heaven). The production had originally been budgeted at £780,000; this was later cut to £670,000, which the makers considered a bare minimum. LWT would only go to £500,000, and while this is small beer compared to the average feature film budget, it is still a considerable outlay in television terms, particularly on a 'prestige' production.

The economic pressures on the single play are likely to increase considerably in the next few years as the result of a combination of factors. First, companies are likely to experience an intensifying cash crisis as costs continue to rise faster than revenues. This is already evident at the BBC where the present licence income falls well short of the level needed to sustain the current range of output. This places the Corporation in a difficult situation. It must continue to attract around half of the total television audience in order to justify its continued claim to the compulsory licence fee and to bolster arguments for an increase. This forces it into aggressive competition with the commercial companies for domestic ratings and overseas sales – which in turn makes market criteria more and more central to administrative calculations. At the same time, however, this increasing emphasis conflicts with the Corporation's traditional role as a patron of the contemporary arts, subsidising excellence and promise out of public funds. The BBC is therefore in a contradictory position. It is expected to fulfil the same functions as the Arts Council at the same time as performing as though it were a commercial concern. It is obliged to operate simultaneously within the ideology of the market and audience maximisation and within the ideology of Art. Up until now, the institutional defence of creativity (although often taking a somewhat élitist and paternalistic form) has provided an important countervailing force to market criteria. As the current Head of Drama Group, Shaun Sutton, recently told a press conference:

> I am determined that our output will continue to reflect every aspect of television drama. The single play will remain as important as the series, the classic adaptation will be matched by the classic play . . . A daily diet of soap opera is not enough.

However, as he conceded, '1981 will be a difficult financial year' and will almost certainly lead to fewer single plays being produced.[39] It may also see an increase in the tendency to package plays in anthologies grouped around a single setting or theme. Moving single plays closer to series in this way may make them easier to schedule and sell and may increase their potential audience, but it also reduces the range of themes and styles they can employ.

The commercial companies are not without their financial problems either, as the cancellation of *The Commune* indicates. As the general economic recession deepens, firms are likely to cut back their advertising budgets and so produce a squeeze on television profits and an increased pressure to go for ratings success rather than 'prestige' productions. Moreover, this emphasis will be considerably reinforced by the television companies need to combat the emerging competition for audiences from video-cassettes (and later discs), Pay-TV, and 'pirate' satellite broadcasts beamed into Britain from continental Europe. While these developments are likely to intensify the pressure on single-play production, they are not likely to provide many alternative outlets since they are all firmly geared to sales maximisation. Some expansion of single-play slots will be provided by the new Fourth Channel. But it is not likely to be as extensive as many programme-makers had originally hoped and argued for, since production will be caught in the same pincer movement of spiralling costs and intensifying competition. Added to which, the new channel will be pushed towards the more popular forms of programming in order to establish itself with an audience share sufficient to guarantee its viability.

How exactly these various pressures will affect drama production in the future is a matter for empirical investigation, but their intensification returns us to the question we started with: what is the relationship *between* ideologies of authorship and organisational imperatives, and how is the balance between them altering in response to ideological shifts and political and economic pressures inside and outside broadcasting organisations? As I have tried to argue, this remains the central question for anyone interested in understanding why it is that we get the television drama we do.

Notes

1. Richard Corliss, *Talking Pictures: Screenwriters in the American Cinema*, New York: Penguin Books, 1975, p. xvii.
2. See, for example, Manuel Alvarado and Edward Buscombe *Hazell: The Making of a TV Series*, London: British Film Institute/Latimer, 1978, and Muriel Cantor, *Prime-Time Television: Content and Control*, Beverly Hills: Sage Publications, 1980.
3. Shaun Sutton, 'The New Television Drama Writers', *EBU Review*, vol. XXX, November, 1979, p. 14.
4. Roderick M. Graham, 'Coming to Terms with Video for Location Drama', *Television: Journal of the Royal Television Society*, vol. 18, no. 3, May/June, 1980, p. 15.
5. Gaye Tuchman, 'Objectivity as Strategic Ritual: An Examination of Newsmen's Notions of Objectivity', *American Journal of Sociology*, vol. 77, January 1972, pp. 660–79.
6. See Peter Burke, *Tradition and Innovation in Renaissance Italy*, London: Fontana, 1974, p. 71.
7. Howard S. Becker, 'Arts and Crafts', *American Journal of Sociology*, vol. 83, no. 4, pp. 864–5.
8. Karl Marx, *Theories of Surplus Value: Part One*, London: Lawrence & Wishart, 1969, p. 401.
9. Karl Marx, 'Debates on Freedom of the Press', in Karl Marx and Frederick Engels, *Collected Works: Volume One*, London: Lawrence & Wishart, 1975, p. 174.
10. I have borrowed this distinction from Herbert Gans, *Popular Culture and High Culture*, New York: Basic Books, 1974, p. 62.
11. See Lewis A. Coser, *Men of Ideas: A Sociologist's View*, New York: The Free Press, 1979, p. 46.
12. See Corliss, op. cit.
13. For a classic statement of this point, see Pierre Macherey, *A Theory of Literary Production*, London: Routledge & Kegan Paul, 1978, Chapter 11.
14. John Sturrock, 'Roland Barthes', in John Sturrock (ed.), *Structuralism and Since*, London: Oxford University Press, 1979, p. 67.
15. Roland Barthes, 'The Death of the Author', in *Music-Image-Text*, London: Fontana, 1977, p. 143.
16. See Raymond Williams, 'The Writer: Commitment and Alignment', *Marxism Today*, vol. 24, no. 6, June 1980, p. 25.
17. This phrase is taken from Bernard Sharratt, 'The Politics of the Popular – From Melodrama to Television', in David Bradby *et al.* (eds),

Performance and Politics in Popular Drama, London: Cambridge University Press, 1980, p. 275.

18. See Phillip Drummond, 'Television Drama: Discursivity and Determination in Hazell', Paper presented to the BFI Television Seminar, March 1980.

19. Colin McArthur, *Television and History*, London: BFI, 1978, p. 40

20. Terry Eagleton, *Criticism and Ideology*, London: Verso, 1978, pp. 58–60.

21. Shaun Sutton, op. cit., p. 14.

22. See Catherine Itzin, 'Production Casebook No 6: *Upstairs, Downstairs*', *Theatre Quarterly*, vol. 11, June 1972, p. 29.

23. Quoted in Charles Barr *et al.*, 'The Making of *Upstairs, Downstairs*, a Television Series', *Movie*, no. 21, November 1975, p. 50.

24. See Alfred Shaughnessy's autobiography, *Both Ends of the Candle*, London: Peter Owen, 1978.

25. Quoted in Charles Barr *et al.*, op. cit., p. 50.

26. Interview with Melvyn Bragg, *South Bank Show*, London Weekend Television, 24 February 1980.

27. Quoted in Charles Barr *et al.*, op. cit., p. 50.

28. Quoted in Catherine Itzin, op. cit., p. 26.

29. See *Communication: A Case Study of 'Days of Hope'*, BBC Audience Research Department, March 1977.

30. See *Variety*, 9 January 1980, p. 171.

31. See 'The Single Play', in *Television and Radio 1980*, London: IBA, 1980, pp. 24–5.

32. 'All the World's a Stage', in *Television and Radio 1979*, London: IBA, 1979, p. 81.

33. Quoted in Sue Woodman, 'The Law, Disorder and G. F. Newman', *Time Out*, no. 535, 18–24 July 1980, p. 19.

34. Quoted in Mairède Thomas, 'A Play for Today: An Interview with Roland Joffe', in *Truth The First Casualty: The British Media and Ireland*, London: Information on Ireland, 1979, p. 12.

35. For documentation, see Colin R. Munrow, *Television, Censorship and The Law*, Farnborough: Saxon House, 1979, pp. 155–160 and W. Stephen Gilbert, 'An Angle on *Solid Geometry*', *Broadcast*, no. 1049, 17 March 1980, pp. 12–16.

36. W. Stephen Gilbert, 'The Television Play: Outside the Consensus', *Screen Education*, no. 35, Summer 1980, pp. 35–40.

37. Kenith Trodd, 'Blue Pencil and Scissor Show', *Broadcast*, 18 September 1978, p. 19.

38. Christopher Morahan, letter to the *Guardian*, 19 September 1977, p. 10.

39. Quoted in *Broadcast*, 21 July 1980, p. 7.

Chapter 9

Planning the Family: The Art of the Television Schedule*

Richard Paterson

So far, most work about television has concentrated on the production of programmes, their analysis as 'texts' and their 'consumption' by audiences. Less attention has been paid to the *circulation* of programmes through the television schedule, the *regulation* of the schedule by legislative and policy concerns, and the way the schedule actually works on the audience. What I want to explore in this article is how what is produced, mapped over the institutional 'needs' of broadcasting, can be articulated with its consumption within the 'domestic world', which is in turn framed by notions of 'healthy' family practice. This means looking at the different pressures – from legislation to censorship lobbies, from economic necessity to an entertainment ethic – brought to bear on the broadcasting enterprise: what emerges is that a concept of 'family' operates in different ways across these and so becomes the keystone of the schedule's architecture. From this perspective, it is possible to examine different types of output, especially the various drama/fiction formats, and to see how they come to be programmed as they are.

* *Screen Education*, no. 35, Summer 1980.

The Family Audience

Raymond Williams has characterised the experience of watching television as a *flow* 'in which the true series is not the published sequence of programme items but this sequence transformed by the inclusion of another kind of sequence';[1] this flow (planned by providers and by viewers) 'operates, culturally, following a given structure of feeling'.[2] Suggestive though this analysis is, it doesn't really explain what is achieved by a television schedule – in part, perhaps, because it is limited by Williams's problematic notion 'structure of feeling'.[3] Equally, John Caughie's amendment that a uniformity of representation is central to programme flow doesn't specify the constitutive differences between programme categories and why they are scheduled differently. My argument is that to understand why the schedules are constructed as they are, it is necessary to think in terms of *audience aggregation* and the ways this is achieved by enlisting particular audience groupings at particular times. Television's consistent, repetitive, plurality – 'producing always variety, always the same thing' – is not a 'pluralism without difficulty'[4] but a central element in enterprise calculations about audience maximisation.

Broadcasting has to amass audiences. American television stations, it has been said, are not in business to produce programmes. They are 'in the business of producing audiences. These audiences, or means of access to them, are sold to advertisers.'[5] Although this may seem applicable only to commercial television in Britain, the perceived need to compete has made it (at least since 1957) equally determining of the British Broadcasting Corporation's (BBC's) output. The quality and nature of the audience are important to market researchers and advertisers, and so there is systematic pressure to produce fairly stable and predictable audience levels. Unlike magazine (and, increasingly, American TV stations), the British broadcasters do not go for 'target audiences', seeking out particular demographic profiles. When advertisers do want to reach a particular type of audience (light viewers, for example, or a specific social class), the present practice is to map the schedule of advertisement onto the programmes schedule, using market research throughout the regional structures of the commercial network to allow full coverage in 'spot placements'.[6] In general, though, the continuing demand for the maximum audience determines scheduling strategy and the sorts of programmes commissioned.

But what is involved in creating this 'mass' or 'popular' audience? Informing the policies involved in constructing an appropriate schedule is a nexus of legislative and economic factors located within a notion of 'family welfare' and 'family health'. Both the BBC and the Independent Broadcasting Authority (IBA) operate a version of the Family Viewing Policy, for example.[7] 'Family', a concept often used as a projection into nostalgia or as a reactionary counter in various discursive formations, thus comes to be used in British broadcasting to unify enterprise strategy. Schedulers take it as axiomatic that the audience is maximised by constructing particular family viewing patterns in the 'domestic situation' – this is how to aggregate the 'popular' audience for offer to the advertisers. At the heart of this strategy is a particular analysis of the domestic – the ideology of the home as haven, the notion of family as site and agent of socialisation. But, as Jacques Donzelot has stressed, the key to understanding the family is *internal differentiation*,[8] whereby different practices single out particular members of different classes for the interventions which play upon it. The same principle applies to the 'family audience' – the schedule singles out the dominant 'voice' of the family at specific times in order to ensure the maximum audience. Whether or not this is a conscious policy, it none the less underlies the conventional practices of both the BBC and the commercial companies.

The policy of the IBA also clearly tends to solidify this scheduling pattern and the work of the schedule on the viewer; thus enterprise calculation of audience reach is overdetermined and augmented by 'authoritative' action. In 1977, the Independent Television Companies Association complained to the Annan Committee that

> the growth of case law in scheduling was now stifling good programming . . . A straitjacket of rules inhibits the scheduler's freedom to set out the day or the week in a way that will best suit the majority of viewers.[9]

They were especially unhappy about the *Television Programme Guidelines* – designed, according to the foreword, 'to help increase good practice' – in which the prescriptions for a Family Viewing Policy are particularly strict.

The Family Viewing Policy crystallises a philanthropic conception of broadcasting; it draws on the accumulated research into the 'effects' of television and the uses to which these have been put by lobbies like the National Viewers' and Listeners' Association. Thus research by both the IBA and BBC constructs profiles of audience availability and audience type. From these an image of Family Life is derived and then is used to prescribe what should be viewable at what times. Four time-bands are specified by the IBA:

1. 16.15 to 17.15 (weekdays) – children's hour;
2. 17.15 to 19.30 – family viewing time, but with all material suitable for children to view alone;
3. 19.30 to 21.00 – no material unsuitable for children viewing with their family;
4. 21.00 onwards – it is considered the responsibility of parents to decide what their children should watch; but allowance has to be made for the possibility of a large (though decreasing) audience of children.

Despite the companies' moans, these timings do them no harm. They rule out the 'unpopular' during prime time (when the highest rates can be charged for advertising) and reinforce the need for a particular kind of output for a particular audience. Thus they give coherence to programme schedules that seek out consumer groups. 'Serious' drama becomes a non-starter in peak viewing time, whereas the popular quiz show and the situation comedy – both highly accessible to the desired audience – can aggregate a large audience with significant buying power. In this way the placing of advertisers' spots in prime time is further encouraged; and notions of public service broadcasting become servant to a notion of suitability.

Scheduling

A striking example of the schedulers' notion of the family audience was London Weekend Television's thinking in launching *Bruce Forsyth's Big Night* in their 1978 Autumn season in an attempt to counter the BBC's domination of Saturday nights. The innovative form of the programme was based on research into viewing habits during that evening. Taking six discussion groups based on families in social class C1 and C2,[10] it indicated that the male of the household controls the choice of channel on Saturday afternoons up until 16.00; at this point – while wrestling is transmitted – there is some family negotiation. After 17.15, it was found, the choice depends mainly on the male and the children, with women apparently busy doing domestic tasks and given little say. Having completed these, though, the woman again becomes significant between 19.30 and 20.00 and is a major influence in the negotiations which continue through the evening. (Hence the radical changes in the second version of *Bruce Forsyth's Big Night*, when its transmission was brought forward from 19.25 to 18.00.) The children were found to remain involved in negotiations after the mythical 21.00 cut-off – at least until *Match of the Day* is broadcast, when once again it is the male who chooses. Late programmes generate a special – predominantly young – audience;[11] thus *All You Need Is Love*, Tony Palmer's history of popular music, was able to aggregate a large but demographically specific audience.

These findings provide the context for the early evening schedule. For many years the hour between 18.00 and 19.00 was 'the toddler's truce' – no programmes were broadcast, so that parents could get children to bed before settling down to an evening's viewing! The BBC broke the truce with *Tonight*, but in a way that took full account of this domestic mythology. Its format of self-contained, easily comprehensible items still continues in its off-spring, *Nationwide* and the regional news programmes. The former toddler's truce is also now the transmission time in many areas for ATV's soap opera *Crossroads* [no longer transmitted], which is 'stripped' across three evenings each week. Its narrative is constructed of multiple short segments, with continual repetition of narrative information but no overall dramatic coherence in any episode. In part, this structure reflects its place in the schedule: continual viewing has to be ensured even though meal times and other domestic interruptions might make it impossible to follow a coherent narrative. A comparison with *Coronation Street* underlines the point. Broadcast twice weekly at 19.30, when the mother/ children family audience is believed to be watching, *Coronation Street* offers a coherent narrative with interweaving major and minor plot lines. The parameters of serialisation still operate, though[12] – the main one being that the percentage of viewers watching from one episode to the next may be as low as 55 per cent.[13]

The point is that the relationship between programme format and audience is not a simple one. The conditions of production and consumption interrelate with the conditions of circulation, the way the product is seen to construct its audience. In the case of the continuous serial, the large and predictable audience, guaranteed by a low-cost production (in terms of additional investment) using high-cost capital equipment in a predictable way, is captured through its slot in the schedule. The logic of this would therefore lead to serials being stripped across the week – a successful ploy for many independent stations in the USA using syndicated material – but their proliferation in British prime time is inhibited by the IBA's misgivings about clogging the schedules and the tenacity of the 'public service' ideology, which raises questions about the 'suitability' of the form.

Serials of finite length, with narrative structures more 'closed' than those of the eternal soap operas, are scheduled more like series – recent examples include *Dallas, Fox* and *The Mallens*.[14] And in fact it is the series that is the typical television fiction product. In Britain its usual form is a 13-episode drama production built around a hero/heroine or a small group of protagonists. Whatever genre may be dominant (the Western, the action series or, more recently, crime series like *Kojak, The Sweeney, Hazell* and *Charlie's Angels*), the series' *repetition* of format and stars dispenses with the need to keep up with a continuing narrative. This is its appeal to the scheduler: it offers predictability to the heavy viewer without putting off intermittent viewers – who not only make up a very large proportion of the audience, but are often the most important for advertisers to reach. How the series is scheduled, then, can be a key to the success or failure of an evening's package. *The Saint* was scheduled on ITV at 19.15 on Sundays in 1978 to attract the children plus males who were seen to dominate channel selection at that time. After 21.00 on weekdays, when the male is important in the family's decisions, crime series consistently have large audiences. The BBC's success on Saturday nights, according to the opposition, has depended on a formula whose 'chemistry' is sensitive to the dynamic of the audience; 'understandable' drama has always been amongst its elements. LWT therefore developed *The Professionals* to combat the slot occupied by *Kojak* and its heirs.

The single play presents peculiar problems for the schedule. Although as conventional in its way as the format series, it is defended as the embodiment of 'creativity' and retains its niche as the most prestigious type of broadcast. On the other hand, it consistently fails to attract large audiences (in television terms) and can seldom be sold abroad (– hence the growing number of television movies by British commercial companies: these have a non-theatrical approach to drama and are more easily exportable). The IBA Annual Report for 1978/9 expressed a continuing concern about the place of single plays in the schedule, given their lack of drawing power, and recommended 'reasonably consistent and easily recognisable slots for them'. They are invariably scheduled after 21.00 – not necessarily because their themes are unsuitable for family viewing but, as LWT made explicit about their Bennett plays, because the language may be considered too difficult. Such 'high-culture' broadcasts often represent the commercial companies' concern for the future renewal of their franchises by the IBA rather than for any particular viewing audience.

Most of my examples so far have been drawn from the scheduling of commercial output. What about the BBC? BBC2, for a long time considered the élitist channel, offers various forms of 'complementary' scheduling to BBC1. Recently, though, the Controller of BBC2 (Brian Wenham) has adopted a more aggressive strategy to increase its audience share by competing against whatever the other two channels have to offer. This has produced high ratings for BBC2 programmes like *Fawlty Towers* and *Pot Black*. It has also involved some experiments in placing drama. The first series of *Empire Road*, for example, was broadcast at 18.40 in order to create an audience for BBC2 earlier in the evening than it had previously tried for; it was supposed to follow alternatives to the news and regional programmes, but the strategy collapsed when the unions prevented early transmission. (The second series went out at 20.00, supposedly a better time for an 'adult' programme dealing with race.) A more successful venture was the scheduling of *Accident* in the ghetto slot of 22.15, which attracted an audience of three million. BBC2 has also been used as a testing ground for innovative serialisations like *I, Claudius* which have later been shown on BBC1.

Commissioning

The scheduler doesn't have an infinite variety of material to select from, of course, but is limited by what is available – which is why the *commissioning* of programmes is so important. Based on organisational practices and precedents, the ways in which this is done in the BBC and in the commercial companies are radically different. In the BBC, the programme controllers of BBC1 and BBC2 consider departmental offers at the beginning of each financial year, and their decisions determine how production money is allocated. These are usually based on common-sense understandings of what sort of programmes should go where in the schedule, and so the system tends to sustain the status quo, with departments being expected to produce much the same quantity and types of programmes as before. Innovation in programme-making may therefore depend less on the 'creative' moment (itself anchored in the social context and intertextuality) than indirectly on the controller's decisions about schedule position, the moment of circulation which influences the type and size of audience. (Such hints will indicate to a department how well its output is being received in the institutional hierarchy.) Although many programmes are commissioned to fill a particular slot, production does sometimes go ahead without this predetermination – *Empire*

Road is an example – and sometimes the nature of the finished programme results in alternative patterns of scheduling. But examples like *Holocaust*, stripped across a week, are rare; the interruption of the series cycle is thought to disrupt audience behaviour and reduce viewing figures.

Commissioning and scheduling are made more complex for the Independent Television network by its structure of five network and ten regional companies. The Big Five (in 1980 ATV, Granada, Thames, LWT and Yorkshire) provide a number of network programmes proportionate to their share of NARAL (net advertising revenue after levy).[15] Four times each year a schedule is drawn up on the basis of what they have to offer (plus some time for the output of regional companies). The power resides with the Programme Controllers' Group – the programme controllers of the Big Five along with the IBA's Director of Television and the director of the Network Planning Secretariat; their decisions have then to be ratified by the Network Programme Committee (the managing directors of the 15 franchise holders) and approved by the IBA. The whole package is offered to all the companies and, although there is no compulsion on them to accept it *in toto*, it is actually unusual for the smaller ('regional') companies not to do so. Network programmes work out quite cheaply for them, as their contributions to production costs are based on their low proportionate share of NARAL; alternative production is expensive in comparison, and the percentage of imported programmes that can be transmitted in any week is limited. The different commercial companies maintain their 'independence' through a limited flexibility of scheduling, based on regional variations in marketing strategy and audience reach.

In 1973 the Select Committee on Nationalised Industries criticised the IBA for its permissive attitude towards the Programme Controllers' Group and their exclusion of 'regional' material and, as far back as 1960, the Pilkington Report commented on the way that ITV's apparent plurality tended to regroup as a unity ordered by the large companies. But these strictures have had little effect on the companies because the system goes on producing audiences and profits for them. An element of mutual trust has also developed about the production of programmes, with different companies specialising in particular categories or genres – Thames for crime and action series, ATV for comedy and so forth. These proven formulae produce a certain rigidity, although attempts will be made to fill any lack that is perceived – as with LWT's innovation of *Bruce Forsyth's Big Night* to tackle ITV's Saturday night problem.

At this stage it's difficult to know how the fourth channel's (at least notional) commitment to independent productions and more demographically specific audiences will change the ecology of British broadcasting. Already some companies are experimenting in the margins of the schedule[16] – LWT's Minorities Unit has produced *Skin* (for blacks), *Gay Life* (for gays) and *Twentieth Century Box* (for youth), for example. And the sometimes antagonistic responses from the 'target groups' have revealed some of the manoeuvre's contradictions. Once the audience is allowed a *political* definition, the hegemonic operation of the 'family audience' concept as the ordering principle of scheduling becomes clear and the plausibility of a 'mass audience' or even of a consensual pluralism is exploded. The broadcasters' present calculations of how to aggregate the largest possible audiences by taking account of the 'domestic' context of viewing may therefore have to be jettisoned. These legislative and political pressures are compounded by technological changes. As channels multiply, as satellite broadcasting gets underway, as video-cassettes and discs become widely available and the number of television sets in each household increases, patterns of viewing and selection and the range of potential target audiences are bound to look quite different. This will in turn require new marketing strategies; and it may even mean the end of 'the family' as we – or rather as Mrs Whitehouse and the schedulers – know it.

Notes

1. Raymond Williams, *Television: Technololgy and Cultural Form*, London: Fontana, 1974, p. 90.

2. Ibid., p. 111.

3. On this see, for example, Stuart Hall, 'The Williams Interviews', *Screen Education*, no. 34, Spring 1980, p. 101.

4. John Caughie, 'The "World" of Television', *Edinburgh Magazine*, no. 2, 1977, pp. 76/7.

5. Bruce M. Owen, Jack H. Beebe and Willard G. Manning, Jr, *Television Economics*, London: Lexington Books, 1974.

6. See Sue Stoessel 'The Real Weight of Light Viewers', *ADMAP*, June 1979, pp. 277–80.

7. For the IBA Family Viewing Policy see *Television Programme Guidelines*, IBA, 1979, para 1.4, p. 1.

8. Jacques Donzelot, *The Policing of Families*, London: Hutchinson, 1979.

9. Lord Annan (Chairman) *Report of the Committee on the Future of Broadcasting*, Cmnd 6753, London: HMSO, 1977, p. 188.

10. This is the main group of consumers that needs to be aggregated

into the audience; research shows that members of social classes D and E watch commercial television anyway.

11. See G. J. Goodhardt, A. S. C. Ehrenberg and M. A. Collins, *The Television Audience: Patterns of Viewing*, Farnborough: Saxon House, 1975, p. 41.

12. On the specificity of its production, format and narrative, see R. Paterson, 'The Production Context of *Coronation Street*', in forthcoming material from the British Film Institute (BFI)

13. Goodhardt *et al.*, op. cit., p. 51; their figure is contested by broadcasters.

14. BBC2's scheduling of *Dallas* across the week in Summer 1980 is an interesting development and indicates the need for further refinement in the analysis of the serial form.

15. For an explanation of NARAL see Annan, op. cit., p. 173.

16. On the economics of minority programming see John Wyver, 'London Programming', in *Time Out*, no. 527, May 1980.

Chapter 10

Broadcasting From Above*

Edward Buscombe

The fourth massive volume of Asa Brigg's *The History of Broadcasting in the United Kingdom* has still advanced the story no further than the birth of ITV in September 1955. Monumental such a work undoubtedly is; but a monument to what exactly? To the BBC, obviously, since although this volume covers in detail the struggle to break the BBC's monopoly which was to end with the creation of ITV, it is with the Corporation that Briggs is largely concerned, and at first sight this seems understandable enough, since for the first 30 years of its history the BBC and broadcasting in this country were virtually synonymous. Some might question whether a history on such a scale is really needed (and presumably there must be at least a couple more volumes to come before the story is brought up to date). Is the BBC that important? The answer must certainly be 'Yes'. The BBC is a major state institution, an Ideological State Apparatus fully deserving of the capitals Althusser bestows upon the term. Till Briggs's work we had only the memoirs of a few of its servants, its annual reports and some other scattered writings from which to construct its history. If he has done nothing else he has at least provided us with abundant material on which to base an understanding of what it is that the BBC represents.

Briggs himself, of course, would not dream of using a term such as Ideological State Apparatus. His work is innocent of anything

* *Screen Education*, no. 37, Winter 1980/81.

remotely like a theory of history or society. What we have here is history in the good old bourgeois sense, a straight narrative of the 'facts'. But as with all good bourgeois history you can learn from it. Brigg's 1000-plus pages are full of meaty data on the role which the BBC has played in British social and political life. As everyone knows, at least since the publication of E. H. Carr's *What is History?*, the selection and indeed the very definition of what constitutes a historical 'fact' is not an operation which can ever be ideology-free and, as we shall see, Brigg's decisions as to what counts as evidence require some comment. But it can certainly be said that much of the material he uncovers can be put to good use – particularly that concerning the relationship between the BBC and the state. It's clear that, despite whatever current notions the BBC may hold about 'balance' and 'neutrality', its historical role, at least as defined by those in control, has been to function broadly as a support for the established institutional forces of society. Thus in 1948 the Director-General Sir William Haley (later to become editor of *The Times* – a fact worth collecting by students of élite networks) stated that:

> We are citizens of a Christian country, and the BBC – an institution set up by the State – bases its policy upon a positive attitude towards the Christian values . . . It seeks to safeguard those values and to foster acceptance of them.

No mealy-mouthed liberal stuff about seeing all points of view here. In areas of cultural policy too the BBC, certainly at the time in question, saw its role as the 'improver' of public taste; it was no part of its duty merely to reflect what public taste actually was. Briggs has a long list of popular songs banned by the BBC on the grounds of bad taste, and there was never any doubt of what section of society was to be the arbiter of taste when it came to decide, for instance, on the suitability for broadcasting of the 'Doin' what comes naturally' number from *Annie Get Your Gun*.

The BBC's role emerges most clearly in the political arena. The External Services have always been the soft underbelly of the Corporation's dedication to neutrality. The then Director of External Broadcasting Sir Ian Jacob (later Director-General) wrote in 1946: 'Success will depend upon the quality of our output, upon the consistency of our standards, and upon the conviction with which we make clear British attachment to truth, freedom and Christian principle'. In 1951 Lord Simon, Chairman of the Governors, wrote more frankly to Attlee that: 'The BBC's Overseas Services are in reality an integral part of national defence, and at a time when defence is being so considerably expanded it is essential that the Overseas Broadcasting Services should at least be maintained'. Probably Simon's statement should not be interpreted as letting the cat out of the bag; it was in any case a piece of special pleading to the Prime Minister not to carry out threatened cuts in the service. Instead it should be seen as one of the terms of a classic contradiction within the BBC, one which found its most acute expression in the External Services. On the one hand there is the obvious fact that if these services did not act in the interests of Britain, the Foreign Office, which finances them directly, would not continue to support them. On the other hand, if the services were not performed according to its own criteria of objectivity then the BBC could not maintain its credibility. The actual services provided are therefore the result of a continuously negotiated balancing act between these two requirements. At any point what is actually broadcast may satisfy both or merely one of them; but it cannot be merely one of them for very long. And the whole juggling act must always depend on the belief of both sides that the BBC's 'neutrality' is ideology-free. Such a belief is possible because each side constructs this neutrality from a common position. The Foreign Office can recognise it as neutrality even though, being itself an arm of government policy, it is not obliged to practice it. Were the BBC to take up its 'neutral' position from another point in the political spectrum, the Foreign Office would of course interpret this as 'bias'.

A similar operation can be observed in the BBC's coverage of domestic politics. Briggs charts in detail the course of the BBC's struggle to maintain its independence from the major political parties. It's not a particularly glorious history on either side. The ridiculous pomposity of Parliament in demanding that it should be the only space in which political debate could take place imposed for a long time on the BBC a ban on discussing any issue for a period of two weeks before it was debated in Parliament. Yet the BBC itself kowtowed to such a view. 'Parliament', Haley maintained, 'is the only grand forum of the nation'. Briggs puts his finger on the reasoning behind the BBC's attitude: 'if it were to seek to become a more active influence there would be so many pitfalls ahead that the independence of the BBC, secured with difficulty during the war, would be in danger'. The BBC's 'independence', then, has always been qualified by its fears of upsetting Parliament, to which ultimately it is subject. Small wonder, therefore, that its notion of political balance has been a scrupulous, even obsessive, preservation of equilibrium between the parties represented in Parliament, combined with an almost total failure to recognise those outside it. Within such a balance one has to recognise that a certain diversity of political views can find expression, more than in the television services of most Western 'democracies'. But this balance can also produce a paralysing enforcement of 'consensus', as the case of N. Ireland (not yet an 'issue' in Briggs's period) has most recently shown. Diversity there may be, contradictions are there to be exploited, but when the chips are down there is never any doubt as to which way the BBC will jump. Long before N. Ireland became the problem for broadcasters it is today, the General Strike episode made that clear. And the other *locus classicus* in the BBC's relations with the state, the Suez affair, which has sometimes been interpreted as an example of the BBC's independence, shows only that the BBC is independent of the government of the day – a very different thing. Can it seriously be thought that if the Labour Party and the Americans had been in favour of the invasion the BBC would have granted expression as readily to those opposing it?

What Briggs's history does, then, is not actually to construct a theory of the relations between the BBC and the state, but to provide in the kind of detail which has not easily been available before chapter and verse for such a theory. That probably is the most that can be expected, if not the most than can be demanded, of it. But there remains the question of whether the book is indeed what it claims to be, a history of broadcasting in the UK. There are reasons why I think it cannot quite be that. One has to do with what Briggs takes broadcasting to be. Broadcasting is what the BBC does, and what the BBC does is largely to be discovered through an examination of its internal records. By far the greater part of Briggs's story is told through the evidence of BBC memoranda, published policy statements, letters, speeches and so on. His book is therefore a history of the BBC's internal workings at the level of policy formation. It is the very opposite of 'history from below'. What we learn is what motivated the Director-General and his senior officials and governors. Now given that the BBC is an extraordinarily hierarchical organisation, that may seem fair enough. What these people thought should happen for the most part did happen.

Thus, through a painstakingly assembled montage of memos, Briggs constructs the (to the modern reader) unbelievably slow and tortuous process by which television, still scarcely begun when this volume opens at the end of the war, was detached from the grip of people whose training had been in radio and who were by temperament and experience unable to adjust to the new medium. It's hardly credible, for instance, that it was not until 1953, some seven years after television transmissions had recommenced, that the BBC moved from having a radio announcer reading the news over a picture of a clock to showing a live newsreader on screen.

But still the news had no pictures of events to accompany the script. To an audience accustomed for years to both cinema newsreels and tabloid newspapers this must have seemed amazingly untelevisual, and can surely only be explained in terms of a rigid dictation of policy from above, as Briggs makes clear. Not until 1955 was a separate Television News Department, distinct from radio, set up.

But the tendency of Briggs's method of relying on internal written evidence is to treat the BBC as an institution whose dynamic is a largely internal one. Memos from the Director-General to the Head of Talks and back again create a picture of an organisation functioning mainly under its own momentum. There is certainly a powerful attraction in this model. The BBC has often been described as a private world (as in the title of Tom Burns's book *The BBC: Public Institution and Private World*). One can plausibly interpret a great deal of the BBC's history simply as the attempt to preserve its own identity, to ensure the means of its own reproduction. For example, the events surrounding the creation of ITV, very fully documented by Briggs, lend support to this view. One of the cardinal principles of the BBC has always been that it is a *public* service, financed out of public funds for the general welfare. For this reason it has always set itself implacably against advertising on the grounds that it would make the public good subservient to the demands of commerce. Or so we have been led to believe. Yet one fascinating fact Briggs reveals is that, when it became clear that the Conservative Government intended to set up a rival organisation to provide an alternative television service, the BBC Board of Management actually favoured, as a way of buying off the pressure for another broadcasting service, a plan which would create a second BBC Television service financed out of advertising revenue. Thus in order to preserve its monopoly the BBC was willing to sell its soul. From this it is indeed tempting to construct a theory of institutions which says that their actions are governed by this fundamental need to ensure their own existence. And the BBC's relations with the state can certainly be seen in this light. To preserve its identity the BBC will not simply broadcast government propaganda, since that would mean it effectively ceasing to be the BBC, becoming instead merely an arm of government. But it will accept Parliament's own definition of what counts as legitimate political expression. This view of the BBC does not in itself offer an adequate explanation, though. That can come only from an understanding of those forces outside the BBC with which it is in continual tension. The BBC changed a good deal during the period covered by this volume, and these changes can only be accounted for from a perspective which relates the BBC's own internal dynamic to that of the wider society. The restrictions inherent in Briggs's method mean that he is unable to produce an analysis of such a relationship. One aspect of this is the almost total failure of his attempted description of the programmes broadcast by the BBC at this time.

It is often assumed, quite wrongly, that the only criterion by which to judge a broadcasting organisation is that of its programmes. The Annan Report was only the most recent of commentators to repeat this fallacy. It certainly doesn't follow that because the BBC produces good programmes that all is well (though there may be grounds for supposing that the converse is true). The relationship between the nature of the institution and the actual programmes is not so direct that any such assumption can be made. Good programmes can happen through a lucky combination of circumstances. And in any case the issues raised by broadcasting are not reducible to the programmes. For example, one of the most interesting things in this book, unfortunately not greatly developed, is the fact that even into the 1950s the possibility of using television as a medium for public exhibition in the way that the cinema had historically developed was still being discussed. The BBC, needless to say, because it had developed as an institution for the public distribution of programmes for private exhibition, was not interested. The implications of the kind of exhibition which emerged go far beyond the question of any particular programmes which may be broadcast. Nevertheless, it is obvious enough that a history of *broadcasting*, as opposed merely to a history of the internal workings of the BBC, ought surely to offer some analysis of the end product. What Briggs provides is for the most part merely a listing of the major shows the BBC put out between 1945 and 1955. One cannot understand the reasons why these programmes took the form they did simply by reference to the minutes of the BBC's Board of Governors. Briggs, despite devoting nearly 300 pages to the programmes, finds little of interest to say about them. All we are given is a brief run-through of titles with a sentence or two of description. Thus of *Take It From Here*, one of the key radio shows of the 1950s, he can only remark lamely that it had 'a brilliant script and offered a new-style mixture of sophistication and corn'.

The sort of history I am asking for may well never be written. Even if all the programmes had been preserved it would be a massive labour to disinter their meanings some 30 years after. But unless something of this kind is done I do not see how we can say that we have a history of broadcasting. The difficulty for Briggs is that not only does he lack, one suspects, the methodology which would be needed for programme analysis, but his reliance on a certain kind of evidence leads him inevitably away from pro-grammes. The official written records are produced by the people in charge. For the most part in the BBC those people were quite remote from production. It is not without significance here that those right at the top have not on the whole been drawn from those areas of production most important to the majority of the BBC's audience. Thus the External Services have been a major supplier of Director-Generals and positions immediately below. When Sir William Haley was considering the question of his suc-cession in 1947 he wrote: 'The posts of Spoken Word, External Services and Management would yield at least three possible can-didates in training for the Director-General's post at any time'. (Briggs comments appositely: 'Home Output was excluded, along with Television: Haley obviously did not see the centre of power there'.) Had Briggs supplemented his written sources with inter-views with producers, writers, technicians and so on we might have, indeed almost certainly would have, been told a different story, one which would have put the actual output closer to the centre of the picture. Such research among those lower down in the hierarchy, involved in programme production, might also complicate and therefore improve our understanding of the BBC's ideological function. While in the end the BBC has generally acted in support of the political and ideological status quo, it must be the case that this position has never been produced merely by *diktat*. There must always have been more or less of a struggle. Indeed the stream of memos and policy papers is at least *a priori* evidence of this. For if there was never any resistance to the line pursued by those at the top, never any questioning of the proper way of doing things, why would the BBC's position need to be spelt out in such detail? A little 'history from below' might have demonstrated with what difficulty, and at what cost, a certain ideological hegemony was achieved and even on occasion, of course, not achieved. An attention both to the actual programmes and to the people who made them would surely have revealed some of the stresses and strains which the BBC had managed to withstand from 1924 to 1955, but which eventually could no longer be contained within it.

This absence in Briggs's work is related, I think, to a second, equally damaging, limitation to the work's claim to be a history of broadcasting – the failure I have already indicated to relate the BBC adequately to the wider society. One instance of this can be given. Briggs relates in exemplary detail the entire history of the BBC's own response to the threat (as it was always seen) of a rival television service. But the forces in society which were eventually to triumph over the BBC's claim to monopoly were rather complex and Briggs does no more than gesture towards them. This is surprising perhaps in one who has made his reputation as a social historian and it might be said in Briggs's defence that an already long book might have been made unmanageably longer had he attempted properly to relate the BBC to the movements of British society in the post-war period. Nevertheless, one has only to consider the list of people who supported the Popular Television Association, the pressure group in favour of ITV, to get some sense of the complex network of ideologies and interests involved. Briggs lists some of them: John Grierson, Alec Bedser, A. J. P. Taylor, Ted Kavanagh, Malcolm Muggeridge, Canon Collins and a variety of Labour politicians. To say that these people were simply the tools of those who hoped to profit from the new service is a gross simplification, which Briggs rightly resists. Even the backbench Conservative Broadcasting Study Group appears to have been motivated as much by a genuine belief that the BBC's monopoly was anti-democratic as by an ideology of free enterprise. Briggs touches on some of the subtleties of this complex, even contradictory alliance without ever putting his finger on one of the most obvious sources of hostility to the BBC. To many people in the country the BBC was, and remains, essentially the instrument of a single class. Maybe they wouldn't put it like that; perhaps they would simply say that the BBC is 'them' and not 'us'. The subsequent greater popularity of ITV, a popularity which the BBC has only dented by becoming more like its rival, can never be understood simply by the fact that it is less squeamish about giving people 'what they want'. Its whole style, its mode of address, has always been more in tune with the working class. Just as the Conservative Party in 1945 was deceived into believing that the war-time popularity of its leader would guarantee continuing electoral support, so a decade later the BBC found that it wasn't nearly as popular as it had assumed. Its belief in its divine right to rule the airways blinded it to the fact that large numbers of the audience, despite their attachment to some of its programmes, did not love the BBC as an institution in the way it thought they did. Perhaps the peculiar status which the BBC attained during the war had blinded it, like the Tories, to an underlying shift in popular attitudes.

Class as a term of analysis is utterly lacking in Briggs's book. He sees the BBC as an institution of state; but the question of whose state is never raised, just as the questions of what the programmes were really like and who they were for are missing. One is bound to conclude that the history of broadcasting, which cannot ignore such questions, remains to be written.

Part III

Education

Chapter 11

Green Paper: Noise of Crisis*

James Donald

> The present offensive against education, in fact a tightening of controls within the dominant system itself, cannot be defeated by campaigns alone. What matters, quite practically, is redefining the issues.
>
> Raymond Williams

The particular clashes and skirmishes of the 'Great Debate' may be over now, but it's hard not to hear that the education system is still 'in crisis'. The administrative machinery of funding, examinations and school government is being stripped down and reassembled. The Tory Right still raises the occasional brouhaha about 'standards'. Battered groupings of Left teachers are renewing their exhortations to rally against the 'attack on education'. Academic observers burrow after the source of the crisis – in the crisis of capitalism, in changes in the labour process and the problems of youth unemployment, in the breakdown of social democratic hegemony. Meanwhile, teachers caught up in all this are liable to lose (at best) their autonomy or (at worst) their jobs. In this hubbub of theoretical debate and political struggle it is difficult to stop and ask the quiet, outrageous question: 'What crisis?'. I'm not saying that there have not been some fundamental changes; some basic contradictions are now clearly having their

* A shortened and revised version of an article first published in *Screen Education*, no. 30, Spring 1979.

effect. The trouble is that 'crisis' is such a loose and baggy notion that it can hold a whole range of undifferentiated changes. That's why I want to ask which things have changed, and how, and why.

Most striking are the changes in state policy on education. These are my concern in this article, particularly as they are embodied in the Labour Government's Green Paper *Education in Schools* (Cmnd 6869) published in July 1977. Just what 'policy' means in this context is not self-evident though. It signifies not only a product (the policy statement), but also two practices – the formulation of policy and its actual implementation. The relationships between these aspects are not as straightforward as is sometimes assumed. The obvious disparities between what the Department of Education and Science says ought to be happening and what is actually going on in schools are usually explained in common-sensical terms of a time-lag, or of the incompetence and/or obstruction of teachers, administrators and students. Both the formulation of education policy and the workings of schools are, it is true, activities of the state; both work, in general terms, to reproduce and modify existing social relations. But there is also a difference between them. They are specific practices of separate institutions and, before it is possible to see how they fit together, it is this specificity that needs to be studied.

The theoretical importance of such a distinction is fairly clear – the distinction between concept and object is axiomatic. To assume that 'education' – one component within a theoretical discourse, significant only in relation to a set of other concepts like 'the state', 'industry', 'nation' and 'family' – is identical with, or simply reflects the actual existence and activities of schools, easily leads to confusion about just what is being studied. The political implications may be less obvious. The separation of questions of knowledge from those of power is deeply ingrained. It is a habit that needs to be broken, though, because there is a relationship between the two which is neither accidental nor simply instrumental. Michel Foucault has made the point that 'there is no power relation without the correlative constitution of a field of knowledge, nor any knowledge that does not presuppose and constitute at the same time power relations'.[1] Implicit in the question of the restructuring of education, then, is the question of how the state exercises and imposes its power in part through the production of 'truth' and 'knowledge' about education. Not to challenge this process cedes to the state the power to define the site, the terms and the limits of struggle. It's not a matter of being gullible or cynical, but of reading (in this case) the Green Paper in a way that recognises this power/knowledge complex and thus may displace other (dominant) readings which block attempts

to bring about changes in education and the wider social formation. It may then be possible to produce a different analysis which
could further that struggle. This article is, I hope, a contribution
to such a radical redefinition of the issues, a salvo in the 'battle
of ideas' around the imposition of a new hegemony on education.

At its simplest, it is possible to identify two processes at work
in 'the education crisis'. What education is for is being redefined
and, at the same time, the institutions of the education system
are being restructured to achieve these new goals and to fit new
patterns of state expenditure. The problem is to see how these
two relate to each other and what are the specific tactics of each.
One barrier, I think, has been the failure to grasp just what is at
issue in the notion of 'crisis'. Most analyses have so far concentrated on the cuts in expenditure and the attempts to gear education more efficiently to the 'needs of industry'. They have identified quite accurately certain empirical causes of the crisis and
some of the consequences of policy changes. That doesn't in itself
explain what the changes mean in terms of the exercise of state
power. The power of the state is not the property of any group
or class. It exists only as it is exercised in what Foucault calls the
'micro-physics of power'. The appropriate model, he suggests, is
not a contract but a perpetual battle. Power is 'a network of
relations, constantly in tension, in activity, rather than a privilege
one might possess'.[2] Focusing just on the centralisation of power
may show where power lies; it cannot explain how it works.

The Green Paper

To challenge the truth of the Green Paper is not a question of
saying it's all lies and mystification, but of showing how it works
as a text and, so, of questioning the definition and effectivity of
its status of knowledge. In the next section I shall examine the
institutional context in which it was produced, regulated, distributed and circulated but here (the distinction is made purely for
purposes of analysis) I shall try to offer some of the tools for a
'reading' which would go against the grain of the paper. A proper
reading would mean breaking it down into fragments and looking
at it 'frame by frame', to use a cinematic analogy, showing its
'truth producing' mechanisms at work. Lacking the space for that,[3]
I shall pick out examples of how 'problems' are selected for the
political agenda and how 'the state' is constructed as a discursive
category.

This last point can be illustrated by investigating the apparently
innocent words 'we' and 'our'. In the paper's Foreword, for exam-

ple, which is signified as by 'the Secretary of State for Education and Science and the Secretary of State for Wales' and signed by 'Shirley Williams' and 'John Morris', it is clearly these named people who are the 'authors' of the comment that

> We hope, therefore, that those who read this Green Paper will do so against this background of much that is exciting and even outstanding.

Compare this with the concluding remark, though:

> But there are times for self-examination followed by the setting down of new objectives and new ways of reaching those objectives. We believe that we have now reached such a time, and this Green Paper is a response to it.

The first 'we' is quite straightforward; it is still the Secretaries of State. But unless the 'self' to be examined is that of Shirley Williams and John Morris the second 'we' cannot simply signify them. The 'self' must be the body politic, so that 'we' signifies not just the authorial subject but author *and* reader, state *and* citizen.

'We' and 'our', then, do not refer just to the paper's authors – it's safe to assume that a fair number of civil servants and politicians had a hand in its various drafts – but to its notional origin and to a definitive relationship between 'author' and 'reader'. The Green Paper seems to speak to its readers in a single, coherent voice, as if engaging them in argument. But it is important to bear in mind that a reader's engagement is with the text and its linguistic structures, not with the mind of the author. The relationship between the 'speaking subject' of an utterance and the 'reader' it implicitly constructs is, therefore, an imaginary one, defined by positions within the text and not with reference to the actual relations between Shirley Williams and any particular reader (you, me, Rhodes Boyson). That's not to say that the 'we' which embodies this imaginary relationship is arbitrary or neutral: its ideological importance – which has implications beyond the confines of the text – lies in the way that it invites certain readings and inhibits others. So, to return to the Green Paper, it is worth asking what subject has the authority to speak of 'our society, our educational system, our Imperial past, our people, our boys and girls'. Each has slightly different connotations – 'our society' and 'our education system', for example, have a social democratic ring to them: not only is society the totality of all 'citizens', but its institutions belong to all its members. But if 'our' signifies the imaginary communality of government and governed, then 'our people' would be a tautology. This is not simply a question of logic, though: 'our people' is an example of how class relations of domination and subordination can be incorporated into a discursive unity. What gives coherence to these variations on 'our', then, is the concept of the State, which itself contains the incompatible meanings of governmental apparatus, community of citizens and antagonistic classes.

In all the examples I have quoted, the source of the enunciation is present within the statements – 'We believe that we have now reached such a time', for example. At many points in the Paper, however, it is suppressed and the very Secretaries of State who are the nominal source become actors within it:

> 2.19 It would not be compatible with the duty of the Secretaries of State to 'promote the education of the people of England and Wales', or with their accountability to Parliament, to abdicate from leadership on educational issues which have become a matter of lively public concern.

That is not to say that there is no speaking subject here: there has to be one for the statement to make sense. Once again in this passage it is the state, although not its temporal embodiments, but a sort of Hegelian ideal of the state. It is a moral category (duty . . . accountability . . . leadership) which provides the overarching form of the state: it mediates the two moments of its agency (bureaucracy, policy) and its functionality (reproduction hegemony), and incorporates both the juridically defined 'state' (Secretaries of State, Parliament) and 'society' (the public). Take, as a final example of the significance of the source of the enunciation, the conclusion of the paper. Here it is acknowledged that 'some anxieties are justified' about education and so the state (as moral category) endorses the actions of the state apparatus:

> 9.2 It is right that the Government should give a lead in making these proposals.

In the final paragraph, though, an overtly ideological 'we' reappears. In a fairly safe bet on who will actually be reading the paper, it is defined in a way that pulls all the different 'we's' of the text into an imaginary coherence (and possibly into political collusion).

> 9.3 Each child's education is a unique experience. We, the

partners in the education service, owe it to our children to provide them with the best education our means allow.

I have tried to show how, within the text of the Green Paper, a field is defined on which the positional relationships of author and reader to that text and to each other are charted. In his book *S/Z*, Roland Barthes has designated this the symbolic, one of five 'codes' which in their interplay create a sense of reality for the reader of a literary text. Although, obviously, there are fundamental differences between the text which Barthes submits to a 'slow-motion reading' (Balzac's short story *Sarrasine*) and a contemporary government document like the Green Paper, the applicability of the symbolic, which is in many ways the most complex, suggests that the same codes can be seen at work in both. Probably the most straightforward of the five is the semic code, which plays on the ascription of characteristics to persons, places, things. Thus teachers may possess 'vigour, imagination, and talent' (Foreword). They may be more or less 'able and experienced' (2.2) or they may be inefficient, incompetent and on the verge of nervous collapse (6.36–8). Parents can be 'inadequate or even uncaring' (1.13) or they may be caring and fulfilled (2.31) and 'involved' (8.5). Schools can be 'exciting' (Foreword), inadequate (1.3) or 'overambitious' (1.3). Closely related to the semic is the 'cultural' code, through which the text refers outwards to 'reality' and to 'common sense'. It invokes the things that everybody knows: Barthes therefore places it 'within' ideology.

> If you collect up all these knowledges, all such vulgarisms, they form a monster, and this monster is ideology. As a fragment of ideology, the cultural code *inverts* its (social and school) class origins into a natural reference, into a proverbial assertion.[4]

The cultural code constructs a familiar 'concrete' world which seems to pre-exist the text, and whose existence justifies and validates it. Thus, in the Green Paper, the idea of a 'background' is repeatedly invoked – 'the background of much that is exciting and even outstanding' (Foreword), 'a background of strongly critical comment in the Press and elsewhere on education and educational standards' (1.2), 'the wider background of recent history and social change, responsibilities, resources and aims' (1.6), 'the background of the resources available' (1.18). The important thing about this 'background' is that it is conjured within and by the text. That does not mean that nothing exists beyond the discourse or that the relationship between the 'source-of-the-represented' and the representation is arbitrary.[5] The point is that in many ways the accuracy with which the 'concrete' is represented is less important than how it is used. It is invoked, in a typical sleight of logic, as both the outside cause of the text and also as its guarantee. Just as ideology in general does not hide 'the real' but creates 'reality', so the Green Paper does not drown out or hide the noise of a capitalist crisis. On the contrary, it is the orchestration of that noise into a politically coherent dissonance. 'Noise' here is not just interference in what would otherwise be 'pure' communication. It is not, as Barthes glosses the term, 'confused, massive, unnameable'; it is a distinct 'cacography'.[6] Its main theme in the Green Paper is 'lively public concern' (2.19) – the noise of 'controversy' (Foreword), 'critical comment' (1.2), 'unease' (2.4), 'misgivings' (6.13) and 'genuine anxieties' (9.1) – and it is in this cultural cacography that ideology is written.

Given this background, the forward movement of the text towards its inevitable conclusion is sustained by the proiaretic and hermeneutic codes. The proiaretic composes the text into already known narrative patterns; the hermeneutic constantly reformulates the problem that is the impulse of the narrative, poses and reposes the teasing enigma which must finally be resolved. In the Green Paper, as for other forms of what Frank Burton and Pat Carlen call Official Discourse, these two codes create a 'discourse of tautology' which appropriates a problem in three stages – (i) it theorises a beginning; (ii) it structures an argument; (iii) it attempts a resolution.[7] This pattern is repeated in the sections on separate topics as well as in the overall structure. Background, for example, starts with an 'apposite history' which establishes when the debate began and who has the authority to initiate it:

1.1   In his speech at Ruskin College, Oxford on 18 October, 1976 the Prime Minister called for a public debate on education.

In the second stage, a perspective is constructed but as if it were neutral, as a natural emergent from the past or, as in this case, from cultural background noise:

1.2   Children's standards of performance in their school work were said to have declined. The curriculum, it was argued, paid too little attention to the basic skills . . . Underlying all this was the feeling that the educational system was out of touch . . .

This allows the state to appear as disinterested and judicious ('1.3   Some of these criticisms are fair . . . 1.2 Other criticisms are misplaced . . .') and to establish the central enigma. This is a lack of knowledge which will be resolved by positivist empiricism and a failure within schools which will be resolved by piecemeal social engineering:

> 1.5 The picture, then, is far from clear. Much has been achieved: but there is legitimate ground for criticism and concern.

A variety of devices are put into play to negate particular problems: straightforward assertion (It is simply not true that there has been a general decline in educational standards); empiricist faith (Recent studies have shown clearly that today's schoolchildren read better than those of thirty years ago); the isolation of failures as an exception rather than the rule (A small minority of schools has simply failed to provide an adequate education by modern standards), the 'fraternal critique' in which human fallibility is mitigated by the recognition of good intentions and/or material constraints (More frequently, schools have been overambitious, introducing modern languages without sufficient staff to meet the needs of a much wider range of pupils, or embarking on new methods of teaching mathematics without making sure teachers understood what they were teaching . . .) and so forth.

The pattern of origin-cause-negation can also help to explain the Labour Government's broader strategy for redefining and restructuring education. From this perspective, the Great Debate should be looked at not as 'fraud' or 'a smokescreen to hide the cuts', but as an elegant political and epistemological manoeuvre to create a rationale for fundamental changes in social democratic social policy. It did not and could not produce new knowledge – its purpose was the validation of existing knowledges through a sort of populist empiricism. The relentless repetition of the process should therefore be seen as a political tactic. The issues selected for discussion in the document *Educating Our Children* set such a rigid agenda for the conferences around the country that by the time of the Green Paper they had become the unarguable constituents of 'the problem of education'. It is in this sense that Barthes says that 'stereotypes are a political fact, the principal aspect of ideology'.[8]

My argument for the need to pay close attention to the language of the Green Paper is based on the principle that contesting its ideology in practice entails exposing the ways in which the 'knowledge' in the text is given credibility. That is, of course, only a first step. But how is it possible to take this opposition to its 'reality' further without appealing to the 'truth' beyond the text which will expose its falsity? This particular trap can be sprung by accepting the need to construct a more coherent theorization than is possible within the Green Paper's own terms, a knowledge produced from a different political position – it is certainly possible to offer accounts of sexual difference and of state expenditure (for example) which expose the partiality and inadequacy of their treatment in the paper. Whereas the first step is deliberately formalist, examining the specific nature of the text as text and the ways in which it institutes a position for its 'speaking subject' (here, I have suggested, the state) and invites or blocks certain readings, the second stage emphasises that such ideological work actually comes into operation as the text is circulated and consumed. And actual readers, of course, bring to bear a diverse range of knowledges, prejudices and resistances: inscribed subject positions are never hermetically sealed into a text but are always positions in ideologies. All readings are therefore negotiated, a conjuncture of two ideological formations, the reader and the text. To see how this process works, it is only necessary to look at some of the ways in which the Green Paper has been read.[9] The Confederation of British Industry (CBI) and the Trades Union Congress (TUC), for example, in their different ways absorb the paper into their existing political discourses and use it as a pretext for reasserting their already known positions. In many ways the most interesting response has come from the National Union of Teachers (NUT), which resists the paper's implicit threat to the power of teachers by reiterating two basic assumptions – that no improvement in education is possible without more resources, and that teachers' professional autonomy must be safeguarded and reinforced. Although the 'knowledge' of the NUT invokes may be 'different', however, it cannot oppose the definitions given by the paper. So firmly bound within those terms of reference is it that the Union actually works through each recommendation and proposal in turn, feebly countering with the discredited stereotypes of the old consensus. Unable to challenge the status of the Paper's truth, reading it as it asks to be read, the Union's discourse is politically ineffective because it has become residual.

The New Settlement

At the heart of the Great Debate was the creation and imposition of a 'new settlement' to replace the old consensus in education. The speed with which the NUT's response was rendered irrelevant suggests that it is in part through its power to define 'truth' and knowledge' that the state is able to secure the ideological conditions of this political settlement – which in turn sustains this produced 'truth'. The NUT's problem was its inability to challenge the Green Paper's status. At the same time, though, revealing the discursive mechanisms inscribed in such a text cannot show how and why its discourse – and no longer the Union's – comes to be 'in power'. 'Discourses cannot be reduced to language', the *Ideology and Consciousness* collective stresses; 'the exercise of power is conditioned at one and the same time by determinate discourses and by the practices and institutions in which they are always invested'.[10] This leads back to my original question of what a 'crisis in education' actually signifies. It means looking not only at the internal logic of the Green Paper, but at the circulation of its discourse, at its correlation with a range of political and economic practices, at the conditions in which its rules became effective and at the ideological work it is supposed to do in rearticulating the forms of state intervention and political representation.

Tracing the path of the discourse embodied in the Green Paper is not the same as looking for its origin or causes. It is a way of bringing to light some of the institutional conditions which made this discourse and not another 'happen' in this particular set of circumstances. From where did the terms and the forms of the new settlement come? Through what institutional practices – apart from the specific signifying mechanisms – have they been imposed and others resisted? What new patterns of social relations has it helped to secure at the same time as they protect its position of dominance? Perhaps most important in this context is the change in the way that the political forces within education are constituted. The old reformist alliance between Labour and the teaching profession was characterised by a commitment to representative parliamentary democracy and a tendency to professionalism. This dyad is now being replaced, it seems, by a new pattern of centralised bureaucratic planning and versions of participatory democracy. One key to understanding this conjunctural connection is the organic contradiction between the state's role in reproducing the labour force and the drain on surplus value that this process represents; this leads to a periodic 'fiscal crisis' of the state.

In the 1960s, for example, there was a growing conflict between the need to control costs and the increasing demands for access to education. Planning and corporate management were tactics to solve this dilemma. In 1961 the expenditure plans of the Department of Education and Science (DES) (as of all other departments) came under the scrutiny of the Public Expenditure Survey Committee. The election of the Labour Government led to the creation of a Planning Department within the DES in 1967. The Tories wound this up in 1970 and replaced it, first, with Programme Analysis and Review and then, in 1971, with a Departmental Planning Organisation. Out of this came the 1972 White

Paper *Education: A Framework for Expansion*. This is interesting not so much in itself but for the mauling it received in the Organisation for Economic Co-operation and Development's (OECD's) review of *Educational Strategy in England and Wales*.[11] Cynical about the mandarin ideology of civil service neutrality on the social functions of education, the OECD examiners deplored the failure of DES planning to transcend the terms of the old alliance. The 'educational community's "consensus" ' (largely formed, no doubt, by the more respectable sociologists), on matters like skewing policy in favour of the disadvantaged, was too readily accepted. Adequate methods had not been found for restricting the power of the teaching profession by imposing 'understandings not based on economic and political power plans'. In place of the DES's weak version of planning, the examiners called for two sorts of change. They wanted more aggressive corporate management, 'the use of greater daring in the delineation of new paths of learning and of new institutional and administrative developments which would allow education to respond and at the same time contribute to changes in society'. This centralisation of power, they recognised, would provoke resistance: 'It will be a challenge to planning how to reconcile the problems arising from the need for such strengthening of central authority with traditional local autonomy seen as essential to the British way of life and politics'.

This is where participation comes in, as the necessary corollary of corporatism. As the chief examiner commented in an aside, 'participation is clearly not the fashioning of policy through mass meetings'. It has an openly hegemonic purpose:

> Apart from presenting a strategy for the rational allocation of resources, an educational plan can serve as a 'third force' in situations of conflict, a rallying point around which a measure of agreement, a consensus, can develop. To do so, however, it must be the product of appropriate public procedures.

What these would be is clear in the critique of DES's 'defensive tactics, excluding an open planning process, public hearings, even participation'. In this move to secure consent at the same time as tightening control, what emerges is the ambivalent significance of the crucial term accountability – financial accountability to the Treasury, public accountability to 'consumers' ('employers', 'parents', 'the community'). This analysis begins to make sense of what may at first sight appear a contradiction between the 'functionalisation' of education for capital (through centralisation of power, standardisation, and so forth) and increasing public participation (in the form of the Great Debate, for example, or the proposals on extending the membership of governing bodies made in the Taylor Report, *A New Partnership For Our Schools*, 1977). It is a pattern repeated at many specific levels within education. In training policy, for example, the rise of the Manpower Services Commission has been accompanied by new forms of involvement of local trade unionists and employers in manpower initiatives. It is also the rationale for the changes in the structure of the Schools' Council.

To recognise within the utterances of the OECD examiners the pattern of the new settlement, though, does not mean that their discourse was immediately and unresistingly accepted. In 1975 it was still emergent, and it became dominant only through a process of political struggle. The year after the review's publication, for example, its criticism was taken up by the House of Commons Expenditure Committee as the starting point for their report on *Policy Making in the Department of Education and Science*. Here again the mutual need for control and consent is highlighted.

> We believe that, within the DES, reforms are necessary. It is no excuse to say that, with an economic crisis on our hands, this is no time to make changes. It is the very time to think ahead. Indeed, with public expenditure on education under severe restriction, it is even more important to create a framework for an informed public debate on priorities.

The point was that the secrecy and conservatism of the DES actually inhibited effective corporate planning: 'it is not so much new consultative machinery which is required as a willingness to open up public discussion on policy issues'. The criticism was not popular within the DES. Maurice Kogan, who was an adviser to the Committee, has noted that 'the Parliamentary study of the DES was briefly dismissed in a departmental reply, and no action on its recommendations was taken'.[12] It is clear, none the less, that the circulation of such fundamental criticism of its ways of thinking and acting marked a shift of the balance of power within the DES, later reinforced by changes in personnel. Its policies and its practices are quite different from those in the period of the old consensus. The Great Debate, in the populism of its form and the corporatism that has followed it, can perhaps be taken as the moment of this break.

The discontinuity it represents is implied in Kogan's comment on the Taylor Report.

> If this passes into law, it will go counter to the institutional

tradition upheld by such a leading Labour politician as Herbert Morrison. He was determined that institutions should not be run by those who work in them or their immediate clientele, but by the local authority that stands for election by the wider constituency.[13]

In the new settlement the losers – as they have quite rightly recognised – will be the local authorities and the representative bodies of the teaching profession. Just as the NUT's response to the Green Paper expressed their resistance to the intervention of central government, so their response to the Taylor Report tries to counter community participation by harking back to the old alliance.[14] They appeal not only to the shibboleth of professional autonomy, but also to its relation to representative democracy. Thus they argue that 'while society has a clear right to indicate its expectations through participation in local government, governing bodies and other means, teachers cannot be held accountable if they are not able to exercise full responsibility for their organization and expertise'. Or again, 'the Union shares the Committee's belief in the importance of representation of community interest, but considers that this should be achieved by inclusion amongst the local authority nominees'. The strongest dissent within the Taylor Committee came from the Chairman of the Cleveland Education Committee, who objected to the direct participation of teachers. He too invoked representation as the true form of democracy. 'I am a very firm believer in local government and would not wish to see any more authority taken away from the local education authority', wrote Mr. Fulton. 'The majority report, if implemented, will devolve to a non-elected unrepresentative body authority without accountability and in my opinion diminishes the role of the local education authority and the headteacher'.[15] This minority report has been endorsed by the local authorities; their opposition combined with the teachers' unions may actually succeed in blocking the implementation of Taylor's recommendations. Similarly, attempts to introduce corporate planning into the local authorities have so far flopped. At the same time, this community approach does open up spaces for tactical opposition.

There are structural contradictions at issue here, not just the conflict of interests represented in the Green Paper. Although financial control and corporate planning allow for the stricter discipline of state employees, they also create the conditions for trade union militancy among teachers. Indeed, much of the pre–1976 expenditure that has been cut was itself an attempt to 'buy' social stability by offering improved welfare facilities and expanding the apparatuses of control and repression. The relation between administrative control and financial control, then, is not only complementary but also contradictory. In a similar vein, Etienne Balibar sees the 'big bourgeoisie' trapped in a dramatic contradiction.

> On the one hand, its political power depends on the mainten-ance of its (hegemonic and uneven) alliance with the 'middle layers' of society, including intellectual wage-earners and even a fraction of the working class. On the other hand, it is becoming absolutely essential to suppress anything that, from the point of view of capital, contributes to the massive *faux frais* or 'privileges' of these same layers; in other words, it is becoming essential to speed up their proletarianisation, beginning with an attack on their security (both Social Security and job security) and their qualification (of which the general cultural level forms an integral part). This contradiction is becoming visible today and is, in the long term, of an explosive character.[16]

In the present critical conjuncture of social relations, this contra-diction brings to light what may appear as another paradox – the connection between the promotion of very localised forms of participatory democracy with the strategic internationalisation of capital. We are not dealing here just with a national state appar-atus. What is at issue are the preconditions necessary for the 'internationalised' reproduction of capital. Werner Olle and Wolf-gang Schoeller suggest that 'just as the process of constituting a total national capital was the result of functions of the national state, so even the tendency towards the constituting of a "true historical world capital" logically and historically presupposes supranational statehood'.[17] This supersession of the national state does not result just from some economic mechanism; it can only be achieved by bringing into play all the bureaucratic and ideological mechanisms through which state power is exercised. Nor does it imply a smooth return to equilibrium. Seeing the pattern of the new educational settlement prefigured in the review of the national apparatus by the OECD (itself a powerful supranational state institution), and strenuously fought by national sectoral interests, shows something of the actual struggles involved.

It is not only through the circulation of discourses that the new settlement is being achieved. Its dominance is also protected by a restructuring of the state apparatus through which it is imposed. One reason that the DES has changed its ways is that it was simply bypassed in the implementation of the sort of policies outlined in the OECD report on *Education and Working Life*.

Instead, new agencies untainted by the old alliance and explicitly committed to the idea of education as training have been created – the Manpower Services Commission, for example, and the Training Services Agency. Other constraints on the national apparatus 'from above' also shape the settlement. Public expenditure cuts, for example, are enforced by the International Monetary Fund as one condition for the national state being given access to the credit necessary, *inter alia*, to meet the costs of reproduction. The problems of social control created by such cuts, I have suggested, have to be tackled by corporate management from the national centre. A similar effect is implied by the dominant themes of 'harmonisation' and standardisation in the European Economic Community. How the particular 'technology' of its power affects education is rather opaque; it is exercised through extremely general 'umbrella' resolutions combined with detailed discussions in the Education Committee of the Council of Ministers. Its effect can be seen, though, in the moves towards trans-European educational qualifications implicit in the current proposals for reforming the English examination system, the standardisation of syllabuses through the 'core curriculum' (an idea which originated in a Council of Ministers' discussion) and even the standardisation of record cards for all the pupils in Europe. It is in this context that the Green Paper's harping on mobility and the need to be able to transfer between schools makes sense.

The implication of this analysis is not that these supranational institutions snap their fingers and the national apparatus jumps. Power doesn't just flow from above down through national and local state to the individual school. There is always a struggle. I have tried to assess some of the forces involved in imposing and resisting the new settlement on English education, and so to highlight some of the contradictions of social democracy in the late 1970s. For example, Labour's control of the state apparatus was originally supposed to reform capitalism in favour of the working class. Education was a major theme in this: it would both equalise opportunities and produce an effective and differentiated workforce. In such ways, the state becomes the vehicle of 'the national interest' above class interests. A crisis throws this act off balance: it is on behalf of capital that the social democratic state has to manage the processes of restructuring. Cuts in expenditure mean that the working class can no longer be incorporated through welfare improvements. The state may continue to expand, but it is to corporatist rather than reformist ends. This opens the ways for a right-wing populism which adds to the traditional Conservative complaint about the dilution of academic excellence by educational egalitarianism – the charge that comprehensivisation has produced neither social change nor industrial efficiency. The alternative offered by Thatcherite Conservatism is parental control allied to a radical anti-statist government.

Notes

1. M. Foucault, *Discipline and Punish*, London: Allen Lane, 1977, p. 27.
2. Ibid.
3. For a more extensive reading, see the original version of this article in *Screen Education*, no. 30, Spring 1979.
4. R. Barthes, *S/Z*, London: Cape, 1975, pp. 97–8.
5. Cf. J. Tagg, 'The means of representation may exist distinct from the source-of-the-represented – they may have their "relative autonomy" – but, if the complex process of constitution of the representation neither allows us to identify the content of the representation and the source of the represented nor to compare the representation and this source, No more does it lead us to the view that the "represented has no existence beyond the process which represents it" ' ('The currency of the photograph' in *Screen Education*, no. 28, Autumn 1978, pp. 55–6).
6. R. Barthes, op cit., p. 132.
7. F. Burton, and P. Carlen, 'Official Discourse', *Economy and Society*, vol. 6, no. 4, November 1977. I have borrowed many of their explanatory categories for this analysis – apposite history, the exception rather than the rule, the fraternal critique, and so on.
8. Barthes, quoted in R. Coward and J. Ellis, *Language and Materialism*, London: Routledge & Kegan Paul, 1977, p. 54.
9. See CBI Education and Training Committee, 'Education In Schools', *CBI Education and Training Bulletin Supplement*, vol. 8, no. 1, 1978; TUC, *Note of Comment on the Government's Consultative Paper 'Education in Schools'* London, no date; NUT, *Education in Schools*, London, 1977.
10. D. Adlam *et al.* 'Debate', *Ideology and Consciousness*, no. 3, Autumn, 1977, p. 125.
11. OECD, *Educational Strategy in England and Wales*, National Reviews, Paris: OECD, 1975.
12. M. Kogan, *The Politics of Educational Change*, London: Fontana, 1978, p. 143.
13. Ibid., pp. 71–2.
14. NUT, *Partnership in Education*, London, 1978.
15. DES and Welsh Office, *A New Partnership for our Schools* (Taylor Report), London: HMSO, 1977, p. 125.
16. E. Balibar, 'Irrationalism and Marxism', *New Left Review*, no. 107, January/February, 1978, p. 4.
17. W. Olle and W. Schoeller, 'World Market Competition and Restrictions upon International Trade-Union Policies', *Capital and Class*, no. 2, Summer 1977, p. 70.

Chapter 12

Class, Culture and the Education System*

Manuel Alvarado

The work of *Screen* over the last six years has clearly had a crucial significance for *Screen Education* – without that journal's commitment to introduce and develop a coherent and systematic theory of film it is certain that *Screen Education* would not be confronting the problems of the cinema in the way that it is now doing. Furthermore, by saying that, I am affirming the debates and disagreements of the last few years as having been a necessary process and one that must be continued not just in the pages of *Screen* but also in *Screen Education* and within the work of the Society for Education in Film and Television (SEFT) as a whole. This is not to encourage an eclectic liberalism, a polemical debate in the tradition of an academic journal, but to suggest that the problems and arguments that SEFT has faced have *not* been the difficulty in constructing a theory of film (a conventional problem that practitioners of a subject discipline have to face) but have rather been concerned with the problems of thinking, analysing and working through problems theoretically rather than empirically.

What does it mean to think and work through problems theoretically, especially for a journal like *Screen Education* that is concerned with a very practical set of problems, that is, those problems involved in the concrete practice of conveying knowledge to (often reluctant) learners? First of all, given our professed

* *Screen Education*, no. 22, Spring 1977.

aim of relating film theory, educational theory and the actual practice of teaching film and television, *Screen Education* needs to take account of, and engage with, the various discourses and practices which are the context of the journal's intervention at present: films; television; critical writings on film, television; film theory; education theory; the education system; the political system; classroom practices; the individual teacher and so on. And from this establish not only approaches to these broad areas but also emphases, points of focus, open to change, development, refinement in as much as they are based on an agreed theoretical position. The problem of theory is not one of how to relate it to practice, that is, how to put this educational filmic theory into our teaching practice, which mainly raises questions such as – what if we can't do it? or, what if it won't work? or, what if the theory is wrong? Rather it is the problem of *how* and *why* to construct a theory of education?

It is perhaps a question of developing a theory of education systems, then looking at our specific educational apparatus; the question of a theory of *education* may only arise because of the nature of the education system, and it is clear that current theories of education (sociological, psychological, interactionist, and so on) are already the product of the structure of education whose processes they seek to explain. It is, then, a recognition of the fact that our elaboration of a particular theory of education and of the place film studies occupies within the education system will determine our understanding of that system, our strategy in relation to it, the manner in which we understand some questions as being fundamental for us to engage with, while others remain of peripheral interest. The educational system is not simply a 'given', a transparently recognisable set of institutions and practices instantly offering themselves for understanding providing we use logic and 'common sense'. Rather, what we see and how we understand what we see, and how we act towards it is a matter of theoretical understanding.

There is no way in which *Screen Education* can hope to 'apply' theory to the educational system and to specific areas of practice within it. On the contrary, our approach must be the development of concepts by which teachers understand their practice, both in the general terms of their functioning as teachers and more specifically in relation to their role as film teachers, and by which they can think the transformation of their practice and of the institutions in which they function. Theory intervenes as a way of correctly recognising and thinking the solutions to specific problems – themselves theoretical constructs.

There would seem to be two aspects to work on a theory of

education; one referring to the problems of ideology – raised, for instance, by the Althusserian notion of Ideological State Apparatuses (in *Lenin and Philosophy and other Essays*, New Left Books, 1971), of which education is a major example. Within this we must consider the question of the relationship of the education system to capitalist modes of production – and here are involved all the questions of the organisation of education, status of knowledge, designation of knowledge, the subjects, curriculum structures, and so on, examination systems, vocational training. The other aspect refers to the problem of learning, socialisation, social skills, the acquisition of knowledge.

It has precisely been *Screen Education*'s concern, in establishing the 'new' subject areas of film/TV/media/images, to confront the implications of the subject as such in schools and in relation to classroom practice, and as a result the problems of 'progressive' versus 'traditional' teaching methods, the status of knowledge about those 'areas', the relationship of students to the content of that knowledge involving questions about 'relevancy' and 'popular culture' (hence this issue) which have all been raised in the journal. This has involved a concern for the position of the student to their class/cultural background, to the containing society and its culture and the relation to the teacher and their mode of insertion into the school system – that is, in the relations between 'their' and 'our' culture.

In this article I raise the problem of one dominant way of discussing popular culture and its relation the dominant society in order to indicate what I feel is an important discussion for *Screen Education* to engage in in the future. I would like to begin by referring to a passage about popular culture in Andrew Bethell's article in *Screen Education*, no. 15 (which Alan Lovell refers to in *Screen Education*, no. 17), where he states:

> A further problem emerges when, for instance, the teacher asks the kids to analyse and dissect the way pop music works, for this is threatening the sanctuary it provides in its aggression and alienation. The whole point about pop music is that it is against and outside all that school stands for; by bringing it into school and by asking the kids to subject *their* music to *our* analysis we destroy its most powerful asset. I believe you can make the same case against many aspects of film and media studies. When we ask kids to analyse films they enjoy frame by frame and help them to peel back the layers of mystification we are also intruding in an area which many of them see as their own.
>
> (*Screen Education*, no. 15, Summer 1975, p. 20)

The key words are obviously the ones that Bethell himself italicised but I would like to ask what is precisely meant if we talk about '*their* music' and '*our* analysis'? The interrelationship of production, distribution, broadcasting, advertising of pop records is such that it is difficult to talk about people's musical tastes without acknowledging the power of those organisations like the BBC to determine those tastes. And certainly if we are talking about 'popular culture' we are not concerned with minority or specialist programmes of experimental groups. We are talking about a music that is internationally marketed and cannot be considered to belong to, or emanate from any one specifiable culture. Obviously an organisation like the BBC (or even the whole set of interdependent organisations) doesn't exert a totally determining and controlling force; within a 'liberal democracy' there will always be sub-cultures and alternative structures operating within the dominant system (for example, West Indian music and clubs, although one must remember the extent to which Reggae, for example, has been recuperated by white culture), but to anyone interested in the concept of ideology, the structures and mode of operation of such organisations are of vital significance when referring to a concept such as 'popular culture' or when talking about '*their* music' in relation to youth culture.

Given the doubts I feel about the extent to which one can call children's culture their own I wish to argue that teachers are responsible not only for extending children's view of the world but also with challenging their perception of it as it has been constructed for them. The notion that the examination of the artefact reduces pleasure is not new and Andrew Bethell is correct to fear the analysis of '*their*' (working-class kids) artefacts with '*our*' criteria, for the alienation process apparent in the education system is something of which teachers should be constantly aware. But one should be equally aware of the dangers inherent in an overloose, benevolent liberalism that seeks to 'protect' one section of the population from the very skills whose absence allows that section to be exploited.

The very existence of the type of debate raised by Bethell's piece has an interesting history, one too long and complex to do anything but here offer a somewhat brief and schematic history. A line of development can be traced through such work as *Education and the Working Class*, *How Children Fail*, Bernstein's work of the mid–1960s, *Knowledge and Control, Tinker Tailor*.[1] Amidst the plethora of educational theories, practice and concern over the last decade, the role of the *Newsom Report* is clearly crucial. Firmly rooted in the philosophy of Peters, it concerned itself with fitting the rounded pegs of *Half our Future* into the

square holes of an established society. I find it depressingly predictable that recent accounts of 'progressive' versus 'traditional'
teaching methods, with whatever other confusions they contain,
seek largely to estimate the success of practice and evade rather
too easily the fundamental question of what constitutes knowledge. In addition the eclecticism inherent in the variety of
approaches and apparent philosophies of education at work in
secondary schools over this period ultimately did no more than
rework the same problems, without recognising the need to
change the nature of those problems by shifting the terms of
reference of the debate.

The debate of the 1960s reminded teachers that for a large
proportion of children, received schooling constituted a frustrating
and alienating experience swiftly shed and largely irrelevant to
the social and economic context in which they would find themselves once outside the classroom. The product of that debate was
a mass of activity calculated to de-escalate the rejection of schooling by children who demonstrated their frustrations in the only
way open to them – negatively – through disruption and truancy.
Thus the concept of 'relevance' was given a central place. This
resulted in an attempt to regroup traditional subjects (for example,
the synthesising of history and geography into social studies), and
the introduction of new areas of 'knowledge' in the form of various
aspects of popular culture, to redress the balance of a curriculum
regarded as too bourgeois and intimidating. Consciences about the
middle-class domination of the working-class child were similarly
salvaged with the introduction of schemes like the Humanities
Curriculum Project, which sought to neutralise the influence of
the teacher as agent in controlling the learning process. Class
distinctions were denied by an insistence on concepts like 'equality
of opportunity' and the development of comprehensive schools
(an anachronism within capitalist society – being demonstrated at
the moment by the various reports proving their 'failure') and the
belief in individual experience and its expression through creative
writing. That the efforts of 'progressive' teachers have manifestly
failed to deal with the frustrations and learning problems of
children or to transform an educational system that is clearly
designed to reinforce and reproduce the class structure of our
society, indicates the urgent need for a radical theory of education
and a radical analysis of the education system and its place within
British capitalism. Meanwhile the reactionary forces of our system
(for example, Rhodes Boyson, the *Black Paper* group) mount yet
another campaign for the reinstatement of 'traditional' methods
indicating the urgency of the need to expose the confusions apparent in the loose bandying of terms like 'traditional' and 'progress-

ive' and ask precisely what we mean by 'education', what its role
and what values are embodied in it. The confusions of the various
positions contained in the so-called progressive/traditional debate
are interestingly demonstrated in a contribution to the second of
the *Black Papers* by Arthur Pollard ('O and A level: Keeping up
the Standards'):

> Freedom without order is dangerous and ultimately brings con-
> fusion and breakdown. But free expression ('creativity') is all
> the vogue, not least in my own subject, English. (It has even
> reached the world of the sub-normal, I am told.) Heaven
> knows, most of the pupils have little enough to be creative
> about. They would be far better occupied with some good old-
> fashioned teaching of grammar, spelling and punctuation. They
> would then at least be able to express somebody else's ideas
> with some coherence and correctness.

It would be useful to indicate that freedom without order is not
so much dangerous as futile and what is of prime concern is, how
is order defined, who imposes it and for what purposes. The anti-
formalist school of the 'liberal' teacher stemmed not least from a
fear that the only future of a study of formal qualities was the
incantation of received values – 'somebody else's ideas'. It is
crucial to recognise that in a sense Pollard is correct (although he
is obviously arguing from a very different political position) – a
grasp of formal skills and the ability to analyse and deal with ideas
is fundamental to our children if they are to understand and
interrogate the structure and operation of the society in which
they live. It is the deliberate avoidance of the concept of indoctrination that has caused the liberal teacher to fail to analyse a
central problematic in the educational debate – that of the status
of knowledge. It may be useful at this point to deal with the
apparent, but deceptive, way in which knowledge has been
remoulded within secondary education. The attack on the organisation of traditional curricula was based on the way conventional
subject divisions were marked. Fundamentally, conventional subject divisions were seen as encouraging the failure of certain
groups of children for a number of reasons. Subject divisions were
seen as being both arbitrary and also as discouraging the potential
for looking across boundaries and perceiving the connections
between what were presented as a disparate set of facts, offered
by different teachers in different lessons. The result of these divisions is finite knowledge, each subject seen as possessing its own
discrete area of concern. In this way, information and ideas
become removed from any understanding of society, their poten-

tial relevance lost in the passive recounting and absorbing from teacher to student. Thus, the apparently significant regrouping of knowledge into areas such as 'integrated studies' and 'social studies' can be highly misleading if the linking of disciplines is no more than telling the facts with a slightly different emphasis. And Bethell's concern about bourgeois intervention into working-class culture becomes a very real one if its dynamism becomes petrified in the process of thoughtless institutionalism – more facts to be learnt in a very particular kind of way.

Of equal concern in the 'knowledge' debate is the interest expressed in the process of communication between teacher and student. Again, traditional methods were seen as encouraging the failure of certain groups of children for a number of reasons. The notion that 'knowledge' was being presented as such at all was seen as problematic because this implied that information was offered as *facts*, with all the seemingly insoluble problems of what we mean by facts, and how we determine their validity. The traditional process of teaching rested in 'facts' being presented in a purely didactic way, the teacher acting as an unquestionable authority, presenting to a silent class necessary information to be committed to memory. And it is this reserve of 'knowledge' which equips the pupils to enter society and find his or her place. The methods by which this ritual was enacted rested on the devices of dictation, directed reading, note-taking, copying the teacher – particularly in practical sessions and, of course, homework. All these methods appeared effective for the bright, the motivated, the middle-class child whose home background reflected the values of school. From the rest emerged a continuing pattern of failure, where even the authoritarian teacher seemed impotent in the face of pupil rejection. And hence the advent of the interdisciplinary approach, project work and the search for relevance – the attempt to locate areas of work nearer to the child's experience, the demise of formal teaching and the potential for dealing with areas of thought not immediately apparent in the experience of the child. For many, the role of teacher became replaced by the role of social worker, attempting to respond to the obviously untheorised problems of children rejecting not only a school system but, by extension, a containing culture. A central problem in all this is that by *seeming* to respect 'their' culture, the teacher is engaged, essentially, in pacifying their emotional frustrations and accepting a system which the teacher is unquestioningly helping to perpetuate.

The challenge to 'knowledge' inherent in all this activity has consisted largely of substituting one set of apparently more acceptable facts for another for which the cultural and political base remains the same. The question which has been consistently avoided is how to deal with the status and context of knowledge, how to encourage pupils to conceptualise and criticise. Such skills are rarely self-evident and to fear the imposition of 'our' bourgeois theories of criticism on to a reluctant proletarian mass, whilst certainly valid, also conveniently avoids the issue of ever offering a large section of the population the skills with which to engage in active debate. The problem is further exacerbated by the misuse of the work of sociologists like Michael Young *et al*. In the introduction to *Knowledge and Control*, Young states that he is engaged in finding a 'direction of research for a sociology of educational knowledge' and thus, by implication, not with the creation of a theory of knowledge. If 'knowledge' is made problematic and treated as an 'object of enquiry rather than a given' it avoids the problem that 'knowledge' will always exist and be transmitted. If Hobbes, Descartes and Marx conceived of 'knowledge' as a product of the informed understandings negotiated among members of an organised intellectual collectivity, then what we have to work towards is *not* the disintegration of the concept 'knowledge' but the creation of a theoretical base from which to produce a 'knowledge' that is not controlled and determined by, or supportive of, a small ruling élite.

The crucial importance, for teachers, of the construction of a carefully conceptualised body of film and television knowledge was clearly argued in a *Screen* editorial (vol. 16, no. 2, Summer 1975):

> However liberal forms of film education based on response may seem to be, however much the teacher attempts to withdraw in favour of his or her students' own personal responses, unless one assumes a complete aesthetic sense innately present in the child, the irrational character of the notion of response will mean that an unarguable taste is being transferred from teacher to student in a process dependent on the authority of the teacher and reinforcing that authority and the ideological formation that confirms it. The existence of some more objective knowledge of the subject about which the students are being taught does not of itself solve this problem; the presentation of a mathematical theorem can be followed by the rhetorical question 'It is so, is it not?' But at least this knowledge provides the student with another authority to turn against that of the teacher, the authority of its procedures of judgement and testing. In this perspective the lack of any established body of knowledge about the cinema puts the film teacher in an even more acute predicament than his colleague teaching literature. This was and is SEFT's

argument for the proposition that a society of film and TV teachers must contribute directly to the production and dissemination of knowledge in the area as well as dealing with the problems specific to teaching about film – hence *Screen* as well as *Screen Education*.

The central project for *Screen Education* at this time concerns a close examination of its field of study. Rather than engaging in a phenomenological study of the sociology of knowledge, we must attempt both a definition and the construction of the subject matter that constitutes Film and Media Studies. And given that we elect to operate within the received educational system, we have to engage with the current debate concerning what we should be teaching and how we should be teaching it without acceding too readily to its terms of reference. Our concern with areas of popular culture and what has been described as 'the consciousness industry' has less to do with the attempted seduction of recalcitrant pupils with lessons concerning topics which afford them immediate pleasure and offer the attraction of 'relevance' – though relevant such areas certainly are – and more to do with a desire to develop critical skills amongst pupils, to afford an understanding of the status of knowledge at any time and the social processes which work to construct and legitimise it. Perhaps the clearest division between the position argued here and that of traditional, subject-based teaching is that whilst the latter appears to accept certain areas of knowledge as intrinsically worthwhile, our concern to establish a body of knowledge for Film and Media studies involves a close consideration of what is revealed by that knowledge. And perhaps the clearest division between our educational polemic and that of the liberal progressive is that whilst we, too, are concerned to affirm the existence of working-class culture, however one chooses to define it, such a commitment should not deflect us from the concern to expose the domination of one class by another.

Acknowledgement

I would like to thank Elizabeth Cowie and Felicity Grant for assistance in the preparation of this article.

Note

1. B. Jackson and D. Marsden, *Education and the Working Class*, Harmondsworth: Penguin, 1966; see B. Bernstein, *Class, Codes and Control*, London: Routledge, 1971; John Holt, *How Children Fail*, Harmondsworth: Penguin 1969; Michael F. D. Young (ed.), *Knowledge and Control*, London: Collier-Macmillan, 1971; Nell Keddie (ed.), *Tinker Tailor – The Myth of Cultural Deprivation*, Harmondsworth: Penguin, 1973.

Chapter 13

Television Studies and Pedagogy*

Manuel Alvarado

I

Len Masterman's book *Teaching About Television*[1] is a key text for all Film and Television Studies teachers. It is a condensation of a long report written for the Independent Broadcasting Authority (IBA) as a result of a Schoolteacher Fellowship awarded in 1976 and it represents the first attempt to offer a book-length study of the problems of teaching about television – it also suggests a range of different ways of approaching many areas of television in the classroom (some of which have yet to receive serious critical attention). The book includes a list of useful periodicals and organisations, an outline of a Certificate of Secondary Education (CSE) Mode III syllabus for Television Studies (although this would require more contextualising material for it to be really useful) and a valuable select annotated bibliography. Many of the suggestions Masterman makes for classroom work are innovative, suggestive and valuable. This is the only book of the sort in the field and there is no doubt as to its value to both practising teachers and to teachers from other disciplines (for example, Arts, Humanities and Social Sciences) and relatively new to Media Studies.

The book is also a key text in that it marks an important stage in the development of television studies in this country. If one

Screen Education, no. 38, Spring 1981.

looks at the published literature concerned with film/television/
media analysis and the problems of how to develop the study of
those areas within an educational situation, it stands virtually
alone. There have, of course, been antecedents, for example,
Stuart Hall and Paddy Whannel's *The Popular Arts*, Jim Kitses
and Ann Mercer's *Talking About The Cinema*, A. J. P. Higgins's
Talking About Television, Stuart Hall, Roy Knight, Albert Hunt
and Alan Lovell's *Film Teaching*, Graham Murdock and Guy
Phelps's *Mass Media and the Secondary School* and Roy Knight's
Film and English Teaching being amongst the better known.[2]
(There are also a number of books which contain sections concerned with this area by people like Stan Cohen and Jock Young,
not to mention those which are primarily concerned with practical
work.[3])

But Masterman's book is separated from these in more ways
than one. First it marks a gap of almost ten years between these
earlier works and *Teaching About Television* – one book to represent the development of such work in the 1970s! Second, unlike
the studies listed above which describe classroom work but which
are often weak in suggesting possible classroom projects, *Teaching
About Television* goes much further by engaging in educational
debate and clearly confronts questions about teaching and learning
– it therefore represents the first attempt within the general area
of Media Studies to engage with the question of pedagogy. This
article is not designed to be a conventional review of Masterman's
book but instead takes issue with a number of arguments and
themes in *Teaching About Television* as a springboard for critically
exploring – in a preliminary way – some of the 'common-sense
wisdoms' which underpin everyday teaching practice.

II

The greater part of the book (Chapters 3–8) takes the form of
a structured series of proposals for classroom work whilst the
introductory and concluding sections (Chapters 1–2 and 9) deal
with the general importance of Television Studies, with educational theory and practice and with educational, cultural and
political principles. Much of what Masterman writes in the first
chapter is useful and, whilst some people might disagree with his
arguments about Film and Media Studies (and their separation
from each other and from Television Studies), they are persuas-
ively presented. Furthermore, his critique of the concept of discrimination might, with luck, conclude that boring debate (despite

Richard Hoggart's attempt to defend it in his review[4]). The following quotation indicates the kernel of his argument:

> The writers are glimpsing what every practising teacher knows: that the objective of arriving at value judgements closes up rather than opens out discussion; that it is too *easy* to obtain evaluative responses from pupils, and therefore too difficult to move beyond them; that as soon as a programme is evaluated as bad (or Processed) or good (or Authentic) then the impetus for further investigation disappears and is likely to be seen by pupils as an unnecessary 'pulling to pieces'; that evaluative responses force students to make individual stands and take personal positions, a more threatening procedure and ultimately one less productive of dialogue than say a systematic group exploration; that one of the keys to unlocking responses is to move students towards making statements which seem to them to have some validity, *irrespective* of their own personal feelings and tastes. If judgement can be suspended and mass-media material simply examined – *seen* more clearly – so that a wider and more complex range of meanings and values can become apparent, then discussion can flow and the necessity for discrimination, an irrelevance to the process of understanding, withers away.
>
> (pp. 19–20)

It is interesting to note that it was this section of the book which was extracted for publication in *The English Magazine*[5] for it would seem to indicate that this debate is still a contentious issue amongst English teachers.

The second chapter (upon which this article will primarily focus) is concerned explicitly with pedagogy and methodology and draws directly from work done in the areas of both television *and* education in the 1970s. From the former, Masterman adopts the notion of television messages as being *ideological* with the responsibility of the teacher being to demystify or decode these messages, that is, rescuing the 'real' from the more 'phenomenal' illusion of ideology: 'A central aim of television teaching is demystification – an examination of the rituals, conventions and practices through which a dominant ideology is disseminated via the medium' (p. 26). The problem here is that an 'ideology' is not an entity which can or cannot be disseminated through a medium, for that medium is itself a part of ideology – a medium is not and cannot be a transparent channel through which meanings pass. Furthermore, recent work which argues for the analysis of the 'rituals, conventions and practices' of the media institutions as

forms of institutional discourse clearly shows the more mechanical
term 'demystification', with its connotations of deliberate and
conspiratorial falsification, to be inadequate.

But the second chapter is mainly concerned with education and
early on the following statement about methodology is made:

> Perhaps the single most important development in educational
> thinking within the past decade has been the elevation of meth-
> odology within the learning process. Good primary school prac-
> tice has for years been based upon the premise that children
> learn most effectively by 'doing', but the full implications of the
> truism have not been clearly articulated until very recently even
> in relation to primary education, while secondary school prac-
> tice still continues to function as though methodology were a
> form of pill-sugaring, a way of making palatable what is really
> being learned, the subject content itself. Media education has
> been no exception to this general trend. Overwhelmingly, writ-
> ing on media studies has been concerned with questions of
> content.
>
> (p. 21)

One of the implications of the first sentence is the notion that one
can teach the same thing (the same 'content') in two or more
different ways. This amounts to suggesting that the modes of
transmitting 'knowledge' are transparent and questions of methodology thereby simply become the problem of how to select the
best teaching strategy. This notion of the possibility of knowledge
being transmitted through the transparent medium of methodology is clearly problematic, particularly to the Media Studies
teacher concerned to critique the analogous version of the conventional communications models.[6] (Perhaps this indicates one reason
why teachers of the media 'seem' to have been more interested
in 'content' than in 'methodology' as Masterman suggests – the
theoretical and critical debates about film and television analysis
with which media teachers are concerned are such as to make
traditional distinctions such as 'form and content', 'content' and
'approach', 'knowledge' and 'methodology' essentially meaningless.)

This is not to say, of course, that the term 'methodology' is
meaningless – there are clearly many different ways of constructing a learning situation. But it is to stress that the distinction
between 'knowledge' and 'methodology' represents only a conceptual difference – nevertheless it is one that in educational debate
often obscures the relationship between certain teaching strategies
and the area of work in which a group is engaged. Undoubtedly

there are different ways of teaching and learning – that is to say, a *range* of methodologies – but what is crucial to recognise is that these methodologies can only be realised as an indivisible part of what is being taught – and vice versa. Thus there can be no such thing as a methodology which is inherently better or more radical than any other. In a situation where a teacher views 'methodology' as itself a process of mediation which is non-transparent then the first problem that she or he faces is, 'What am I going to teach and why?' That much is unexceptional! However, the second problem to be addressed will not be, '*How* am I going to teach that area?' but rather, 'What are the possibilities and *implications* of the apparent diversity of ways of teaching about that area? – given the recognition that the area will be transformed and *different* as a result of that decision. The important recognition is that it is impossible to teach exactly the same thing in two different ways – there will always be differences. Thus in all teaching situations it is necessary to maintain a flexibility about modes of approach in the classroom situation. This position is being stressed because a dominant way of understanding 'progressivist' philosophies of education has resulted in the overlooking of those areas which require 'direct teaching', that is, those areas which require a direct informational input. This is not to suggest that 'direct' teaching represents a transparent method but simply that such a mode of presentation, with all its implications, constitutes an important and necessary part of a teacher's skills. This matter will be returned to in the next section of the article.

The second sentence quoted above provides a good example of a piece of conventional educational wisdom, that is, '. . . children learn most effectively by "doing" . . .'. Far from being a 'truism' it would seem that what children learn most effectively by *doing* things is largely going to be *how to do* things. Obviously at the primary levels such activities are important in teaching certain cognitive skills and in developing children's understanding of certain conceptual relationships. However, the same would not seem to hold true for the secondary age levels and above. There are clearly a whole range of theoretical and analytic problems which require mental activities far removed from physical ones (other than those concerned with mental discipline, for example, concentration). The final sentence of the above quotation states that people involved in media education have been primarily 'concerned with questions of content'. The problem here is not just the impossibility of practically separating 'content' from 'form' (alluded to earlier) but additionally the recognition that all 'knowledge' and 'experience' – two central terms in debates about educational 'content' – involve positions and stances. 'Knowledge' and 'experience' are never neutral or objective. Masterman recognises this:

> What the television teacher can do is to work outwards from the concrete television images themselves towards a recognition of and feeling for – if not always a precise understanding of – the institutional and industrial contexts within which they are encapsulated. The process begins with a reading of the total communication of the television image and an exploration of the values implicit within it, and ends with speculation upon four questions. Who is producing the images? For whose consumption? For what purposes? And what alternative images are thereby excluded? The teacher and his pupils must tread with care. Glib answers – the kind of crude determinism which equates commercialism with cynical audience manipulation for example – are easy; accurate ones more elusive and complex.
>
> (pp. 6–7)

Whilst one must beware of crude determinism it is not clear from what Masterman writes that the teacher would necessarily reach the important areas of the structures of broadcasting and the political economy of the media. An understanding of these areas does not require either a 'feeling' for them or 'speculation'. The four questions listed are important but the first three don't rely on conjecture at all and even the fourth can be dealt with more precisely than is suggested by the use of the word 'speculate'. The use of that word does seem to be particularly significant, however, for it reinforces a notion that exists implicitly throughout the book, that is, Masterman is always more interested to construct 'discussion' situations rather than 'direct teaching' ones.[7]

The questions will be independently and briefly considered. The first requires basic research which could be done by the teacher, a pupil, or a group of pupils, to be presented to the rest of the class. The second is more speculative if one attempted to answer it purely through textual analysis, that is, if one attempted to determine the 'intended' audience inscribed into the text. (Even this approach, however, requires the teacher to teach pupils sophisticated analytical concepts.) There are more direct and empirical approaches to answering this question which would involve (if it were possible) asking key television personnel. The third is similar to the second (that is, it could be treated speculatively or empirically although its vagueness makes it a little difficult to know precisely what would be involved in asking it). Overall, however, it is not so much a matter of deciding whether questions invite speculative responses or not but rather of questioning the implications of asking questions which invite such responses. One worrying implication, for example, would be that it can encourage vague, general and liberal responses – it encourages a situation where everybody has something to say and yet which leads to 'a kind of opinionated lethargy'.[8]

There is a quite separate strand to Masterman's discussion of 'methodology' in which important questions about 'competitiveness' and 'help' are invoked. For example, Masterman discusses Jules Henry and the case of Boris. Henry explains how Boris's failure at the blackboard was the source for another child – Peggy – to succeed. Henry writes:

> To a Zuni, Hopi or Dakota Indian, Peggy's performance would seem cruel beyond belief, for competition, the wringing of success from somebody's failure, is a form of torture foreign to these non-competitive cultures.
>
> (p. 22)

Henry clearly implies that western culture is 'competitive' – a somewhat vague and generalised notion but nevertheless something that can be recognised in a range of social practices and situations – particularly those of the school. The school system is organised on the basis of encouraging personal development and individual achievement with an emphasis being placed on the importance of the rights of the individual – 'competitiveness' is never conceived of in terms of group work or struggle. And, despite the advances progressivist teachers have made in terms of children being treated more humanely and with greater respect, individualist notions are still being reinforced. Henry's rejection of 'competitiveness' is wrong because it is necessary to transform the notion not simply to reject it. Whilst it would be a crude and over-brutal response to the statement quoted above to say 'yes, and look what happened to the Zuni, Hopi and Dakota Indian', it is necessary to recognise that the concept of 'competitiveness' is necessary to the process of *successful* struggle and it is also important to recognise that there are many aspects of our society which need to be struggled against. It is this general rejection of the notion of 'competitiveness' that indicates one reason why Masterman takes such an antagonistic position to examinations. He begins with a statement with which one would totally agree: 'The purpose of a teacher's comments should be to help his pupils' learning and not to judge, rank and discriminate between them' (p. 30), but then continues:

> Examinations exist to divide and discriminate between people; they create and institutionalise failure; important qualities that

ought to be at the centre of any worthwhile education – self-understanding, aesthetic and social sensitivity, intellectual curiosity and creativity – get pushed to the fringes because they are not conventionally examinable and wither away when they are measured not in personal terms, but against other people's or a mythical norm.

Examinations are divisive and do encourage discrimination between people individually but they also divide and discriminate groups or classes of people. It is the crucial position the examination system occupies within the educational apparatus which needs to be analysed in order to reveal more clearly the regulatory function examinations fulfill in terms of the reproduction of a work-force with diversified skills.[9] To look at examinations in these terms would mean not simply rejecting them because of the individual harm they do (Masterman naïvely suggests that individual schools could opt out of the examination system) but rather analysing more precisely the complex of relations that exist between the state, the education apparatus and the social formation.

This point is made because it relates to what is possibly the central weakness of Masterman's book, which is the lack of interest (verging on antagonism) expressed in developing work on the structures of broadcasting and the political economy of the media – an absence noted by Graham Murdock in his short review of the book.[10] What in 'academic' terms is an omission is educationally and politically a very serious lack. It is the first chapter which contains the crucial statement:

> All of the arguments in favour of studying the media collectively stem from a prior commitment to uncover for students either the institutional bases or the structures of ownership and control of the media. I have a great deal of sympathy for these commitments but there are great difficulties in urging their centrality to the study of the media *in schools*. The major problem lies in the distinct differences which are likely to exist between what is considered important and interesting by the teacher, and what is of interest to his [sic] pupils.
>
> (p. 5)

From what he writes in the book it is far from clear why Masterman believes what he states here, for the problem presented is unsatisfactorily answered. If a teacher works on the basis of what is of interest to his or her pupils it immediately poses the difficulty of how to get beyond talking about (let alone teaching about) students' *experiences*. (Experience is clearly a key concept which will be returned to in the next section.) Furthermore, by implication, an area for work that might be central at a further level than the secondary school is considered too difficult to handle with younger people. Unfortunately this essentially patronising position is all too familiar amongst teachers. Masterman continues:

> Like most articulate people who don't possess much of it, teachers and lecturers tend to be fascinated and even preoccupied with questions of power and control. It is not, by and large, a preoccupation which is likely to be shared by many of their pupils. And even assuming that pupils are able to see its significance there is a genuine difficulty in relating questions of organisational structures or patterns of control to the direct experience of the pupil. Pupils buy records of course; they watch television, read magazines and some of them go to the pictures. Connections can be made and investigations can even be undertaken of who owns the local papers, cinemas, bingo halls and the like, but the fact remains that media *products*, because they are immediate, concrete and involving are more intrinsically interesting to most pupils than media structures which are necessarily covert and abstract.

Ignoring the patronising tone of the first sentence it would be easy to make an equally unsubstantiated assertion, that is, that in fact the situation is exactly the opposite. I would suggest that it is precisely questions about power and control which are ignored by most teachers and that it is because the power and influence of, for example, the multinational corporations are not felt or experienced directly, that they are not analysed in schools. It is not enough to analyse the superstructural levels of the media – TV ideology – for it is also necessary to teach about the material and economic bases of the television institutions as it is necessary to teach about the bases of the other state apparatuses.[11] In addition, media structures are no more covert and abstract than television ideology. Overall, it would seem that Masterman is allowing what he would term 'methodology' to determine what is being taught. In believing that it is possible to think of 'methodology' as a separate concept to 'content' he is able to ignore this area of work because it is so information-laden – the only way of presenting it would be directly, which is a procedure of which he clearly disapproves.

III

How can one take further the key notions of 'experience', 'methodology' and 'institutional structures'?

Experience

The problem of 'experience' is central to many intellectual debates whether they be philosophical, political, cultural, or educational.[12] In being critical of the concept one is not denying the validity and importance of experience – that would obviously be an extremely naïve thing to do. The questions are: 'How do we make sense of our experiences', and 'How do we make them useful?' In order to respond one needs to rethink the concept of experience theoretically! Why? First, how do we distinguish between 'good' and 'bad' experiences and what does that mean (for example, how does a teacher deal with a situation where a pupil enjoys experiences which involve other people suffering?)? Second, personal and emotional responses to empirical situations must always be limited and restricted and therefore are unlikely to offer the bases necessary for the construction of analytic and conceptual tools. Third, personal experience does not necessarily teach one very much about matters ideological, or about intellectual, theoretical or conceptual problems.

Many progressivist notions about teaching are theoretically related to a phenomenological position and practically based on a notion of the importance of expressing personal experiences. The problem is, for example, an experience of racism doesn't necessarily help one to understand, explain or fight it – and it is vital that people learn how to analyse, understand and explain in order to fight things of which they have no personal experience. Boys can have no personal experience of being girls and therefore cannot write about sexism through experience – they have to learn about and confront the problem of a sexist society analytically (as do girls, but that is a different discussion). Thus it is necessary to construct a pedagogy that precisely does not *depend* upon personal experience and, in certain ways, critiques it.

Methodology

As Masterman points out, 'methodology' has been the crux of much debate amongst teachers and educationalists. 'Methodology' seemed to offer the possibility of addressing the problem of how to present a subject area to a class of pupils more precisely and has, in certain books, been placed as an area of academic study in its own right. On the other hand it has been derided by teachers prone to making statements such as 'nothing works with 4G anyway'. Ultimately, in most debates, teaching is treated as an intensely practical activity about which it is virtually useless to theorise. In such a context methodology is what is studied and discussed during teacher-training only to be thrown out of the window when a person first takes up employment as a qualified teacher. Ironically, the result of this attitude is that by default 'methodology' achieves the status of 'theory'. Furthermore, it would seem that we have reached the stage in educational debate where 'methodology' has come to mean anything other than *direct teaching*. By 'direct teaching' I refer to those situations where a teacher talks/dictates/reads to a silent class – a situation which in current discussion is considered to be at best amethodological or, at worst, authoritarian, reactionary and traditional. (And 'authoritarian' is a popular word of abuse used far too freely and loosely when what is required is the drawing of careful and precise distinctions between the authoritarian teacher and the teacher as authority, for example.)

It is not a matter of returning to traditional 'methods', for they were not only bad but often damaging. Rather, it is a matter of arguing that the political and ideological shifts undertaken by 'progressivists' have emphasised questions of 'method' at the expense of a concern with *what* was being taught. That is to say, it was crucially necessary to critique and replace educational thinking and practices as dominantly and traditionally organised up to the late 1960s but ultimately what was changed were largely classroom structures and procedures and the nature of pupil/teacher relationships. The new 'progressive' developments in teaching didn't mean, for example, that teachers began teaching about the economic and political factors that underpinned historical events like the Crusades as opposed to the conventional 'wisdom' about those events, that is, that they represented a Holy War.[13] What is being argued is that the conventional wisdom of education needs to be interrogated, uncovered and critiqued as well as some of the classroom practices of traditional education, but that also, in reconstructing the educational processes of the classroom, *all* modes of address need to be deployed and exploited. I suspect that no 'progressivist' would disagree with the unexceptional statement that types of presentation and activity in the classroom should be varied in order to maintain pupil interest. The point is however, that it is necessary to keep changing the activity not just (or even) to maintain interest but because one is teaching different types of things within each kind of activity. I also suspect that in the range of activities many teachers offer, 'direct teaching' is often overlooked and that 'progressivists' would certainly stop short of using dictation in a lesson!

Institutional structures

Teaching about the film industry and about the structures of broadcasting has historically been recognised as an important area of work within Film/TV/Media Studies courses. The rationale, at one level, has been clear, that is, the mass media represent major institutions and industries and therefore should be taught about. The implications of work in this area do not, however, seem to have filtered through to other subject areas in the curriculum. For example, how many English teachers include in their syllabuses (in the teaching of all age groups) work on the production, circulation and reading of texts and on the organisation, ownership and interrelationships of the various publishing houses? Or do work on book advertising and the retail distribution system? Or on copyright law and the interrelationship between authorship, ownership and copyright?

Many teachers would no doubt respond to these questions by arguing that children would not be interested and would find the researching for, or provision of, such information boring. One response which can be made is to say that to have access to a publishing house is to have access to a certain power and, what is more, children know that they, in the main, don't enjoy such privilege. The questions then are, why not? who does? how? and why? In my experience, these are questions which interest children greatly. Another response one could make would be to question the notion of 'boredom' and the idea that it can define what work is done, what ground covered. The implication is that children are only prepared to engage in what provides fairly immediate gratifications, which is also fairly unlikely to have any relation to what might be considered hard work. The problem is that if one doesn't teach about the areas indicated above, it would seem to be impossible to introduce key concepts such as 'cultural hegemony' – key because without it it is unlikely that many children are going to recognise the importance and significance of engaging in cultural struggle in order that, for example, working-class/black/female/children's texts are distributed more widely and influentially.

Furthermore, is such work so boring? Is it boring to know why some people struggled to establish the 'alternative' bookshops which now exist across the country (like the Walter Rodney Bookshop, Sisterwrite, Centreprise)? Is it boring to know why 'alternative' publishing houses were similarly established (like Bogle L'Ouverture, Women's Press, Readers and Writers)? Is it boring to think through the implications of the policies of the major publishing houses in relation to the hegemonic maintenance of a particular cultural heritage – one that is fed and reinforced by university English departments, book reviewers in the press, on radio and television and by a bookshop chain like W. H. Smith? Is it boring to try to understand why certain authors and certain topics are extensively published and distributed and others hardly at all? Is it boring to analyse the inadequacy of the conventional response to these questions – which is that publishers and booksellers are merely responding to public demand? And finally, suppose that one accepted that such work was inherently boring. Why should work be easy, why do we kid 'kids' that they only need to do the pleasant and easy things at school when we know that life is unlikely to be easy for them when they leave?

An important point here, however, is that if children do find such work boring it may be because the teacher has not located and contexted the material in the most pertinent way. If information about institutional structures is simply provided as a list of 'facts', then pupils will correctly find such information irrelevant – but, if such information is placed within the broader context of children understanding more fully about *our* social formation, about *their* position within it and about how it might be otherwise then they are likely to be much more interested than Len Masterman would seem to believe. To ignore this area of work is implicitly to keep pupils in a position of ignorance, and ignorance is a form of powerlessness. If this seems merely a truism, I will relate a chilling anecdote. Recently, an Inner London teacher showed a racially mixed class of 15/16 year-old boys and girls Programme 8, 'Show Business', from the first series of *Viewpoint*. (This is the episode that both helped to get the series withdrawn[14] and which also prompted Masterman to write the following footnote – 'My own experience of the excellent *Viewpoint* series, for example, was that the programme dealing specifically with the business side of the media was one of the least popular with pupils'.) One of the group was a white boy who openly declared his National Front membership and whose response to the programme was that he knew all that stuff anyway but that what the programme didn't say was that it was all a Jewish conspiracy for it was they who controlled the media. The point is that he possessed a 'knowledge' – an odious and racist knowledge – and that it represented material which he could martial and use in an argument. In order to combat that sort of response a teacher obviously needs to be well-prepared and knowledgeable but he or she also needs to be prepared to respond *directly* and not simply to suggest that the group has a discussion of that viewpoint.

It is not being suggested that the direct offering of information will necessarily change this Fascist view of the world which is often clung to emotionally, for '. . . students never take the teacher's messages straight but always submit them to resistances and transformations'.[15] Recognising the social relations in the classroom and the ideologies students bring with them to the classroom, we have to be aware that there can be no perfect pedagogy. However, it is important to recognise that the process of teaching and learning should always be a struggle – and that the classroom is recognised as being a central, but not the only, site for that struggle – and that the provision of information is part of that struggle. Furthermore, whilst that provision won't necessarily change the attitudes of the young Fascist mentioned above, it might, at the very least, provide useful information for the other members of the group who work with him. There is one final point I will make about media teaching in the area of institutional structures. If we, as teachers, avoid teaching about this area, who will teach it and to whom? Unless one believes in the early demise of the BBC, the IBA and the ITV and ILR (Independent Local Radio) companies, then their maintenance will depend upon continuing recruitment *and* a public that accepts them as they are. If they are ever to change then a critical scrutiny of their structures and financing as well as of their programmes and practices will be required. Although this piece has concentrated upon teaching about the structures of broadcasting there are obviously many significant content areas with which a critical pedagogy must deal and which involve the consideration of abstract concepts, theoretical models and modes of discourse.

IV

I will conclude this article by making two general points about pedagogy. Firstly, it should be axiomatic that a teacher be absolutely clear with a class about what the proposed areas of work will be and how they intend to cover those areas. For example, it is fundamental that a teacher present to a class what work needs to be covered that year at the beginning of, and throughout, the year. In my experience so few children seem to have a sense of the total structure of the work in which they are engaged or to really understand why they are doing it. (Needless to say, if a teacher has problems justifying what he or she is doing then maybe he or she should be doing something else.) My response to the anticipated protest – ah yes, but then the teacher is totally determining what the class will do and is not allowing the children a say in what is important to them – will constitute my second general point.

There should always be two major strands running through every classroom situation: (1) a recognition of the power and importance of the structures of the present social formation and a recognition of the need for all people to work within those structures successfully, and (2) a recognition of the importance and *potential* power of all forms of oppositional knowledge and groupings. Working-class or West Indian cultures and language, for example, are important and must not be denied *but* they don't, as yet, provide anything more than forms of resistance – they don't provide what is necessary to contest and transform the dominant cultural, social, economic, political and linguistic formations which therefore have to be analysed, studied and understood. Thus, in the preparation for examinations, for example, it is crucially important that pupils learn how to pass them whatever the teacher feels about the intrinsic value of the questions and also that the pupils know why it is important. If, say, GCE English papers require debates about a text like *Othello*, then that should not only be taught, but could also be done relatively economically, that is, directly. To deal with the historical conjuncture within which the play was written and first performed, to discuss the question of race in the Elizabethan social formation and to deal with the ideological and political problems of presenting it in the conjuncture which is Britain in 1981 is more important intellectually and should provide the focus for classroom work, *but* only if dealt with in tandem with what is going to be more directly important for the exam. I would suggest that a much better and harder working relationship is likely to be established between teacher and pupils if this duality is made explicit, discussed, kept in tension and used analytically.

Notes

1. Len Masterman, *Teaching About Television*, London; Macmillan, 1980.

2. Stuart Hall and Paddy Whannel, *The Popular Arts*, London: Hutchinson, 1964; Stuart Hall, Roy Knight, Albert Hunt and Alan Lovell, *Film Teaching*, London: British Film Institute, 1964; Jim Kitses and Ann Mercer, *Talking About The Cinema*, London: BFI, 1966; A. J. P. Higgins, *Talking About Television*, London: BFI, 1966;

Graham Murdock and Guy Phelps, *Mass Media and the Secondary School*, London: Macmillan, 1972; Roy Knight, *Film and English Teaching*, London: BFI/Hutchinson, 1972.

3. Stan Cohen and Jock Young, *The Manufacture of News*, Constable, 1972. The books I am referring to about practical work include Douglas Lowndes, *Film Making in Schools*, London: Batsford, 1968; Robert Ferguson, *Group Film Making*; London: Studio Vista, 1969; Keith Kennedy, *Film in Teaching*, London: Batsford, 1972.

4. Richard Hoggart, 'Reading the Instructions on the Box', *Guardian*, 15 April 1980.

5. Len Masterman, 'Appreciation and Discrimination', *The English Magazine*, no. 5, Autumn 1980.

6. For example, Harold D. Lasswell, 'The Structure and Function of Communications', in Lyman Bryson (ed.), *The Communication of Ideas*, New York: Cooper Square Publications, 1948; Claude Shannon and Warren Weaver, *Mathematical Theory of Communications*, Champaign: University of Illinois Press, 1949; David. K. Berlo, *The Process of Communication*, New York: Holt. Rinehart & Winston, 1960.

7. For a critique of this position see Bob Ferguson, 'Media Education – Discussion or Analysis'. *Screen Education*, no. 25, Winter 1977/78.

8. See Bob Ferguson. 'Liberal Education, Media Studies and the Concept of Action'. *Screen Education*, no. 22, Spring 1977.

9. See James Donald. 'Examinations and Strategies', *Screen Education*, no. 26. Spring 1978; also, for different but related arguments see Geoff Whitty, 'Teachers and Examiners', in Geoff Whitty and Michael Young (eds) *Explorations in the Politics of School Knowledge*, Driffield: Nafferton, 1976, and Samuel Bowles and Herbert Gintis, *Schooling in Capitalist America*, London: Routledge & Kegan Paul, 1976.

10. Graham Murdock, book review in the sociology section of *British Book News*, 1980.

11. Louis Althusser, 'Ideology and Ideological State Apparatuses', in *Lenin and Philosophy and Other Essays*, London: New Left Books, 1971.

12. Of particular interest here is Perry Anderson's recent and invaluable discussion of the term in his *Arguments Within English Marxism*, London: New Left Books, 1980, pp. 26–9.

13. For a critique of 'progressivism' in primary education see Rachel Sharpe and Anthony Green, *Education and Social Control*, London: Routledge & Kegan Paul, 1975.

14. See 'The Viewpoint Controversy', *Screen Education*, no. 19, Summer 1976.

15. Editorial in *Screen Education*, no. 34, Spring 1980, discussing Richard Johnson's important article 'Cultural Studies and Educational Practice' in that issue.

Chapter 14

Sex, Power and Pedagogy*

Valerie Walkerdine

In this paper I want to address certain issues about the position of girls and women within the education system with reference to an examination of some observations collected in two nursery schools.[1] I shall draw out certain contradictions for traditional Marxist approaches to the relations of power within educational institutions. One such view is that education as a bourgeois institution places teachers in a position of power from which they can oppress children who are institutionally powerless. To somewhat overstate the case, the teacher, powerful in a bourgeois educational institution, is in a position to oppress children whose resistance to that power, like all resistance, is understood as ultimately progressive rather than contradictory. Children's movements have tended to understand resistance in terms of 'rights' or 'liberation'. Similarly, certain feminist accounts have used the psychological concepts of 'role' and 'stereotype' to understand women and girls as unitary subjects whose economic dependence, powerlessness and physical weakness is reflected in their production as 'passive', 'weak', and 'dependent' individuals. While such accounts have been extremely important in helping to develop Marxist and feminist practices, I want to pinpoint some of the reasons why such analyses might not be as helpful as we might previously have supposed in understanding the phenomena presented in this paper. I want to show, using examples from

* *Screen Education*, no. 38, Spring 1981.

classroom practice, that in both the case of female teachers and of small girls, that they are not unitary subjects uniquely positioned, but produced as a nexus of subjectivities, in relations of power which are constantly shifting, rendering them at one moment powerful and at another powerless.[2]

Additionally, I want to argue that while an understanding of resistance is clearly important, we cannot read every resistance as having revolutionary effects; sometimes resistances have 'reactionary' effects. I want to argue that resistance is not just struggle against the oppression of a static power (and therefore potentially revolutionary simply because it is a struggle against the monolith) but that relations of power and resistance are continually reproduced, in continual struggle and constantly shifting.

An Example of Boys' Resistance in a Nursery School

The following interchange between teacher and children comes from a series of recordings which were made in a nursery school. The teacher who is a woman about 30 is seated with a group of children aged 3 and 4 around a table. The children are making constructions from Lego; we are concerned here with the actions of three children: a 3-year-old girl, Annie, and two 4-year-old boys, Sean and Terry. The teacher's name is Miss Baxter.

The sequence begins when Annie takes a piece of Lego to add on to a construction that she is building. Terry tries to take it away from her to use himself and she resists. He says:

> Terry: You're a stupid cunt, Annie.

The teacher tells him to stop and Sean tries to mess-up another child's construction. The teacher tells him to stop. Then Sean says:

> Sean: Get out of it Miss Baxter paxter.
> Terry: Get out of it knickers Miss Baxter.
> Sean: Get out of it Miss Baxter paxter.
> Terry: Get out of it Miss Baxter the knickers paxter knickers, bum.
> Sean: Knickers, shit, bum.
> Miss B: Sean, that's enough, you're being silly.
> Sean: Miss Baxter, knickers, show your knickers.
> Terry: Miss Baxter, show your bum off.
> (they giggle)

Miss B:	I think you're being very silly.
Terry:	Shit Miss Baxter, shit Miss Baxter.
Sean:	Miss Baxter, show your knickers your bum off.
Sean:	Take all your clothes off, your bra off.
Terry:	Yeah, and take your bum off, take your wee-wee off, take your clothes off, your mouth off.
Sean:	Take your teeth out, take your head off, take your hair off, take your bum off. Miss Baxter the paxter knickers taxter.
Miss B:	Sean, go and find something else to do please.

Various people on reading this transcript have commented that they are surprised and shocked to find such young children not only making explicit sexual references, but having so much power over the teacher. What is this power and how is it produced? Here it is the case that, although the teacher has an institutional position, she is not uniquely a teacher, nor are the boys *just* small boys. Particular individuals are produced as subjects *differently* within a variety of discursive practices. A particular individual has the potential to be 'read' within a variety of discourses. We cannot say that the limit of the variety is determined in any direct or simple sense by the economic.[3] However, the 'materiality' of the individual does have particular effects, though those effects are not solely determined by that materiality, but by the discourse in which it is 'read'. In this case the teacher is a woman and while that itself is crucial, it is only because of the ways in which 'woman' signifies that we can understand the specific nature of the struggle.[4] The resistance of the boys to her can be understood in terms both of their assertion of their difference from her and their seizing of power through constituting her as the powerless object of sexist discourse. Although they are not physically grown men they can take the positions of men through language and in doing so gain power which has material effects. Their power is gained by refusing to be constituted as the powerless objects in *her* discourse and recasting her as the powerless object of *theirs*. In their discourse she is constituted as 'woman as sex-object' and as that object she is rendered as the powerless object of their oppression. Of course, she has not in a sense ceased to be a teacher, but what is important is that she has ceased to *signify* as one: she has been made to signify as the powerless object of male sexual discourse. The boys' resistance takes the form of a seizure of power in discourse such that despite their institutional positions they achieve power in this instance.

It does not seem reasonable to assert a monolithic and ahistorical view of sexism and oppression in which the boys are *simply* either to be understood as powerless children oppressed by the control of an oppressive bourgeois educational institution or *simply* as the perpetrators of patriarchal social relations. The important word here is simply. For, indeed they have the potential to be produced as subjects/objects in *both* discourses, but inherent in the discursive positionings are different positions of power. Individuals, constituted as subjects and objects within a particular framework are produced by that process into relations of power. An individual can become powerful or powerless depending on the terms in which her/his subjectivity is constituted. The importance of this argument is in the way that we can assert that relations of power are not invested in unitary individuals in any way which is solely or essentially derived from their material and institutional position. This should not be taken as implying that the material or economic has no importance or force. However, the material and economic do not appear to be acting as unique and linear causes of the production of power relations in this example. The gender and the ages of the participants clearly have major effects which serve to displace other 'variables'. (The two boys are not yet capable of physically assaulting the teacher, but it may be only a matter of time.) Since the boys are both children and male, and the teacher is both teacher and female they can enter as subjects into a variety of discourses, some of which render them powerful and some of which render them powerless. It is important to note the way in which the boys refer to the teacher and to the 3-year-old girl, Annie, in the same terms. They call Annie a 'cunt'. In this way they bring the teacher down to size: she and a small girl are in discourse but the same thing – sex objects. The power of their discourse is one which renders all females, typifications of the same qualities, in this case possessors of tits, bums and cunts. However, it is important that this argument is not just a concern for theoretical distinctions. The issue which I have raised would appear to have important consequences for practice. In this example we can understand the boys as both subjects in patriarchal discourse perpetrating patriarchal oppression upon their teacher and at the same time children oppressed/controlled by the authority of the teacher. Are we then to choose as our course of action, one which wishes to potentially liberate them from their oppression,[5] or are they to be suppressed as sexist perpetrators of a patriarchal order?

The Pedagogic Discourse of the Teacher

An important effect of this power struggle between the teacher and children is the way in which the teacher interprets the children's discourse so as to lessen its oppressive effect upon her, and to justify her failure to stop them as correct. To understand this we have to be aware of the psychological and pedagogic terms in which she understands herself as teacher and the children as learners. In particular, what concerns us here is the discourse on childhood sexuality. It was not by accident that the teacher waited so long to stop the children, nor that when she did so it was with a fairly gentle rebuke which did not take issue with the content of their talk.

When I discussed the incident with her later she explained what had happened in the following way:

> The kind of expressions are quite normal for this age . . . As long as they're not being too silly or bothering anybody, it's just natural and should be left . . . coming out with that kind of expression is very natural.

How does she come to 'read' the children's actions as a harmless expression of a sexuality which is normal and natural? What are the main strands characterising childhood sexuality? To understand that question it is necessary to examine the formation of those discourses and practices which inform and constitute 'progressive education'. We can understand the formation of the practices which make up progressive education in terms both of the necessity to reformulate a pedagogy which produced individuals who were controlled but not regimented. We can understand the insertion of psychoanalytic discourse as a way of understanding those concerns which were around at the time of the formation of the new education, that is in the second two decades of this century.

Take, for example, the following remarks made by Margaret Lowenfeld in 1935 at the end of a book on the educational importance of play:[6]

> Play is to a child, therefore, work, thought, art and relaxation, and cannot be pressed into any single formula. It expresses a child's relation to himself and his environment, and, without adequate opportunity for play, normal and satisfactory emotional development is not possible . . . Emotional satisfactions, which the mind has missed at the period to which they properly belong, do not present themselves later in the same

form. The forces of destruction, aggression and hostile emotion, which form so powerful an element for good or evil in the human character, can display themselves fully in the play of childhood, and become through this expression integrated into the controlled and conscious personality. Forces unrealised in childhood remain as an inner drive, for ever seeking outlets, and lead men to express them not any longer in play, since this is regarded as an activity in childhood, but in industrial competition, anarchy and war.

We can see in the end of this quotation the specific link made between the capitalist ethic, struggles and war, and the stifling of expression of emotion. The rise of totalitarianism (of the left and right) was attributed very clearly to the failure of current education and child-rearing to produce the right kind of individuals. It was felt that over-regimentation had produced the phenomenon described at the time as 'Prussianism'.[7] Psychoanalysis understood this failure as the result of repression. In relation to this a new discursive formation was produced, 'scientific pedagogy', based on a view of the production of control through self-control and self-regulation. The pedagogy took the form of the monitoring of the form and structure of development and of steering it along the right lines by provision of the right environment. Clearly, this is not the place to expand on the details of this pedagogy, but it is important here to understand the way in which it served to produce the terms and categories which provide the teacher's understanding of her experience. Central to the pedagogy was the unfolding of child development, understood as natural, and as a central part of this, the *expression* rather than *repression* of natural childhood sexuality.[8] And, of course, according to the Freudian discourse this natural sexuality was essentially male.

The practice of the teacher here conforms to this 'scientific pedagogy'. While some activities are provided for the children, they are allowed to 'choose'. They are never coerced into doing something that they do not want to do, nor rarely taken away from activities in which they are engaged. They are natural normal children who should be left alone to develop at their own pace. This discursive formation, which constitutes the pedagogy and the experience of this teacher should be seen as neither 'knowledge' in her control, with which she can consciously oppress the children, nor a transparent 'experience' which will give the children access to knowledge which is liberating because they have produced it themselves. The knowledge is not inserted in the context of the school and set to work in the interests of the teachers to control the children. Conversely, its purpose is to

produce better control through self-control and that ironically is
what helps to produce the space in the practice for the children
to be powerful. In this situation, the children have the power to
define what they do within the limits of the pedagogy, that is,
they can *choose* and they cannot be stopped in their choosing.
The children recognise quickly that the uttering of the magic
words 'I don't want to' quickly produces a situation in which they
can control the flow of events. Thus the very discourse helps to
produce the children as powerful. The space is already there for
their resistance. Similarly, the discourse of the naturalness of male
sexuality to be expressed not repressed produces and facilitates
in the teacher, collusion in her own oppression. Since, if she reads
actions as normal and natural, and suppression of those actions
as harmful, she is forced into a no-choice situation. She cannot
but allow them to continue, and she must render as harmless their
power over her. The very practice which is supposed to liberate
('progressive education') produces the possibility of this discursive
power in the children. There is no counter discourse and the
children know it.

The pedagogy of 'choice' is a tool in the production of the
rational ideal. Rationality, rational choice and decision-making is
the ideal, the goal of the pedagogy. It assumes (following Piaget
and many others) that this rational individual can be produced by
leaving children alone to 'grow out of' their base animal sexuality,
their aggression, that is, the non-rational. Left alone this will be
worked out and not pushed down to fester in the unconscious.
Through this process children will come to act in a civilised
manner. They will become agents responsible for their own
actions, whose interactions are based on rationality alone, having
left the irrational behind them. Thus education serves to produce
them as unitary subjects making logical and rational choices.

But, as we have witnessed, this rational ideal is doomed to
failure from the beginning, in both its assertion of rationality and
its picture of the unitary subject. What particularly concerns us
here is that the very discourse aimed to set the children free from
over-regulation permits any activity as a natural expression of
something: something 'better out than in'. It is in this sense that
the children, as children, in the terms of 'progressive education'
cannot be understood as produced in discourses which have
oppressive effects: they simply have experiences, and experiences
are transparent, the context incidental. Leaving the children alone
to their own devices means that they will reproduce those positions in those discourses with which they are familiar, and are
thus not open to scrutiny and transformation. Neither the children
nor the teacher can change without the production of different

discourses in which to read their actions, and to produce different actions and different subjectivities. Thus we can understand the complexity of the production of the social relations in this small exchange between teacher and children. The individuals in this exchange do not appear to be produced in some static and unitary reflections of social forces. Neither are they given power as a simple function of their institutional position. The discursive forces which shape the pedagogy of the classroom produce a space which promotes the power of children and asserts the naturalness and harmlessness of their actions. They show us how the teacher is rendered powerless to resist the power of the boys and how she fails to understand this as an example of their oppression of her: we can only so understand it with the superimposition of a feminist discourse. We can understand that the individuals are not produced as unitary subjects but as a nexus of contradictory subjectivities. These contradictions are produced by the way in which the 'material' of the individual provides the potential to be the subject and object of a variety of discourses which produce that individual as sometimes powerful and sometimes powerless. There is in this model neither the unitary rational subject of progressivism who sloughs off the irrational, neither is the individual a 'real' and essential kernel of phenomenological Marxism, whose outer skins are just a series of roles which can be cast off to reveal the true and revolutionary self.

Girls and Boys in the Classroom

I want to extend this analysis to examine more interactions involving small boys, but this time in play with girls in the classroom. We can apply the kind of model that I have signalled above to understand the production of girls as subjects within pedagogic practices. Sex-role socialisation accounts of the reproduction of girls understand them as produced as a reflection of traditional female sex roles. The economic dependence and oppression of women will produce girls whose personalities are passive and dependent, dominated and not dominant. Yet as I have asserted earlier, individuals are powerless or powerful depending upon which discursive practice they enter as subject. Recent work within the women's movement[9] has pointed out that the oppression of women is not unitary, and that different discursive practices have different and often contradictory histories. This means that in some practices women are relatively powerful, for example, in those practices in which they signify as mothers (for example, in custody cases). These practices are reproduced by the children in their play in the nursery classroom. This means that the girls are not always passive and dependent, just as their mothers are not, but are constantly struggling with the boys to define their play and to redefine it into discursive practices in which they can be powerful. To understand the power and resistance in the play of children we have to understand those practices that they are recreating in their play. These help to produce the children both as recreating the, often reactionary, discourses with which they are familiar, but also serve to constitute them as a multiplicity of contradictory positions of power and resistance.

Let us examine one small piece of play taken from the same classroom as before. This time, the children are playing hospitals. They have been given all the necessary equipment by a nursery nurse, and she has seen to it that the boys get the doctors' uniforms and the girls the nurses'. The nursery nurse constantly helps to maintain the power of the doctors over the nurses by constantly asking the nurses to 'help' the doctors. One girl, Jane, changes this into a situation where she is to make cups of tea for the patients. She goes into the Wendy House and has a domestic conversation with another girl and then the following sequence ensues:

One of the doctors arrives in the Wendy House and Jane says to him:

Jane:	You gotta go quickly.
Derek:	Why?
Jane:	'Cos you're going to work.
Derek:	But I'm being a doctor.
Jane:	Well, you've got to go to work doctor 'cos you've got to go to hospital and so do I. You don't like cabbage do you? (he shakes his head) . . . Well you haven't got cabbage then. I'm goin' to hospital. If you tidy up this room make sure and tell me.

Jane has managed to convert the play situation from one in which she is a powerless and subservient nurse to the only one in which she has power over the doctor, that by controlling his domestic life by becoming the controlling woman in the home. It is important that the other way in which she could have had power within that game, by, for example, playing a more senior doctor than Derek, is denied her by the nursery nurse's action and it is unlikely that she would be able to take that position by herself.

In another example of play between children in another nursery school we can examine another situation of struggle for power between girls and boys. This time the boy, Dean, is struggling for power to define and control the game. He comes to join Diane and Nancy, who are already playing mothers and daughters in the Wendy House. Diane is playing mother and controlling both the sequencing of the game and the actions of Nancy, who like any dutiful daughter, goes along with mother's wishes. They are playing happily until Dean intervenes. Diane tries to tell him what to do as her son, but he tries to take over her commanding position. Diane says:

> Diane: Well I'm playing mums and dads and girls. You're not. Or my, or my sister'll tell you off if you come in my house. She'll tell you off if you, if you come in my house. She will 'cos I'm making 'er bed and if you get in 'er, in 'er bed she'll tell you off she will.
> Let's go and get the baby, come on then, you've got to go to bed now darling. You ain't been to bed yet have you?
>
> Dean: (to Nancy) You don't like . . . you don't want to play with 'er do you?
>
> Nancy: Yes, she won't let me go . . .

Diane pushes Nancy a bit on the rocking horse and then tries to retrieve the domestic discourse:

> Diane: Darling . . . I made the bed for you. Look what she's done. She'd made it all dirty. All all new, I've made it all clean. Now I'll have to tidy up. Let's see my money, see if there's money. Here's your food. Meat, chicken and bacon and steak. Now d'you want the telly on? D'you want the telly on? I put it on for you. Here y'are I put the telly on for you. You can't turn it off.
>
> Dean: What?
>
> Diane: Can you?
>
> Dean: I know you can't.
>
> Nancy: She's our mum, she's our mum, yeah she's our mum.
>
> Dean: (to Nancy) if you're playing with 'er I'm not gonna be your friend any more . . . not ever play with you. So what you gonna do?
>
> Nancy: (she looks first at one and then at the other, and 'turns tail') I'll play with you.

Diane: Nancy, get off that horsey and go to bed now 'cos you're being naughty.

In both of these examples the struggle on behalf of the powerless child, the resistance of that child, takes the form of reading the individual as the subject/object of another discourse, just as in the Miss Baxter sequence. In both cases the girls' power is produced by their setting up the game as domestic, in which they, like their mothers, traditionally have power, though of course it is power produced through contradiction and paid for by their domestic labour: it is therefore severely limited and limiting, but not without effects. It is true that this is precisely what is asserted by sex-role stereotyping arguments, but there are several important points which, it seems to me, stereotyping arguments cannot explain. First, the girls are not always weak and dependent, but appear to be engaged in a *struggle* with the boys to read and to create the situations as ones in which they are powerful. The boys equally struggle to remove the play from the site of the domestic in which they are likely to be subservient. It is interesting to note that in the large number of play sequences recorded in these two nurseries, there were very few in which boys played powerful fathers *when girls were present* though they did so when playing with other boys.

The Position of Girls in Early Education

Relative to boys, the academic performance of girls in the whole of the primary school is superior. Stereotyping arguments traditionally separate the domestic and the academic, arguing that girls fail in school because of their insertion into traditional feminine and not academic roles. The academic is counterposed to the domestic. However, such a position does not appear to be able, readily, to explain why girls should actually be relatively successful in early education. I want to raise some speculations about how we might be better able to account for this phenomenon, using the notions of power and discourse outlined above.

The fact that girls can and do take up powerful positions in play appears at first sight to be contradictory. Girls appear to struggle to obtain power in precisely those situations which are the site of resistance for boys. The girls try to manoeuvre the situation so that it becomes domestic play and the boys try to move it to a non-domestic situation. The domestic situation is precisely a site for opposition and resistance of the power of women in the home lives of these boys. It is unlikely that either at home or in play it would be sanctioned for them to 'identify' with their mothers by taking a position of similarity, that is as acting as a sub-mother in either the home or in school, and it also seems unlikely that their fathers would take 'mothering' positions within the domestic sphere. The girls on the other hand can precisely so identify with the positions occupied by their mothers within domestic practices. Thus, it is not surprising that the power of the domestic is a site of resistance for these boys and one in which their resistance takes precisely that form of transforming the situation in discourse to one in which the girls and women are constructed as weak in relation to men.

However, for these young children the domestic is not the only site of apparent female power. Their school lives are controlled by female teachers. There are many ways in which the discursive position adopted by the teachers is similar to that of mothers. Indeed, the nursery school provides a context in which good mothering and good pedagogy are seen as part of the same process – of aiding child development. I would argue that the very power of women in this transitory situation, between the domestic and the academic, is precisely what permits the early success of girls. It may be the similarity between these discursive practices, both sites of female power, that allows girls to take up positions of similarity with the powerful teachers. Indeed, the girls who are considered to be the 'brightest' by the teachers do indeed operate as subjects within the powerful pedagogic discourse. Within that discourse they take the position of the knower, they become sub-teachers.[10] For example, in one of the nurseries, Nancy, considered to be bright by the teacher, constantly asserts that she 'knows'. She continually finishes her work before the others to shrieks of 'Done it' and 'That's where it goes 'cos I know it does'. The boys in these exchanges are, by contrast, for the most part almost totally silent. They seem to be engaged in a resistance of silence, which is, of course, another way of resisting the discourse. Another example from an infant school will show just how the 'bright' girls act as sub-teachers. This is a typical conversation between Sally and a girl whom she has been helping with her work:

> 'Put your book away, come on. That's good work for today . . . slow to do everything. You take a minute to do it!'

I would argue that it is the relation between the domestic and the pedagogic and the way in which women signify as mothers and teachers, taking positions of power within those practices which provides the space for the early success of girls. This success is achieved precisely because successful school performance requires them to take up such positions in pedagogic discourses.[11] On the other hand, this is equally a site of struggle for the boys, a struggle in which they must work to redefine the situation as one in which the women and girls are powerless subjects of other discourses. It could well be this very resistance to that quasi-domestic power which results in the failure of the boys to do well in early education.

Concluding Remarks

I would suggest that the kind of analysis towards which I have gestured provides a potentially better alternative explanation for understanding the relation of girls and women to early education. Understanding the individuals not as occupants of fixed, institutionally-determined positions of power, but as a multiplicity of subjectivities, allows us to understand that an individual's position is not uniquely determined by them being 'woman', 'girl' or 'teacher'. It is important to understand the individual signifiers as subjects within any particular discursive practice. We can then understand power not as static, but produced as a constantly shifting relation.

However, having said that, there remain certain problems of determination which do not seem to be totally resolved by this analysis. Although this paper does raise problems for arguments which advocate direct and linear cause, the economic and the material are clearly crucial to these examples. The confining of women to the quasi-domestic, while discursively powerful, remains a site of economic dependence. While this dependence does not directly produce a passive and dependent subject, it is not without effects. Similarly, the girls and women do not take up *any* position in *any* discourse. Their signification as girls and women matters. It means the positions available to them exist *only* within certain limits. These limits are material. Not in the sense that they are directly *caused* by the materiality of the female body, but certainly by the limits in which that body can signify in current discursive practices. Nor are they directly 'caused' by the economic, but it does serve to produce women as confined to the domestic. However, the contradictions, the struggles for power, the shifting relations of power, all testify to the necessity for an understanding of subjectiv*ies* not a unique subjectivity. These contradictions also point to the necessity to rethink our strategies for action within education. It shows too how resistance on the part of children is not necessarily progressive in and of itself, and that the consequences of resistance are, to say the least, contradictory.[12]

While I do not find it possible to present easy answers or immediate political strategies, I think the presentation of the complexity is important. The teachers' guilt at the possibility of oppressing children is something which may have been shared at one time or another by many of us. It no longer seems enough to believe that we are in the process of simply oppressing children. Neither can we be comforted by the thought that 'progressive education' will free children to explore their own experience, without understanding precisely how that experience is understood and how that produces the children as subjects.

Notes

1. The observations were made as part of the projects on developmental psychology and nursery education and girls and mathematics in the early years of schooling. The latter work was carried out jointly with Rosie Eynard and further details are contained in the project report: R. Eynard and V. Walkerdine, *The Practice of Reason: Investigations into the Teaching and Learning of Mathematics*, vol. 2, *Girls and Mathematics*, University of London, Institute of Education (mimeo).

2. For example, see criticisms of the notion of the unitary subject of psychology and the assertion of the necessity for an understanding of individuals as a 'nexus of subjectivities' in Adlam *et al.* 'Psychology, Ideology and the Human Subject', in *Ideology and Consciousness*, no. 1, 1977.

3. For example, the following (amongst others) raise the problems of 'economistic Marxism': Adlam *et al.*, 1977 op. cit.; M. Foucault, *Power, Truth, Strategy*, Sydney: Feral Publications, 1979, and *Discipline and Punish*, Harmondsworth: Penguin, 1977.

4. See, for example, the article by Fran Bennett, Rosa Heys and Rosalind Coward in *Politics and Power*, no. 1, 1980, in which they argue for an understanding of the complex and contradictory signification of 'woman' in a variety of legal and welfare practices.

5. See, for example, Shulamith Firestone, *The Dialectic of Sex*, London: Cape, 1971 and Julian Hall (ed.), *Children's Rights*, London: Panther, 1972.

6. M. Lowenfeld, *Play in Childhood*, London: Gollancz, 1935, pp. 324–5.

7. See, for example, R. J. W. Sellick, *English Primary Education and the Progressives 1914–1939*, London: Routledge & Kegan Paul, 1972.

8. For example, see Denise Riley's article, 'War in the Nursery', *Feminist Review*, no. 2, 1979.

9. See note 4, and also, for example, Julia Brophy and Carol Smart,

Family Law and Reproduction of Sexual Inequality, British Sociological Association Conference, Aberystwyth, and certain recent work within the journal *m/f*, 1981.

10. See Eynard and Walkerdine, op. cit.

11. Madeleine MacDonald argues that accounts of education as reproduction are problematic in relation to the contradictory nature of women's education because of the relations between the domestic and the academic: 'Socio-cultural reproduction and Women's Education' in R. Deem, *Schooling for Women's Work*, London: Routledge and Kegan Paul, 1980. See also Carolyn Steedman's article, 'The Tidy House', in *Feminist Review*, no. 6, 1980, in which she talks about girls' contradictory relations of power and powerlessness in relation to the home and child-rearing and asserts the possibility of using an awareness of this to produce change.

12. Using a different theoretical framework, certain 'youth and counter-culture' studies reveal that resistance can be contradictory, for example, in relation to Paul Willis (*Learning to Labour: How Working-Class Kids Get Working-Class Jobs*, Farnborough: Saxon House, 1977), 'lads' who resist school only to be confirmed in a 'macho' masculinity and the necessity of physical labour.

Chapter 15

The Diversion of Language: A Critical Assessment of the Concept 'Linguistic Diversity'*

Diane Adlam and Angie Salfield

Although in the mid–1960s a comprehensive survey of socio-linguistics could be contained in a single review article,[1] the discipline has grown so rapidly over the past decade that an exceedingly long book would now be needed. One reason for this expansion has undoubtedly been its applicability to practical problems in education – in particular to the consequences of desegregation in American schools. The failure of this policy to solve the problem of 'underachievement' among pupils from minority ethnic groups has, in part, been explained in terms of the 'communicative interference' arising from the contact (and clash) of different linguistic patterns. Important in this context is the work of Harold Rosen as director of a research project on 'linguistic diversity' at the Institute of Education in London.[2] Rosen also has a wider importance in British educational debates about language and culture: he is a leading opponent of 'deficit' theories and his work is often invoked in attempts to formulate a 'progressive' or 'socialist' pedagogy.[3] In fact, we shall argue, Rosen himself conceptualises both teaching and politics almost entirely in terms of consciousness-raising; we shall attempt in this article to see

* *Screen Education*, no. 34, Spring 1980.

how he draws on general socio-linguistic concepts to justify this conclusion.

One difficulty for this investigation is that Rosen rarely discusses his conceptual framework, preferring to place the commitment to educational policy at the centre of his work. Teachers and pupils are involved at all stages of the 'linguistic diversity' project, for example, and this classroom orientation is contrasted to the abstruseness of theory and to the pointless disruption which university research teams usually bring to schools. In preference to books or articles, short papers or summaries of conferences are published: they are directed to people practically involved in education and are not easily available to others. The political implications of this choice are spelt out by Rosen in some of the work that is available: middle-class, white researchers with fancy equipment and nothing to say beyond what is written down on their standardised interview protocols will inevitably produce a distorted picture of the language of working-class and ethnic minority children. An 'accurate' picture requires other means.[4]

Given this explicit concern to ground research in practical problems, why discuss – as we shall – conceptual issues relatively separately from matters of policy? Why attempt to unravel and assess the orienting concepts and forms of argument that govern this work on linguistic diversity? In part it is precisely *because* it is so deeply entrenched that the framework needs to be opened up for questioning. In addition the general concepts of 'linguistic diversity', 'multicultural education' and 'collaborative learning' do not always correspond with the more specific recommendations about changes and interventions in education, and they need to be challenged. There is, for example, an incongruity between Rosen's sometimes flamboyant moralising and the more modest tone of the document *Linguistic Diversity: The Implications for Policy and Curriculum* produced by his research team.

Antecedents of 'Linguistic Diversity'

In the late 1960s, notions of innate differences in intelligence were given a new lease of life by psychologists like Arthur Jensen and were then taken up in a resurgence of the 'nature/nurture; controversy. Conceptualisations of culturally-mixed classrooms being crossed by 'communicative interference' emerged as a more progressive explanation of the 'causes' of educational inequality. They also called into question the parameters of the debate in the old polarities of genes *or* environment, biology *or* socialisation; these tended to be replaced by analysis of structural and ideological determinants. In explaining inequalities in terms of a clash between the language of the school and the language of the pupils, such work denied any inherent deficit in any child and so was consonant with the 'environmentalist' position. Nevertheless, its susceptibility to the psychologism of arguments in which IQ was a central explanatory concept soon became clear, because to say that certain groups of children suffered from linguistic 'deprivation; or 'deficit' was not so very different from arguing that they suffered from an *intellectual* deficit. The 'deficit/difference' debate that followed was therefore part of a growing tendency to assert that the question about linguistic competence, ability or whatever being 'innate' or 'acquired' was in many respects a false one. By assuming the *inferiority* of some children (whether laid down in genetic material or picked up in environmental material), both hereditarians and environmentalists failed to look beyond the individual child and analyse the political reasons for educational organisation. Some studies did try to locate questions of language and education in a Marxist framework of economic and historical determination,[5] and others conceptualised language variation as an element in the 'cultural reproduction' undertaken by the school on behalf of the bourgeoisie.[6] More influential than these, though, were the various versions of the 'sociology of knowledge' – Michael Young's and Nell Keddie's, for example[7] – which contrasted ideologically-biased educational knowledge with the apparently untainted non-school experience of working-class children. This, they argued, should be the starting point for radical teachers. Although this approach avoided the 'individualism' of psychological explanations of educational inequality, it tended to lapse into the inter-subjectivism of phenomenological sociology and into a moralistic assertion that all linguistic patterns are different-but-equal. In addition to empirical evidence, arguments from theoretical linguistics were marshalled in opposition against concepts of linguistic deficit or deprivation. The consensus that emerged among progressive socio-linguists was therefore that western industrialised societies are characterised by a wide range of different-but-equal linguistic patterns – by a considerable *linguistic diversity*.

Linguistic Diversity and Educational Inequality

'Linguistic diversity', then, draws on three main influences. It was developed in opposition to – yet on the same terrain as – the concept of linguistic deprivation; its central concern remained educational inequality; and it was rooted in analyses of classroom communication and interaction. In place of a notion of a 'homogeneous speech community', it emphasised the multiplicity of different linguistic patterns in any society – thus in studies of education, for example, the criteria of differences have included different languages, different dialects and different accents as well as different 'rules for use' in the same 'language'. (The lack of precision in explaining how these differences can be identified and so in defining linguistic diversity is, we shall argue, inevitable in socio-linguistics.)

The crux of the socio-linguistic analysis of education is that linguistic patterns correlate both with identifiable social *groups* (ethnic, sex or age groups, for instance) and with identifiable social *situations* (classroom, family, street-gang and so on).[8] The stratification of social groups is paralleled in a hierarchy of language use and those patterns which diverge from the ones accepted by the school are devalued and excluded: pupils using them are regarded as stupid, unmotivated or rebellious. Along with this ascription of differential value to linguistic patterns goes a complex set of miscommunications and misunderstandings by both pupils and teachers, the result of mutual ignorance of each others' habitual uses of language to convey meaning. Sociolinguistics therefore seeks to show that negative attitudes to any particular linguistic patterns are an *error*, a failure to perceive that really these are all different-but-equal. The error results from ethnocentrism and prejudice (according to non-Marxist explanations) or from ideological conditioning (according to Marxist explanations) and because it is committed by groups with power, like teachers and educational policy-makers, it has certain consequences. Non-standard speakers suffer both by learning little and, more crucially since this is seen as the source of the problem, by having their self-respect and self-confidence shattered.

The general solutions proposed by socio-linguists therefore tend to be in terms of admitting and encouraging the gamut of linguistic patterns at present excluded from the school. This would enable non-standard speakers to value the worth of their own background and overcome their relative educational failure, and would also lead to the cultural enrichment of the classroom. To counteract the ways that the linguistic values of the school disturb the processes of communication, language needs to be restored to its true status as the transparent means whereby human experience is expressed. According to this argument, then, it is a combination of prejudice and ignorance about the communication patterns of other people which turns cultural difference into social division. This position fails to take account of the complexity of language, relying on the orthodox view of it as simply an instrument of communication.

Concepts of Language

We have noted that socio-linguistic studies tend to be imprecise and arbitrary in identifying the linguistic and quasi-linguistic variations which are argued to be of social significance and which, when misrecognised, result in communication breakdown. The range of categories is enormous,[9] switching between languages (for bilingual speakers), variations in lexical and grammatical categories associated with 'dialect', phonetic variations ('accent'), difference in the incidence of grammatical categories (especially subordinate clauses and various sorts of modifiers), mood and aspect of verbs, changes in the number, length and location of pauses, rate of speech and patterns of intonation, the 'function' of the speech, aesthetic judgements and assessment of logical structure, the presence of speech at all as opposed to silence. Although this list is not exhaustive, there seems to be no set of theoretical categories that could govern all these aspects; and even in linguistically detailed and sophisticated analyses, it is seldom possible to discover the theoretical rationale for examining one set of speech phenomena rather than another.

This confusion, we would argue, is the result of what seems to be a paradox: that analysis of language as a system (the traditional object of linguistics) is regarded as outside the domain of socio-linguistic investigation.[10] This does not constitute a rejection of 'pure' linguistics – on the contrary, many socio-linguists regard it as a body of knowledge whose truths can be drawn upon but whose field is delineated so that it has little to say about language 'in use'. Similarly, socio-linguists tends to regard semantics, the study of *meaning*, as an activity undertaken in other departments. Dell Hymes's distinction between 'referential' meaning (the concern of theoretical semantics) and 'social' meaning (the concern of socio-linguistics) is usually taken as axiomatic:[11] whereas the referential meaning of language concerns the expression of ideas, thoughts or experiences past and present, its social meaning expresses aspects of the speaker as a member of society and in relation to others. This social or 'indexical' information is conveyed by *linguistic variation*: it is therefore implicit that the distinction between types of meaning presupposes a stable semantic core for any language. This is clear in William Labov's definition:

By 'social', I mean those language traits which characterise various sub-groups in a heterogeneous society . . . [this is] included in 'expressive' behaviour – the way in which the speaker tells the listener something about himself and his state of mind in addition to giving representational information about the world. Social and stylistic variation presuppose the option of saying 'the same thing' in several different ways: that is, *the variants are identical in referential or truth value, but opposed in their social and/or stylistic significance.*[12]

This division between 'language as such' and 'language in use' is open to many theoretical objections – not least because it suggests that 'representational' meaning is *non-social*. Here, however, we want to examine how this basic distinction and others that accrue to it function, often implicitly, in socio-linguistic argument.

The idea that social meaning is carried in optional *ways of speaking* suggests an explanation of the heterogeneity of categories in socio-linguistic research. Studies of how speech variations signify formality or informality, respect or disrespect, submissiveness or dominance, uncertainty or control are governed by usually unquestioned sociological categories like *status* and *role*. Linguistic variation merely 'realises' aspects of social or interpersonal relations: analysis therefore becomes a matter of discovering which linguistic phenomena perform this function. In this argument, the relation between social and linguistic categories is systematic for any given culture but none-the-less contingent in principle: any variable linguistic pattern might be 'chosen' by a community to express features of its social organisation. In contrast, it is supposed that necessary relations hold between the organisation of representational meaning and the core linguistic structure; these are epitomised by the relation between the logical nature of reasoning and the logical nature of certain syntactic structures. Theoretical linguistics, then, is justified in having recourse to *a priori* reasoning, whereas socio-linguistics should confine itself to ethnographic investigation. This does not mean that descriptive socio-linguistics is free from theoretical presuppositions, of course: most investigations are based on the prior assumption that, in general, variations in language use *express the organisation of social status and interpersonal relations in a society*. The trouble is that 'status' and 'role' are *not* social arrangements awaiting description but are rather weak sociological concepts. Empirical work within this conceptual framework can therefore all too easily become merely studies in impression formation and interpersonal attraction.

The influence of such research has nevertheless spread beyond the confines of a small anthropological and sociological community to inform many progressive analyses of education, particularly since it began to offer accounts of 'communicative interference' in classrooms – showing, for instance, that a child's hesitant speech to a teacher may express respect rather than the resistance he had taken it for, or that a teacher's tone of voice may signal anger to her pupils rather than the intended enthusiasm. The argument was that pupils can be caught in a downward spiral of educational failure if their speech patterns are misunderstood or rejected. Although we do not consider it unimportant to show that such misunderstandings occur nor underestimate how miserable and boring they can make school for children, this work simply cannot be accepted as constituting a theory of language and education. It may differ from purely descriptive socio-linguistics in *what* it analyses, but the mode of analysis and the governing concepts remain the same.

Some socio-linguists, it should be pointed out, consider what we have characterised as shortcomings to be positive insights. Peter Trudgill, for example, who has written extensively on education and addresses his writings explicitly to teachers, argues that attitudes to language variation are not linguistic attitudes at all:

> They are *social* attitudes. Judgements which appear to be about language are in fact based on social and cultural values, and have much more to do with the social structure of our community than with language . . . They are judgements about speakers rather than about speech.[13]

This shows how closely socio-linguistic analyses of education resemble the accounts based on 'labelling theory'. Speech variations are considered as signals that are interpreted or misinterpreted as conveying information about the speaker's person, social background and relation to the addressee. In certain circumstances, therefore, they may provoke habitual responses of rejection or denigration. This *might* be prevented by rooting out the prejudice involved, which *might* make life pleasanter for some people. It cannot guarantee an end of educational inequality because that, after all, is not caused by inter-individual prejudice. Nevertheless, other socio-linguists, including Harold Rosen, appear to claim, not only that their work may mitigate educational inequality, but that it can open the way for a definitively socialist pedagogy. What remains unclear is whether (or how) Rosen's political allegiances lead to different forms of argument from the liberal socio-linguistics of someone like Trudgill.

Rosen has never analysed 'language in use' with the precision and detail of Hymes, Labov and others. This is perhaps not surprising in relation to the current linguistic diversity project, which is concerned with identifying the range of language and dialects spoken in London schools[14] rather than with differences in the use of the same language. But even in his earlier studies of working-class speech, which were concerned with intra-language variation, extracts were assumed to 'speak for themselves' and to require only minimal analytical commentary pointing out their 'vitality' and 'expressiveness'.[15] In his critique of Basil Bernstein's methods of analysis, Rosen was cavalier in his treatment of M. A. K. Halliday's theory of language on which they were based – he reduced this to an oversimplified question of contexts which allow some children to express themselves and cruelly constrain others. Here he commented that:

> the relationship between class and speech cannot be described and understood by the usual sociological methods. Working-class speech has its own strengths which the normal linguistic terminology has been unable to catch. There is no sharp dividing line between it and any other form of speech, but infinite variation in the deployment of the resources of language.[16]

Rather than analysing this infinite variation, Rosen usually just points out (using the normal terms of literary criticism like 'expressive' and 'vital') that these strengths do exist for some speakers in some situations and then generalises this into an argument about 'working-class speech'. Although the 'usual sociological methods' certainly need to be criticised, the collection of bits of spoken language from supposedly random individuals is not an obviously superior form of evidence. However much he may criticise slavish allegiance to linguistic analysis – and despite an obfuscating political rhetoric – Rosen himself remains entirely within the socio-linguistic orthodoxy when it comes to social analysis:

> there is that other assumption about society which corrodes our thinking, that the great working class of this country with its largely unwritten history, its heroism, its self-transforming engagement with life, its stubborn refusal to be put down, is nothing but a deprived inarticulate herd. Even the new radical teacher sensitive to the language of working-class pupils and armed with political theory can be corroded by the social assumptions which abound in current educational and sociological literature.[17]

Rosen, it is true, is more explicit than most socio-linguists about

the social basis of prejudice and, on occasion, even has recourse
to theories of ideology.

> As the scholarly scrutiny of the life-habits of the working class
> proceeds, more and more attention has focussed upon their
> language (which as everyone knows distinguishes them from
> others much more effectively than, say, horny hands and
> overalls) . . . on the one hand there are honest and devoted
> people who are trying to answer the question, 'Why do so many
> working-class children fail in schools and how can we change
> things so that they do not?'; and on the other hand . . . there
> are people who, in the effort to guard their privileges and power
> within the educational system, seek tirelessly for new and better
> theoretical justifications.[18]

Language differences are a *clearer* object of prejudice than horny
hands or overalls, but not different in kind. Although negative
attitudes are based on the – unspecified – 'social system' and serve
particular interests, they *operate* intersubjectively. That is the logic
of Rosen's attempts to 'reveal' to teachers how pernicious and
entrenched are their presuppositions about the working class and
their language. One article by Rosen ends in the following
way: 'Suppose I tell you that there is a little known story by D.
H. Lawrence, which contains this . . .' He then quotes a passage
about life as a miner's wife, told in the first person. Finally he
pulls his guilt-evoking rabbit out of the top hat:

> How did you read that? What kind of careful, reverent attention
> did you give it? What can you say about its dialogue, its sense
> of felt life and so on? But now read it again but bear in mind
> that it is not in fact by D. H. Lawrence but is the spontaneous
> language of a Yorkshire miner's wife which appears in *Language
> and Class Workshop No. 2* . . . Give material like this the same
> loving attention you have lavished on literature and you will
> extend your humanity.[19]

This outrageous moral piety is inadequate both conceptually and
politically. Conceptually, Rosen's analysis has not moved beyond
the social psychology of labelling theory – his case rests on humanistic notions about the consequences of an oppressor's attitudes
and behaviour for a victim. Politically, change is conceived as the
result of individual guilt and self-criticism. Decking this out in
Marxisant terminology makes no difference: mechanistic theories
of ideology are quite consonant with ideas of oppression as an
intersubjective process. Language is not being conceptualised here

as a complex set of structured meanings, but simply as a general mirror of *human experience*. This is the real focus of Rosen's work – how social situations admit the 'culture' of some individuals and exclude the experiences of others. The only importance of linguistic diversity is thus that it reflects and exemplifies the ways in which cultural and individual differences are turned into social divisions and individual injustices.

Rosen's work, it becomes clear, is concerned less with the *diversity* of linguistic forms than with the *equivalence* of human experience. It relies on the old idea of universal human goodness ready to flourish once the causes of its present suppression have been removed, but backs this up with a selective reliance on the evidence and scientific claims of socio-linguistics and, in potential and undefined ways, of linguistics. To criticise Rosen for according language only a residual place in his analysis is not to defend linguistics as an adequate science. The real problem is that the distinction between 'language as such' and 'language in use' allows socio-linguists to retain both an orthodox philosophy of language and an orthodox sociology and so to conceive of *meaning* as socially neutral. It is this basic distinction that needs to be disrupted.

Language and Culture

In the 'deficit/difference' debate, one element of the anti-deficit case was the demonstration by theoretical linguistics that no language is superior to any other – that they are all equally grammatical and rule-governed, that they are all complex systems equally valid as a means of communication. Some versions of this argument made explicit reference to Transformational Generative Grammar (TGG), to the concept of linguistic universals and their supposed innateness to the human mind. The deduction from these arguments was that no individual speaker could be deemed linguistically 'deficient' for speaking, for instance, Black English Vernacular (BEV) rather than Standard English. At the political level, this general argument about the 'grammaticality' of all language varieties was both important and effective, particularly when buttressed with the sort of empirical evidence collected by Labov. But shifting it from the level of theoretical linguistics to use it as proof of the equal validity of all *experiences* and *cultures* entails several problematic assumptions. To begin with, linguistic diversity comes to be conceptualised as a matter of different ways of expressing *the same thing*; this is consonant with the distinction between social and referential meaning. What is expressed, though, is not the truth value of a proposition but the *fundamental commonality of human experience.* Languages and language varieties in general are taken to express human experience in general: because languages are 'equal', the argument goes, so is all human experience.

Second, language is not simply conceptualised as the instrument for expressing experience in general, but the experience of an individual consciousness. This is rooted in the notion that the source of language is based in ideas, in the cognition of a human subject. The communication of thought from one mind through language to another is possible because the form of its message – experience – is everywhere the same. If languages are equal then the origin of this equality must be the universal attribute of an experiencing consciousness. This position is congruent with Chomskyan notions of innate linguistic universals and the fundamental rationality of the mind but, like them, it also entails a speculative leap from a theory of universal structures of *grammar* to the location of an origin for those structures in the universal human mind. It therefore fails to take account of the contemporary critique of such a privileging of the category of the subject, which argues, not that the subject is constitutive of language, but that *subjects are actually constituted in language.*

These assumptions then become tangled up in socio-linguistics with an evaluative slippage between *equality* and *equivalence.* The debate about linguistic deficit cannot stop with the theoretical assertion of equivalence of all languages at the level of universal structures. If it did, socio-linguistics would become redundant and so the emphasis shifts to the notion of *different-but-equal.* A tension is thus set up between notions of equivalence, diversity and equality. One problem here is the ambiguity of 'linguistic diversity'. In one sense, it refers to variant forms of an identical structure; but at the same time, the distinction between 'language as such' and 'language in use' assumes that these two aspects – and the determinants acting upon them – are fundamentally different. Thus the contention that all forms of 'language use' are equal cannot be derived from the premise that all languages are 'equal' – the two statements are at entirely different levels of abstraction. The equality of language is based on the conception that they all share certain universal properties; since 'rules for the use' of language are argued to have *no* universal properties, abstract linguistic arguments cannot be used as 'proof' of the equality or equivalence of all patterns of linguistic variation.

This point, however straightforward, is often obscured by the heterogeneity of what counts as 'language in use'. Sometimes it is acknowledged that the term encompasses two relatively distinct concepts – language varieties (dialects, accents and distinct languages) and variations in speech patterns according to the social context (markers of formality, respect and so forth). Whereas the argument that non-standard dialects were not linguistically degenerate had a definite pertinence in the debate about language varieties, it is simply irrelevant to the question of contextual variation in forms of 'language use' because these are defined as particular, contingent and devoid of universal linguistic properties. The inappropriateness of abstract assessments of 'deficiency' or 'equivalence', however, tends to be ignored. The distinction between language varieties and language in use is blurred by the assumption that language varieties are themselves socially patterned – for bilinguals different languages carry different social meaning, for example. Both variations in the *language* used and variations in the use of *a language*, then, are said to realise social meaning: both can therefore be analysed in the terms of attitudes we discussed earlier. But because this perspective treats language varieties as if they were variations within a language (or a 'linguistic reportoire'), for socio-linguistics it must be extrinsic to the question of the grammaticality of a variety considered as a general linguistic system. On the rare occasions that this point was made in the 'deficit/difference' debate,[20] it was always hedged around with qualifications about the fundamental equality of all languages. The recognised theoretical weaknesses did not lead sociolinguists to question the deficit/difference polarity itself.

Indeed, the dichotomy was strengthened by relativist arguments against the notion of *cultural* deprivation introduced from the 'new sociology of education'. The arguments about language and about culture became part of each other's armoury: since the opposite pole of linguistic deficit is linguistic universality, so it seemed to follow that the opposite pole of cultural deprivation must be cultural equivalence. Transposing this position from a phenomenological sociology of knowledge to the socio-linguistic debate meant satisfying two conditions. First, the distinction between the variety of language and variations within a language would have to be ignored. Second, on the premise that language is the expression of experience, it had to accept the logic that, because all languages are equivalent, then so must be the varieties of human experience. This connection is clear in two quotations from Norbert Dittmar:

Linguistics refutes the theoretical presuppositions of the Deficit Hypothesis and its methods. Its starting point is that Standard and Non-Standard are two different systems which have their own equivalent possibilities of expression and correspond to an equivalent logic.[21]

What would be the source of this 'equivalent logic'?

There are a multitude of cognitive universals which are not influenced by social class and ethnic membership. The fact that there are still some differences occurring consistently in superficial measurements can be interpreted in a way that has already been mentioned several times: it is not the *common abilities* but the *norms* for those abilities that are different.[22]

In such ways the concept of linguistic *diversity* is continually undermined in these debates: different-but-equal becomes not-different-but-equivalent as the socio-linguistic distinction between 'language as such' and 'language in use' is confused and priority is (ironically) given to the former. Referential meaning – nominally the object of theoretical semantics – reappears in its simplest version, language as the mirror of mind, as the *raison d'être* of the socio-linguistic enterprise. Variations in use become obstacles to potentially *perfect communication*. Were all patterns of linguistic variation mutually intelligible – if, in other words, a society could rid itself of prejudices between social groups – then the free interchange of thoughts would become possible. Language could then be restored to its true status as the transparent bearer of ideas. The various *forms* of expressing experience would continue, but would now be universally intelligible; so would the different *contents* of experience, because the form and potential of all human experience is everywhere equivalent. The political implication is clear: let experience speak. But so is the opposing theoretical position that explodes the entire framework: that representational meaning is itself socially organised; that this organisation is internal to discourse; and that it is never the product of individual experience. Socio-linguistics cannot confront such positions unless it also confronts the concept of differences in meaning which are not guaranteed by an underlying equivalence and which require *real* interventions (rather than the removal of blinkering prejudices) if they are to be transformed.

None of this diminishes the decisive importance of socio-linguistics in countering 'deficit' positions; nor do the theoretical problems altogether undermine the value of the empirical work that was central to its contribution. The problem arises, as it were, 'beyond the deficit/difference debate.' The concepts forged within it have prevented socio-linguistics from conceptualising language as systems of meaning *diverse* in their differences. To conceptualise language as simply a means of expression renders meaning unproblematic; this makes it difficult to view language other than in evaluative terms like 'adequacy' and 'validity'.

Rosen's 'Socialist Pedagogy'

Drawing on the work of Labov and others rather than making the linguistic argument point by point himself, Harold Rosen continues to denounce simplified notions of linguistic and cultural deprivation. Socialist teachers still need to be reminded that working-class language and culture exist, he seems to think, and to be warned against oppressive thoughts and deeds:

> What I am speaking of is that tendency in progressive opinion of all kinds, including all kinds of socialists, to see working-class life as a horrifying ulcer springing from the unwholesomeness of capitalist society, a deforming disease which a new and better society would purge and cleanse . . . The alternative view amounts to this, that out there in the 'social context' there is a culture which is alive and kicking. Just as we have discovered that children do not come to school to be given language but arrive with it as a going concern, we need to discover that children come with this too. Indeed, their language, the despised vernacular of great cities and industrial towns, is part of it.[23]

It seems to us that socialists today don't need to be taught the same lessons as the Jensens of 1970. The political implication of Rosen's unchanging position is that prejudice simply needs rooting out and that an existing language, experience and culture should be admitted to contexts that now exclude them. This applies to race as well as to class – Rosen sees 'multicultural' education as the analogue of linguistic diversity:

> For if the school appears to be turning its back on the languages and cultures of a large part of the community it serves, it is in danger of offering instead what can only be an impoverished and unrealistic education for children who are growing up to be members of a multi-racial and, therefore, multi-cultural and multi-lingual society.[24]

The conceptual differences and relations between 'race', 'culture' and 'language' are ignored: they are all given a common status as objects of prejudice. This enables Rosen to avoid the major problem in socio-linguistics already noted – the non-transferability of the notion of the equivalence of all languages to concepts of language use. Rosen's two principal sets of 'linguistic' categories also help him to gloss this over. The first comprises languages varieties (dialects, accent, and so on) which are susceptible to the demonstration of grammatical complexity, but at such a level of abstraction that this says nothing at all about the organisation of meaning: it is mere theoretical speculation or an act of faith to claim that they demonstrate the equivalence of all experiences. Rosen's second set of categories is taken from the discourse of literary criticism – terms like 'expressive' and 'vital'. Even more than the first set, these are used to show that, given the right context, working-class children 'can speak' and do 'have culture'. But whereas this demonstration of the *presence* of language and culture was necessary only in the very specific context of the deprivation debate, Rosen elevates it to an argument for universal equivalence. Again the political – or rather *moral* – implication of the abstract assertion of an equality which exists already but remains unrecognised is that the oppressed should be allowed to speak. If they can't or won't, then prejudice (especially that of teachers) is to blame. But, we would argue, politics can never take this form. Political interventions always imply positive transformations in the discourses and social practices with which they emerge.

The same problems undermine Rosen's prescriptions for teaching. He quotes Chris Searle with approval:

> The English teacher in the schools is probably in the best position to give back to the child his own world and identity in education, to reaffirm it, to share it himself, support it and strengthen it.[25]

The first aim, then, should be to perfect communication amongst pupils and between teachers and pupils. Only thus could the free expression and interchange of experiences be achieved. This perfect communication, Rosen contends, could be achieved if the *intention to communicate* were strong enough to overcome the obstacles. Hence the advocacy of 'collaborative learning' by his research team: this would entail changing the hierachical and competitive interpersonal relations in the classroom and so a renunciation by the teacher of any notion of his or her superiority. The assumption is that, by restoring self-confidence, this would automatically promote better learning and enrich the classroom:

> We would see students change through such learning. We would

witness the growth of self-esteem as they assumed the responsibility for their own learning and for themselves.[26]

But what if such changes don't product the effects that Rosen's
theory predicts? Again, it would simply mean that the teacher
has not been committed enough. The circularity of the dogmatic
assertion of an essential human equivalence thus emerges: if it
surfaces, it proves the theory correct; if it does not, it is because
insufficient effort has been made to uncover it.

In pedagogic terms, this sidesteps attempts to reform the curriculum which might entail *teaching* children something which
directly conflicts with their cultural identity and experience. More
broadly, we would argue that, from the point of view of a socialist
politics, the abstract assertion that all cultures are equal is meaningless and potentially harmful. Aspects of certain 'cultures', for
example, are clearly reactionary, and Rosen himself warns against
romanticising working-class culture.

> In all that I have said I may possibly have given the impression
> that I believe that working-class speech is as fine an instrument
> as could be devised for communicating and thinking, and that
> middle-class speech is pretentious garbage. That would be an
> absurd romanticism.[27]
>
> It is not a matter of asserting that working-class culture is
> infinitely superior . . . but rather of demonstrating that it is
> there at all, that it is pertinent to our concerns, that we build
> on it or build nothing.[28]

Although the tone is muted here, for Rosen change still entails
no more than sweeping away ideological excrescences by altering
interpersonal relations. The stress and primacy given to 'identity'
demonstrate that culture is taken as equivalent to the contents of
consciousness. But what happens if a working-class or middle-
class adolescent refuses to give up the racism that is part of his
or her identity? This can never ben an insurmountable problem
because of the guarantee of an already existing homogeneous and
egalitarian human essence.

Rosen's contention that politics must take the form of liberating
the culture, history and experience of a humanity rendered inaud-
ible by oppressive social relations draws on a long tradition of
libertarian socialism which is perhaps best exemplified today in
the writings of E. P. Thompson. Indeed, Rosen cites his work as
the approach which should be developed in a socialist analysis of
education. Thompson's analysis is clearly governed by general
epistemological categories of experience and rationality and, as

a result, is caught in the inescapable circularities of traditional philosophy.[29] Similarly, Rosen's conception of *language* is determined by the privileging of experience as an epistemological category. To criticise these arguments is not to deny that people have experiences: it is to insist that as a general philosophical category experience cannot be made the guarantee of political change. If it is, as by Rosen, socialist interventions in education are reduced by questions of pedagogy (understood as teacher/child interaction) and vital sites of struggle are dismissed as secondary – economic determinants and effects, legislative conditions, the structure of education as a profession and the nature of teacher training, control over the organisation of the curriculum and so forth.[30]

Rosen's position, of course, does have implications for the curriculum, but the changes he envisages would be of a uniform and singular type; he does not consider how a socialist policy towards pedagogy would differ radically under different social conditions. Indeed, we would argue that the idea of an homogeneous 'socialist pedagogy' is a chimera; nor can (or should) socialist teachers be given the job of training cadres of organic intellectuals by rearranging their classrooms and their attitudes. There are two points here. The first concerns the question of different calculations under different conditions. It would, for example, be quite possible for socialists to consider the introduction of political education into schools as a primary objective: the point would not be to transmit a particular ideology but to provide access to understanding about how political power is organised and distributed, about how policies are formulated and decisions taken. Teaching about mass media might also be central, if it emphasised not stereotyping and distortion but the ways in which forms of reporting and the telling of stories (fictional or 'non-fictional') construct their varied messages. It would certainly be possible to calculate that literacy is a central goal: there is an odd contrast between applauding socialist regimes in poor countries for introducing literacy campaigns and assuming that giving priority to literacy and numeracy in industrialised societies is necessarily the mark of a reactionary concern with 'standards'. The idea of a 'socialist pedagogy' as a general raising of consciousness blocks the discussion of such issues.

This brings us to the second point: that the attempt to free and to nurture an already present experience is doomed to impossibility. Schools are organised as specific institutions, sets of practices and discourses governed by principles which necessarily differ from the discourses and practices outside them. A classroom cannot be made into a playground, a youth club or a family any more than it can be made into a court of law or a prison. If classrooms are regarded as oppressive simply by virtue of denying the experiences given by other social relations then, though we strongly disagree, the advocates of deschooling have a certain logic on their side. Rosen's position always entails a certain paralysis stemming from the anxiety that teaching will involve the exclusion of parts of a child's non-school life or the introduction of changes from 'outside' rather than developments of which that experience is itself the author. But education (including Rosen's pedagogy and like all other organised social practices) always entails inclusions, exclusions and transformations. The real problem is formulating decisions about what direction these should take. The last thing we are suggesting is that education should be severed from other social practices; but we are saying that the connections and relations can never be linear and homogeneous. The idea that they are relies, as we have tried to show, on a transcendentalist view of the category 'experience'. Although Rosen might consider such philosophical problems irrelevant, they undermine both his theoretical position and the forms of progressive teaching he endorses.

Although we have concentrated here on Rosen's pedagogic prescriptions, this framework has not hegemonised all the specific policy proposals made by the linguistic diversity project. The range of languages spoken in inner city schools clearly does pose an enormous problem, and attitudes towards languages are part of it. But this by no means exhausts the problem of language and education. Attempting to homogenise the diverse linguistic phenomena studied by socio-linguistics under the general rubric 'attitudes to language' grossly oversimplifies the issues at stake.

Language and Social Relations

In this article, we have shown how Harold Rosen's misleading claims to offer a 'socialist pedagogy' draw on certain types of socio-linguistic work, which themselves rely on a concept of language as a transparent instrument for the expression of experience. This has inevitably meant eliding some quite diverse modes of analysis – there is at least one socio-linguistic theory, for example, which does not start from this assumption. M. A. K. Halliday's stated concern is with language as a socially-governed *semiotic* system, and so his work can be presented as an alternative to the dominant socio-linguistic view that the relationship between language and social relations can be reduced to questions of prejudice. Although he goes along with the general argument that judgements about language are 'social' rather than 'linguistic', for him this is the beginning of the problem and not the end, as it is for someone like Trudgill. Halliday tries to explain attitudes to language as an effect of the ways in which conflicts in meaning are related to the organisation of society:

> The problem of educational failure is not a linguistic problem, if by linguistics we mean a problem of different urban dialects, though it is complicated by dialect features, especially dialect attitudes; but it is at bottom a semiotic problem, concerned with the different ways in which we have constructed our social reality, and styles of meaning that we have learnt to associate with various aspects of it.[31]

In so far as he contends that all meaning is social, Halliday displaces the socio-linguistic distinction between 'language as such' and 'language in use': linguistic variation is not a matter of optional ways of saying the same thing because it is always a question of variation in meaning. This leads to another difference from most of the work we have discussed. Although Halliday does employ a notion of language use, for him it refers to the meanings selected from an overall 'meaning potential'[32] and how this is governed by forms of social relations. He is therefore able to give a theoretical specification to the connections between social structure and the patterning of meanings. Although Halliday's work does represent an advance beyond most socio-linguistics, however, it is not without major difficulties. Because its theoretical basis, in contradistinction to other socio-linguistics, lies in the Firthian school of 'fundamental linguistics', it is beset with the problem of positing pre-given functions which any language must fulfil. This in turn leads to the setting up of a distinction between 'ideational' and 'interpersonal' meaning which does not in fact escape the problems we have identified in the analogous distinction between referential and social meaning. So despite his insistence that ideational meaning is social, Halliday's crucial concept of 'register',[33] which is supposed to specify different meaning patterns, is only sustained at the general level of linguistic theory. When concepts like register are related to sociological theory, the specificity of meanings which they are designed to encapsulate dissolves and language once more becomes a mediator: society, meaning and linguistic forms are conceived as different levels, each of which *realises* the one which precedes it. Thus although Halliday confronts the question of the systematicity of meaning and its intrinsic connections to forms of social organisation, his work does not really avoid the general problems we have discussed throughout this article. The point of mentioning it is to indicate that these difficulties have been challenged at least minimally from within socio-linguistics.

The most obvious theoretical challenge to the whole conceptual framework from outside comes from semiotics. By this we do not mean a ready-made theory which could be applied to education: semiotics has in any case fragmented over the past decade into distinct theoretical camps with often quite antagonistic political allegiances. Rather it would be a question of explaining how socio-linguistics has failed to provide a means for conceptualising the range of discourses that cohere around education through ignoring the fundamental premises of semiotics – the idea that all meaning is social; that language is not an instrument of expression but a system within which meanings are produced; that therefore human experience and identity can never be the origin of meaning but are rather its effect; that the real and its 'representation' are in no sense separate realms with the latter mirroring the former. The questions raised by these semiotic perspectives (and by current concepts of discourse) should be central to a rethinking of the analysis of education. But even this could only clear the way for rethinking pedagogic practices in relation to language. Rosen's use of socio-linguistics to justify his own position may serve as a warning against an opportunistic appropriation of linguistic theories: it nevertheless remains important to think through the implications of semiotic and discursive analyses in a constructive way. One reason that this project has hardly begun yet may be that socio-linguistics appears never to have heard of semiotics – but then the opposite is also the case.

Notes

1. Susan Ervin-Tripp, 'Sociolinguistics', in L. Berkowitz (ed.), *Experimental Social Psychology*, no. 4, 1969. By socio-linguistics we mean that concern with *linguistic variation* and its social correlates associated with, for example, Hymes, Fishman and Labov in the US and Trudgill and Rosen in Britain. The omission of Basil Bernstein's work may seem surprising, but that has an entirely different theoretical basis. His writings are not subject to many of our criticisms here: a critical assessment of the theory of codes would require a separate paper.

2. The project of mapping the range of languages and dialects spoken in London schools is a politically important part of the contemporary concern with multicultural education and, particularly, with the question of mother-tongue teaching – itself the focus of controversy because of the EEC directive (77/486/EEC, 25 July 1977) that all member countries should make provision for it.

3. They are particularly influential among secondary English teachers:

see the many publications of the National Association for the Teaching of English and the London Association for the Teaching of English.

4. See H. Rosen (ed.), *Language and Class Workshop*, nos 1 (1974) and 2 (1975).

5. See Norbert Dittmar, *Sociolinguistics*, London: Edward Arnold, 1976.

6. See Pierre Bourdieu and Jean-Claude Passeron, *Reproduction*, London and Beverly Hills: Sage, 1977.

7. M. F. D. Young (ed.), *Knowledge and Control*, London: Collier-Macmillan, 1972; N. Keddie (ed.), *Tinker, Tailor: The Myth of Cultural Deprivation*, Harmondsworth: Penguin, 1973.

8. Also termed 'social context', 'setting' or 'speech domain'. The concept is usually defined by means of a mixture of the physical, social and social-psychological 'attributes' of the settings in which communication takes place. It is an ethnographic concept.

9. See, for example, Pier Paolo Giglioli (ed.), *Language and Social Context*, Harmondsworth: Penguin, 1972; J. B. Pride and J. Holmes (eds), *Sociolinguistics*, Harmondsworth: Penguin, 1972; C. B. Cazden, V. P. John and D. Hymes (eds), *Functions of Language in the Classroom*, New York and London: Teachers College Press, 1972.

10. This is something of an oversimplification. Socio-linguists disagree about whether their work is part of sociology or part of linguistics. Those who take the second position (like Trudgill and Labov) argue that linguistics requires a socio-linguistic analysis if it is to develop a complete theory of language. However, even Labov admits that linguistics can proceed in major aspects of its work without referring to socio-linguistics. And whatever the position taken on this question, the basic linguistic *and* sociological categories are rarely questioned – they are merely juxtaposed.

11. See D. Hymes, 'Socio-linguistics and the ethnography of speaking', in E. Ardener (ed.), *Social Anthropology and Language*, London: Tavistock, 1971.

12. W. Labov, *Sociolinguistic Patterns*, Oxford: Basil Blackwell, 1978, p. 271; emphasis added.

13. P. Trudgill, *Accent, Dialect and the School*, London: Edward Arnold, 1975, p. 27.

14. The project reports discuss the difficulties of identifying boundaries between different languages; between language and dialect and between dialects. None the less they seem finally prepared to use fairly simple categories and to leave the identification of which speakers belong to which categories up to teachers' judgements. This cannot fail to have an effect on the results of their survey work.

15. See *Language and Class Workshop*, op. cit.

16. H. Rosen, *Language and Class*, London, Falling Wall Press, 1972, p. 19.

17. H. Rosen, 'Out There or Where the Masons Went', in Martin Hoyles (ed.), *The Politics of Literacy*, London: Writers and Readers Publishing Co-operative, 1977, p. 205.

18. Rosen, 1972, op. cit., pp. 1–2.

19. Rosen, 1977, op. cit., pp. 209–10.

20. See, for example, Dell Hymes, 'Introduction', in Cazden *et al.*, op. cit.

21. Dittmar, op. cit., p. 95.

22. Ibid., p. 91.

23. Rosen, 1977, op. cit., pp. 208–9.

24. H. Rosen, Appendix One in *Language Diversity: the Implications for Policy and the Curriculum*, London: University of London, 1979, p. 26.

25. Quoted in Rosen, 1977, op. cit., p. 208.

26. Dale Spender, 'Collaborative Learning: Feminist Statement', in A. Lee and D. Spender, *Collaborative Learning*, London Institute of Education, mimeo, 1977.

27. Rosen, 1972, op. cit., p. 19.

28. Rosen, 1977, op. cit., p. 210.

29. For a more detailed critique see Paul Hirst, 'The Necessity of Theory: A Review of Edward Thompson's *The Poverty of Theory*', *Economy and Society*, vol. 8, no. 4, 1979.

30. This problem is not unique to Rosen but is shared by positions on education rooted in a phenomenological sociology of knowledge. For critical accounts of these see Jack Demaine, 'On the New Sociology of Education', *Economy and Society*, vol. 6, no. 2, 1977; James Donald, 'Green Paper: Noise of Crisis', *Screen Education*, no. 30, Spring 1979; and Athar Husain, 'The Economics of Education', *Economy and Society*, vol. 5, no. 4, 1976.

31. M. A. K. Halliday, *Language as Social Semiotic*, London: Edward Arnold, 1978, p. 163.

32. M. A. K. Halliday, *Explorations in the Functions of Language*, London: Edward Arnold, 1973, Chapter 2 and Halliday, 1978, op. cit., Chapter 6.

33. See Halliday, 1978, op. cit., and Ruquaiya Hasan, 'Code, Register and Social Dialect', in Basil Bernstein (ed.) *Class, Codes and Control, Vol. 2*, London: Routledge & Kegan Paul, 1973.

Part III

Cultural Studies

Chapter 16

Cultural Studies and Educational Practice*

Richard Johnson

It seems to me that there are two ways of introducing a discussion of cultural studies and educational practice.[1] One can either proceed by review or by argument. The method of review implies some attempt to describe the field of cultural studies or those parts of it most relevant to 'popular culture'. We might start by considering, for example, the different uses of the terms 'popular' and 'culture'. We might consider some parallel couplets: mass culture, working-class culture, subculture, even dominant culture. We might note the presence of other opposed or complementary terms: older ones like values, myth or consciousness, newer or refurbished ones like ideology, the symbolic, representation, signification or, the favourite of the day, discourse. Reviews like this may produce useful maps, indispensable to explorers – especially over such bumpy ground as this is! By concentrating on the variety of definitions, they perform a useful relativising function. They remind us that educational practices are inextricably connected to language and to the choice of categories. 'Theory', in this sense, need not be abstruse, but is, rather, a part of making us critically self-conscious of what is implied by the use of certain words and concepts. The danger is that such cartography foregrounds a tiny bit of social process, especially the activities of specialist intellectuals. We may become entranced by the lines and squiggles on the maps and never reach a more direct investigation of broader

* *Screen Education*, no. 34, Spring 1980.

social and cultural processes. So I shall not try to draw a map of this kind, but shall conduct an argument. This will include some detours (which will look uncommonly like 'theory') but under the discipline, I hope, of practical questions.

There are three main strands in the argument, two of which concern difficulties along the way. I want to argue, first, against some mental habits in the pursuit of cultural studies which I'll call 'theoretical absolutism'. I mean the tendency to contain the subject within one preferred approach. This may be a preferred theoretical paradigm or it may be a conventional 'disciplinary' boundary. I'll concentrate mainly on theoretical partisanship, but the other theme is also important: the narrowing that results, for instance, from an exclusively literary or sociological approach to problems better grasped in a more open interdisciplinary or non-disciplinary way. Actually most practitioners do have a disciplinary entry-point, and, as a basis for transformations, this may be very useful. My own entry-point, for example, has been via history. But I have become acutely aware, not only of drawing usefully on 'historical' virtues, but also of being blocked by other features of 'being an historian': hence the need, sometimes, to turn back and criticise *that* practice.

The second argument is against all partial, piecemeal and therefore trivialising conceptions of culture and cultural studies. There is, for example, what I'd call the 'literary reduction'. Here the concern is primarily with cultural products of a particular kind, text-like products, nicely lying there, inertly awaiting analysis or appreciation. I think that there are some subtle carry-overs here from high literary pursuits which are mainly located in universities. This produces, in other educational contexts, different objects but similar 'readings'. This literary inheritance has been extremely important in the foundation of cultural studies; it only becomes really problematic when it limits or contains the objects of the study by defining them exhaustively in this way. Early cultural studies combined a fine appreciation of the text with an interest in the cultural forms that were lived and experienced by concretely-placed social groups – a more sociological or social-historical definition. Some histories and some sociologies, on the other hand, are prone to a parallel reduction: the reduction of the cultural to popular pursuits, especially to 'leisure-based' practices which have a peculiar popular salience – football or pop music, for instance. These cultural forms too are very important; but they must not be taken to define the sphere of the cultural as such, as in the common equation: culture = leisure = 'freedom'.[2]

The third theme is the mutual dependence of cultural studies and educational practice. I am not arguing here for some unique privilege for formal educational institutions. Thinking about the history of 'education' (in the equation: education = school = knowledge) I'm committed to the need for alternative educational activity, outside and in contest with the dominant pressures of the institutional sites. I mean, rather, the need to link what we are beginning to learn about cultural processes with the ways we learn and teach. This means seeing formal education as a cultural process; and seeing culture as centrally including education. It means using the experiences of schooling as a way of learning about culture. As teachers we are centrally involved in cultural processes. We are implicated in them, in and around the schools. So are the pupils we teach. The object of study exists there in front of us. We do not have to 'bring it into the classroom'. At one level this is obvious enough, though hidden, perhaps, by the disciplinary specialisms of *educational* studies. But I still think it is something which is persistently difficult to grasp, and when securely grasped, may help to transform cultural studies *and* educational practice. It is certainly no accident that the study of the cultural has been associated not only with new contents or curricula, but also with a more open, critical, explorative and collective educational dynamic.

Out of Absolutism?

The first problem, then, is the tendency to approach culture within the narrowly disciplinary or theoretical frame. It is best illustrated by recapitulating, as briefly as possible, some aspects of an intellectual history. Work in cultural studies is influenced, willy-nilly, by one or other or both of two competing paradigms. The first of these belonged, historically, to the late 1950s and early 1960s. That at least was the generative moment, founding traditions very much alive today. It might be described, indeed, as the birth of cultural studies, though it also marked a break in history, literary criticism and sociology too. Politically this was the moment of the old New Left, of CND, of the crisis within the post-war Communist Party and of the launching of the political experiments around the early *New Left Review*. More widely it marked an exit-point, especially for left intellectuals, from the oppressions and frustration of the 1950s. Younger people now know this period mainly through some key texts. They include Richard Hoggart's *The Uses of Literacy* (1957), Raymond Williams's *Culture and Society* (1958) and *The Long Revolution* (1961) and Edward Thompson's *The Making of the English Working Class* (1963). At the centre of this movement were developments within a Marxist intellectual and political tradition (especially in Marxist history), but there were parallel shifts within non-Marxist intellectual traditions (such as an empirical sociology) and social-democratic politics too.

At the risk of considerable simplification (and subsequent chastisement) we might list the main features of early cultural studies.[3] The main concern was with lived experience, especially of subordinated classes and social groups. But there was also an interest in those intellectuals constituting the 'culture and society' traditions. The new field was defined, theoretically, through the elaboration of the notion of culture and its historical accretion of meanings (Williams) or through a re-working, in the light of 'culture' or 'experience', of the older Marxist category of 'class consciousness' (Thompson) or, more descriptively, through cultural memory and a certain nostalgia (Hoggart). There was a primary commitment to the concrete recreation of cultures and struggles, usually located in past time. History was the characteristic mode, whether histories of words or of social movements. This went along with an abiding suspicion of abstract categories, of hard and fast analytical distinctions, of 'base and superstructure', of aprioristic and mechanical reasoning, of theoretical impositions on experience. The preferred method was experiential, even autobiographical: witness Hoggart's personal memories and childhood vision, Williams's deeply autobiographical way of approaching larger questions, even Thompson's personalised polemic and deeply political historical partisanship. These styles went along with a popular, democratic, anti-élitist politics that centralised personal feelings and moral choices. The political style of the period, indeed, prefigured, in important ways, the 'new' politics of the 1960s and 1970s, especially the movements among students, among black people and the modern Women's Movement. It was also the earliest phase in a post–1950s development: the creation of broad radical strata drawn mainly from the college-going populations. Any account of the development of cultural studies needs to recognise this history and the recurrent political problem thus posed: the relation between radical cultural workers of this kind and the declining popular support for left politics more generally. The problem of the old New Left remains the problem today – the generalisation of popular transformation of elements first developed within a particular and restricted social milieu. Educational practices of all kinds are clearly at the forefront of these struggles.

This takes us to our second moment which I will call 'the moment of Theory'. I understand this as a development of the period from the late 1960s to mid–1970s. The main feature was a heightened – some would say fevered – encounter with new intellectual currents, often imported from other intellectual cultures. The role of particular centres, especially the newer *New Left Review*, was often crucial here. The consciously-pursued internationalisation of Marxist theory certainly transformed the debate about culture but it also tended to divorce it still further from common-sense understandings and from indigenous traditions. There were many strands in the importations, more or less assimilable to the older terms. The least digestible of these are usefully summed up, again risking over-simplification, as various kinds of 'structuralism'. I include here the Marxist structuralism of the French Communist philosopher, Louis Althusser and his collaborators, but also allied strands in French linguistics, including 'semiology' (in its successive modes) or the structuralist 'science of signs'. I include too the various modern schools of formalistic literary and filmic criticism represented in *Screen* and elsewhere and the development of work associated with the influence of the French historian, Michel Foucault.[4]

Again, we might list some key features. The most familiar of these has been the tendency to very abstract debates: a concern with general theoretical and epistemological questions – the nature of science and ideology, of language and of myth, of societies or 'social formations' in *general*. One characteristic abstraction from larger social processes has been that of ideological, symbolic, linguistic or 'discursive' practices or systems which are then analysed, mainly, in terms of their *internal* logics and processes. Much structuralist analysis has taken this form: the concern is with the ways that these systems, treated as texts, structure or position their (ideal and, more rarely, actual) readers or 'subjects'. This is a very different preoccupation from that of the older traditions with the cultural forms of life of particular historically-situated social groups and classes. Different too, in some variants, from a characteristically Marxist or sociological concern with 'social relations'. The preference is for an altogether more abstracted analysis of systems of representation – though this notion too has often been challenged by more thorough-going semiologists. Again, in some variants, one might note a reproduction of literary modes of analysis: again the main empirical object is the 'text', whether in the form of writing, image or film. It is an interesting speculation to ask how many of those now preoccupied with sign-systems and discourses, came to this interest through literary discipline, half breaking from them, half preserving them.

Even without a full familiarity with these debates, formidable in extent and 'difficulty', the oppositions that now largely define the field of cultural studies will be apparent.[5] 'Structuralism' did interrupt the older cultural studies, not least because it shared a concern with, in the largest sense, 'consciousness' or subjectivity. On the other hand, there was plenty of room for well-founded 'culturalist' ripostes. Hence the tendency to absolutist modes of argument, in which we are invited to take sides along the main lines of this opposition. I include here the many structuralist attacks on the 'humanism' or 'empiricism' of older paradigms and the more polemical counter-blasts from the other side. And since both structuralism and semiology were, in many variants, associated with Marxism, both were implicated too in the broader intellectual and political crisis of *this* tradition, sometimes promoted as solution, sometimes attacked as an un-materialist degeneration. The tendency to 'absolutism' was reinforced by one understandable (and, with reservations, useful) reaction to all this, a desire to return to 'fundamentals', represented by some preferred reading of the works of Karl Marx.

If we look optimistically at all this, it is possible to see that absolutist stances of all kinds – on behalf of 'history' or a rational epistemology, or of 'ideology' – are becoming more difficult to sustain. There has been a revival of interest in those Marxists of the past whose work promises some resolution of the contemporary oppositions. Gramsci has been especially important here as an unambiguously Marxist intellectual who broke from an older scientism and dogmatism, whose work had a historical reach similar to Marx's, and whose terms of analysis and commitment speak directly to the political dilemmas of today.[6] But there are many other hopeful currents too. Feminism is making its own distinctive contributions, initially by marking out an intellectual and political territory of its own, latterly moving out from this necessary autonomy to transform old politics and old categories. Because feminism had no developed theoretical tradition of its own, women have been forced to think more freshly in the light of experiences made more conscious by their own forms of personal politics. There is also, if I read the signs aright, a marked move back to concrete studies and to 'history' in that sense, but informed now by what has been learned in structuralist and theoretical detours. There is much more mixing too of codes and disciplines and media: of autobiography, fiction and history, of historical re-creation and filmic practice, of radical theatre, humour, song and intellectual analysis. It is becoming more exciting to teach again as it was, for me, even in a conventional Redbrick university, in the late 1960s and early 1970s. Above all, perhaps, despite the widespread sense of guilt and frustration, intellectual energies are turning again to the need for a really living popular connection –

a return to the problems of the late 1950s, but with new tools and new possibilities.

Combining Insights

So it has become easier than it was two or so years ago, to argue that practical needs are best served by combining, in an imaginative, careful and reasoned way, elements from different intellectual and political traditions. Intellectually, there are perhaps two especially useful tasks. The first is to stress the *common* elements, including the common problems of different traditions (always present but hidden by an over-polemical relation); the second is deliberately to promote the understanding of *particular contemporary problems* over the overvalued pursuit of theoretical purity or partisanship. These problems, especially those concerning the relation between the 'intellectual' and the 'popular', have always in practice set the agenda, but ought now to do so self-consciously. That is not a recipe for abandoning intellectual or general concerns, though it should certainly lead to a questioning of the social divisions of labour of intellectual *functions*. But to abandon 'theory' is an impossible project anyway, since the categories we think in always have a particular intellectual location and historical origin. I want to argue first around some common problems and then give some instances, mainly from work I'm currently involved in, of the need to combine insights. I'll then try to draw some conclusions for educational practice.

One common set of problems is posed by the inclusiveness of the chief categories of both structuralist and culturalist accounts. In the English tradition this is indicated by the persistent fuzziness of the key term culture itself. Williams's 'whole way of life' certainly broke decisively with élitist or narrowly genre-based conceptions of culture. But what was embraced, in turn, was a generalised notion of human practice, production or creativity. Williams, a great transformer of categories, including his own, has in his later work put struggle back into the heart of his theorisations, but as Thompson pointed out in 1961 and as other critics have noted, in this conception of culture the distinction between cultural and other forms of production is blurred.[7] It therefore becomes difficult to talk about the structural or material determinations on cultural form, cultural difference and cultural relations, to relate culture to not-culture-at-all. Thompson himself attempts to solve this problem by re-working a distinction in Marx between 'social being' and 'social consciousness' or, more typically in his historical writing, to charge the term 'experience' with a double meaning. 'Experience' denotes the material conditions of different forms of consciousness. It also indicates the sense that is made of these conditions. Such formulations – 'Experience 1' and 'Experience 2' in his most recent clarification – still permit of great ambiguity.[8] I have argued elsewhere that the English tradition, even in its overtly Marxist forms, is persistently dogged by a lack of clarity, that derives from a refusal to abstract even as a moment of analysis. Without some more developed notion of ideology or of the internal rules of cultural production, these formulations remain, for me, insufficiently theorised.

If we transpose this problem into one of pedagogic practice, the point may be clearer. There is a long-established pedagogy that emphasises the role of the teacher, especially, perhaps, of the teacher of English, as enabling the self-expression of the pupil. Like some notions of culture or 'experience', this pedagogy may be inadequate on its own. The products of self-expression or the act of expression itself are taken unproblematically and may acquire, indeed, a peculiar authenticity. Of course, there is a sense in which such accounts *are* both the beginning and the end of such a practice, and rightly: they are a direct route to practical skills and confidence. But they also arise from definite material conditions and especially from asymmetrical relations of power and dependency, particularly those structured by class, race and gender. They also represent a particular individual (or collective) appropriation of the terms of making sense in our society, including dominant elements properly called ideological. The fuller pedagogy therefore consists of a further labour upon the products of self-expression, not by the teacher alone but by readers and writers too, in which this text becomes a route for exploring both structural conditions and ideological representations. We could only think about teaching in this way (if indeed it is useful and intelligible) if we took that notion 'experience' as in some way problematic, and really (not just 'theoretically') fissured.

Structuralisms in their purer forms, however, have no ready answer to this problem. Indeed, there is a parallel slide by which ideology or discourses come to cover the whole sphere of the social, threatening a relapse into quite idealistic formulations. 'Experience' quite disappears in either of its primary meanings. Either that, or it is seen entirely as the product of ideology and ideological subordination. The classroom text, in the pedagogic example, becomes worthless, except perhaps as wholly deconstructed by the teacher. In fact, I find it very difficult to conceive of any effective pedagogy based upon these principles alone. In more materialist versions, as in a classic Althusserianism for example, material conditions ('the economic') are certainly present.

The problem here is that each kind of social relation or social practice – the economic, the ideological and the political – acquires such an autonomy of its own that it becomes difficult to explore the effective relations between them. The point of intersection of these 'instances' – experience if you will – is, again, absent.

The suggested solution to this, implicit in the pedagogic example, is twofold. We need to distinguish the cultural and ideological from other aspects or practices; but we need also to make distinctions *within* the general sphere of the cultural or ideological. There is already, within Marxism, a general term – 'consciousness' – that makes the primary distinction. Marx's notion of consciousness (not consciousness of class but consciousness-in-general) denotes that specifically human attribute, evident in all history.[9] Just as human beings have always won a living from nature and sustained their material existence, so also they 'possess consciousness'. The characteristic feature of the cultural/ideological, then, is the production of forms of consciousness – ideas, feelings, desires, moral preferences, knowledges, forms of consciousness of self. If we understand 'culture' in this way, the full distancing from partial and trivialising versions becomes apparent. There is, for instance, no separate institutional sphere of social life in which forms of consciousness arise: mentalities and subjectivities are formed in every sphere of existence, in all social sites. They are formed very powerfully, for example, in processes of economic production. Economic practices – production *and* consumption – depend, indeed, upon cultural conditions. As Foucault's notion of discourse recognises, political or regulatory practices are also always practices involving knowledge.[10] Such a notion has nothing in common with culture as a residuum, left over when other things have been subtracted. Nor is it in any way similar to culture as limited to certain specialised activities – reading, writing, watching films or playing football. But it includes all these, looked at from a particular aspect: the production of forms of consciousness.

Like all simple abstractions of this kind, though, 'consciousness' only provides the basis for further analysis. It bounds a particular object of inquiry. It also has certain useful connotations: of the conscious and the not-conscious, of activity and engagement, of coming or raising *into* consciousness. But the key task of cultural studies (in this definition) is to specify the social and the historical *forms* of consciousness and, more analytically, the processes or circuits through which they are produced.

The second suggested solution is to employ the terms of cultural and ideological analysis not as opposed terms but as complementary ones. And at this point, if only to break the abstractness or the argument, it is useful to pose the problem in relation to a concrete case.

Ideology, Culture and Schooling

The concrete case is the problem of the transformation of the whole field of debate and effective relations of force in educational policy in the 1970s. A group of us at the Birmingham centre have been preparing a book about this.[11] We wanted to look both at the dynamic of public debate itself (what we called 'ideologies of schooling') and at the lived experience of schooling (what we called 'the culture of schools'). We adopted this approach because we wanted to know how the new Conservatisms of the 1970s acquired their contemporary dominance, enabling the current restructuring of formal education. We wanted to think about an adequate response which would also be a popular response. The primary question, then, was how had this ground been won, and how deeply, how securely? What *was* the popular purchase of Thatcherism's educational variant? How had Thatcherite ideologies connected with a grass-roots experience of schooling and turned the tables on the dominant 1960s tendencies? Some parts of this were easier to deliver than others. We early reached the conclusion that part of the answer lay in the character of the preceding phases, patently in crisis at the time when we started the research. The New Right succeeded, in part, by colonising the absences in 1960s 'social-democratic' orthodoxies and by working on their contradictions. Economic crisis accelerated and deepened this process, underway long before the Labour Government lost the election. All this involved looking closely at public discourses of all kinds: political programmes and debates ('great' and puny), media representations and the professional knowledges of the field, especially the sociology and economics of education. We had, perhaps, a stronger sense of the 'non-discursive' than is sometimes the case.

We were particularly interested in the social basis of the 1960s settlement: who were the most active protagonists, who benefited most from the policies, which groups and classes were virtually excluded, as 'problem' populations, from the 1960s alliances? We were also concerned to show how promises of equalisation or expansion or 'growth' were precisely promises – not realised, differentially realised, often unrealisable. It was more difficult to make the connection with the popular experience of schooling, though we were committed, theoretically, to seeing this as a generative aspect, more than merely an effect. But the point to stress is that we found it completely illegitimate to infer the character of popular experiences from the field of ideological representations. Research in or near the group, which focused on the deeply contradictory experience of schooling for working-class girls and boys, showed that, even within the school, one entered a whole new domain of transformations.[12] These could not be grasped or inferred from even a developed history of schooling, sensitive to specifically ideological processes. It was not possible, in particular to infer the popularity Thatcherism from an analysis of the public debates and policies. A different kind of research was required.

If we now stand back from the case, it is possible to theorise this in relation to our general argument. The terms culture and ideology actually refer to different moments or aspects of a larger process. They require different forms of analysis and of research. Cultural analysis concerns those shared and lived principles of life, characteristic of particular classes, social groups and social milieux. It is always particular, located, observational. It attempts to grasp forms of consciousness as ensembles of lived beliefs and their modes of expression. It has always to concern particular groups of persons. Paul Willis's or Angela McRobbie's accounts of the masculine and feminine cultures of school students are good examples here, but the usage is very close to those of the English tradition in its less literary forms. It is especially close to Hoggart's. It is similar too to what Gramsci called 'common sense' – 'the spontaneous philosophy that is proper to everyone'.[13] Common sense, or culture, is intimate with practical activity. It suffices, for most of the time, to manage the world of practical action. Since this world itself is problematic, culture must perforce take heterogeneous and sometimes contradictory forms. The analysis of ideologies (or all forms of the analysis of systems of signification or representation) takes a different, but related, object: conceptions of the world, of the self or of nature in a different moment of their circulation. The *possibility* of this form of analysis rests upon particular conditions: that thought and evaluation may be concretised in 'texts' or objects and may be there analysed in another more abstracted way. In particular the possibility of this arises wherever 'conception' is separated from other activities and becomes thereby the province of 'intellectuals'.[14] This particular division of labour has, in modern societies, acquired immensely elaborated institutional forms, especially in the educational curricula and in the whole range of the media. Conceptions are carried in the minds of social individuals but are also written down, communicated, inscribed and coded in different ways. This real abstraction allows us to take ideologies or ideological fields as a definite object of critical study though it provides no warrant to forget their actual connection with wider processes, or indeed to vacate the other 'cultural' ground. It is only in combination, indeed, that cultural and ideological analysis approaches a more complete account of the ways in which specific forms of consciousness are produced.

Debates on education, then, are a classic example of the ideological moment of this circuit. The way in which the *Daily Mail*, for instance, a key intellectual instrument for the Right, ripped its *causes célèbres* out of their living context in the schools and constructed them into its own argument of crisis, would provide (if space allowed) a compelling illustration! But we could also follow through the analysis of the two moments into the schools themselves. We could certainly conduct, for example, an ideological analysis of the formal curricula of school. We could also look at the morning assembly of the infants' department of an English primary school from this perspective, attending to the stories and prayers which the headmistress chooses and their preferred accounts of infant happiness, of school, or of God. We could also be concerned with the particular bodily and social regime that prescribes that children sit cross-legged, in reasonable but informal order, inside a large chalk circle drawn upon the floor or occupy chairs in serried ranks as is more common in the secondary school (and appropriate to less pliable bodies and minds). But such analysis could not deliver, on its own, any account of the effect of such practices on the consciousness of the children, or, indeed, a judgement about their controlling or liberating tendency. *It is tempting, but completely illegitimate, to infer lived effects from structural analysis.* We would have to look, with a different sort of curiosity, at all those shuffles and exchanges inside the circle of chalk. We would have to learn more about the broader cultural and material contexts of these childhoods and the way in which groups of children, boys and girls, black and white, working-class and middle-class, produce their own meanings. We now know that this process *always* involves transformations, blocking, inversions, complex reproductions. And we'd have to ask similar kinds of questions about the lived cultures of teachers and about the parents (predominantly mothers) who are present at these particular proceedings every Wednesday. We would soon exhaust, especially in the necessary or symptomatic absence of the fathers, what could be learned from this particular event. And we would have to take account of what *they* were doing, and the chains of consequences that followed from that.

One further general point which is of key importance for the educational implications: the culture/ideology relation is not merely analytical or descriptive; it is also social and political. All groups develop their own common senses of the world; but they have radically different relations to public or formal representations – to the 'dominant culture' in this special sense. This is partly a matter of access: of the visibility, in something like its own terms, of the cultures of dominated groups. But there are more active oppressions involved since black people, women and working-class 'representatives' do actually appear in media discourses but only in certain ways and contexts. The culture/ideology relation is, therefore, an important site of domination and oppression and reinforces the asymmetry of other social relations. This is the principal reason why the culture/ideology relation always involves struggles and transformations, and why there can never be, in societies structured in this way, a system of perfect communication, that persistent liberal dream. The same is true, for that matter, of the search for a 'perfect' pedagogy though here, among all the other transformations, are those particularly associated with age and the social construction of 'childhood'. Age – rank relations are, in themselves, sufficient to guarantee that the messages of the teacher and of the school will never be taken 'straight', but always played with, according to the resistances of childhood.

Educational Implications

Perhaps there are two sorts of implications: those for teaching cultural studies (or anything like it) and those for pedagogies in general. But in both cases these *are* only 'implications', untested in practice in the schools.[15]

The various aspects of cultural studies are mutually dependent, requiring each other for completion. If we want to know the conditions under which particular ideologies (from Thatcherism to a new popular socialist-feminism!) become principles of life, we have to attend both to public representations and lived cultures. But we won't understand these aspects of consciousness unless we also investigate the structural and historical position, in different social relations, of particular social classes and groups. We can't understand black cultures and white racisms without a structural account of the position of black people today or some knowledge of a long history of slavery and colonial plantation or conquest and Empire. We can't understand femininity or masculinity as cultural products without an analysis of patriarchy's structural supports and a history of (at least) post-war struggles. We won't succeed in working with or across class-cultural forms without some concept of class and some historical account that takes us deeper than the common-sense of 'stratification', or the idea that 'class' is a residual cultural feature (like pin-striped trousers or posh accents).

That means, in the classroom, that there are many different starting-points but that the struggle should be to move round the whole circuit of determinations. Certainly one starting-point is to treat everyday public representations – newspapers, adverts, television programmes, films, and popular literary forms – as objects of relatively detached critical analysis. There *are* relatively independent questions to ask here: what is the image/report/programme 'saying'? What effect or 'reality' does it construct? What is the 'world' of reporting on soccer 'hooliganism', of *Jackie*'s stories, of the advertisers' images of the feminine? But of course the classroom work can't and shouldn't end there. What the image 'says' has also to be posed for a particular, structured audience or readership. What the image says is also itself constructed and produced by processes that don't show up in the text. Two obvious moves, therefore, are into the cultural experience of readership and into the process of cultural production: the first leads to discussion and the attempt to record and understand responses; the second to some form of cultural practice – writing, video or whatever.

Alternatively, a start could be made with sources that are of a richer more experiential character. (Popular representations *may* be fruitfully read in this way too but that would be a very complex place to start.) These might, centrally, be autobiographical, or fictional sources with a strongly autobiographical character, including the school students' own productions. Again, as I suggested earlier, the notion that these are 'experiential' texts, disguises the artifice and conditions that affect their production, but there is now a wealth of material that *is* more directly rooted in popular experience – I mean the whole range of popular autobiographies, oral histories, community history projects. The educational implications of the evocation of such materials are, in themselves, extremely interesting. I've already noted how such materials could be used. The important thing is actually to *use* them, *develop* them, *work* on them, not expect them to deliver up a message simply. Such sources, in other words, should be treated as a *product*, a social – historical product, not just as an individual 'statement'.

We can best pose the larger pedagogic questions through the cultural studies case. We might predict two sorts of results in such teaching: first, that the teacher's aims will be systematically transformed in the consciousness of the children and (if we get that far!) in their productions; second, that the transformations will take systematically different and partially contradictory forms. It follows, from the first prediction, that all pedagogies should be experimental or explorative, in the sense that they take the transformations themselves as a further object of study. In 'cultural studies', of course, this is not only a legitimate but an absolutely necessary moment of practice which should, moreover, be pursued collectively, by the whole group. This means the development in a group or a class of a degree of self-consciousness about its own interactions, unusual wherever a more abstracted curriculum is used. Part of the object of study lies in the structured interactions of the group or class itself.

The point about difference and contradiction is more difficult. But it is clear that lessons on the media, say, that raise the issues of racism and sexism will mean completely different things to black and white children and boys and girls. Girls 'know' about sexism in a way boys don't: a lot of such a lesson would be 'obvious' or worse. The same is true of black children, white children and racism. If the teacher sets the aim of encouraging boys and white children to question their own attitudes, there is a danger that black children and girls become, in this discourse, passive bearers of problems. Such a lesson would involve, then, a different pedagogy for black children or girls encouraging them, for example, into an active role in challenging the racism or sexism of their classmates. One clear prerequisite here (and there are certainly more radical conclusions to be drawn) is that the teacher must take, or be capable of taking, the standpoint of the oppressed.

Notes

1. This paper was given at a day school on Popular Culture held at the Inner London Education Authority (ILEA) English Centre, in conjunction with the Society for Education in Film and Television (SEFT) on 10 November 1979. It ought to be read alongside Hazel Carby's article, hers being the more concrete working through of problems.

2. One effect of these identifications is to exclude women from 'culture', since the term 'leisure' is of doubtful application to women's experience: this question is explored in a forthcoming Course for Contemporary Cultural Studies (CCCS) paper by D. Hobson, C. Griffin, T. MacCabe and S. Mackintosh. On the concept of leisure in cultural analysis, see Simon Frith's article in this issue.

3. For a recent exchange on these questions see Edward Thompson, 'The Politics of Theory', in the forthcoming volume of Ruskin History Workshop Papers. For a longer analysis see Richard Johnson, 'The Three

Problematics', in J. Clarke, C. Critcher and R. Johnson (eds), *Working Class Culture*, London: Hutchinson, 1979.

4. For a fuller identification see *Working Class Culture*, op. cit; for a more extended review see Rosalind Coward and John Ellis, *Language and Materialism*, London: Routledge & Kegan Paul, 1976, and Tony Bennett, *Formalism and Marxism*, London: Methuen, 1979.

5. For a longer account of the opposition see Richard Johnson, 'Histories of Culture/Theories of Ideology', in Michele Barrett *et al.* (eds) *Ideology and Cultural Production*, London: Croom Helm, 1979.

6. For an interesting review of recent work on Gramsci see Bob Jessop, 'The Gramsci Debate', in *Marxism Today*, February 1980.

7. E. P. Thompson, 'Review of *The Long Revolution*', *New Left Review*, nos. 9–10, 1961.

8. In Thompson, 'Politics of Theory', op. cit.

9. They key source here is the *German Ideology*, but there are important references also in Marx's 'mature' work, especially *Capital*.

10. See, for example, M. Foucault, *Discipline and Punish: The Birth of the Prison*, London: Allen Lane, 1977, p. 27.

11. *Unpopular Education: Schooling and Social Democracy in England since 1944*, London: Hutchinson, 1981.

12. See especially Paul Willis, *Learning to Labour: How Working-Class Kids Get Working-Class Jobs*, London: Saxon House, 1977, and Angela McRobbie, 'Working-class Girls and the Culture of Femininity', in CCCS Women's Studies Group *Women Take Issue*, London: Hutchinson, 1978.

13. Quintin Hoare and Geoffrey Nowell-Smith (eds), *Selection from the Prison Notebooks of Antonio Gramsci*, London: Lawrence & Wishart, 1971, p. 323.

14. Using 'intellectuals' in the expanded sense in which it is used by Marx ('active conceptive ideologists') and by Gramsci (all those with an 'educative' or 'directive' function).

15. Teachers already working from the sort of perspective I outline here (or who would like to develop this sort of work) may be interested in two collections of materials relevant to schools which are now being prepared by people associated with the Centre for Contemporary Cultural Studies – a book for girls (contact Trisha McCabe or Angela McRobbie) and a book for teachers of cultural studies (contact me, Mike Shaughnessy or Hazel Carby). We would also welcome responses from teachers to this article and to the one by Hazel. The address is CCCS, University of Birmingham, P.O. Box 363, Birmingham B15 2TT.

Chapter 17
Multi-Culture*

Hazel Carby

Anti-racist teachers are faced with a dilemma: how should they respond to the range of new policies that are affecting black students in British schools? On the one hand, 'multi-culturalism' offers one of the very few remaining areas in which resources are being made available for curricular innovation. As Clara Mulhern argues in a document produced in November 1979 by ALTARF (All London Teachers Against Racism and Fascism):

> In a climate of retrenchment and defensiveness in education, when many of the curricular innovations of the Sixties are under attack, practically the only present source of progressive perspectives on the curriculum is the concept of multi-culturalism.[1]

But in the same month, the Organisation of Women of Asian and African Descent pointed tellingly to a different aspect of policy.

> It is no coincidence that the cuts in education will not mean a reduction in the number of disruptive units. Some boroughs are even considering building more, despite their reduced budgets.[2]

The problem often seems to be that discussions about the nature of curricular changes that could adequately reflect a multiracial society tend to avoid – or at least to address only implicitly –

* *Screen Education*, no. 34, Spring 1980.

issues of discipline and control which are central to education practice. The twofold strategy of educational policy at the moment is apparently to win consent in the classroom and, if and when that fails, to bring coercion into play; and increasingly it is black students who are subjected to coercive strategies. What therefore need examination are not just courses and curricula, but also the social relations of classrooms and schools in relation to the wider material and ideological structures within which both teachers and pupils are located. A distinction has to be drawn between attempts to confront racism by changing educational policy and an understanding of educational racism as one instance of institutionalised racism in the context of other forms of institutionalised racism within a racist society. Policy, in short, cannot be divorced from politics.[3]

In current educational debates, multi-culturalism is generally accepted as a positive practice with which teachers committed to an anti-racist society should be engaged. But despite the useful teaching produced from this perspective and the importance of ALTARF in creating a space in which white, anti-racist teachers can assess their work, there seems to be little questioning of what multi-culturalism is. In this article I shall therefore address the limitations of the approach – the exclusive way that the concept poses questions about race and its implications, as an educational theory, for educational practice.

Policy and Educational Theory

The terms in which the argument for a multi-cultural curriculum is usually posed are not new; they are drawn from earlier debates about the need to counteract working-class educational failure. Theories of 'deficiency' and 'deprivation' were mobilised in these to support policies of channelling increased resources to inner-city schools and creating Educational Priority Areas. A similar strategy of positive discrimination was embodied in the Race Relations Act, 1976, which obliged local authorities to take positive action to promote equal opportunities. In this context education is seen as central in forging a new, more egalitarian and more democratic society. The Inner London Education Authority's (ILEA's) 1977 report, *A Multi-Ethnic Education*, asserts that:

> Unequivocally the commitment is to all. Just as there must be no second class citizens, so there must be no second class educational opportunities.[4]

The purpose of educational policies is thus to promote tolerance between social groups and so produce a society displaying an equilibrium among ethnic groupings and between classes. The school is made a site for containing the effects of racism.

The need for multi-cultural education has not been regarded only as an ideal, however. According to the 1977 Green Paper *Education in Schools*, it is a practical necessity for constructing the society of the future.

> Ours is now a multiracial and multicultural country and one in which traditional social patterns are breaking down . . . the comprehensive school reflects the need to educate our people for a different sort of society . . . the education appropriate to our Imperial past cannot meet the requirements of modern Britain.[5]

This reference back to 'our Imperial past' does hint at the basis of interracial conflict in social relations of exploitation, but this is presented as a historical rather than a structural consideration. The 'breaking down' of 'traditional social patterns' is presented as a natural, evolutionary progress; the antagonism, conflict and contradictions inherent in the process are disguised. The specific contribution of schools to the development of a racially just society is to 'tackle with sustained enthusiasm the problems of children from other cultures or speaking other languages and make a microcosm of a happy and co-operative world.[6]

A similar perspective informs the work of educational theorists like Robert Jeffcoate, whose book *Positive Image* draws on his involvement in the (so far unpublished) Schools Council report on multiracial education; he now works in the Racial Minorities Unit at the Open University. The multiracial classroom, he argues, should be 'a place where pride in race is affirmed and where inter-racial friendship and understanding are celebrated'.[7] By dismissing 'tensions and animosities', the multiracial curriculum is supposed to create an environment in which 'the kind of racial slurs . . . traded in the playground [are] not traded in the classroom',[8] Jeffcoate assumes it can achieve these effects in isolation from 'negative and divisive outside pressures'. Such sentiments, common to both Jeffcoate and the Green Paper, are based on a shared assumption that schools somehow *reflect* society, that a classroom can be a microcosm of society. But schools are also seen as a catalyst – the creation of 'happy and co-operative classrooms' *will* influence the wider society and help to bring about a 'happy and co-operative world'. In justifying (and celebrating) his optimism, Jeffcoate 'pins his hopes' on the generation

now at school rather than on any structural – political or economic
– changes. He leaves unexplored the relationship between (a) his
students' display of multiracial co-operation in his classroom, (b)
their trading of 'racial slurs' in the playground and (c) the 'tensions
and animosities' outside the school. He fails to conceptualise the
students – and their teachers – as living in and subject to these
'negative and divisive outside pressures'.

It is this account of the school/society relationship in educational
policy that needs to be called into question. Both the Green
Paper and the ILEA report from which I have quoted are official
documents produced within state institutions. One of their ideological effects is to conjure up a 'national interest' based on an
assumed consensus of social interests, problems and solutions.
Through a range of discursive techniques,[9] this apparent unity is
imposed upon and subsumes inherent contradictions and conflicting economic and political interests within and between racial,
sexual or class groupings. This normative pluralism not only
ignores the institutional differentiation of interests but actually
makes it impossible even to raise the question of the *construction*
of inequality. Increasingly rigid immigration laws designed to limit
black entry into Britain, police harassment and inequalities in
housing and employment are not just detrimental to the interests
of the black community, but they actually construct certain racial
groups as 'less equal' than others. In these material conditions,
black students *know* that they are second-class citizens – in school
as much as anywhere else.

It is here that the theoretical insights of Cultural Studies, as
described by Richard Johnson in his article elsewhere in this issue,
are important. By insisting that 'culture' denotes antagonistic
relations of domination and subordination, this perspective under-
mines the pluralistic notion of compatibility inherent in *multi*-
culturalism, the idea of a homogeneous national culture (innocent
of class or gender differences) into which other equally generalised
Caribbean or Asian cultures can be integrated. The paradigm of
multiculturalism actually excludes the concept of dominant and
subordinate cultures – either indigenous or migrant – and fails to
recognise that the existence of racism relates to the possession
and exercise of politico-economic control and authority and also
to forms of resistance to the power of dominant social groups.
Based upon liberal, humanistic notions of the individual experience of other cultures, multiculturalism proposes the classroom as
the locus in which the cultures of racial minorities in contemporary
Britain should be shared. The greater understanding achieved at
this level is then meant to flow outwards to create a more harmoni-
ous society. In this account, schools are expected to affect wider

social relations but are paradoxically granted autonomy from the effects of that society. The social relations of schools and classrooms are reduced to the single question of the transmission of a curriculum. But, as Richard Johnson argues, the material being worked on in a classroom – the texts – is separate from the cultures as lived in the school, the lived experiences brought to the school and lived in the social relations of the school by both teachers and students. Multiculturalism assumes that it is only the material taught that is problematic.

Robert Jeffcoate dismisses as 'pathological' and 'tendentious' any argument that sees racism as endemic in Britain or as a cultural norm which moulds children's attitudes. He also complains that debates about race have 'become confounded' with debates about immigration.[10] To argue that the two debates should not be confounded, though, actually ignores their structural and historical interrelationship. Imperialism used race as a mechanism for economic, political and socio-cultural forms of exploitation and dominance. At present a different form of exploitation is being experienced within the Mother Country of that colonial system. Although the specific nature of the relationship has changed, of course, race is still seen as 'the issue'. In the terms of common sense, white immigration is effectively disregarded: the policies of successive governments have been designed to prevent non-whites from entering Britain; there's no doubt about who 'they' are in comments like 'we don't want any more of them'. 'Immigrant' has become synonymous with 'black'. It is not therefore a question of the issues of race and immigration being confounded: rather, the immigration laws and the dominant forms of representation in this area of debate are profoundly racist.

The central proposition here is that 'blacks are a problem'. The Green Paper refers to the '*problems* of children from other cultures'; the ILEA report addresses the *problem* of black students as low achievers, which has become associated with the corollary *problems* of black crime and unemployed black youth; Robert Jeffcoate sees the *problem* of black students' negative self-images as central. Thus black educational failure is taken to guarantee that the root problem is that of the ethnic minorities themselves.[11] Black people are constructed as a social problem; the concept of multi-culturalism mobilises a 'race relations' discourse and a range of social (educational) policies to 'deal with' the problem.

Texts

The aspect of policy that I am mainly concerned with in this article is the use of texts in the multicultural curriculum to promote 'racial harmony' by creating an unproblematic understanding of the culture of 'others'. Robert Jeffcoate argues for a fairly common but oversimplified methodology: he implies that the complexities of racism can be reduced to a simple binary opposition of positive/negative and that negative images can be reversed, like a photograph, and displaced by prominent and positive representations. (The cover of his book is an effective metaphor for this argument.) If they accept this logic, even teachers who would normally eschew the use of filmic, televisual or fictional literary texts to solve 'real-life' problems can find themselves arguing that the use of texts which represent blacks positively somehow reflects the needs of ethnic minorities and would allow teachers to combat racism in the classroom. This notion of an imbalance in the curriculum which needs rectification ignores both the social, political and economic determinations on the school as an institution and also the class, gender and racial positions of subjects within that institution. In Richard Johnson's terms, the texts to be worked on and the 'lived relations' present in the classroom are not held separate; they therefore become obscured and are reduced to equivalents.

If these two elements are not distinguished, it is impossible to take proper account of how both of them determine and constrain what teaching and learning can effectively be achieved. The reasons for a white student's refusal to read a 'Paki book' or for students' resistance to watching a play by black girls cannot be deduced just from the 'positive' texts. Nor can these 'positive' texts be assumed (though they often are) to show 'blacks as they really are', as against the misrepresentations in ethnocentric or racist texts – a notion which would appear ridiculous if applied so simplistically to white characters. Teachers should therefore not be as surprised as they sometimes have been when, say, Farrukh Dhondy's short stories provoke a hostile response; when white students harden their racist responses and black students adopt strategies to exclude whites in the classroom from the availability of certain meanings. This increased divisiveness, rather than the expected cooperation, cannot be understood or explained if the 'culture of the classroom' is seen as separate from 'outside' tensions and from the determinations upon the attitudes students and teachers bring to the texts and which are being lived in the classroom in spite of, not *because* of, the texts. The point is not that the texts have no effectivity or that they should not be analysed in terms of their reconstruction of dominant ideologies (that's the pedagogic purpose): on the contrary, it is to draw attention to the unargued psychological assumption that *these* texts will have *these* effects on any individual student, and to question quite radically the notion that actual responses to a text are wholly determined by the way it 'positions' its 'reader'. Because, as Paul Willemen argues in his 'Notes on Subjectivity', the inscribed reader

> is itself already an imaginary unity, a mapping onto each other of different You's produced by the plurality of discourses that constitutes the text, the construction of that unity will differ according to the discourses (knowledges, prejudices, resistances, etc.) brought to bear by given readers on that place. It is in this sense that inscribed subject positions are never hermetically sealed into a text, but are always positions in ideologies. Texts can restrict readings (offer resistances), they cannot determine them.[12]

Multiculturalist approaches to the examination of black cultures in schools generally tend to be as reductionist as their use of texts. The main purpose often seems to be to do no more than prove that 'blacks have a culture too'. Thus the case is made for including established West Indian and Asian authors in an O level syllabus (see the *Times Educational Supplement*, 13 October 1978) – 'established' here indicating literary texts which can be assimilated into the pantheon of a high cultural tradition. Alternatively, the introduction of black culture is seen in terms of the *ad hoc* incorporation of forms considered 'relevant' to pupils' 'lifestyle' – reggae, the poetry of Linton Kwesi Johnson, young black people's own writing, Rastafarianism. Again, the tendency in such teaching is to reduce 'black culture' to the artefacts produced within a limited number of 'cultural' sites – the arts, religion and so forth. These manifestations are thus divorced from the political and economic struggles of being black in Britain, whether in school or in the labour market; the ways in which a culture is produced from and about the social relations of these sites and struggles remain unexplored. To take one of the most common examples, much contemporary reggae music can be said to be about the forms of resistance of urban black youth, about their refusal to be perpetual victims. Many songs voice the need for this resistance: but they can lose any political relevance if they are treated as a purely 'cultural' artefact that is 'popular' as opposed to 'high'. It is also misleading to assume that these records unproblematically represent the students' own culture that can be brought into the classroom. As soon as questions about production and consumption are raised, it becomes obvious that urban black youth have no control over their marketing or distribution. Other interests are involved – multinational record companies seeking a mass audience for their product, for example, will consider the music's appeal to white consumers as well as a black audience. An expression of black consciousness can equally well be good to dance to at a white middle-class party.

Similarly, language itself should be seen as a site of struggle over meanings: this makes it possible to understand the relation between a white teacher's use of standard English and a black student's use of an alternative form as a mode of resistance. A teacher may be excluded from understanding through the student's use of patois or the student may be labelled as insolent by the teacher for rejecting the required set of meanings:

> 'And no blue and green tights. I want all the girls to wear flesh coloured tights'.
>   'Whose flesh, miss?' Lorraine asked.[13]

The struggle over whose terms will be definitive is not restricted to texts, and these broader contexts also need to be explored. How are superior/inferior or correct/incorrect attitudes inscribed within language in and through the social relations between dominant and subordinated groups? Why do non-racist texts produce racist readings – refusals to accept the preferred reading encoded at the point of their production? Once we recognise that texts have to *work* to neutralise contradictions and produce imaginary resolutions, we then need to examine not only the way texts are produced but also the differential nature of the responses they evoke. Instead of assuming that all texts are incorporated into a dominant ideology, we should ask what contradictions are present and how they are being handled. Why, for example, is romance mobilised in the BBC series *Empire Road* to resolve (at an imaginary level) racial conflict? Rather than asking how accurately it represents black life, *Empire Road* could be questioned in the light of a comment by the show's leading actress, Corinne Skinner-Carter.

> Writers don't like writing for women – even Michael [Abbensetts] . . . I've always accused him of being a chauvinistic pig. The women in *Empire Road* are passive. I'm only there because Norman must have a wife – because if he wants a cup of coffee he can't make it for himself.[14]

Invisible Woman

From the pedagogic point of view, the really important question
is the specific ways in which texts are used, where and by whom.
In the context of multi-cultural education, black or anti-racist
books, films and television programmes are used mainly by white
teachers for the purposes of understanding black cultures: the
black voice is noticeably absent from the debate about the multi-
cultural curriculum. I can illuminate these points by looking at a
specific question – the 'invisibility' of black women. Courses in
Black Studies or Black History are usually male-centred and relate
to white patriarchal society; in the same way, Women's Studies
courses focus almost exclusively upon aspects of white women's
lives. In sociological and cultural research, it is the forms of
subcultural resistances by black male youth that are analysed.
Sexism is implicit in the stories of Farrukh Dhondy and, despite
a contradictory sequence showing the Grunwick dispute, the
woman's voice is not heard in the film *Blacks Britannica*. Black
women are seldom recognised as a particular socio-cultural entity,
nor as important enough to merit serious academic consideration.

How could a white woman teacher rectify this omission? There
now exist texts in which black women write about the influence
of white societies and confront the past and present in personal
and historical terms; they address the need to reverse the present
order through an increasing awareness of self and understanding
of the political and economic pressures that underlie present conditions. The writings of Ama Ata Aidoo, Toni Cade Bambara,
Buchi Emecheta, Rosa Guy, Joyce Ladner, Toni Morrison, Alice
Walker and Amrit Wilson are part of the struggle to challenge
dominant white conceptions of black women and to voice the
need for economic, political and personal power to change the
fantasies that limit and construct the black woman.[15] They are
part of a growing body of work which can be used by women
teachers to explore, not just the process of growing up female in
a patriarchal society, but also the ways in which growing up female
and black means coping with racial oppression at an early age
and developing self-reliance and resilience. The spectre of white
beauty can here be seen as hauntingly destructive:

I destroyed white baby dolls. But the dismembering of dolls
was not the true horror. The truly horrifying thing was the
transference of the same impulse to little white girls. The indif-
ference with which I could have axed them was shaken only by
my desire to do so. To discover what eluded me: the secret of
the magic they weaved on others. What made people look at

them and say, 'Awwwww,' but not for me . . . The best hiding place was love. Thus the conversion from pristine sadism to fabricated hatred, to fraudulent love. It was a small step to Shirley Temple. I learned much later to worship her . . . knowing, even as I had learned, that the change was adjustment without improvement.[16]

The point of this extended example is to illustrate the potential and also the problems of introducing such texts. They should certainly help white teachers to understand the culture of black women. But this does not mean that they can be granted a privileged status. They do not simply express the experience of black women; like the other texts I have mentioned, they represent that experience in particular ways that have to be worked on by readers. Returning to Richard Johnson's two moments of a culturally-informed pedagogy, the continuing absence of such texts from schools and from Women's Studies courses means that useful teaching about how black women are constructed as a category cannot even begin. Including these texts in a teaching programme is only half the problem, though, because Johnson's second moment, the cultures brought to bear by students, still obtains. For example, a white woman teacher, maybe for feminist reasons, may care about the position of black women and want to learn about them, understand them and teach them. Nevertheless, it would be important that she should recognise the implications of white womanhood for black womanhood, clarify what are the social relations with those she teaches, and understand the nature of their responses to her teaching. Inevitably in this process, the anger evoked by texts representing the oppression of black women could not be separated from anger directed at the white teacher, herself implicated as a direct source of oppression. This conflict-ridden duality in the pedagogic role will remain unperceived if teachers interested in black culture are too comfortable or complacent in their own anti-racism.

It is also these hierarchical relationships that are misrecognised in the unifying concepts of 'national interest', 'community' and 'multi-culturalism'. The 'black' of *Blacks Britannica* and its use in this article to designate 'non-white' should be seen in the context of a political consciousness which threatens these integrative concepts and their implication of an equality that is all too obviously a myth:

I mean, it's something that was sort of generated from school. They were saying, 'You're gonna want a car, you're gonna want a house, and you gotta do this and you gotta do that, and you

wanna earn a wage about a certain amount.' It's all drummed
into you, you know, time after time. 'You're gonna need this,
and you're gonna want that, and so on – you're gonna need a
holiday at least once a year, and all them things; and you gotta
study, you know.' And what they didn't tell you was that 'you're
black, and we're going to stop you doing all this, we're going
to do our best to stop you getting all this'.[17]

Notes

1. Clara Mulhern, 'Multicultural Education and the Fight Against
Racism in Schools', *Teaching and Racism*, London: ALTARF, 1979.
2. 'Education Cuts, from sin-bins to social security', *Fowaad, News-
letter of the Organisation of Women of Asian and African Descent*,
London: OWAAD, 1979.
3. For a fuller account of some of these arguments see my stencilled
occasional paper *Multicultural Fictions*, Centre for Contemporary Cultural Studies, Birmingham University, 1980.
4. Inner London Education Authority, *A Multi-Ethnic Education:
Joint Report of Schools Sub-committee and Further and Higher Education
Sub-committee*, London: Waterlow, 1977.
5. Department of Education and Science and Welsh Office, *Education
in Schools*, (Cmnd 6869), London: HMSO, 1977, paras 1.10–1.11.
6. Ibid.: Foreword
7. Robert Jeffcoate, *Positive Image: Towards a Multiracial Curriculum*, London: Writers and Readers Cooperative, 1979, p. 122.
8. Ibid., p. 63.
9. Among the most common of these is the play on 'we' and 'our';
for a detailed exploration of this process see James Donald, 'Green
Paper: Noise of Crisis', *Screen Education*, no. 30, Spring 1979.
10. Jeffcoate, op. cit., p. 26.
11. Other theories of deprivation also have the failing or problem child
at their centre through causative factors: the urban environment, poor
living conditions, a family structure regarded as inadequate, and so on.
The school's role is one of compensation; compensating for all the inadequacies focused in the student. For example, linguistic deprivation theories of the working-class child are applied to the black child whose language becomes regarded as not adequate for the learning processes.
Increased resources are then considered needed for remedial provision.
Essentially the argument is for a more intense application of schooling
rather than a structurally different form of an education system.
12. In *Screen*, vol. 19, no. 1, Spring 1978, pp. 62–3.
13. Farrukh Dhondy, *Come to Mecca*, London, Fontana Lions, 1978,
p. 67.
14. In *Radio Times*, 18–24 August 1979.
15. See Ama Ata Aidoo, *No Sweetness Here*, London: Longman,
1970, and *Our Sister Killjoy*, Longman, 1978; Toni Cade Bambara, *Gor-*

rilla, My Love, New York: Random House, 1972; *The Seabirds Are Still Alive*, Random House, 1977, and (ed.) *The Black Woman*, New York: Mentor, 1970; Buchi Emecheta, *In the Ditch*, London: Allison & Busby 1979; *Second Class Citizen*, London: Fontana, 1977; *The Bride Price*, London: Fontana, 1976; *The Slave Girl*, Fontana, 1979, and *The Joys of Motherhood*, London: Allison & Busby, 1979; Rosa Guy, *The Friends*, Harmondsworth: Puffin, 1977, and *Ruby*, New York: Bantam, 1979; Joyce Ladner, *Tomorrow's Tomorrow: The Black Woman*, New York: Doubleday Anchor, 1971; Toni Morrison, *The Bluest Eye*, New York: Pocket Books, 1972; *Sula*, New York: Bantam, 1975, and *Song of Solomon*, Signet, 1978; Alice Walker, *In Love and Trouble*, New York: Harvest/HBJ, 1973; *The Third Life of George Copeland*, New York: Harvest/HBJ, 1977, and *Meridian*, New York: Pocket Books, 1977; Amrit Wilson, *Finding a Voice*, London: Virago, 1978.
    16. Morrison, 1972, p. 22.
    17. Draft transcription of *Blacks Britannica* quoted in A. Paris, '*Blacks Britannica:* Race Cinema and the Public Sphere', *Socialist Review*, no. 48, November – December, 1979, pp. 4–5.

Chapter 18

Revaluations*

Richard Collins

It is logical for the debased and commercialised mass culture to be replaced by a true culture for the masses. It cannot be forgotten that for the greater completeness of that culture the social and intellectual participation of the masses themselves must be secured. To achieve this a powerful amateur cultural movement must have been developed.[1]

Alan Lovell's brief article 'The Searchers and the Pleasure Principle',[2] his critical positions in the revised Don Siegel American Cinema booklet and the paper by Jim Cook and Jim Hillier, 'The Growth of Film and Television Studies 1960–1975'[3] mark the course of an important contemporary current in Film Studies. The current these articles signal is one of opposition to the way in which relations between culture, art and society had traditionally been made in Britain, and of espousal of the formula 'Popular Culture' that it is hoped will offer a potentiality for study of the cinema unvitiated by the governing principles of the British tradition of cultural studies; its élitism, conservatism, and individualism. Cook and Hillier construct the tradition thus:

Crudely the position might be expressed as follows: modern society is unsatisfactory because its industrial mechanistic nature prevents it from meeting the essential human needs like contact

* Screen Education, no. 22, Spring 1977.

with work, nature and other human beings; great art as the direct creative expression of the individual offers a critique of modern society and embodies accordingly moral values; since the mass media are products of technology, one of the most important features of the industrial system, they cannot possibly be art and are in fact corrupting in that they express false moral values.

They find its principal articulation in the work of Matthew Arnold and F. R. Leavis. Noting their relative distance from the line they construct around Arnold and Leavis because of its blocking of interest in the cinema, Cook and Hiller plot a different, and for them preferable, line through the work of Richard Hoggart, Raymond Williams, Stuart Hall and Paddy Whannel – a line of interest in 'Popular Culture' that for them makes possible:

> A new sort of interest in mass culture – one which was neither dismissive nor, at best, neutral, but which through the Leavisian inheritance looked at the material positively, examining its values and making judgements in ways analogous to those which operated for high art.

Lovell poses the issues rather differently, invoking not the procedures of the study of high art, that is, as I understand Cook and Hillier's usage, the readings of an authoritative critic or scholar, but makes the responses of a hypothesised audience, their 'pleasure' and 'entertainment' the central analytic and legitimising concepts for the pop culture current. These writers then take a notional audience's positive response or pleasure as axiomatic; given this axiom and the American Cinema as object for study then clearly the ways of thinking the relations of art, culture and society of the British tradition had to be rejected. *Vis-à-vis* writers like Wordsworth, Carlyle, Ruskin, Arnold, T. S. Eliot, the line Williams tracks in *Culture and Society*, the pop culture current's critique has an interesting and useful potentiality, but not (or at least not as Lovell/Cook and Hillier formulate it) *vis-à-vis* Leavis and *Scrutiny* who are taken, wrongly, I think, as representative of the tradition and as a kind of *ne plus ultra* of its horrors.

Customarily culture is thought to get worse as time goes on. All the British writers of the dominant tradition are governed by hostility to division of labour, mass production and mass society, to values and behaviour uninformed by and unlegitimised by high culture. Accordingly there's consistently a sentimental and conservative pining for the world before the rot set in – for Eliot it ended when the English Church split with Rome, for Ruskin the

golden age was the era of Gothic, for Arnold, Classical Greece
and Rome. For all of them, knowledge of the past and access to
the tradition that is in continuity with the past is, as Arnold says,
'the help out of our present difficulties'. That knowledge, that
culture, is for these writers necessarily the prerogative and property of a minority, an élite or (as Eliot argues with a coherence
that's notably absent from the general muddle of the nineteenth-
century writers) an aristocratic patrician class:

> It is an essential condition of the presentation of the quality of
> culture of the minority that it should continue to be a minority
> culture. No number of Young People's Colleges will compen-
> sate for the deterioration of Oxford and Cambridge,[4]

whose social policy, in the interests of 'sweetness and light', should
be:

> As for rioting, the old Roman way of dealing with that is always
> the right one. Flog the rank and file and fling the ringleaders
> from the Tarpian rock.[5]

Leavis and *Scrutiny* share the general pessimism and hostility to
industrialisation of this tradition, but unlike Eliot who saw in the
seventeenth century a 'dissociation of sensibility' stemming from
the schism with Rome as the source of rot or Arnold who saw
strong doses of 'sweetness and light' as the remedy (that is, both
construct the argument in terms of superstructure) – Leavis saw
the means of production, the base, as finally determining:

> The great agent of change, and, from our point of view, destruc-
> tion has of course been the machine-applied power. The
> machine has brought us many advantages, but it has destroyed
> the old ways of life, the old forms, and by reason of the contin-
> ual rapid change it involves, prevented the growth of new.
> Moreover the advantage it brings us in mass production has
> turned out to involve standardisation and levelling down outside
> the realm of mere material goods.[6]

The distinction between locating cultural and social decline – and
its possible reversal – at the level of base or superstructure is
important though Leavis never questioned, nor did the antecedent
writers, whether the form industrialisation took on in British capitalism was a necessary form, or one specific to the social relations
of capitalism. He talks of 'the means of production' not the
'relations of productions'. In his first editorial for *Scrutiny*, 'Under

Which King Bezonian?'[7] Leavis engages with Marxism – that is, with the major challenge to the tradition's thinking about culture and society. He says: 'There seems no reason why supporters of *Scrutiny* should not favour some kind of communism as the solution of the economic problem,' and (with some barbed disclaimers about where unorthodox Marxist thought is to be found) discusses Trotsky's ideas about culture and society. Essentially, it seems to me, Leavis rejects Marxist ideas about culture because of what he saw as a doctrine of mechanical determinism of superstructure by base:

> There can be no doubt that the dogma of the priority of economic conditions however stated means a complete disregard for – or rather a hostility towards – the function represented by *Scrutiny*.

There is no doubt that Leavis was right to resist this economism although the centrality of the notion of base in any formulation is worth bearing in mind, particularly at a time when current work derived from psychoanalytic concepts seems to be constructing itself outside of any notions of class consciousness and of the relation of consciousness to the material world.

Leavis formulates later in the essay a notion that maintains the relative autonomy of the realm of culture – its capacity to have an uneven relation in its development to the finally determining relations of production.

> It is true that culture in the past has borne a close relation to 'the methods of production'. A culture expressing itself in a tradition of literature and art – such a tradition as represents the finer consciousness of the race and provides the currency of finer living can be in a healthy state only if this tradition is in a living relation with a real culture shared by the people at large. The point might be enforced by saying (there is no need to elaborate) that Shakespeare did not invent the language he used. And when England had a popular culture, the structure, the framework of it was a stylisation so to speak, of economic necessities, based it might fairly be said, on the 'methods of production', was an art of living, involving codes, developed in ages of continuous experience, of relations between man and man, and man and the environment in its seasonal rhythm. This culture the progress of the nineteenth century destroyed in country and in town; it destroyed (to repeat a phrase that has been used in *Scrutiny* before and will be, no doubt, again) the organic community. And what survives of cultural tradition in

any important sense survives in spite of the rapidly changing 'means of production'.

Ultimately Leavis's ideas were more pessimistic than those of the tradition – if culture had a limited autonomy but was finally determined by the means of production then there remained no room for it to function as the 'great help out of our present difficulties'.

The tragic disintegration of Leavis's own work into more and more petulant and contradictory rhetoric stems from the fundamental unsurmounted contradiction in the *Scrutiny* analysis and to say to the reader weaned on recent writings. 'Nor shall my sword' and so on, that one of the principal thrusts of the *Scrutiny* critique, up until say the 1940s, was to attack, examine and propose reconstruction of the institutions of mass culture is doubtless surprising and paradoxical. But the absence of distinction between the means of production and the relations of production, between industrial society and capitalism, did nothing to inhibit the fight against 'the ideological state apparatus'. Consistent loci for *Scrutiny*'s attack were the education system, mass communications, particularly advertising and the press, the British Council and so on. The hostility towards mass society and espousal of a vague Utopian communism manifested itself in unfocused (though explicitly anti-Marxist) attacks on capitalism itself. But against monopoly capitalism was pitted an increasingly embattled and hopeless strategy of cultivating the capacity for personal discrimination in cultured individuals.

Robin Wood, whom Cook and Hillier describe as 'probably the single most influential writer on film in English', has emphasised the later aspect of Leavis. Wood takes the strategy of searching for an enobling and revivifying tradition to be absorbed by individuals who proselytise its values, into his own work as a film critic, and defines works of value:

> All one asks for Hitchcock is that people *look* at his films, allow themselves to react spontaneously and consider their reactions; that for example, instead of assuming that *Vertigo* is just a mystery thriller . . . they look without preconceptions at the sequence of images Hitchcock gives us and consider their first-hand responses to those images. They will then be led, very swiftly by the straightest path, to the film's profound implications.[8]

In adopting the model of identifying the ennobling and revivifying culture, that is, following Leavis's/*Scrutiny*'s later practice, Wood short-circuits the enquiry into the relations of culture and society and the central assertion of the relative autonomy of the realm of culture. His notion of the firsthand response has as a necessary entailment an idea of the innocent eye guaranteeing access to the world of those uncorrupted by social living, culture, and which necessarily conceives of representation as unmediated, innocent of convention and unproblematically equivalent to reality. In modelling his work on the axiom:'A tradition of literature and art . . . can be in a healthy state only if this tradition is in a living relation with a real culture shared by the people at large'. Wood finds in Hollywood, because Hawks and Hitchcock worked there, a conjuncture similar to that of Mozart's Vienna or Shakespeare's London. (Wood does offer some qualifications to his argument especially in his more recent writing,[9] but I think it's substantially as I represent it – see particularly the introduction to *Howard Hawks*.[10]) That is, he adopts, and stands on its head, the mechanical model of determination linking base and superstructure that Leavis rejected. Leavis's model provoked analysis of the base, of the containing society and its conditions of production, Wood inhibits it. Where great art exists then, axiomatically, there is a sustaining culture.

It's perhaps a good moment to confess my crimes; in my 'The Film' in the revised edition of *Discrimination and Popular Culture*[11] there's a similar mechanical equivalence made between culture and society, base and superstructure and a characteristic recuperation of the notionally popular culture, here the American cinema, by 'high culture' analysis, essentially it seems to me the same mistaken tendency as that of Robin Wood. For all their quite considerably differing degrees of emphasis and context, there is then at certain points shared by Wood, by Cook and Hillier, and by me in 'The Film', a notion of popular culture as a set of phenomena which lies outside high culture, which high culture improperly ignores but which is to be studied with the same apparatus as high culture. It is a reformist aesthetic that argues for the inclusion within the aesthetic realm of art objects that have been excluded from its privileged zone. It's reform that rejects criteria of originality and uniqueness and points instead to the properties of recurrent motifs in genres but which does not question the privileged realm of art or scrutinise its place in social relations.

Lovell offers his espousal of mass culture as a challenge to the 'passive/manipulative account of mass culture' that is seen to stem from Leavis. Lovell sees the positive quality of mass culture as evidence against the pessimistic and conservative ideology of *Scrutiny*:

the *Scrutiny* current about the nature of mass culture. The original account of mass culture offered saw it as the debased product of mass industrial civilisation. The developing process of industrialisation had deprived the lives of the mass of people of meaning and value and made it possible for them to be exploited through the new means of communication (cinema, newspapers, radio, television).

As it makes a positive response to the medium very difficult, the unattractiveness of this position for anybody interested in the cinema is obvious. More importantly the political position implicit in it is a conservative and static one. The mass of people are seen as the victims of social developments over which they have no control.[12]

His desire to reformulate dominant notions about mass culture and develop a theory that will encompass enthusiasm for Don Siegel and enable him to reject élitism and conservatism, leads him, I think, into populism. First, though Lovell's central categories of 'pleasure', 'entertainment' and 'positive response' are categories that refer to the audience and its experience and thus his system shifts the focus of attention from text to audience, he is in fact silent as to how the audience is constituted, how we know when it experiences pleasure and how that experience relates to the text. The populist tendency in Lovell's ideas comes in a formulation like: 'The mass of people are seen as the victims of social developments over which they have no control.' The *Scrutiny* current then is rejected because it adopts a particular historical analysis. Yet the position Lovell rejects in favour of a faith in the mass of people as controllers of their own destiny and an enthusiasm for their perception of the world seems to me to be preferable to his. The mass of people in Britain have been 'victims of social developments over which they have no control'. Certainly that process of development has been attended by fierce struggle and has been distinguished by major achievements but it was one in which the mass of people were and are constituted as a subordinate class. To validate the perception and ideas of that class, 'pleasure' 'entertainment', 'their culture', as if that subordination did not exist, is to stand élitism on its head – populism is as myopic a basis for understanding culture and society as elitism – and does no more to challenge the governing relation of domination and subordination.

In *Screen Education*, no. 17, Lovell states that some place, some path, must be found that mediates between 'acceptance of the children's authentic experience and a rejection of it as a form of "mystification" '. It seems to me that there is no contradiction between respect for, and understanding of, the function and meaning of anyone's enthusiasm – their authentic experience – for mass culture, and understanding and developing an understanding in others, of mass culture's mystification. There is only a possibility of popular culture, 'their culture' (though I see no reason why it shouldn't be 'ours'), in a society where culture and its means of production are owned and controlled by the people. To argue as Lovell does, for the legitimacy of mass culture, because of the 'pleasure' and 'entertainment' it yields to the audience, is to abandon the possibility of criticism of mass culture, the values it propagates, its modes of organisation and control, its function in capitalist society. This abandonment is implicit in his use of the category 'mass culture'. The massness of contemporary mass culture is one of *consumption:* not of the mass but from the ruling class to the mass. This is not to say that there are not contradictions, progressive currents, material for profitable study and some possibility of positive action within mass culture and its institutions. This is the objective reality of mass culture. Lovell's usage though is one that affirms a genuine or mass or popular base to mass culture of which I see no evidence. His argument runs the danger of being incorporated into that of the Independent Broadcasting Authority (IBA) and commercial television companies: that because something is widely consumed it is what consumers want; such lines of argument mystify patterns of organisation and control, and thus hinder analysis of meaning. Lovell's category of entertainment further runs the danger as it stands, and without greater elaboration and sophistication, of relegating works to a realm where the view of the world they define is non-pertinent:

> If the interest in them (films) is what they tell audiences about the world (in this context it's of no odds whether what is communicated is conceptualised as 'themes' or 'ideology' or 'world view' or 'artistic vision' or 'moral values') film education is made into something with very close affinities to subjects like history or social studies.

Again I would have thought that there is no necessary incompatability of the two notions Lovell opposes; an interest in, and analysis of, the world view defined in a film does not preclude attention (indeed I think it necessitates it) to the mediations and transformations filming produces. It seems to me that the false dichotomy Lovell operates necessarily makes more difficult his task of giving an account of how and why, for instance, 'hardhat' ideology and its contradictions are managed in *Dirty Harry*.[13] The question of why the killer wears a peace badge as a belt buckle is not one that can be answered with a formal analysis, that is an immanent analysis. And that demand for formal analysis anyway presupposes a different mode of understanding which (in the terms in which it's posed) is incompatible with the audience-based aesthetics of Lovell's central categories.

'Popular Culture' then is a formulation that defines a long moment in British cultural analysis. It can be seen to have been produced by the élitism of a particular tradition, the élitism from which its *raison d'être* of resistance comes, though that tradition's translation into film culture by Robin Wood has invested F. R. Leavis, in a misleading teleology, with a mantle that sits better, perhaps, on the shoulders of T. S. Eliot. The problems that analysis from the category 'Popular Culture' generates are those of the tradition stood on its head – what both tradition and critique (though not Leavis) share is a problematic that is all superstructure and no base. Otero's statement, at the head of this piece, indicates that there can be no 'Popular Culture' without a new social order, and that is Leavis's analysis too.

To understand our national popular culture, we have to enquire how its discourses are produced and consumed, by whom, for whom, what place do they have in the totality of social relations, how do the worlds these discourses construct represent and interpret the material world; what relation do they bear to human activity both as the expression of that activity and as an informant to it?

The categories of base and superstructure that language equates and balances-equalises, in practice bear on each other unequally and discontinuously. They define an area in which social relations of capitalism and its dominant culture reproduce themselves and in which no successful struggle can be waged within the bounds of the symbolic defined by the category 'culture'. Cultural and intellectual struggle need both concrete alliances and an analytical framework that includes categories that transcend those immanent within 'culture'.

Culture is a mode of cognition formed in determinate social relations, its understanding and transformation needs activity and ideas within the parameters defined both by 'superstructure' and 'base', 'culture' and 'society'. To understand how it constructs, conceives and represents the world we have to attend to the agencies through which the frames of reference of the dominant culture, that of state monopoly capitalism, generalise themselves and naturalise the social relations of capitalism. We require a model of culture that sees the domination of ruling-class ideology in, *inter alia*, mass communications and the education system, not phenomenally – as inherent features of an autonomous (or relatively autonomous) system, and which are to be contested (or not) within the problematic of the system, but dialectically as a theatre of struggle which bears on the lives of human beings and their conditions of being and in which struggle can only effectively be prosecuted when its analysis and programme for action comprehend the mutual determination of social relations and their representation, superstructure and base.

For us then, enquiry must be directed to the frame of reference in which human understanding and action are formed. The absence in Leavis's model of a notion of the reciprocal determination of base by superstructure left none of the space for action, and we need rather an analytical model that is adequate to the totality of social relations in which culture, its primary object for study, is located; one that, to put it modestly, attends to the absence of free play in culture, that recognises the dominance of ruling-class ideology in mass communications, and the function of mass communications in propagating and naturalising the world view of the ruling class.

Notes

1. Lisandro Otero, *Cultural Policy in Cuba*, Paris: UNESCO, 1972.
2. Alan Lovell 'The Searchers and the Pleasure Principle', *Screen Education*, no. 17, Winter 1975/76.
3. BFI mimeograph, 1975, obtainable from the Education Advisory Services of the British Film Institute.
4. T. S. Eliot, *Notes Towards a Definition of Culture*, London: Faber, 1948.
5. Matthew Arnold, *Culture and Anarchy*, Cambridge: Cambridge University Press, 1963.
6. F. R. Leavis and D. Thompson, *Culture and Environment*, London: Chatto & Windus, 1933.
7. F. R. Leavis 'Under Which King Bezonian?' *Scrutiny*, vol. 1, no. 3, 1932.
8. Robin Wood, *Hitchcock's Films*, London: Zwemmer, 1965.
9. See Steve Neale's review of *Personal Views* (Gordon Fraser 1976) in *Screen*, vol. 17, no. 3, Autumn 1976.
10. Robin Wood, *Howard Hawks*, London: Secker & Warburg, 1968.
11. D. Thompson (ed.) *Discrimination and Popular Culture*, Harmondsworth: Penguin, 1973.
12. Alan Lovell, *Don Siegel*, British Film Institute monograph, 1976, p. 1.
13. Alan Lovell, op. cit., pp. 38–45.

Chapter 19

Up Aporia Creek*

John O. Thompson

I

Concluding his 'Reflections in Conclusion' to *Aesthetics and Politics*, Fredric Jameson counsels us to embrace the aporia – 'an enigma for thought' – left behind by the failure of the political aesthetics on display to resolve any of their 'extinct but still virulent intellectual conflicts'; the aporia 'contains within its structure the crux of a history beyond which we have not yet passed'.[1] The Oxford English Dictionary, if you look up 'aporia' in it, quotes a lovely 1589 definition of the term as a figure of rhetoric:

> Aporia, or the Doubtful. [So] called . . . because oftentimes we will seeme to cast perils, and make doubt of things which by a plaine manner of speech we might affirm or deny him.[2]

And Henry More, the Cambridge Platonist, had occasion in 1667 to remark, 'The greatest Wits in the World have been . . . Sceptical or Aporetical'. The word comes from the Greek for no passage or way; and some readers may be tempted to murmur 'No way!' as they observe how the high eloquence and sinewy argumentation of these great wits of the Marxist intellectual world – Bloch, Lukács, Brecht, Benjamin, Adorno – are marshalled to put each other's positions endlessly in doubt.

How keen you are to cherish the aporia in question may depend

* *Screen Education*, no. 31, Summer 1979.

285

on your reaction to Jameson's version of radical gloom. 'In our present cultural situation . . . both alternatives of realism and of modernism seem intolerable to us': the large depressive gesture is eloquent, and kept at a safer distance from talk about actual works than the less prudent debaters of the 1930s and 1940s managed. (Though it's taken to be self-evidently disgraceful that 'Schoenberg's Hollywood pupils used their advanced technique to write movie music'.) But Jameson is not unaware that 'a political and historical despair that . . . finds praxis henceforth unimaginable' won't do; so 'some provisional last word for us today' is wrung from a reconstructed Lukács, and a sketch for 'a new realism' is offered – to which we'll return.[3]

It seems more and more debatable what good has come from the long-standing tendency within Marxist aesthetics to condemn most of what is being done in the arts at a given moment in the name of a model to which committed or progressive art should conform. It always turns out 20 years later that, though no one came forward to realise the programmatic hopes, not only 'good' but politically-effective work was produced where it was least expected. One plain lesson from the German debates is that Lukács was *wrong* about Joyce and Brecht (and 'socialist realism'), and Adorno was *wrong* about popular music and the cinema (and, probably, Schoenberg) in a way which could have been avoided and should not be repeated. 'Wrong as he might have been in the 1930's,' says Jameson of Lukács before giving him his provisional last word – a kindly gesture but a dangerous one, given *how* wrong he was.

What fuels this tendency within Marxist aesthetics towards a dour prescriptivism? Certain propositions recur:

1. Capitalism is in crisis, in decay: decaying societies produce decadent art.
2. Capitalism has so contained its crisis as to produce a 'total system' which can coopt virtually all art to serve it – resulting in servile art.
3. Capitalism generates ever falser consciousness, hence ever more misleading or blinkered art.
4. Capitalism produces an ever more immiserated, or corrupted, proletariat, and provides them with ever cruder art. (Meanwhile, the mandarin elements of the bourgeoisie develop an ever more effete, precious inaccessible art.)

At this level of generality there is virtually no Marxist content to such propositions. This can be demonstrated by replacing 'capitalism' by 'the USSR', 'atheism' or 'popery', and imaginatively adopting the positions of a Cold Warrior, a fideist, and a seventeenth-century Protestant. On the whole, the resulting statements seem no less plausible under these transformations. Note at the same time how they retain a power to make it seem disloyal to deny them. They are not Marxist but *partisan* propositions: plausible deductions on the part of partisans facing a large evil thing which surely cannot but have nasty effects.

Partisan propositions have their uses. The danger is that when more detailed work from a Marxist standpoint gets undertaken, of such quality that no Marxist can simply ignore it, such work can still remain imprisoned within the bounds these propositions set. Yet it is clear that they are all deeply idealist, in that they posit a relay ('mediated', no doubt – but are the mediations allowed really to matter?) from an essence of capitalism (or some stage of it) to the essences of the works of art produced under it. Perhaps the most dangerous level on which such a Marxist discourse can operate – if only because it provides such rich opportunities for waxing eloquent – is one of intermediate generality. There are avowedly partisan modes of address which energise, call to arms, and present themselves openly as such.[4] There are analytic discourses in close touch with the materiality, diversity, plurality of cultural production. Between them lies a level of discourse which both the texts and the commentary in *Aesthetics and Politics* often favour. Take this extract from the 'Presentation' of the Brecht-Lukács debate: how much more concrete, nuanced and persuasive it seems than proposition (4) above, or than the Chiang Ching passage quoted in note 4 below!

[The] dispute between Benjamin and Adorno over modern cultural practice . . . was concerned with the relations between 'avant-garde' and 'commercial' art under the dominion of capital. The continuity and intractability of this problem has made it a central focus of aesthetic controversy on the left ever since, where the contradiction between 'high' and 'low' genres – the one subjectively progressive and objectively élitist, the other objectively popular and subjectively regressive – has never been durably overcome, despite a complex, crippled dialectic between the two . . . The fragility of Brecht's synthesis . . . has only been confirmed by aesthetic development since. The collapse of the cinema of Jean-Luc Godard, in many ways the most brilliant and ambitious revolutionary artist in the last decade, when it attempted a political turn and ascesis not unlike that effected by Brecht's theatre in the thirties, is the most recent and eloquent testimony to the implacable antinomies of cultural innovation in the imperialist world.[5]

Yet it is enervatingly sweeping in its magisterial pessimism. And must it not be rejected as any sort of serious summary of 40 years of artistic production in which works, audiences and history have never ceased to be in motion in respect to one another? Writing off the effectivity of Godard's 1970s work *just like that* is symptomatic of how far such a discourse has to insulate itself from the detailed labours of artists and audiences and the various apparatuses in between.

II

In one sense it is hardly possible to review *Aesthetics and Politics* fully – accurately and constructively – because of its status as a sort of sampler: it is meant to whet your appetite. If Adorno 'clicks' for you, presumably you will search elsewhere for less compressed and gnomic statements of his (dare one say positive?) aesthetic proposals than those on offer here. Bloch appears only as a sparring-partner for Lukács: is he worth following up? Benjamin figures as (i) a friend of Brecht who keeps a diary, and (ii) under friendly 'attack' ('friendly' attack?) from Adorno. The two roles might as well have been performed by two people who never met, so distant do they remain from one another here: only a Complete English Benjamin will give us the material to bring them into productive relation.[6] The Brecht-Lukács confrontation (direct, and as extended in Adorno's critiques of both) does seem able to stand on its own, but I suspect that this too may be an illusion.[7] The useful New Left Books (NLB) contextualising 'presentations' do not attempt to disguise how this selection has as its anchoring referent the greater textual body which is the Bloch/Lukács/ Brecht/Benjamin/Adorno *Gesammelte Werke*.

But most of us can't read everything, so we search for the focus of this particular selection. Modernism-versus-realism is a tempting candidate for the central debate. (This involves setting Benjamin to one side, which I will regretfully do.) It is especially tempting for teachers: many of us have discovered how productive questioning 'realism' can be, if only because students at all levels have views on the subject which, though strong, are not too difficult to shake up. At a tactical level, of course, the best way to unsettle or trouble the assumptions inhibiting this questioning will vary, depending on where teachers and students are starting from. Rather different orthodoxies need to be undermined by (i) an art college teacher whose students seem 'naturally' to favour high modernist doctrine; (ii) a comprehensive school teacher whose students find the literary 'great tradition' of realism pretty inaccessible but who are even more remote from high modernism; (iii) a teacher in higher education whose students find the 'great tradition' 'naturally' congenial – or at least are docile faced with it – and distinguish it sharply from both 'mere entertainment' (such as Hollywood) and not-yet-canonised modernist works. Such teachers and others will all find arguments with *Aesthetics and Politics* to ponder and to use. But will they in the end have to admit that any larger strategy which their rethinking-realism tactics are to serve remains agonisingly aporia-ridden, as Jameson and the Presenters imply? Such would be the case if the overt aim of much of this material were to be accepted at face value.

This aim is to define a certain sort of text: one which would be not only equal to the world, but equal to changing it. If such texts dependably existed, the duty of all progressive teachers would presumably be clear, wherever their students might be starting from: they should facilitate students' access to these texts, and steer students away from other texts which at worst might delude them and at best would waste their time.

Most of *Aesthetics and Politics* relates in some way to Lukács's views of how the Progressive Text should operate. He sees it as necessarily *realist*, in a sense of that term which opposes realism to *modernism* and *naturalism*, twin errors which undermine the capacity of the art-work to provide us with a cognitive grasp of the world. (Modernism does so by valuing distortion in representation or by refusing representation altogether, naturalism by attempting to render appearances exactly rather than delving beneath appearances to grasp the essential.) This position leads to invigorating judgements which usefully challenge the orthodox triumph-of-modernism accounts of recent cultural history common *in some circles*. But almost nobody can rest satisfied with Lukács's views, for (at least) two reasons. They violate our intuitions about texts: most of us have some pet modernism-naturalist texts which we would be reluctant to condemn. This may just be bourgeois of us, of course; the less circular reason for abandoning Lukács is that his account of how realist texts operate reads today, in the light of subsequent work of signification, as confused, vague and pretentious. How much is really being said in a passage like this?

> Great realism . . . does not portray an immediately obvious aspect of reality but one which is permanent and objectively more significant, namely man in the whole range of his relations to the real world, above all those which outlast mere fashion . . . [I]t captures tendencies of development that exist only incipiently and so have not yet had the opportunity to unfold their entire human and social potential. To discern and

give shape to such underground trends is the great historic
mission of the true literary avant-garde. Whether a writer really
belongs to the ranks of the avant-garde is something that only
history can reveal, for only after the passage of time will it
become apparent whether he has perceived significant qualities,
trends, and the social functions of individual human types, and
has given them effective and lasting form.[8]

For this to amount to anything we could work with, we would need
to know much more about what signifying operations 'portray',
'capture', 'give shape to' and 'give form to' are gestures towards.
I don't think that Lukács anywhere provides a satisfactory account
of this (though his work on specific texts might be worth examining
to see if his critical practice allows us to reconstruct such an
account for him); certainly *Aesthetic and Politics* leaves us in the
dark.[9] Pending clarification, we would seem to be free to defend,
say, Joyce against Lukács (if we like Joyce) either by claiming
that Joyce in fact fits Lukács's criteria (as Adorno does) or by
simply dismissing these criteria as incoherent.

Brecht's (posthumously published) anti-Lukácsian remarks are
agreeably miscellaneous, full of the sort of 'plain good sense'
which the NLB Presenters rather anxiously warn us against being
too impressed by, and funny. Adorno weighs in against Lukács
on other grounds. Roughly, Brecht challenges Lukács's calculus
of political effectiveness (taking over from his opponent the trick
of treating 'realist' and 'politically effective' virtually as synonymous), while Adorno presents us with a different (and difficult)
notion of how art and the world confront one another.[10] Adorno's
views look interesting, and could probably be cut free from his
unattractive contempt for this century's popular culture. But it
must have been felt that it is as a spokesman for an élitist-modern-
ist position that he best keeps the aporia fires burning, and texts
have been selected accordingly, so his own view of the cognitive
status of art is only very sketchily displayed.[11] This leaves the
collection with the (somewhat deceptive) air of being, *as a whole*,
'about' the political effectiveness of art, with the relation of art
to truth as a vital but subordinate question.

III

Much film study and film teaching at the moment is bent on
challenging a certain realism's dominance in the cinema, where
modernist textual strategies have been allowed to operate only at
the edges of mainstream production and distribution. Whether or

not Lukács would have accepted Hollywood as 'realist' in his sense (one suspects he could have brought himself to endorse a film fully only if it had been directed by Thomas Mann), there is in fact a good deal of overlap between what Lukács recommends and how the dominant cinema operates.[12] But matters become terminologically confused now that attacks on quasi-Lukácsian 'classic realism' are carried out by writers sympathetic to Brechtian polemics which use the term 'realism' to designate a Good Thing. In these Brecht texts, realism equals truth-telling, and truth is a weapon. 'Anyone who is not a victim of formalistic prejudices knows that the truth can be suppressed in many ways and must be expressed in many ways'. The case against 'classic realism' is that it is a strategy for expression which regularly operates to suppress truths the oppressed need.

One of the most interesting things about Terry Eagleton's uneven review of *Aesthetics and Politics* is how he characterises Brecht's views on assessing the militant realism of a text:

[F]or Brecht, realism can only be . . . retrospective. You thus cannot determine the realism of a text merely by inspecting its intrinsic properties. On the contrary, you can never know whether a text is realist or not until you have established its effects – and since those effects belong to a particular conjuncture, a text may be realist in June and anti-realist in December . . . A text may well 'potentialise' realism, but it can never coincide with it . . . Texts are no more than the enabling or disabling conditions for realist effectivity.[14]

A text has effects; 'realism' is a pertinent concept for characterising these effects; but such effects cannot be assessed in isolation from the particular conjuncture to which they contribute. Recently Dick Hebdige and Geoff Hurd have in a similar spirit accused 'the *Screen* critique of realism' of trying to assess effects on the basis of an inspection of films' intrinsic properties. They fear that too often:

the theory is pitched at an 'in-general' level ('the cinematic apparatus', 'ideology-in-general', the 'subject-spectator', and so on) which makes the analysis of specific texts produced and consumed in concrete historical circumstances difficult, if not impossible.[15]

This essentialism leads, they claim, to a blanket rejection of 'classic realist' texts as intrinsically incapable of adequacy to the real (now Lacanianly rendered as that-which-resists).[16] In effect, they agree with Eagleton in seeing here something of the same sort of dogmatism attached by Brecht: the many ways the truth can be expressed are arbitrarily restricted. For *Screen*, according to Eagleton, 'in a comical inversion of the aesthetics of Lukács, realism is now the ontological enemy', and the text's own properties declare its enemy status.[17]

The Hebdige and Hurd polemic was specifically directed against an article by Tony Stevens;[18] nuanced though Stevens's reply is, it does declare firmly that 'it would be extremely difficult to produce a progressive content, one that gave the audience a real grasp of its historic situation, within the form of 'classic realism'.[19] Stevens, however, is as determined as Eagleton or Hebdige and Hurd to theorise the text's properties in relation to the conjuncture. The sort of critical attention he urges as the goal of film education

> relies as much on a theory of how (and therefore what) a film can mean as on a full account of the historical scene into which that film is inserted. Why should this be held to involve a denial of history? Only the *fullest* attention to the text in fact leads back to history.[20]

In the terms of Eagleton's formulation: attention to the text in itself is necessary for the assessment of the text's effective potential, which is then variously (but not randomly) actualised in specific conjunctures.

Another recent piece in *Screen Education* might seem even more open to Hebdige's and Hurd's challenge. Gill Davies concludes her analysis of the 'reactionary affirmation' lurking beneath the surface pleasures of *The Big Sleep* with a broad claim.

> [T]he realist text . . . initially poses problems or puzzles and subsequently re-orders them in a balanced or symmetrical way. This seems to lead the reader/audience *inevitably* to a point of fullness and closure.[21]

Yet she too claims that her analysis

> reveals features which can be accounted for in the conjuncture of Hawks and America in 1946 . . . The structure of the narrative reveals a deeply conventional affirmation of certain American values which were being preached overtly during this period.[22]

On her account, the classic realist text produces, inevitably, closure; but the contents into which the audience is to be locked are conjuncturally specific.

Two areas for debate seem to emerge. Is the classic realist text really as unlikely to potentialise a progressive engagement with the real as Stevens and Davies claim? What relative weights should one assign textual and extra-textual factors in assessing the effects produced by a given text in a given conjuncture? However, both debates find their participants agreed on the cogency of the text-conjuncture-effect triad. And what may need to be queried is that triad itself.

IV

If you took a child's-electric-set view of Eagleton's formulation, you might fantasise about some day building a large Marxist machine called an Effectometer. When you're presented with a text, you feed it into the Effectometer, which is wired to the Conjuncture. The machine's analysis of the text, plus Conjuncture input, produces a read-out. Eagleton envisages the machine as set to calculate the value of the text's militant realism; it might be more straightforward to equip it with a dial giving a direct Progressive Effect reading. Stevens's and Davies's predictions are easily expressed in Effectometer terms: when you feed the machine a classic realist text you keep getting a zero or a minus reading. Eagleton, and Hebdige and Hurd, on the other hand, warn against prejudging the issue: each work needs to be tested anew in each conjuncture.

How do you tell if your Effectometer is working? Presumably you check it regularly against the effects a given work has actually had on those who have read or seen or heard of it. Indeed, is not the Effectometer simply a robot audience? Conversely, is not the audience a sort of human Effectometer? The audience too is plugged into the Conjuncture; it too parses the text. But whereas the Effectometer produces a reading, the audience *acts*. The Effectometer's reading is an index of the progressive value of the work's audience's acts. But if a measurable Progressive Effect involves an audience's *doing something* (the caricature examples – building barricades, or at least joining the Party – need not be invoked), then it is immediately clear that politically, except in very freakish circumstances, the audience of a single work always does nearly nothing. It would be mad if it did more: what sort of meaningful political act would one have any business undertaking *purely* on the basis of having just seen *The Caucasian Chalk Circle* or *Days of Hope* or *History Lessons*?

Thus to the extent that the Effectometer is successful in modelling the audience confronting a single text, it will keep coming up
with just the negative readings Stevens and Davies predict.
Indeed, texts which Stevens and Davies might wish to privilege
will fare no better. Modernism and realism will, just as Jameson
gloomily suggests, vie with one another for zero Progressive Effect
ratings. The shadow of this result falls across Eagleton's review:
concluding it, he writes, 'our own polemics about the desirable
character of "revolutionary" film or theatre stumble not so much
over theoretical divergencies as over a rather more recalcitrant
fact: what revolutionary film or theatre?' He agrees that there *are*
revolutionary or at least progressive texts and performances (for
he goes on, 'I do not mean to suggest that there is no such
phenomenon at all'); but still there can't be *really*, since work by
work the Effectometer keeps reading roughly zero.

V

The insistence that the text be assessed conjuncturally was meant
to discourage persistent determinist, dogmatic attempts to read
off a text's political effects directly from its formal characteristics.
As such it seems attractive. What I am suggesting is that such a
strategy is nevertheless deeply unsatisfactory so long as it partici-
pates in anything resembling the Effectometer fiction. The Effectometer's central defect is that it is set up to produce an individual
reading for each text. *But on the political level texts can only
operate in aggregate, and as elements of cultural formations of
great heterogeneity*. The search for the text that would, on its own,
produce progressive effects is doomed. On the other hand, finding
texts which under certain conditions can join other texts, theoretical work and experience to produce change (changed subjects,
changed ideological formations) is not at all difficult, since almost
any text with a certain amount of force may serve (just as *The
Big Sleep* itself presumably serves in the defamiliarising context
of Gill Davies's teaching). What remains elusive (but not imposs-
ibly so) and conjunctural (but less vaguely so) is the specification
of the conditions under which texts can aggregate to progressive
effect.

When you consider the political effects of texts one by one, you
are trapped as in one of Zeno's paradoxes of motion: moment by
moment, the arrow cannot be in flight and the tortoise is unbeat-
able. But things move, physically and historically. Given the fact
of motion in political and ideological formations, it seems

unreasonable to assume that the texts we encounter (realist *or* modernist) have nothing to do with it.

A preconception which Tony Stevens does seem to share with Lukács is that the burden of giving the audience 'a real grasp of its historic situation' has to be borne by each text singly and anew. Neither seems prepared to admit that effects in themselves much smaller but cumulatively benign could be welcomed; or for that matter that the audience might already have a grasp of its situation such that the autonomous reflecting work (Lukács) or the deconstructive unsettling work (Stevens) is not of such vital concern to them. On any account of the real, it seems likely that access to it is gained as much through the differences between texts as through individual texts themselves. Especially at a political or ideological level, the difference between film A and film B (or between film A and lived experience X or unexperienceable-as-such structural fact Q)[23] may be the bearer of crucial information. Since no text is itself the bearer of that difference, text-bound analyses, as they construct the text's ideal reader (the reader ideally bound to the text's formal operations), can produce no model of the reader *moving from text to text* – distrusting some, subordinating others, even perhaps gripped equally by contradictory texts. Of course nothing guarantees that the reader's movement from text to text will have a radicalising or even an informative effect. What is most valuable in the tradition of left culture-critique is its demonstration of how at a given moment the favoured aggregation of dominant texts operates oppressively. But it is crucial that we do not import the despair which ideal-reader (ideally-bound reader) theories can generate into the calculations we make in trying to radicalise the existing cultural aggregate. The effectivity of intratextual differences is incalculable enough to resist any 'total system's' programming; two or three texts gathered together are a potential powder-keg.

VI

To illustrate how single texts rather than texts-plus-differences-between-texts are the central concern of much of *Aesthetics and Politics*, here are some passages with brief comments.

1. Bloch v. Lukács

What material does Lukács then use to expound his view of the Expressionists? He takes prefaces or postscripts to anthologies,

'introductions' by Pinthus, newspaper articles by Leonard. Rub-
iner, Hiller, and other items of the same sort. So he does not
get to the core of the matter, the imaginative works which
makes a concrete impression in time and space, reality which
the observer may reexperience for himself.[24]

Plural *works* make a single *impression;* this single *reality* is the
core of the matter. The work has some sort of right to be encountered on its own, or at least in the congenial company of similar
'imaginative' works, free from the ephemeral discourses which
surround it. The work itself endures over time, self-identical,
independent of discourse: it is always available for re-experiencing
by the single observer.

2.   *Lukács* v. *Bloch*

> Only when the masterpieces of realism past and present are
> appreciated as *wholes*, will their topical, cultural and political
> values fully emerge. This value resides in their inexhaustible
> diversity,   in   contrast   to   the   one-dimensionality   of
> modernism . . . The wealth of the characterisation, the pro-
> found and accurate grasp of constant and typical manifestations
> of human life is what produces the great progressive reverber-
> ations of these works . . . In realism, the wealth of created life
> provides answers to the questions put by the readers themselves
> – life supplies the answer to the questions put by life itself![25]

The *whole* work is a realm of *wealth*,[26] *inexhaustible* like *life*. It
is, in fact, a microcosm. Within the microcosm, all is not-the-
same: the little world holds difference and contradiction *inside
itself*. Between the unified little world and the unified big world
communication is possible: life answers life in a full, untroubled
speech. (Avant-garde art, on the contrary, makes it impossible
for 'ordinary people' to '*translate* these atmospheric *echoes* of
reality back into the *language* [singular] of their *own experience*
[singular].[27]

3.   *Lukács* v. *Bloch* – On montage techniques in modernism:

> The details may be dazzlingly colourful in their diversity, but
> the whole will never be more than an unrelieved grey on grey.
> After all, a puddle can never be more than dirty water, even
> though it may contain rainbow tints. This monotony proceeds

inexorably from the decision to abandon any attempt to mirror objective reality, to give up the artistic struggle to shape the highly complex mediations in all their unity and diversity and to synthesise them as characters in a work of literature.[28]

Mirroring is the only operation that can hold unity-and-diversity together; it allows plural *characters* (themselves *syntheses*) to inhabit a single *work* (world). A 'dirty', bad unity (monotony) is the result of unsynthesised, uncomposed diversity within the work. Montage can produce only a body-in-pieces (*corps morcélé:* Lacan). Such a production is inadequate to the unity of the real. ('Marx says: "The relations of production of every society form a whole".[29] The single work must be cognitively and sensuously a match for this scientifically guaranteed unity.

4. Adorno v. Lukács

[T]aken to its logical conclusion, loneliness will turn into its opposite: the solitary consciousness potentially destroys and transcends itself by revealing itself in works of art as the hidden truth common to all men. This is exactly what we find in the authentic works of modern literature. They objectify themselves by immersing themselves totally, monadologically, in the laws of their own forms. It is this alone which gives the works of Joyce, Beckett and modern composers their power. The voice of the age echoes through their monologues: this is why they excite us so much more than works that simply depict the world in narrative form. The fact that their transition to objectivity remains contemplative and fails to become praxis is grounded in the nature of a society in which the monadological condition persists universally, despite all assurances to the contrary.[30]

Each *authentic* work is a *monad*, through which sounds the *voice* (singular, monologue-like) of an age in which reification, loneliness, the monadological condition are *universal*. Monotony is an effect of the sort of mirroring depictions Lukács privileges, but this is because such depictions have not sufficiently exorcised the spectre of the body-in-pieces in the text: the truly exciting text will subject each moment of itself to its own 'total', internally-generated lawfulness. The text's logic 'is not that of subject and predicate, but of internal harmony'.[31] A work so harmonised will always stand as a *reproach* to actuality, with all its 'unreconciled' objects.[32] Yet the modernist text to be authentic must feel anxious; this is because it also somehow captures (mirrors, 'echoes') the horror of the *false* reconciliations, the *bad* totality of, in the Presenter's phrase, late capitalism's 'all-inclusive "administered universe".'[33]

Even this brief dossier should suggest how, while Bloch, Lukács and Adorno differ in how they define the individual great work and in how they handle their desire for it, such a work plays an unduly crucial role in their thought. Giving up the individual great work (and its 'bad object' counterpart, the failed or delusive work) as central to political aesthetics would entail a salutary upheaval within the *Aesthetics and Politics* debate as they define it.

VII

Once we shift our attention from individual texts to groups of texts, and from how texts resemble one another to how they differ, the bringing into existence or promoting of the Perfectly Progressive Text ceases to look either possible or desirable. Instead, relations of juxtaposition and dominance within the textual aggregate become politically pertinent. Which texts/genres/media are given precedence over others, within 'common sense', at a given moment? What troubling of that consensus can be achieved by promoting a despised or ignored text, of challenging an admired or widely-promoted one? Can troubling that consensus in a given instance really be articulated with other, more politically central, struggles?

Jameson's concluding proposal for building a politically effective art of the left in America today makes better sense in terms of this sort of tactical calculation than it does as he himself justifies it. The heart sinks when we read that the realism he favours, though it would 'incorporate what was always most concrete in the dialectical counter-concept of modernism – its emphasis on violent renewal of perception in a world in which experience has solidified into a mass of habits and automatisms', is supposed 'to reinvent that category of totality which, systematically undermined by existential fragmentation on all levels of life and social organisation today, can alone project structural relations between classes as well as class struggles in other countries, in what has increasingly become a world system.'[34] (Thus is Lukács given his provisional last word.) The 'fragmentation' which is to be combated derives from 'reification', defined as 'a process that affects our cognitive relationship with the social totality . . . a disease of that mapping function whereby the individual subject projects and models his or her insertion into the collectivity'. As human relations take on the appearance of relations among things, 'confusion as to the nature and even the existence of social classes' increases. Individual subjects cannot any longer (presumably they once could) easily perceive that 'the fundamental structure of the social "totality" is a set of class relationships – an antagonistic structure such that the various social classes define themselves . . . by opposition with one another'. Jameson's recommendation is that art be used to reverse this loss of a sense of class:

> If the diagnosis is correct, the intensification of class consciousness will be less a matter of a populist or *ouvrierist* exaltation of a single class by itself, than of the forcible reopening of access to a sense of society as a totality, and of the reinvention of possibilities of cognition and perception that allow social phenomena once again to become transparent, as moments of the struggle *between* classes.[35]

Since all this talk of totality begins after a while to sound rather gestaltist, perhaps it would not be inappropriate to discuss Jameson's proposal in terms of the famous rabbit-duck line drawing. A shift in gestalt lets us see the drawing now *as* a duck, now *as* a rabbit. The new realism will engineer this sort of gestalt shift: what had been perceptually reified as rabbit is to have its duckness unblocked, as social phenomena are presented *as* effects of or moments in the class struggle. This is to be accomplished, as far as I can tell, by progressive artists presenting us with a succession of overt, unambiguous duck-pictures, which are however rabbit-like *enough* to lead us at some point to look at that particular 'rabbit'-picture which is our own experience with new eyes as its full duckness dawns on us. Realism-as-verisimilitude is a tactic designed to fulfil the 'rabbit-like *enough*' clause; realism-as-science involves a claim that the pictures produced will be most valuable if they are as accurately and analytically duck-like as possible.

But the duck-rabbit analogy suggests that 'totality' need not be in question at all. The duck is not more 'total' or 'together' than the rabbit: it is *another thing*. All that Jameson needs to show is that American society is another thing from how it is dominantly represented, and that adversary texts should be promoted which render it *other than classlessly*. This need not, indeed had better not, amount to demanding that all pictures be class-embodying pictures. And it may turn out, despite Jameson's sudden optimism as reflected in his use of 'transparent', that to be a class-embodying picture is a non-popularist/*ouvrierist* way while retaining verisimilitude, attractiveness, and so on, is peculiarly difficult. Nevertheless, it seems plausible that according a certain privilege to texts that attempt this could constitute *one* useful de-depoliticising intervention in America today.

Here in Britain it may be less clear that such works (*as such:* obviously a work might accord with Jameson's requirements while doing other things too) have much change of disturbing an all-too-familiar textual aggregate wherein 'class' is a theme only too easily domesticated, whether as part of a 'centrist' congratulatory-nostalgic package (*Upstairs Downstairs*, and many a BBC2 adaptation of just the sort of novel Lukács most admired), as part of a 'left-defeatist' package (*Days of Hope*), or as part of a 'documentary' package ('workers' chosen to be interviewed because they so perfectly incarnate *workers:* consensus *typage*). Of course there is room for argument on this: all I want to suggest is that *Aesthetics and Politics*, necessary reading though it doubtless is, does not represent a gift from the past which deserves to dominate that argument. Jameson speaks of 'the aesthetic controversy between "Realism" and "Modernism", whose navigation and renegotiation is still unavoidable for us today'.[36] An idealist river with essentialist rapids? There must be other routes.

Notes

1. Ernst Bloch, Georg Lukács, Bertolt Brecht, Walter Benjamin and Theodor Adorno, *Aesthetics and Politics* (with a conclusion by Fredric Jameson), London: New Left Books 1978, p. 213.
2. George Puttenham, *The Arte of English Poesie*, London, 1589.
3. *Aesthetics and Politics*, op. cit., pp. 211–2.
4. Two examples:

1. Karl Radek, in 1934 (speaking against defence of Joyce): Should we really tell the artist at the present time – the revolutionary artist here or abroad: 'Look at your inside'? No! We must tell him: 'Look – they are making ready for a world war! Look – the fascists are trying to stamp out the remnants of culture and rob the workers of their last rights! Look – the dying capitalist world wants to throttle the Soviet Union!' This is what we must say to the artist. We must turn the artist away from his 'inside', turn his eyes to these great facts of reality which threaten to crash down upon our heads.

(*Soviet Writers Congress 1934*, London, 1977, p. 179).
2. Chiang Ching, in 1966:
Capitalism has a history of several centuries. Nevertheless, it has only a pitiful number of 'classics'. Some works modelled after the 'classics' have been created, but these are stereotyped and no longer appeal to the people . . . On the other hand, there are some things that really flood the market, such as rock-'n-roll, jazz,

> striptease, impressionism, symbolism, abstractionism, fauvism, modernism – there is no end to them – all of which are intended to poison and paralyse the minds of the people. In short, there is decadence and obscenity to poison and paralyse the minds of the people.

(quoted in D. W. Fokkema and Elrud Kunne-Ibsch, *Theories of Literature in the Twentieth Century*, London, 1977, p. 109)

How should one assess such texts? Clearly not just on their 'intrinsic' merits; Radek may carry the reader with him. Chiang Ching probably doesn't – but in the contexts of preparations for Zhdanovism and the Cultural Revolution respectively, shouldn't these evaluations be reversed?

5. *Aesthetics and Politics*, op. cit., pp. 66–7.

6. To get a sense of the complexities involved, see Irving Wohlfarth, 'On the Messianic Structure of Walter Benjamin's Last Reflections', *Glyph*, vol. 3, 1978, pp. 148–212.

7. The *Aesthetics and Politics* material can now be supplemented by Georg Lukács, 'On Walter Benjamin and Bertholt Brecht', *New Left Review*, no. 110, July-August 1978. pp. 83–92.

8. *Aesthetics and Politics*, op. cit., p. 48.

9. It would be unfair to Lukács to leave the impression that somewhere there exists a good account of 'capturing', or that the problem of accounting for our sense that some artists 'capture something' and others don't has somehow been dissolved by recent work on signifying practices. Critics such as Leavis, or John Bayley (see Terry Eagleton, 'Liberality and order: The Criticism of John Bayley', *New Left Review*, no. 110, July-August 1978, pp. 29–40), are as hopeless on this as Lukács. The trouble with such critics is not so much that they haven't yet explained 'capturing' as that they seem not to realise how puzzling the phenomenon is; they blithely make evaluative use of the criterion most in need of further analysis, to predictably dogmatic effect.

10. 'In art knowledge is aesthetically mediated through and through. Even alleged cases of solipsism, which signify for Lukács the regression of an illusory immediacy on the part of the individual, do not imply the denial of the object, as they would in bad theories of knowledge, but instead aim at a dialectical reconciliation of subject and object. In the form of an image the object is absorbed into the subject instead of following the bidding of the alienated world and persisting obdurately in a state of reification. The contradiction between the object reconciled in the subject, i.e. spontaneously absorbed into the subject, and the actual unreconciled object in the outside world, confers on the work of art a vantage-point from which it can criticize actuality. Art is the negative knowledge of the actual world' (p. 160).

11. Can it be found elsewhere? The NLB Presenter claims that 'the fundamental categories of Adorno's aesthetics remain opaque: . . . none of [its] crucial terms is assigned a clearly delimited meaning' (p. 146). It isn't clear whether the Presenter is speaking only of the texts included in *Aesthetics and Politics* or of the Complete Works.

12. Consider, for instance, Lukács's contention that the artist 'must

artistically conceal' the relationships revealed by his initial abstracting process in order to produce an effect of 'immediacy', of 'life as it actually appears' (p. 39). Textual practice must deny its own action in order to position the reader securely in front of the life-like: all traces of the theses governing the representation should be effaced. 'What matters is that the slice of life shaped and depicted by the artist and re-experienced by the reader should reveal the relations between appearance and essence without a commentary' (p. 33–4). Readers construing the piece of 'life' before them, in discovering the 'real relations' hidden there for them to find, accomplish their own commentary: it's like those ads which conceal the name of the product so that you are forced to supply it yourself, giving it your own voice.

13. *Aesthetics and Politics*, op. cit., p. 83.

14. Terry Eagleton, 'Aesthetics and Politics', *New Left Review*, no. 107, January-February 1978. p. 28.

15. Dick Hebdige and Geoff Hurd, 'Reading and Realism', *Screen Education*, no. 28, Autumn 1978, p. 72.

16. See Colin MacCabe, 'Principles of Realism and Pleasure', *Screen*, vol. 17, no. 3, 1976.

17. Eagleton, op. cit., p. 24. For the record, recent writings in *Screen* by Heath, Willemen, MacCabe and others are full of cautions against just this sort of 'ontologising'.

18. Tony Stevens, 'Reading the Realist Film', *Screen Education*, no. 26, Spring 1978, pp. 13–34.

19. Tony Stevens, 'Renovating Eng Lit', *Screen Education*, no. 29, Winter 1978/79, p. 86.

20. Ibid., p. 85: Stevens's emphasis.

21. Gill Davies, 'Teaching About Narrative', *Screen Education*, no. 29, Winter 1978/79, p. 76; my emphasis.

22. Ibid., pp. 75–6.

23. Cf. Brecht: 'Whether a work is realistic or not cannot be determined merely by checking whether or not it is like existing works which are said to be realistic, or were realistic in their time. In each case, one must compare the depiction of life in a work of art with the life itself that is being depicted, instead of comparing it with another depiction' (*Aesthetics and Politics*, op. cit., p. 85).

24. *Aesthetics and Politics*, op. cit., pp. 18–19.

25. Ibid. pp. 56–67; Lukács's emphasis.

26. Cf. Brecht: 'In a certain sense, we hear from our critics the fateful slogan, once addressed to individuals: "Enrich yourselves" ' (ibid., p. 78).

27. Ibid., p. 57; my emphasis.

28. Ibid., p. 43.

29. Ibid., p. 29.

30. Ibid., p. 166.

31. Ibid., p. 168.

32. Ibid., p. 160.

33. Ibid., p. 147.

34. Ibid., pp. 212–13.
35. Ibid., p. 212.
36. Ibid., p. 196.

Chapter 20

The Williams Interviews*

Stuart Hall

Politics and Letters: *Interviews with New Left Review*
Raymond Williams, New Left Books 1979

This is a somewhat unusual review – more a commentary on some of the major themes and issues posed by this long and intense interrogation of Raymond Williams's work than, in any strict sense, a critical review of *Politics and Letters*. There are several reasons for adopting this approach. First, the form of the book invites it. Readers will know that it is in the form of a series of extended interviews conducted with him by Perry Anderson, Anthony Barnett and Francis Mulhern on behalf of the *New Left Review (NLR)* editorial board. I comment on the success of this form below. But here I simply note that the interrogative form, when well done, invites the reader to become involved in what is in any case a dialogue – with Raymond Williams, but even more importantly, with his work. The second reason is that my own work in cultural studies has so often followed, and in many instances been guided by, those key points which mark out Williams's own development, that I feel the strictly objective and external critical eye would be inappropriate here. The third reason is closely related to that. It is simply the fact that, apart from the influences which have naturally arisen in the course of working in closely cognate areas, there are several strategic points at which

* *Screen Education*, no. 34, Spring 1980.

our careers have intersected. At very significant points in my own intellectual and political life, we have found ourselves shaping up to the same issues, or crises: and shaping up, if by no means in identical ways, then certainly from the same directions. I read an early essay of his, 'The Idea Of Culture', which enunciated some of the themes of *Culture and Society*, in *Essays in Criticism* at exactly that moment when I had decided, on other grounds, that my intermittent interests in questions about 'culture' had to assume something of the nature of a more committed project. The essays of his which we were privileged to publish in *Universities and Left Review* were amongst those from external contributors which most closely resonated with the internal project of that venture. His dispassionate wisdom and support sustained me through some of the rougher passages of the early *New Left Review*. In the depths of the recoil from the manifest taming and political defeat of the 1964–6 Labour Government, we found ourselves in the same room again, working on the draft of the statement which eventually became the *May Day Manifesto*. And so on. I put this somewhat too weakly and hesitantly. The fact is that in a broader, intellectual sense, I have often had the uncanny experience of beginning a line of thought or inquiry, only to find that, apparently coincidentally, he had not only been travelling much the same road but had given the issues a clearer, more forceful and clarifying formulation. *Politics and Letters*, the first, long overdue, attempt at a 'retrospective' seemed to call for something other than the usual balancing of accounts.

I have mentioned the form of *Politics and Letters*. I am not over-fond of the extensive interview form. It tends, on the whole, to a looseness of formation: extensiveness at the expense of depth and penetration. However, on this occasion, I think the form has been deployed with extraordinary success. There are three reasons for this. First, it isn't a set of interviews in the usual sense at all, subsequently transcribed for publication. It is an extended conversation. The *NLR* editors have entered into the dialogue as full partners to the conversation. They have interpreted their brief as not merely to interview well, but to probe; to expand their questions into statements which are worth considering in their own right. They have formulated critical remarks and alternative positions, to which Williams has had to react positively. On many occasions I find myself disagreeing either with the form in which a criticism is made or with the direction in which the dialogue is turned. Often I have felt myself gaining an unexpected insight into the collective mind of the *NLR* editorial team as much, if not more, than I am learning something about the development of Williams's work. But that is a minor point. The degree to which

they have made themselves partners to the exchange has paid off.
Second, their ability to become part of the dialogue in this way
is clearly the result of extremely conscientious and careful preparation. They know Williams's work in all its detail. They have
a comprehensive grasp of the turning points, the main lines of
development. They have done their homework. The results show
up in the text.

But the principal reason for the success of the form is undoubtedly the manner in which Williams has responded to the challenge.
The self-reflexivity which the form demands suits him well. He
has seized the opportunity to meditate and reflect. He has a
remarkable ability to treat himself and his own work dispassion-
ately, from the outside, as it were, without losing his line or
his characteristic 'voice'. His capacity to respond affirmatively
to criticism offers a most positive contrast with the intellectual
defensiveness and the polemic search for an impossible retrospective consistency which characterises so many of his contemporar-
ies. And this is due, in the last resort, to a virtue which is to be
found, not only in these interviews but in all his work – especially,
perhaps his most recent work. I mean his capacity simply *to go
on thinking*, to go on developing and changing in response to new
intellectual challenges. In *Politics and Letters* he gives a quite
exemplary demonstration of this quality of mind.

Biography

The book is divided into six sections: Boyhood, Cambridge; then
the major intellectual themes – Culture, Drama, Literature;
finally, Politics. Readers will know more of Williams's personal
background and boyhood than they would with comparable intellectual figures because he has written of them in fictional form in
his 'Welsh Trilogy', *Border Country, Second Generation* and *The
Fight for Manod*. His father was a railway signalman, but he
lived in a village where more than half the population were small
farmers. He comments here on the unusual way in which the rural
pattern of small farmers interlocked with the unionised and waged
world of the railway. The strong and rooted sense of community
– a concept which has taken on a peculiarly resonant meaning in
all of Williams's writing – and his double attachment to country-
side and the world of the railway workers are strands in his early
formation which have been continuously re-worked as themes in
his later work. But for me the first arresting exchange in the book
occurs at the beginning of Chapter 2 – 'Cambridge' – where, in
response to the question as to what the impact of Cambridge was

like on the young, bright, already politically-committed young man from the Welsh valleys, Williams simply responds: 'I was wholly unprepared for it. I knew nothing about it'.

Though I myself came from a very different background, to Oxford not Cambridge, and a decade later – beginning of the 1950s rather than the 1940s – those stark sentences carried enormous reverberations for me. I still feel a strong sympathy for that way in which the bright young lad from the 'periphery', coming to Oxford as the idealised pinnacle of an *intellectual* path, first experiences the actual *social* shock of discovering that Oxbridge is not only the apex of official English intellectual culture, but the cultural centre of the class system. I know at once what Williams means by remarking, in his usual understated way, that 'the class stamp of Trinity was not difficult to spot'; and also that inevitable path which led, in the search for some kind of refuge, to the discovery of the Socialist Club – 'a home from home'. In the Oxford Socialist Club of a decade and a half later, there was also a moment when the Welsh, Scots and colonials took a look around the room and came to the startling conclusion that 'There is not an Englishman among us'. Williams arrived in Cambridge at the end of the 1930s as the bright 'scholarship boy' from the valleys. He records with feeling how that brash, radical certainty was constantly broken against the effortless assumption of superiority of the system: the sense, as he put it, that any critical statement he made could be immediately beached by a knowing reference to a comparative text he had not read; the sense of being 'continually found out in ignorance'; and being forced to look at himself, increasingly, with radical doubt. I still experience that indefinable sense of being absolutely placed and put down even today, whenever I cross the threshold between Oxford railway station and Broad Street, gateway to the 'dreaming spires'. In the light of these pages, I now know just what is meant by thinking of this as a 'colonial' experience. Williams, being made of sterner stuff, has remained his own man through very long sojourns in both places.

By the time Williams returned to Cambridge at the end of the war, the 'break' had already occurred. In 1939–40 his project had seemed 'confident and unproblematic'. By 1945–6, it had become 'incredibly problematic'. It is difficult, even in the light of these pages, to distinguish between the elements of the personal, the political and the intellectual within this break. But, not surprisingly, for Williams (as for many of us a generation or two later), this 'sense of the complexity of things' was, in its own complex way, intertwined with the impact of Leavis. It is difficult now to convey to those who only know the conservative after-glow of Leavis and the *Scrutiny* tradition, the paradoxical nature of the influence of what Williams quite rightly calls Leavis's 'cultural radicalism'. For those who were part of the privileged Downing-*Scrutiny* circle, things were always different. They were committed, not only to the culturally conservative programme, but to following every twist and turn of the Great Man's idiosyncratic critical judgements, and to imitating the ascetic, non-conformist ethic and a mimicry of that highly distinctive style of writing, with its peculiar involutions. But why on earth should such a formation have had so powerful an impact on others of a more radical political temper, committed to an egalitarian educational practice? Williams cites in explanation Leavis's attack on the metropolitan literary and commercial cultural scene, the excitement of the discovery of practical criticism and the *Scrutiny* emphasis on education. But I wonder if these things didn't resonate more because of the immediately dominant ethos of Oxbridge itself (themselves?)? Certainly, in the 1950s, *Scrutiny's* 'seriousness' about serious issues contrasted favourably with the dilettantism of the Oxford approach to literary and cultural questions. Practical criticism seemed to offer some sort of discipline with which to combat the effortless exercise of 'good taste' which passed for the critical enterprise. Leavis discussed cultural issues as if they mattered. Finally – to repeat a point which Williams made with force in *Culture and Society* and which he makes again here, at a later point in the argument: If your field happened to be literary and cultural questions, *Scrutiny* offered a sort of 'complexity' much more adequate to the complexity of the forms one had to deal with than anything which at the time passed for a 'native' Marxist literary or cultural criticism or theory. Practical criticism was the practice which condensed this value in its most available form. Williams is right, both in identifying its weakness (its evasion of the problems of structure, ideology and belief) and in acknowledging its persistent hold on those who were trained in it. Somewhere in there the commitment to 'a new cultural politics' was born.

But the break was also a political one. The sense of the loss of impetus in the 1945 Labour Government, coupled with the impossibility of rejoining the Communist Party (which he had joined within a month or two of arriving at Cambridge), left Williams, objectively, in what later we would have called a 'New Left' position – if any such thing had existed. 'You are a Communist, not a member of the Party, but still a Communist,' people said to him. 'I did not know what to reply. Neither no nor yes was the right answer.' But, of course, there was no such political space then between the intolerables. And the collapse of his first venture into active cultural politics – the breakup of the group around the short-lived *Politics and Letters* (the journal which gives its title to this volume) – Williams appears to have experienced as a personal crisis. 'I pulled back to do my own work. For the next ten years I wrote in nearly complete isolation'. *Culture and Society* was, in part, the fruit of this 'retreat'. But, as others have suggested, the isolation took its toll, as certain notes and tones in *Culture and Society* itself attest.

The *NLR* interrogators do not hesitate at this point to pose the awkward political questions. Why didn't *Politics and Letters* nail its socialist colours to the mast? Why didn't it go for a more direct intellectual-political form of engagement? Williams does not duck the issue here. He bravely identifies the costs of a prolonged sorting-out of the 'emerging terms of the collaboration between left politics and "Leavisite" criticism'. This is true; and honest of him to say so – as anyone who has gone through that painful 'sorting-out' will testify. Yet, from a different point of view, the question is too *politicised*. There was radically important work to do, precisely in the space which *Horizon* then and *Encounter* a decade later occupied so effectively: a contest of the struggle for intellectual hegemony over the liberal intelligensia in the polarising climate of the Cold War. It was a task which the Communist Party should have filled but could not. The historians clearly could and did for a time win some space within the orbit of the Party for a different and telling kind of intellectual project: accordingly, amongst those who, between 1946 and 1956 did stop and fight inside the Party for a separate position, the most significant formation was the historians, tutored and sustained by the elusive Dona Torr. But, as Williams frankly and correctly puts it, 'The Party had absolutely no implantation of a kind I could respect in any of the fields of work I was involved in'. Start of a new chapter . . .

Culture and Society

The 'new chapter' was, of course, *Culture and Society* – which Williams shows here to have been a genuine voyage of intellectual discovery, not a mere reworking of an old Cambridge 'Moralists' course. It was an oppositional enterprise, attempting to redress the appropriation of a long line of thought about 'culture' to reactionary positions. In short, another episode in the engagement with the Leavisite inheritance: that is why the reassessment of Arnold, though still too muted for my taste, is one of the main pivots of the book. Yet *Culture and Society* is profoundly marked by the imprint of the tradition to which it was counterposed: and nowhere so much as in its *method*. I am thinking of the preference for text over general argument or theory; the procedure by way of the 'local instance' and particularity: 'I shall try to do this by examining, not a series of abstracted problems but a series of statements by individuals'. This is the long shadow of 'practical criticism' . . . There is also the obliqueness of the approach to political questions – via, so to speak, the displacements of 'culture'; and the privileging of 'complexity of response' over position. If one asks what constructs the unity of this 'tradition' it is certainly not a unity of positions adopted by the writers who compose it. Rather, it is a unity of an *idiom* – the posing of the right, qualitative question; the priority given to the complexity of an articulated response to experience ('politics saturated with thought').

Of course, Williams is not wrong to have identified this underlying commitment, amongst writers who would have sharply disagreed with each other, to a particularising, empirical-moral, anti-generalising idiom of discourse about culture and society. The problem is that its presence in the book is over-determined from at least three directions: the force of the idiom itself amongst 'culture and society' writers; the preferring of this idiom in the qualitative side of the Leavisite appropriation of them; its underpinn·ng in the method of analysis which Williams adopted – which carried the idiom, so to speak, in its very bloodstream, but as a *methodological* rather than a substantive imperative. It is this, I believe, which gives the book, ultimately, its undertow towards a certain 'inadvertent conservatism', despite the many other tendencies in it. The difficulty is that, since Williams's method underpinned the idiom it was analysing, the book itself offered no rallying point outside this empirico-moral discourse from which its limitations (as well as its strengths) might have been identified. Actually, of course, this was not only a *cultural* question: in the English context, it was precisely the manner in which a particular set of political and social values had sedimented into a habitual inflexion of language and thought. This the book does not and could not place because it remains, in some ways, methodologically trapped inside the discourse.

Something of this comes across in Williams's forthrightly self-critical response to a question from the *NLR* team, when he identifies in the book what he calls the way it is 'negatively marked by elements of a disgusted withdrawal . . . from all immediate forms of collaboration'. Perhaps this goes too far, now, in the other direction: for, as he also insists, this very 'drawing back' allowed him to reintroduce themes and issues which have since become crucial, politically, but which were 'absent from what I knew then and often know now as politics'. Still I think Williams has put his finger on a sensitive point in the *Culture and Society* project, though he has attributed it to too personal a cause.

His interlocutors take him to task, undoubtedly, for the 'absent traditions' and influences in the book; no French Revolution, or popular radicalism, or sociology; the lack of an international perspective and of Marx. Finding what *Culture and Society* left out has become, over the years, something of an intellectual game. Including them all would have required a book four times the length of the existing one. Perhaps it is a measure of the book's achieved stature that its critics expected it to be comprehensive. Yet these *are* convenient ways of trying to isolate some of the weaknesses of the book, even recognising its properly limited scope. A comprehensive account of the French Revolution was certainly not on the cards. But its absence as a precipitating intellectual force within the corpus of English ideas means that, not only is there little indication of the radical character, the growth and challenge of popular radicalism, and the quite striking non-intellectual culture which sustained it; but also, the book lacks, as a dramatic episode, the sharp ruptures in the very liberal-intellectual climate of thought which *is* the centre of the book's concerns which Jacobinism provoked. The absence of 'sociology' is less surprising. Not only did it not manifest itself at the time when *Culture and Society* was being written as a comparable intellectual formation. Those who knew of its existence barely understood that the issues arising from 'the twin revolutions' were actually what the 'science of society' addressed. (This was the hey-day of American structural-functionalist gobbledegook.) As a result, the book could literally not address the questions as to why what, in Germany, was sustained in a historico-philosophical mode, and in France a 'positive social science' one, should have been sustained in England in so pre-eminently a *literary-moral* mode of discourse. But I confess that my own candidate of omission is none of these – though I do think the failure to recognise the non-literary culture of popular radicalism is both a product of *Culture and Society*'s literary centredness and contributes to the book's over-literariness. What I have always regretted most in *Culture and Society* is the absence of any developed reference to the *dominant* intellectual formations of the time – political economy, political individualism, liberalism, empiricism – against which the 'culture and society' tradition was pitched. It is the ideas which formed the great heartland of the 'English ideology', and a sense of the profound sedimentation of these ideas into the habits and idioms of everyday life – the weight of English 'common sense' and its roots in the thought of the previous century and a half (Hobbes, Locke, Adam Smith and Bentham, to cite a few key names almost at random) – which needed at least to be sketched in, if we are to understand the force, within the culture-and-society tradition, of the conservative critique of utilitarian possessive individualism (to coin a phrase). This would have given us a better sense of the somewhat 'exceptional' character of the literary-moral social critics, and placed them, as a formation, more appropriately, socially and historically. Williams makes a small gesture in this direction towards the end of this discussion in *Politics and Letters* where he regrets not yet having written up his early lectures on Hobbes. But it is a line I wish the *NLR* interviewers had pressed harder. Its relation to what the book is actually about is more organic: hence, in my view, its presence in the book only as an eloquent absence (what everybody in 'the tradition' was, implicitly, *against*) is rather more damaging.

The Long Revolution

The exchange achieves a particular pitch of intensity in the debate about *The Long Revolution* – and rightly so, since its project was so thoroughly innovatory: a difficult, not always successful, but in its way *heroic* attempt to break, finally, with the idiom and method of *Culture And Society*: and, on the back of a mode of discourse militantly hostile to the very idea of generalisation, to begin to construct a cultural *theory*. In a radical sense, *The Long Revolution* is a 'settling of accounts' – a text of the break. Its notorious 'difficulty' stems, I believe, precisely from the ambitiousness of its project. Often, the attainment of a genuinely-sustained mode of theorising falters, and the argument falls back on a sort of abstract generalising. But the pressure to formulate was exemplary.

The main controversial themes are all touched on here. The tendency towards too evolutionary a notion of 'culture' – 'way of life' – which provoked E. P. Thompson's famous and strategic response – 'way of struggle' – is openly acknowledged. (The polemical manner in which this revision was advanced is noted, in a characteristically understated aside.) This leads Williams to a reformulation, expanding the difference between the permanent and inevitable presence of 'class conflict', endemic in a capitalist social order, and those moments of 'conscious and mutual contention, an overt engagement of forces' – 'class conflict' – which may not always be to the forefront. Actually, I would myself prefer to reverse Williams's proposed usage: using the more classic term, 'class struggle' to identify the general process, and 'class conflict' for those moments of more sustained and open contention. But this may be just a quibble. Thompson was undoubtedly correct to force the absolute centrality of these dimensions for any socialist definition of 'culture' to the forefront. Nevertheless, Williams here does rescue an important qualification, while conceding the general argument. He notes that the stress on 'struggle', appropriate for heroic periods of class conflict in history, may be less satisfactory for dealing with 'unheroic decades'. In the context of the 1950s, and later – indeed, perhaps from the 1920s onwards – not only do we have to confront 'unheroic periods'; but the nature and causes of their 'unheroic' character constitutes *the* absolutely key and prior issue for socialist analysis. In fact the problem of 'reformism' and containment is inadequately addressed by either an heroic emphasis on 'struggle' or Williams's more evolutionary 'way of life'.

Then there are the two characteristic stresses in *The Long Revolution*, for which Williams, despite his openness to the critical comments which his interviewers address, provides a tougher defence. The first is the stress, in *The Long Revolution*, on the impossibility of separating out the different lived systems and according any one prior determinacy, the theoretical basis of the radically interactionist conception of the social totality which the book advanced. The second is the complementary stress on 'experience' as the authenticating test of cultural analysis, as well as the privileged object which it attempted to 'produce in thought'. Williams receives a strong challenge on both questions from the *NLR* team. On both he has conceded something – especially, with respect to the first; making a sort of return, in more recent work, to a stronger sense of 'determinacy' than the 'interaction of all practices on one another' which marked his position in *The Long Revolution*. Nevertheless, I see a striking continuity of basic position on these issues even in his more acceptable recent formulations. Both a marked disparity between different systems and a temporal unevenness in social formations are now more openly acknowledged. But Williams continues to resist any attempt at the analytic separation of grounding structures and practices. He acknowledges that his earlier 'appeal to experience' as a way of grounding this unity of structures was unsatisfactory. But he stands by the reformulation of this position which achieved its clearest statement in *Marxism and Literature*: 'indissoluble elements of a continuous social-material process'.

This is an area where I continue to take issue with him. I do think that the indissolubility of practices in the ways in which they are experienced and 'lived', in any real historical situation, does not in any way pre-empt the *analytic* separations of them, when one is attempting to theorise their different effects. The ways in which everything appears to interconnect in 'experience' can only be a starting point for analysis. One has to 'produce the concrete in thought' – that is, show, by a series of analytic approximations through abstraction, the concrete historical experience as the 'product of many determinations'. Analysis must deconstruct the 'lived wholeness' in order to be able to think its determinate conditions. I believe this necessary use of abstraction in thought is quite mistakenly confused, in current debates, with a sort of 'fetishisation of theory' (theoreticism, of course, exists, and is a plague on all our houses: but so is empiricism). And I do think that this confusion, which persists even in Williams's later work, is predicated on an uninspected notion of 'experience' which, in the earlier work, produced the quite unsatisfactory concept of 'a structure of feeling' and which continues to have disabling theoretical effects. However one attempts to displace the plenitude which the term 'experience' confers, and however much one allows for 'marked disparities' and 'temporal unevenesses', so long as 'experience' continues to play this all-embracing role, there will be an inevitable theoretical pull towards reading all structures as if they expressively correlated with one another: simultaneous in effect and determinacy because they are simultaneous in our experience. Here I find myself in agreement with the *NLR* questioners: 'structures can be temporally simultaneous, but they need not thereby be causally equal'. The more recent emphasis on 'indissoluble socio-material practices' does, of course, go a great deal of the way towards a more materialist theory of cultural practice. But what I think, without being unfair, we can call the 'experiential' paradigm does continue to cause some theoretical fluctuations in Williams's work around such key problems as determination, social totality and ideology. Williams is admirably clear on these questions in this section; and always open to critical argument. But he does not concede much ground.

Literature

In the hot-house climate of theoretical sectarianism through which we have recently passed, it has often been assumed that a theory which *tends* towards the correspondence between different practices (or the dissolution of them all in 'material praxis', which is a variant of the same position) would necessarily produce a corresponding problem when applied to more local instances. But this is to deploy the theory of 'symptomatic reading' in a hopelessly theoreticist way – reducing all of every text to its 'problematic'. In fact, when we come to Williams on literature, there has never been any simple parallelism of this kind. Indeed, as we move from the discussion of literature and society in the 1840s, in *The Long Revolution*, through *The English Novel from Dickens to Lawrence* to *The Country and the City* – one of his finest but most neglected works – we move farther and farther from any such correspondences. In part this is because of a rich, deeply organic, but non-formalist conception of 'form' – a theme, first enunciated in rather organicist terms in *The Long Revolution*, which has undergone progressive transformations since.

I wish I had more space to devote to the passages in *Politics and Letters* which deal with literature, literary theory and drama, because they are among the richest in the volume. In the early 'Cambridge' section, it comes as something of a shock to find that the literary intellectuals in the Communist party at the time were regarded by their comrades as 'aesthetes' because of their commitment to the project of a modernist literature (Williams cites Joyce in particular here). For much of his work in this area, the common view would be that which notes his strong attachment to and vigorous defence of the *realist* tradition. He means 'realism' in the Brechtian sense. And his critique of the absolutist manner in which the debate about realism had been conducted (the worst excesses have been in film theory) and his gentle reproof of the ahistorical way in which an immovable correspondence has been assumed between modernist aesthetics and revolutionary socialism is well made, and timely. But, his reflexive remarks on *Dickens to Lawrence* – apart from many illuminating asides – are important primarily because of the manner in which the term 'form' is deployed. The distinction between an attention to the 'form' of the work (for example, the contrast between the reproduction of 'known forms' in Trollope, and the 'formally disturbed novels' of George Eliot and Hardy) and a formalist criticism, is a highly relevant one for contemporary debates in aesthetics. It has not, I think, been sufficiently noticed how systematically, in these more 'traditional' works of literary criticism, Williams has tried to fight his way – not always successfully – out of the pull towards the 'practical critical' approach towards a different kind of critical practice.

My own view is that this break is not fully made until *The Country and the City*. The difference here consists, primarily, of two elements. First, the formalised and conventional nature of much 'pastoral' literature has *forced* a more sustained attention to displacements and disjunctures, which earlier work on more 'naturalistic' and 'realist' forms did not. But the more significant element is the sustained and detailed historical work, and its integration into the thematic of the book, which radically and irretrievably interrupts any residual pull towards 'practical criticism'. The *NLR* interviewers put their finger on this point very precisely when they note how prolonged and how full of subtle reformulations have been Williams's efforts to define what constitutes the literary text. In *Reading and Criticism* the documentary aspect was still paramount: the text was 'a record of human experience'. *Culture and Society* added a more active element: there it is both 'record' and 'response'. The 'response' side is developed in *The Long Revolution* in theoretical terms: literature provides the most intense kind of 'response' to cultural change; but it is also placed as a 'special kind of communication' and therefore part of a more general 'creative' process. *The English Novel* describes literary texts as a 'dramatisation of values' – 'an action'. We can see the movement here from the characteristically Leavisite inflexion – record-response-expression – to a more 'Brechtian' conception of literary production. But it is only in *The Country and the City* that these two warring conceptions are brought into direct confrontation: and what produces this is the fact that 'for the first time literature is distanced and contrasted against a history that is systematically and separately analysed'. Williams's response to this point is very direct. The project was 'to show simultaneously the literary conventions and the historical relations to which they were a response . . . to see together the means of production and the conditions of the means of production'. This remains the most challenging of Williams's efforts in this field to put to use his own, specialised notion of what is involved in seeing literary forms *historically*. Interestingly, then, the discussion in this section does not remain at the 'literary' level, but is obliged to engage very central historical and theoretical questions: the relationship of classical Marxism to 'city' and 'country'; and the vexed issue of whether or not one can speak of 'progressive' literary forms. The question of rural and urban is one of the 'lost' themes in Marx. Williams's approach to this question – informed as it is by his own background and experience – is one of his most creative moments.

It is nevertheless the case that, theoretically at least, *Marxism and Literature* takes the notion of 'literary production' several stages on even from the positions adopted in *The Country and the City*. The former is one of the clearest statements we have of Williams's current position – a masterpiece of condensed formulation. It takes his earlier conception of the 'continuum of creative practices of communication' several steps further than the earlier volume; and it produces some challenging theses, mainly grouped around a new, provisional definition of his own project as that of clarifying and developing a 'cultural materialism'. The first thesis evokes from the *NLR* team a somewhat outraged and scandalised defence of 'the received idea of literature' – a piquant moment for *NLR*-watchers, this. But the second leads to one of the most provocative exchanges in the book – around the 'cultural materialism' thesis. The exchange deserves to be read in full. The important point seems to me to be the fact that Williams is still on surer ground when he identifies negatively the positions against which 'cultural materialism' is defined ('a totally spiritualised cultural production' on the one hand; on the other, its 'relegation to a secondary status') than he is in clarifying the positive content of his thesis. Clearly the challenge of recent debates around 'material practice' have stimulated him to a whole new phase of thinking – a welcome sign of the continuing vigour and freshness of his mind; even if one could have wished that *Marxism and Literature* fingered its opponents in a more open way. The question of determination continues to be the theoretical thorn in his side. Only those who have not suffered from this continuing irritant could afford to be cavalier with the problem, even if they also recognise that the definition of 'determinacy' as 'limits and pressures' is nothing more than a holding operation.

Politics

The *NLR conscience collective* bristles again at what they somewhere describe, with alarm, as a 'veering towards a radicalism of the ultra-left' in Williams's current position. The actual course of the closing discussion on 'Politics' must be reassuring in at least this respect. The emphases are characteristic: the break with 'Labourism' (which leaves open the question of strategies towards the Labour Party), the need to bypass received models of socialism, the question of self-management. If this is 'ultra-leftism' it is only in the mildest of doses – and a thoroughly necessary tonic. In fact, alerted as we are by the ruffling of *NLR* feathers, what surprises us most about this concluding section is the steady and persistent way in which Williams sticks to his guns: I mean, responding to the more overtly 'political' issues by having at his disposal all the complex themes of his particular preoccupations with broadly 'cultural' questions. In others this may have appeared as an evasion. In this instance it provides a sort of demonstration that, properly understood, the distinction politics/culture is, for him, an irrelevant one. To sustain *that* point while facing up to questions *inter alia* about the Labour Party, the tender issues surrounding the transfer of power between the 'New Left' Marks I and II, the 'October Revolution' and the future of socialism, is a remarkable testimony to his single-mindedness, his absolute singularity of tone and address.

I return, in closing, to my original starting-point. Both in form and content, *Politics and Letters* does not ask for, and should not get, blanket affirmation. This would be a hopeless exercise, since the book is instinct with revaluations, reformulations, taking criticisms, opening new lines of thought. There is no 'position' here to subscribe to. It is not a book for the religious. What is consistent is a *project*: the project of working through some of the most difficult and thorny problems in Marxist cultural theory. What the book is evidence of and for is the capacity to sustain a project at full intellectual strength: or, more simply, what I called his determination simply *to go on thinking*. On this matter, *Politics and Letters* is simply an exemplary performance.

Author List and Contents of *Screen Education* (*SE*) and *Screen Education Notes* (*SEN*), nos 1–41, Winter 1971/72 to Winter 1981/82

ADLAM, Diane

'The Diversion of Language: A Critical Assessment of the Concept "Linguistic Diversity" ' (with Angie Salfield), *SE*, 34, Spring 1980, pp. 71–86.

ALVARADO, Manuel

'Report – *Young Screen 1973*', *SEN*, 8, Autumn 1973, pp. 33–6.

'Outline Proposal I' (with Sheila Mullen), *SE* 10/11, Spring/Summer 1974, pp. 60–62.

'Draft Proposal for CSE in Media Studies' (with David M. Barrat), *SE*, 12, Autumn 1974, pp. 51–7.

'Simulation as Method', *SE*, 14, Spring 1975, pp. 21–6.

'The *Viewpoint* Controversy' (with Richard Collins), *SE*, 19, Summer 1976, pp. 74–81.

'Class, Culture and the Education System', *SE*, 22, Spring 1977, pp. 49–55.

'Teaching Television', *SE*, 31, Summer 1979, pp. 25–8.

'Photographs and Narrativity', *SE*, 32/33, Autumn/Winter 1979/80, pp. 5–17.

'Note in Response to Kevin Halliwell', *SE*, 37, Winter 1980/81, pp. 85–6.

'Television Studies and Pedagogy', *SE*, 38, Spring 1981, pp. 56–67.

CATTO, Mike
'Simulacra Et Anobile – Misrepresentation in Image Reproduction', *SE*, 23, Summer 1977, pp. 39–49.

CAUGHIE, John
'Teaching through Authorship', *SE*, 17, Winter 1975/76, pp. 3–13.
'Glasgow SEFT Group', *SE*, 22, Spring 1977, p. 76.
Book Review: '*BFI Distribution Library Catalogue* (Julian Petley)', *SE*, 24, Autumn 1977, pp. 60–62.

CHALMERS, Martin
'Notes on Nazi Propaganda', *SE*, 40, Autumn 1981, pp. 34–47.

CHAMBERS, Iain
'Rethinking "Popular Culture" ', *SE*, 36, Autumn 1980, pp. 113–17.
'Pop Music: A Teaching Perspective', *SE*, 39, Summer 1991, pp. 35–46.
'Silent Frontiers: An Italian Debate on the "Crisis of Reason" ' (with Lidia Curti), *SE*, 41, Winter 1981/82, pp. 26–33.

CLARK, John
Book Review: '*Japanese Cinema: Film Style and National Characters* (Donald Richie)', *SEN*, 5, Winter 1972, pp. 32–3.

CLARK, Maureen
'Liberation, Action or Radical Education? Three Educational Journals', *SE*, 30, Spring 1979, pp. 95–102.

CLARKE, Alan
'Vandals, Pickets and Muggers: Television Coverage of Law and Order in the 1979 Election' (with Ian Taylor) *SE*, 36, Autumn 1980, pp. 99–111.

COCKPIT Arts Workshop
'Photo-Essay, 2', *SE*, 38, Spring 1981, pp. 100–4.

COLLEY, Iain
'*Pennies from Heaven*: Music, Image, Text' (with Gill Davies), *SE*, 35, Summer 1980, pp. 63–78.

COLLINS, Richard
Book Review: '*To Encourage the Art of the Film – The Story of the British Film Institute*', *SEN*, 2, Spring 1972, pp. 33–4.
'Structures of Broadcasting', *SEN*, 3, Summer 1972, pp. 15–20.
Book Review: '*Von Stroheim* (Thomas Quinn Curtis)', *SEN*, 3, Summer 1972, p. 30.
Book Review: '*Film as Film* (V. F. Perkins)', *SEN*, 5, Winter 1972/73, pp. 35–7.
Book Review – '*Working Papers in Cultural Studies*, no. 3', *SEN*, 6, Spring 1973, pp. 35–7.
'Mythic Knowledge and its Mediation in the American Cinema', *SEN*, 7, Summer 1973, pp. 9–16.
'A Diploma Course in Film Study at the Polytechnic of Central London', *SEN*, 9, Winter 1973/74, pp. 11–21.

Book Review: '*Light Entertainment* (Richard Dyer)', *SEN*, 9, Winter 1973/74, pp. 31–4.

'TV Practice in TV Studies', *SE*, 12, Autumn 1974, pp. 46–50.

'Television and the People: Access, Participation and Assimilation' *SE*, 14, Spring 1975, pp. 8–13.

'The Education Cuts' (with Jim Grealy), *SE*, 16, Autumn 1975, pp. 41–6.

'The *Viewpoint* Controversy' (with Manuel Alvarado), *SE*, 19, Summer 1976, pp. 74–81.

Book Review: '*Bad News* (Glasgow University Media Group)', *SE*, 21, Winter 1976/77, pp. 80–82.

'Revaluations', *SE*, 22, Spring 1977, pp. 31–7.

Book Review: '*Facing the Nation: Television and Politics 1936–76* (Grace Wyndham Goldie)', *SE*, 24, Autumn 1977, pp. 62–8.

'Panic Among the Baked Beans', *SE*, 31, Summer 1979, pp. 61–7.

CONNELL, Ian

'Broadcasting: Democracy or Pluralism?', *SE*, 30, Spring 1979, pp. 69–74.

'The Political Economy of Broadcasting: Some Questions', *SE*, 37, Winter 1980/81, pp. 89–100.

COOK, Jim

'Inner London Education Authority Film Study Course for Sixth Form Students' (with Cary Bazalgette, Jane Corbett, Christine Gledhill, Jim Hillier, Chris Mottershead, Mike Simons), *SEN*, 5, Winter 1972/73, pp. 12–18.

'Book Review: *Film in English Teaching* (Roy Knight, ed.)', *SEN*, 6, Spring 1973, pp. 32–5.

'An Account of the Second Term of the ILEA Film Study Course for Sixth Forms and an Assessment of the Course' (with Cary Bazalgette, Christine Gledhill, Jim Hillier, Chris Mottershead, Mike Simons), *SEN*, 8, Autumn 1973, pp. 4–10.

'An Outline Proposal III', *SE*, 10/11, Spring/Summer 1974, pp. 73–78.

'The Role and Function of a Teacher Advisor', *SE*, 15, Summer 1975, pp. 43–46.

'Teaching the Industry', *SE*, 16, Autumn 1975, pp. 4–18.

'Film and Television Education in Great Britain' (with Jim Hillier), *SE*, 18, Spring 1976, pp. 40–5.

COOK, Pam

'Teaching Avant-Garde Film: Notes Towards Practice', *SE*, 32/33, Autumn/Winter 1979/80, pp. 83–97.

CORBETT, Jane

'Inner London Education Authority Film Study Course for Sixth Form Students' (with Cary Bazalgette, Jim Cook, Christine Gledhill, Jim Hillier, Chris Mottershead, Mike Simons), *SEN*, 5, Winter 1972/73, pp. 12–18.

HEBDIGE, Dick
'Reading and Realism' (with Geoff Hurd), *SE*, 28, Autumn 1978, pp. 68–78.

HILLIER, Heather
' "Film as Industry" in the ILEA Sixth Form Film Study Course' (with Richard Exton), *SE*, 16, Autumn 1975 pp. 36–9.

HILLIER, Jim
'Introduction to Papers from the Conference "Film and Youth" Mannheim-Ludwigshafen, October 1971', *SEN*, 1, Winter 1971/72, p. 3.
Book Review: '*Talking about Television* (A. P. Higgins)', *SEN*, 3, Summer 1972, pp. 35–6.
'Inner London Education Authority Film Study Course for Sixth Form Students' (with Cary Bazalgette, Jim Cook, Jane Corbett, Christine Gledhill, Chris Mottershead, Mike Simons), *SEN*, 5, Winter 1972/73, pp. 12–18.
'An Account of the Second Term of the ILEA Film Study Course for Sixth Forms and an Assessment of the Course' (with Cary Bazalgette, Jim Cook, Christine Gledhill, Chris Mottershead, Mike Simons), *SEN*, 8, Autumn 1973, pp. 4–10.
'Outline Proposal V', *SE*, 10/11, Spring/Summer 1974, pp. 81–8.
'Film and Television Education in Great Britain' (with Jim Cook), *SE*, 18, Spring 1976, pp. 40–45.

HOLMES, Peter
'Report on the SEFT Summer School 1972, at Stockwell College of Education: "Television and Education" ', *SEN*, 4, Autumn 1972, pp. 28–31.

HOOD, Stuart
'Arbeiterfilme: The Collins-Porter Monograph', *SE*, 37, Winter 1980/81, pp. 68–72.

HORROCKS, Tim
'Film-Making As Training for the Professional', *SEN*, 2, Spring 1972, pp. 16–20.

HORROX, Alan
'*Our People*', *SE*, 31, Summer 1979, pp. 83–8.

HUNTER, Fred
'Fine Tuning the News', *SE*, 22, Spring 1977, pp. 71–3.

HURD, Geoff
'*The Sweeney* – Contradiction and Coherence', *SE*, 20, Autumn 1976, pp. 47–53.
'Reading and Realism' (with Dick Hebdige), *SE*, 28, Autumn 1978, pp. 68–78.

JAMESON, Fredric
'Class and Allegory in Contemporary Mass Culture: *Dog Day Afternoon* as a Political Film', *SE*, 30, Spring 1979, pp. 75–92.

LUMLEY, Bob
'Notes on Some Images of Terrorism in Italy', *SE*, 40, Autumn 1981, pp. 58–66.

LUSTED, David
'Appraisal of a Study Unit: *The Western*', *SEN*, 2, Spring 1972, pp. 26–7.
'GCE Mode III "O" Level in Film Study', *SEN*, 5, Winter 1972/73, pp. 19–20.
'Film as Industrial Product – Teaching a Reflexive Movie', *SE*, 16, Autumn 1975, pp. 26–30.
'*The Searchers* and the Study of the Image', *SE*, 17, Winter 1975/76, pp. 14–26.
'What Would Constitute a Critical Pedagogy?', *SE*, 25, Winter 1977/78, pp. 16–36.
'Review of Robin Wood's *Howard Hawks*' *SE*, 40, Autumn 1981, pp. 93–9.

LYONS, Harry
'A First and Second Year Course in Image Education' (with Stephen Neale), *SE*, 13, Winter 1974/75, pp. 36–9.

MacDONALD, Ian
'Select Bibliography on the "One-off" Play', *SE*, 35, Summer 1980, pp. 95–105.

MacDONALD, Madeleine
'Cultural Reproduction: The Pedagogy of Sexuality', *SE*, 32/33, Autumn/Winter 1979/80, pp. 141–53.

MacRAE, Alan
'Film-making in the English Class – A Canadian View' (Extract), *SEN*, 2, Spring 1972, pp. 21–5.

MacSHANE, Denis
'Reporting Race', *SE*, 31, Summer 1979, pp. 91–6.

MALE, Peter
'For Those with Eyes to See', *SE*, 13, Winter 1974/75, pp. 22–30.

MARTIN, Angela
'A Report on the 1974 Summer School in TV Studies at the Polytechnic of Central London', *SE*, 12, Autumn 1974, pp. 61–5.

MASTERMAN, Len
'Film and the Raising of the School Leaving Age', *SEN*, 6, Spring 1973, pp. 21–4.
Book Review: '*Film in English Teaching* (Roy Knight, ed.)', *SEN*, 6, Spring 1973, pp. 29–31.
'Football on Television: Studying the Cup Final', *SE*, 19, Summer 1976, pp. 14–27.
'TV Pedagogy', *SE*, 40, Autumn 1981, pp. 88–92.

MORRIS, Hugh
'Practical Studio Work in Television Studies', *SE*, 21, Winter 1976/77, pp. 13–19.

MORSE, David
'Teaching the American Cinema', *SEN*, 7, Summer 1973, pp. 28–30.

MORT, Frank
'The Domain of the Sexual', *SE*, 36, Autumn, 1980, pp. 69–84.

MOTTERSHEAD, Chris
'Film-Making in a College of Further Education', *SEN*, 2, Spring 1972, pp. 9–12.

Book Review: '*Communications* (Raymond Williams)' and '*The Popular Arts* (Stuart Hall and Paddy Whannel)', *SEN*, 3, Summer 1972, pp. 36–7.

'Inner London Education Authority Film Study Course for Sixth Form Students' (with Cary Bazalgette, Jim Cook, Jane Corbett, Christine Gledhill, Jim Hillier, Mike Simons), *SEN*, 5, Winter 1972/73, pp. 12–18.

'Report on the London Association of Teachers of English Conference "Word and Image" ', *SEN*, 7, Summer 1973, p. 31.

'An Account of the Second Term of the ILEA Film Study Course for Sixth Forms and an Assessment of the Course' (with Cary Bazalgette, Jim Cook, Christine Gledhill, Jim Hillier, Mike Simons), *SEN*, 8, Autumn 1973, pp. 4–10.

'Regional Film Centres', *SEN*, 9, Winter 1973/74, pp. 23–25.

'Problems over Practice: Relating Film-making to Film Study', *SE*, 10/11, Spring/Summer 1974, pp. 24–8.

'Comments on "A Draft Proposal for a CSE in Media Studies" ', *SE*, 12, Autumn 1974, pp. 57–60.

Book Review: '*Television, Technology and Cultural Form* (Raymond Williams)', *SE*, 14, Spring 1975, pp. 35–8.

'The Role and Function of the Teacher Advisor: Report 2', *SE*, 16, Autumn 1975, pp. 47–51.

Book Review: '*Sixguns and Society* (Will Wright)', *SE*, 19, Summer 1976, pp. 61–4.

'Practical Work: Positions and Problems', *SE*, 21, Winter 1976/77, pp. 4–12.

'The Corporate Control of Broadcast News', *SE*, 27, Summer 1978, pp. 78–81.

MULHERN, Francis
Book Review: '*Media, Politics and Culture: A Socialist View* (Carl Gardner, ed.)', *SE*, 32/33, Autumn/Winter 1979/80, pp. 135–7.

'Notes on Culture and Cultural Struggle', *SE*, 34, Spring 1980, pp. 31–5.

MULLEN, Sheila
'Outline Proposal I' (with Manuel Alvarado), *SE*, 10/11 Spring/Summer 1974, pp. 60–62.

'Planning the Family: The Art of the Television Schedule', *SE*, 35, Summer 1980, pp. 79–85.

'Real Entertainment: The Iranian Embassy Siege' (with Cary Bazalgette), *SE*, 37, Winter 1980/81, pp. 55–67.

PEARCE, John (pseudonym for **Trevor Pateman**)
'Day by Day by Day by Day . . .', *SE*, 14, Spring 1975, pp. 27–34.

PERKINS, T. E.
'Remembering Doris Day: Some Comments on the Season and the Subject', *SE*, 39, Summer 1981, pp. 25–34.

PINES, Jim
'The Study of Racial Images: A Structural Approach', *SE*, 23, Summer 1977, pp. 24–32.

POLLOCK, Griselda
'What's Wrong with Images of Women?', *SE*, 24, Autumn 1977, pp. 25–33.

'Three Perspectives on Photography', *SE*, 31, Summer 1979, pp. 49–54.

PORTER, Vincent
Book Review: '*The American Film Industry* (Tino Balio)', *SE*, 24, Autumn 1977, pp. 53–7.

'Video Recording and the Teacher', *SE*, 35, Summer 1980, pp. 87–9.

PRINGLE, Ashley
Book Review: '*Structures of Television* (Nicholas Garnham)', *SEN*, 9, Winter 1973/74, pp. 29–31.

PURDON, Noel
Book Review: '*The Cinema of Carl Dreyer* (Tom Milne)', *SEN*, 1, Winter 1971/72, pp. 35–6.

PYE, Douglas
'Film and English Studies at Berkshire College of Education', *SEN*, 4, Autumn 1972, pp. 3–8.

'*The Searchers* and Teaching the Industry', *SE*, 17, Winter 1975/76, pp. 34–48.

RICE, Philip
'Critical Practice', *SE*, 38, Spring 1981, pp. 86–8.

'Quizzing the Popular' (with Adam Mills), *SE*, 41, Winter 1981/82, pp. 15–25.

RICHARDS, Chris
'Classroom Readings', *SE*, 40, Autumn 1981, pp. 67–79.

RIDGE, Christine
'Reflections on the ILEA 6th Form Film Course', *SEN*, 8, Autumn 1973, pp. 11–12.

ROCKETT, Kevin
'Constructing a Film Culture: Ireland', *SE*, 27, Summer 1978, pp. 23–33.

'Cops, Consensus and Ideology' (with John Dennington), *SE*, 20, Autumn 1976, pp. 37–46.
'The Annan Report', *SE*, 23, Summer 1977, pp. 50–54.
'Television, Trade Unions and Media Studies', *SE*, 38, Spring 1981, pp. 68–79.

TURNBULL, Les
'The Use of Film in the Teaching of History', *SEN*, 6, Spring 1973, pp. 9–20.

TURPIE, Jonnie
'Photo-Essay 1', *SE*, 38, Spring 1981, pp. 26–32.

WAKSMAN, Daniel
'*Plaza Sesamo* and an Alibi for the Author's Real Intentions' (with Armand Mattelart), *SE*, 27, Summer 1978, pp. 56–62.

WALKER, Michael
' "Film as Industry" in the GCE Mode III "O" Level in Film Studies' (with Ian Gilman), *SE*, 16, Autumn 1975, pp. 31–5.

WALKERDINE, Valerie
'Sex, Power and Pedagogy', *SE*, 38, Spring 1981, pp. 14–24.

WALSH, Martin
'Film at the University of Western Ontario', *SEN*, 8, Autumn 1973, pp. 25–31.

WATKINS, Roger
'News on Television', *SEN*, 3, Summer 1972, pp. 12–14.

WEAVER, Mike
'Film in the Context of American (and Commonwealth) Arts' (with Mick Gidley), *SEN*, 7, Summer 1973, pp. 21–7.

WEBBER, John
'Production versus Criticism: An Account of the BA Course in Film at California State University, San Francisco', *SEN*, 4, Autumn 1972, pp. 24–7.

WEX, Marianne
'Photo-Essay', *SE*, 39, Summer 1981, pp. 47–55.

WHANNEL, Garry
'Broadcasting Institutions and the "National Interest" ', *SE*, 27, Summer 1978, pp. 73–7.

WILLEMEN, Paul
Book Review: '*The Films of Akira Kurosawa* (Donald Richie)', *SEN*, 1, Winter 1971/72, pp. 34–5.

WILLIAMS, Christopher
'Film Education and the ILEA Course', *SEN*, 8, Autumn 1973, pp. 21–24.

WILLIAMS, David
'Bandaging the Cuts: News from the North-East' (wtih Sylvia Harvey and Philip Simpson), *SE*, 23, Summer 1977, pp. 55–8.

WILLIAMS, Raymond
'Television and Teaching' (an interview with Raymond Williams conducted by: Richard Collins, James Donald, Simon Frith and Jim Grealy, uncredited), *SE*, 31, Summer 1979, pp. 5–14.

WILLIAMSON, Judith
'How Does Girl Number Twenty Understand Ideology?', *SE*, 40, Autumn 1981, pp. 80–7.

WIMMER, Gunter
'*Pacific 231* A Unit for Teaching about Media', *SEN*, 1, Winter 1971/72, pp. 21–5.

WOLLEN, Peter
'Film Studies at the University of Essex', *SE*, 19, Summer 1976, pp. 57–60.

WOOD, Robin
'Film Studies at the University of Warwick', *SE*, 19, Summer 1976, pp. 51–4.

WREN-LEWIS, Justin
'The Story of a Riot: The Television Coverage of Civil Unrest in 1981', *SE*, 40, Autumn 1981, pp. 15–33.

Uncredited

1. 'Objectives for Media Education in the Subject Swedish in the Swedish Elementary School', *SEN*, 1, Winter 1971/72, pp. 26–7.
2. 'SEFT One-day Conference at Ormskirk', *SEN*, 1, Winter 1971/72, pp. 32–3.
3. 'Film Education in Yugoslavia', *SEN*, 5, Winter 1972/73, pp. 21–3.
4. 'Revised Scheme of Study for the Certificate and Diploma in Film Study', *SEN*, 9, Winter 1973/74, pp. 7–10.
5. 'Three Charts for Film Study', *SEN*, 10/11, Spring/Summer 1974, pp. 46–51.
6. 'The "Field" of Film Study', *SEN*, 10/11, Spring/Summer 1974, pp. 52–7.
7. 'Communication Studies at N and F level: SEFT's comment to the Schools Council', *SE*, 32/33, Autumn/Winter 1978/79, pp. 154–60.

Editorial Boards

SEN 5, Winter 1972/73

Editors: Edward Buscombe, Tom Ryall;
Editorial Board: Elizabeth Cowie, Richard Exton, Christine Gledhill, Jim Hillier, Andrew McTaggart, Chris Mottershead.

SEN 6, Spring 1973

Editors: Edward Buscombe, Tom Ryall;
Editorial Board: Elizabeth Cowie, Richard Exton, Christine Gledhill, Jim Hillier, Andrew McTaggart, Chris Mottershead.

SEN 7, Summer 1973

Editor: Edward Buscombe;
Editorial Board: Cary Bazalgette, Richard Collins, Jim Cook, Richard Exton, Felicity Grant, Jim Hillier, Chris Mottershead.

SEN 8, Autumn 1973

Editor: Edward Buscombe;
Editorial Assistant: Elizabeth Cowie;
Editorial Board: Cary Bazalgette, Richard Collins, Jim Cook, Richard Exton, Felicity Grant, Jim Hillier, Chris Mottershead.

SEN 9, Winter 1973/74

Editor: Edward Buscombe;
Editorial Assistant: Elizabeth Cowie;
Editorial Board: Manuel Alvarado, Cary Bazalgette, Richard Collins, Jim Cook, Richard Exton, Geoff Goldstein, Felicity Grant, Jim Hillier, Chris Mottershead.

SCREEN EDUCATION (*SE*), numbers 10–41, Spring 1974–Winter 1981

A troika system was introduced at this stage whereby three members of the Editorial Board took responsibility for an issue. Many issues were also thematically based from this date.

SE 10/11, Spring/Summer 1974: 'CSE Film Study: Problems and Approaches'

Issue Editors: Jim Cook, Jim Hillier, Chris Mottershead;
Editorial Assistant: Elizabeth Cowie;
Editorial Board: Manuel Alvarado, Cary Bazalgette, Edward Buscombe, Richard Collins, Jim Cook, Richard Exton, Geoff Goldstein, Felicity Grant, Jim Hillier, Chris Mottershead.

SE 12, Autumn 1974: 'Special Number: TV Studies'

Issue Editors: Manuel Alvarado, Edward Buscombe, Richard Collins;
Editorial Assistant: Elizabeth Cowie;
Editorial Board: Manuel Alvarado, Cary Bazalgette, Edward Buscombe, Richard Collins, Jim Cook, Richard Exton, Geoff Goldstein, Felicity Grant, Jim Hillier, Chris Mottershead.

SE 13, Winter 1974/75: 'Image and Context'

Issue Editors: Cary Bazalgette, Richard Exton, Felicity Grant;
Editorial Assistant: Elizabeth Cowie;
Editorial Board: Manuel Alvarado, Cary Bazalgette, Edward Buscombe, Richard Collins, Jim Cook, Richard Exton, Geoff Goldstein, Felicity Grant, Chris Mottershead.

From this point a paid editor was employed, who also doubled as the Society for Education in Film and Television's (SEFT's) Education Officer.

SE 14, Spring 1975: 'Media Studies – Methods and Approaches'

Editor: Manuel Alvarado;
Editorial Assistant: Elizabeth Cowie;
Joint Editor for the issue: Richard Collins;
Editorial Board: Cary Bazalgette, Edward Buscombe, Richard Collins, Jim Cook, Richard Exton, Geoff Goldstein, Felicity Grant, Jim Grealy, Jim Hillier, Chris Mottershead;
Advertising Manager: Ann Sachs.

SE 15, Summer 1975: 'Education: the System and Classroom Practice'

Editor: Manuel Alvarado;
Editorial Assistant: Elizabeth Cowie;
Joint Editors for the issue: Cary Bazalgette and Jim Hillier;
Editorial Board: Cary Bazalgette, Edward Buscombe, Richard Collins, Jim Cook, Richard Exton, Geoff Goldstein, Felicity

Grant, Jim Grealy, Jim Hillier, Chris Mottershead;
Advertising Manager: Ann Sachs.

SE 16, Autumn 1975: 'Teaching the Film Industry'

Editor: Manuel Alvarado;
Editorial Assistant: Elizabeth Cowie;
Joint Editors for the issue: Jim Cook, Geoff Goldstein, Chris Mottershead;
Editorial Board: Cary Bazalgette, Edward Buscombe, Richard Collins, Jim Cook, Richard Exton, Geoff Goldstein, Felicity Grant, Jim Grealy, Jim Hillier, Chris Mottershead;
Advertising Manager: Ann Sachs.

SE 17, Winter 1975/76: '*The Searchers*: Materials and Approaches'

Editor: Manuel Alvarado;
Editorial Officer: Elizabeth Cowie;
Joint Editors for the issue: Richard Exton, Jim Grealy;
Editorial Board: Cary Bazalgette, Edward Buscombe, Richard Collins, Jim Cook, Richard Exton, Felicity Grant, Jim Grealy, Jim Hillier, Chris Mottershead;
Advertising Manager: Ann Sachs.

SE 18, Spring 1976: 'Media Education in Europe – UNESCO Survey'

Editor: Manuel Alvarado;
Editorial Officer: Elizabeth Cowie;
Joint Editors for the issue: Cary Bazalgette, Felicity Grant;
Editorial Board: Cary Bazalgette, Edward Buscombe, Richard Collins, Jim Cook, Richard Exton, Felicity Grant, Jim Grealy, Jim Hillier, Chris Mottershead;
Advertising Manager: Ann Sachs.

SE 19, Summer 1976

Editor: Manuel Alvarado;
Editorial Officer: Elizabeth Cowie;
Joint Editor for the issue: Richard Collins;
Editorial Board: Cary Bazalgette, Edward Buscombe, Richard Collins, Jim Cook, Richard Exton, Felicity Grant, Jim Grealy, Jim Hillier, Chris Mottershead;
Advertising Manager: Ann Sachs.

Drummond, Bob Ferguson, George Foster, Simon Frith, Jim Grealy, Madeleine MacDonald, Philip Simpson, John Tagg; *Advertising Manager:* Ann Sachs.

SE 37, Winter 1980/81: 'The State and the Law: Images and Narrativity'

Editor: Angela McRobbie;
Editorial Officer: Susan Honeyford;
Additional editorial help: James Donald;
Editorial Board: Manuel Alvarado, Tony Bennett, Edward Buscombe, Hazel Carby, Richard Collins, Elizabeth Cowie, Phillip Drummond, Bob Ferguson, George Foster, Simon Frith, Jim Grealy, Madeleine MacDonald, Philip Simpson, John Tagg; *Advertising Manager:* Ann Sachs.

SE 38, Spring 1981: 'Pedagogics: Practice and Problems'

Editor: Angela McRobbie;;
Joint Editors for the issue: Manuel Alvarado, Bob Ferguson, Philip Simpson;
Editorial Board: Manuel Alvarado, Tony Bennett, Edward Buscombe, Hazel Carby, Richard Collins, Elizabeth Cowie, Phillip Drummond, Bob Ferguson, George Foster, Simon Frith, Jim Grealy, Madeleine MacDonald, Philip Simpson, John Tagg, Judith Williamson;
Advertising Manager: Ann Sachs.

SE 39, Summer 1981

Editor: Angela McRobbie;
Editorial Board: Manuel Alvarado, Tony Bennett, Edward Buscombe, Hazel Carby, Richard Collins, Elizabeth Cowie, Phillip Drummond, Bob Ferguson, George Foster, Simon Frith, Jim Grealy, Madeleine MacDonald, Philip Simpson, John Tagg, Judith Williamson;
Advertising Manager: Ann Sachs.

SE 40, Autumn 1981

Editor: Angela McRobbie;
Editorial Assistance: Manuel Alvarado, Martin Chalmers;
Editorial Board: Manuel Alvarado, Tony Bennett, Edward Buscombe, Hazel Carby, Richard Collins, Elizabeth Cowie, Phillip

Notes on Contributors

Diane Adlam worked at the Sociological Research Unit, Institute of Education, University of London. She was a founding editor of the journal *Ideology and Consciousness*, with Angie Salfield.

Manuel Alvarado was editor of *Screen Education* from 1975 to 1978. He taught at all levels of the British education system and is currently Head of Education at the British Film Institute. He has published numerous books on the media and education including *Learning the Media* (co-authored with Robin Gutch and Tana Wollen), *The Media Reader* (co-edited with John O. Thompson) and *Media Education: An Introduction* (co-edited with Oliver Boyd-Barrett).

Edward Buscombe was a founding editor of *Screen Education* and remained on the editorial board throughout the journal's existence. He was also on the board of *Screen*, 1971–6 and 1982–3. He is currently Head of Trade Publishing at the British Film Institute and is editor of *The BFI Companion to the Western*.

Hazel Carby is Professor of English, African–American and American Studies at Yale University. She is author of *Reconstructing Womanhood: The Emergence of the Afro-American Woman Writer* and is currently completing a book on black women in music, film and fiction in the United States of the 1920s and 1930s.

John Caughie is Senior Lecturer in Film and Television Studies at Glasgow University and co-director of the John Logie Baird Centre. Subsequent to the article reproduced here, he edited the BFI/RKP Film Studies Reader, *Theories of Authorship*, and has also published widely on television theory, criticism and history. He is a member of the editorial group of *Screen*.

Richard Collins was a member of the editorial board of *Screen Education* from 1973 to 1981. He has written several books on television and is Senior Research Associate in the Department of Media and Communications of Goldsmiths' College, University of London. His research concerns the Europeanisation of television.

Pam Cook is Associate Editor of *Sight and Sound* magazine at the British Film Institute. She edited and co-wrote *The Cinema Book* and is presently working on the construction of national identity in Gainsborough costume melodrama.

Elizabeth Cowie was administrative officer with the Society for Education in Film and Television from 1972 to 1976 and was a member of the editorial boards of *Screen Education* and *Screen*. She co-founded and co-edited *m/f*, the journal of feminist theory, from 1978 until 1986, when it ceased. Since 1981 she has taught film studies at the University of Kent and is the author of a forthcoming book on psychoanalysis, film theory and the representation of women.

James Donald edited *Screen Education* from 1978 to 1980, when he moved to the Open University. Among the courses he worked on were *Popular Culture, Beliefs and Ideologies* and *Race, Education and Society*. He is now Senior Lecturer in Media Studies at the University of Sussex. His most recent books are *Sentimental Education, Race, Culture and Difference* (with Ali Rattansi), *Psychoanalysis and Cultural Theory: Thresholds* and *Fantasy and the Cinema*.

Umberto Eco is Professor of Semiotics at the University of Bologna. His publications include *A Theory of Semiotics*, *The Role of the Reader*, *Travels in Hyper-Reality* and two novels, *The Name of the Rose* and *Foucault's Pendulum*.

John Ellis has been an independent television producer since 1982, running Large Door Ltd, which has produced over sixty hours of documentaries about cinema and popular culture. Previously he taught film studies at the University of Kent, where he wrote *Visible Fictions*. He was appointed Visiting Professor of Mass Communications at the University of Bergen in 1991.

Stuart Hall has written extensively on the media. He was Director of the Centre for Cultural Studies at Birmingham University until 1979 and is now Professor of Sociology at the Open University.

Richard Johnson who was Director of the Centre for Contemporary Cultural Studies, University of Birmingham, 1980–8, now teaches part-time in the Department of Cultural Studies.

Graham Murdock is Reader in the Department of Social Sciences at the University of Loughborough and Professor of Mass Communications at the University of Bergen. He has written widely on the political economy of the communications industries, on the sociology of youth and on the dynamics of political communication. His books include, as co-author, *Demonstrations and Communication* and *Televising Terrorism* and, as co-editor, *Communicating Politics*. His current interests centre upon the reorganisation of the television industry, the sociology of consumption, and the relations between communications and society.

Steve Neale is Senior Lecturer in Film Studies at the University of Kent. He is the author of a number of articles published in *Screen*, *Framework* and elsewhere, of *Genre* and *Cinema and Technology* and, most recently, co-author of *Popular Film and Television Comedy*.

Richard Paterson is Deputy Head of the Research Division at the British Film Institute. He has had a close involvement in recent BFI research initiatives on the future of the British film and television industries. His most recent book was an edited collection, *Organising for Change*, in the Broadcasting Debates series.

Angie Salfield worked at the Sociological Research Unit, Institute of Education, University of London. She was a founding editor of the journal *Ideology and Consciousness* with Diane Adlam.

John O. Thompson works for the BFI as MA Course Director/Education Officer (HE). He edited *Monty Python: Complete and Utter Theory of the Grotesque*. He is co-author (with Ann Thompson) of *Shakespeare: Meaning and Metaphor* and (with Antony Easthope) of *Contemporary Poetry meets Contemporary Theory*.

John Tulloch is Principal Lecturer in Journalism in the School of Communication, Polytechnic of Central London. He has contributed to *Monogram*, *Screen Education* and *Media, Culture and Society* and is currently engaged in research on government information and news management policy.

Valerie Walkerdine was a primary school teacher who then went on to study psychology, film and fine art. She is currently Professor of the Psychology of Communication at Goldsmiths' College, University of London, and a practising artist and film-maker. Her latest book is *Schoolgirl Fictions*.

Index

P 91 .S37 1993 c.1

The Screen education reader

DATE DUE